Learn the answers to these questions in
ECONOMIC LITERACY

❏ What do economists mean when they talk about **"real" dollars**?

❏ What is the difference between the **deficit** and the **national debt**?

❏ Why does the **stock market** sometimes *drop* when good news is announced?

❏ What makes up the nation's **money supply**?

❏ What are **junk bonds,** and who buys them?

❏ How can having a **strong currency** hurt a nation's economy?

❏ What are the pros and cons of raising the **minimum wage**?

Economic Literacy

What Everyone Needs to Know About Money & Markets

Jacob De Rooy, Ph.D.

Three Rivers Press
New York

Published by Three Rivers Press, a division of Crown Publishers, Inc.,
201 East 50th Street, New York, New York 10022.
Member of the Crown Publishing Group.

Originally published in hardcover by Crown Publishers, Inc., in 1995.
First paperback edition printed in 1996.

Random House, Inc. New York, Toronto, London, Sydney, Auckland
www.randomhouse.com

THREE RIVERS PRESS and colophon are trademarks
of Crown Publishers, Inc.

Printed in the United States of America

Library of Congress Cataloging-in-Publication Data
De Rooy, Jacob.
  Economic literacy : what everyone needs to know about money &
markets / by Jacob De Rooy.
    1. Economics. 2. Money. I. Title.
HB34.D38   1995   330—dc20   95-5140

ISBN 0-517-88683-9

10 9 8 7 6 5 4 3

Dedicated with Love to
Martha and Catherine

Contents

Acknowledgments

I am indebted to students in my undergraduate and MBA classes who have asked me questions, or written specious exam essays, that challenged me to do a better job of conveying the essentials of economics. I am also grateful to many interviewers and reporters from the media who have asked me to face a microphone or TV camera and, in a minute or two, make sense of something that might take an hour to cover in a classroom. Many of the questions and answers in this book were motivated by working with students and reporters who needed clear responses faster than you can pick up a meal at a drive-through window.

But equally challenging is scrutiny by one's academic peers. I am thankful to Dr. Jeanne C. Hey, who read the entire book, and to Drs. Stephen Mathis and Janet Koscianski, who each read parts of this book. They all tried to put me back on track when I strayed and gave me helpful comments. I may not always have been true to their direction, so I can only hold myself responsible for any remaining errors.

Preface

Economic Literacy for Writers and Speakers . . . and Their Audiences

Your **economic literacy** is the ability you have to read and to write about the economic conditions that affect your material well-being. It is the ability to understand, to discuss, and to react to the events that shape your economic environment.

Economic literacy is not just for economists. The successes you enjoy in your profession and in your investments are only partly determined by your skills, experience, and accumulated wisdom. Even the important people you know (assuming they like you) deserve only partial credit for your accomplishments. Your success is significantly influenced by the economic environment.

Your economic environment gives you both constraints and opportunities. No matter what business interests you have, somehow your career and wealth will be affected by the elements of the economic environment: business cycles, unemployment, wages, inflation, interest rates, financial markets, banking, taxes, govern-

ment regulations, economic policies, and foreign trade and investment. Economic literacy gives you the ability to understand and to
deal with these elements.

   You certainly do not have to be a master mechanic to drive a car
and do it well. You do not have to be a botanist to grow a flower, or
a physician to take care of your body. By the same token you do not
have to be a professional economist to have a basic understanding of
your economic environment. This understanding would certainly
help you to make intelligent evaluations and decisions as a businessperson, as an investor, and as a voter.

   The 1990s is the decade of the market economy. Soviet-style economies in Europe and Asia have broken down; they are being replaced
by economies that are market oriented. Many Southern Hemisphere
nations are also moving in this direction. In advanced economies
there is a trend toward privatization of industry. The United States
and other leading nations have taken bold steps toward deregulation
of businesses. All of these developments create the need to know
more about the market economy and how it works. That is what this
book, *Economic Literacy*, is about.

   In the popular musical *My Fair Lady*, Professor Henry Higgins
was so expert in phonetics that he could detect a person's social status (which was so important in his Victorian England) just by listen-
ing to him or her talk. On a bet, he gave speech lessons to the flower
girl Eliza Doolittle to launch her in high society and to establish her
in a career.

   Economic literacy is important in the office. In the business world
of today competition is so sharp that speakers and writers with only
a loose grasp of economics are quickly discredited. The economic
literacy you need for success is not the use of pretentious vocabulary
and diction, which Eliza could employ to mislead others. *Economic
literacy is a sound understanding of how our market economy works, and a
familiarity with its current condition.*

   Economic Literacy is a collection of short pieces on economics. Each article
discusses what you need to know to get a clear understanding of business conditions, of economic policies that influence our economy,
and of concepts that help you to understand how the economy works.
Using simple English, it makes sense of those "ten-dollar terms" that
make up much of the modern jargon of economics.

Economics is really about people and about the things they do. The fancy jargon that economists use among themselves and in public obscures this important fact. *Throughout the book vignettes illustrate basic economic concepts on a personal level.* To make sure you see the human side of economics, each article has short examples about things people do. You will meet Felicia, Bob, Juan, Terry, and others who may seem familiar to you. You will see how they behave and how their behavior, when added to the actions of many others like them, influences the conditions of our economy (our economic environment).

Many of the illustrations will remind you of people you know. However, to save real individuals from possible embarrassment, or undeserved credit, they are all fictitious. This case method has been used for years in teaching law.

This is not a textbook in economics. There are lots of those and some of them are pretty good, too, but this is not a textbook. They are fine if you have the time and commitment to learn the technical side of economics and to study theories, equations, and graphs. But remember, you do not have to be a mechanic to understand how a car works. You do not have to be an economist to understand the basic elements of your economic environment.

This book will not make you an expert on economics any more than an easily readable book on home gardening can make you a professional botanist. But if it gets you started on the subject, and if you really want to dig deeper, a college course in economics is the way to go from here.

Because this book is about people, and people are sometimes funny, there is a little humor in *Economic Literacy*, too. Economists are not known for their wit, nor are they a colorful lot. I know many economics professors who can cure insomnia just by lecturing! But I want to show that economics is a very human subject and that economists have important things to say about a lot of familiar things people do.

Unfortunately, there is a lot of economic illiteracy in America and in other market economies. Even though the United States is the world's leading market economy, the economic literacy of Americans is low.[1] In 1992 the National Center for Research in Economic Education and the Gallup Organization conducted a poll entitled the

National Survey of American Economic Literacy. They found that only 39% of the American public could correctly answer questions on concepts and relationships that concerned current economic issues. Even college seniors scored only 51%. These are not passing grades for a nation that is experiencing increasing competitiveness at home and abroad.

About 75% of the respondents relied on the popular news media (radio, television, and newspapers) for information about economics. Unfortunately, thirty-second news bites and two-hundred-word newspaper articles cannot be relied upon to give people adequate explanations and background for today's economic events. That is where this book, *Economic Literacy*, fills in the gaps.

If economic literacy is poor in the world's largest and wealthiest market economy, we can expect it to be lower in the nations that are only now struggling to develop their own market economies.

Economic literacy is more than familiarity with buzzwords and fancy terms; it is understanding. You already "know" much of the language of economics because you come across it every day in newspapers and magazines, on television news programs, during business meetings, and even from politicians. But if these are the places where you picked up most of your economic vocabulary, your economic literacy rests on a rickety foundation. *Economic Literacy* uses straight talk to address such questions as

- How can **rational expectations** help you to understand changes in **stock market prices**?
- Can the **Federal Reserve** control our nation's **money supply** and **interest rates**? Has it lost some of its muscle?
- What does a **weak dollar** mean for the economy?
- What is the average length of **recessions** in the United States?
- How does **human capital** effect earnings?

This handy book will give you insights you cannot pick up from the media, and that you may have missed if you dozed off in that dull "econ" course you took in high school or in college.

Many of the economically illiterate are clever about hiding their handicap; they nod knowingly, throw around fancy vocabulary, or quote economists (which can be like asking Phyllis Diller for beauty tips). Most people who are economically illiterate can read and write, otherwise it would be easier to spot them. Others may not know they are economically illiterate. The best way to help is to know the modern language of economics yourself. This means more than recognizing words; it means having an understanding of basic concepts.

A *Pop Quiz on Economic Literacy*

If your eyes get heavy when you have to read about economics, or if you doze off when you hear an economist, go right to the introduction of this book. Don't waste time on the quiz.

But if you feel you really know your stuff, then try this pop quiz on economic literacy right now. It is not for the fainthearted.

Once you have read this book, you will be able to tackle the quiz with no sweat. You may not find economics to be as exciting as a video on MTV, but at least you will no longer think the arcane jargon of economics is puzzling, and you might just find that economics is really not so drab after all.

Pick the answer that you think is correct. What is your economic literacy score? See scoring instructions after the last question.

1. A recession occurs when
    A. personal income falls for three consecutive months
    B. real gross domestic product falls for two or more quarter-year periods
    C. the unemployment rate rises above the natural rate of unemployment
    D. your successful brother (the one your mother brags about) loses his job

2. When the nation's workers are "fully employed," the nation's unemployment rate is equal to
    A. the inflation rate
    B. the natural rate of unemployment
    C. 0%
    D. the unemployment rate in Washington, D.C.

3. Suppose IBM proudly announces that its earnings this year were 15% higher than earnings last year. But in response, the stock market price of IBM shares may fall if
    A. investors in the stock market are not always guided by rational expectations
    B. investors had expected earnings to rise more than 15%
    C. investors had expected earnings to increase less than 15%
    D. the report is believed to be the result of computer error

4. Economists closely watch the important federal funds rate. This is the interest rate
    A. charged by the Federal Reserve Banks when they lend money to commercial banks
    B. the U.S. Treasury pays on government bonds
    C. charged by federal employees when they lend government money to their relatives
    D. that commercial banks charge when they make short-term loans to other commercial banks

5. The gross domestic product of our nation is the
    A. income received by all workers in the economy
    B. market value of all manufactured goods
    C. market value of all goods and services that are not used to make other goods and services
    D. nasty stew your mother-in-law makes from leftovers

6. The widely followed Consumer Price Index is used to measure
    A. changes in the cost of living
    B. changes in consumer spending
    C. inflation
    D. how much it costs to live beyond your means

7. If a nation has a market economy, then
   A. prices of essential goods and services are set by government agencies
   B. governments do not produce any goods or services
   C. its politicians can be bought
   D. most of the things we use to produce goods and services are owned by individuals and private firms

8. Examples of externalities in our economy include
   A. automobile exhaust fumes
   B. fish killed by industrial pollutants
   C. both of the above
   D. portions of the body exposed by French-cut bikinis

9. When the value of the U.S. dollar declines in international trading, then it is likely that
   A. American people will prefer to make purchases by cash rather than by credit card
   B. U.S. exports will rise
   C. U.S. exports will fall
   D. this book will become more expensive

10. During the 1990–91 recession in the United States the unemployment rate for the nation reached a high level of about (select the closest value)
    A. 24%
    B. 11%
    C. 7%
    D. 2%
    E. 0%

Scoring the quiz: You can find the correct answers at the end of this section.

Rating Your Score on the Pop Quiz	
NUMBER OF CORRECT ANSWERS	EVALUATION OF YOUR SCORE
9–10 correct	You are a pro! Give this book to all your friends and colleagues so they can talk about economics with you.
7–8 correct	Your conversational economics is good, but you could get tripped up on a few terms. Skim through the book to strengthen your weak points.
5–6 correct	Avoid talking with professional economists, and take a low profile at business meetings, until you read this book. You show promise.
3–4 correct	You probably break out in a cold sweat when you hear an economist talk. This reaction will fade as you use this book to master the language of economics.
1–2 correct	Chances are that when you read economic news, your lips get tired. *Economic Literacy* will enable you to make sense of economic jargon.
None correct	Maybe you should run away from it all and paint landscapes in Mongolia.

Warning: This short pop quiz is certainly not a complete test of your economic literacy. Many important topics in economics were not mentioned in the quiz, although they are covered by articles in this book. So if you did well on the quiz, browse through the table of contents or examine the index to locate any topics you are still not comfortable with. If you missed several answers, however, take this book and wear it out!

Answers to the Pop Quiz

1.	B	6.	C
2.	B	7.	D
3.	B	8.	C
4.	D	9.	B
5.	C	10.	C

Introduction

How to Use This Book

This book has two uses. You can use it as a reference book ready to give you specific information on demand. If you have more time, however, you can use the book as a short course in economic literacy, focusing on an understanding of the economic environment and the workings of a market economy. Either way you use it, you will find the book has user-friendly features that are described in this introduction.

Economic Literacy is an easy-reading collection of short articles that you can pick up and peruse at your own pace and according to your own interests. Each article covers a topic in economics that is important for understanding the economic environment.

Each of the seven chapters contains a group of related articles. Each article is divided into questions with answers. This format makes it easy to develop your economic literacy.

Economic Literacy has much of the same information you might otherwise have to look for in dictionaries, textbooks, and business almanacs. It pulls together the essentials and presents them in a more user-friendly way.

This book has an extensive index with references and cross-references. The index enables you to quickly find economic terms you find in the media today and for which you need a definition or explanation, such as the **Consumer Price Index** or **unemployment rate**. The table of contents enables you to locate material on broader topics, e.g., **inflation**, which is the topic of an article.

Suppose you want to learn how to interpret a news item on changes in the nation's **money supply**. Looking up this term in the index will lead you to two articles in which it is discussed. Secondary terms in most index listings help you to pinpoint aspects of the topic you want to study. For example, the index entry "**money supply**: components of" will lead you to a specific page in the article "Money and Banking." The index entry "**money supply**: influence of the Fed on" will lead you to specific pages in the article "The Federal Reserve."

If a term is the principal topic of an article, it will be capitalized in the index, followed by the article number, for example, MONEY AND BANKING (Article 17), followed by the page numbers where it appears (221–35). Of course, article titles also appear in the table of contents.

Beside listing the principal terms that appear in each article, the index includes common substitute words and related terms. You will be referred to the article "The Unemployment Rate" if you look up the term **unemployment** or if you happen to look for the terms **joblessness** or **employment**, because these terms are often associated with the unemployment rate.

You can skim through an article to find the specific information you need. Each article contains a number of **bold-faced** provocative questions, followed by one or more paragraphs of information. The answer to each question includes one or more *italicized summary statements*. If you are familiar with a given term, then use the fast-track approach: merely skim through all of the italicized statements in an article. Pause only to dig deeper by reading the question and answer on the topic you are interested in exploring.

Of course, numbers are an important part of economics. Most articles use simple information tables so you can get a feel for economic quantities and important economic statistics. Economic literacy means more than knowing definitions. It means knowing about the condition of our economy and getting a sense of size and proportion.

Most terms in economics represent measurable values. **Personal income** is measured in dollars, the **inflation rate** is measured in percent, **employment** is measured in persons, etc. All articles in the book that describe terms that can be measured include a table with current statistical information. These short tables tell you about the economy.

What's more, the data lets you put into perspective statistical information reported in the media. The tables give you a feel for significant values and let you make meaningful comparisons. Then when you see a news story about the unemployment rate or economic growth, for example, you will be able to compare new statistics with what went on before.

The book will give you comprehensive understanding of the economic environment because it is a short course in economic literacy. Start your short course with Chapter 1, "Aerial Views of the Economy." The articles in this chapter discuss the broadest measures of the condition of the economy. Then go on to study the role of human labor in the economy in Chapter 2, "Jobs and Wages of People at Work." These articles discuss employment of people, which, after the measures in Chapter 1, usually attract the most interest. Other chapters cover prices and markets, international trade, business investment, financial markets, economic policy, and other subjects.

The sequence of chapters and articles presents a logical and orderly progression in the coverage of economic concepts, going from the most general to the most specialized.

The chapters and articles can be read in any order. However, if you use the book as a short course, begin with the first chapter, which introduces the basic measurements of the state of a nation's economic environment. The other chapters can be covered in accordance with your interests.

Articles within each chapter are arranged to gradually develop your understanding of a specific subject. The early articles present you with the elements of a subject. Succeeding articles develop more advanced and specialized concepts. To get the most out of the book as a short course in economic literacy, read the articles in each chapter in the order they appear.

To accommodate those who use the book as a reference, some key definitions and explanations are repeated throughout the book, with references to related articles indicated by a pointer (☞ Art.). The repetition may be a minor inconvenience to those who read the book from beginning to end, but it may be helpful to those who read articles in isolation.

If you use the book as a short course, you should read the introduction to each chapter to guide your study. The introductions tell you what to look for and explain how each article relates to the others in the chapter.

The articles are divided into questions and answers, with each question leading into the one following. To help you, the book contains *italicized summary statements*, which are brief responses to each question. Use the italicized summaries in each article for review or to help you set your pace. You can take a fast track in each article by skimming through the summary statements, pausing only to read the full text of each answer when you want a full explanation of the material.

Most of the articles are self-contained; they do not require any preparation. There are a few exceptions. When you would benefit from reading a pair of articles in sequence, you will find Reading Suggestions at the beginning of the article.

Generally, the articles can be read in no more than ten to twenty minutes.

FEATURES IN EACH ARTICLE

Bold-faced terms: Terms in the language of economics that are introduced in an article are written in bold-faced type when they appear for the first time. These terms are also listed in the index.

Italicized summaries: All key points are written in italicized type for emphasis and to enable you to skim through articles for review.

☞ This symbol points you to another article in the book where you can learn more about this subject. You may wish to read it *after* you have finished the current article. However, the articles in the book can be read in any order unless there is a Reading Suggestion at the beginning of the article.

Economic
Literacy

1

Aerial Views
of the Economy

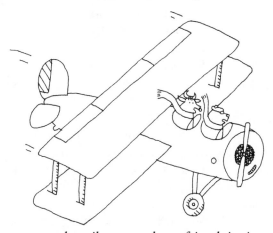

How can you describe your best friend in just a few
words? A complete description involves so much more.
The nation's economy is no different; it is too complex
for any single number to adequately account for its
condition. This chapter tells you how to use and to understand the
broadest, and most widely used, yardsticks for assessing the economic condition of the nation. These important yardsticks together
give you an aerial view of the economic environment, just as a satellite picture gives an overview of the topography and weather conditions of a large landmass. The later chapters in this book focus on
specific parts of the economy.

The first two articles in this chapter discuss gross domestic product, commonly designated as GDP. This is the official comprehensive measure of economic activity in most of the nations of the
world. The old yardstick of the U.S. economy, gross national product, or GNP, was replaced by GDP in 1992, so most Americans are

not yet familiar with it. Article 1 tells you what GDP is and how it measures various types of economic activity.

There are a few numbers that you should know to be literate about current GDP, and you will see them here. Since nearly every nation now uses GDP, this statistic is great for comparing the sizes of economies around the world. You will see some comparisons of size in Article 1, which will also explain how the new GDP compares with the old GNP. (Despite its demotion, GNP is still calculated, and you can learn something about an economy by comparing its GDP and GNP numbers.)

Article 1 is one of the most important in the book and an appropriate starting point in developing your economic literacy. This is a "must read" item.

Article 2 continues our coverage of GDP. It is intended for those who want to take a harder and closer look at this important statistic. It focuses on different ways of valuing economic activities and also on what GDP does not tell us about the economy. Here you will learn how the economy is divided into parts, called sectors, and how the economic activity of each sector is measured. You will see how the activities of governments, charities, educational institutions, and religious groups are included in GDP (more or less). This article also talks about drug dealers, gamblers and prostitutes, housekeepers, and baby-sitters and how their respective jobs affect the GDP numbers; despite their markedly different contributions to society, they are treated very much alike by the government's economic statisticians.

Articles 1 and 2 both discuss important ways of getting "snapshots" of our economy; they describe statistics that tell us about the condition of the economy during a particular year. But economists are also concerned with the way conditions change. They need "motion pictures" to tell them about our progress from one year to the next. Articles 3 and 4 discuss economic growth and the ups and downs of the business cycle. Article 3 explains how economic growth is measured and what real growth rates say, and do not say, about our progress. The article identifies the factors responsible for growth. You will also get an understanding of what a healthy growth rate is, and you will see the growth rates of some important countries.

Article 3 also discusses the measurement of long-term economic growth. Article 4 is a natural sequence to this article because it discusses business cycles that interrupt or accelerate growth over short periods. Growth is never even; it proceeds in a sequence of economic expansions and recessions (which might take the form of dramatic "booms" or "busts") that affect nearly everyone in the economy.

An important feature of Article 4 is the discussion of recessions and depressions. How long is a normal recession? When do recessions begin and end? How "great" was the Great Depression of the 1930s? These are just some of the questions answered in this article.

The four articles in this chapter will give you a good start in evaluating and in improving your economic literacy. They discuss the "big picture" of the economy, where it is and how fast it is moving.

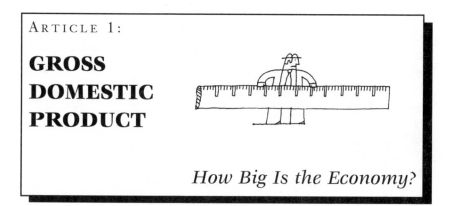

ARTICLE 1:

GROSS DOMESTIC PRODUCT

How Big Is the Economy?

What is gross domestic product?

The shorthand for **gross domestic product, GDP**, is becoming the best-known abbreviation in economics. GDP is our broadest measure of the economic activity that goes on in the nation during the year. It measures the value of all of the TV sets, cars, toys, bricks, frozen foods, paper clips, and the millions of other things that are consumed, or acquired for use, during the year. It also measures the value of all of the bus rides, stage shows, plumbing repairs, hairstylings, package deliveries, funerals, and the many other services that people do for each other.

But how can we come up with a single number that counts all of these different things? One feature that most of them have in common is that they have a dollar value, and dollars can be added together. *GDP is the total market value of all final goods and services that are produced within the borders of a nation within a year.* That definition sounds neat and tight, but it's really not. Let's take it apart and see what it says . . . and what it doesn't say.

What are "final goods and services" and how do we know what they are worth?

GDP is the value of **final goods and services**. *Final goods and services are things that are produced, and services that are performed, that are not used to create other goods and services.* Let's start by seeing what a "final good" is. Meet Juan, who enjoys taking color pictures.

JUAN'S FINAL GOOD: Juan bought some rolls of 35mm camera film this year for $35. He used the film to take pictures for the pleasure of his family and friends. Because he is the end user of the film, it is a final good and the $35 he spent for it is added to the nation's GDP.

The dollars we use to measure GDP are determined by the **market value** of what is produced. *The market value of a final good is whatever the end user actually pays for it. GDP includes the total amount of money paid for final goods.* The value of the film was $35 because that is what Juan paid and that is the least it was worth to him (he may have been willing to pay more for it). We must use the market value because that is the value society places on a good or service. What makes this film a final good is what it is used for. Juan only wants to use it for his own benefit, not to make money, so he is the end user.

Now let's meet Helga, who is using her weekends to start her own photography business. We will see that when she buys similar film, its value is not added to GDP, simply because of how she uses it.

HELGA'S INTERMEDIATE GOOD: Helga is a part-time photographer who takes pictures, for fees, at special events. Dan and Hillary hire her to take pictures of their wedding. In preparation for this job Helga bought rolls of 35mm film for $69. Later she put the developed pictures in frames and an album and sold them to the couple for $700. The amount of money she spent on this film is not added to GDP.

Helga's film becomes what economists call an intermediate good. *Intermediate goods are used to produce another good or service.* That does not mean that the rolls of film are ignored in accounting for our economy's activity: she used the film to take wedding pictures that she sold to her customer, and her fee of $700 is added to GDP. The package of pictures is a final good. Her rolls of film are part of the value of the pictures, just as sugar is an ingredient that adds to the value of a cake sold by a bakery. GDP includes only the value of final goods. **Intermediate goods and services** are left out of GDP to avoid double counting. If we had added Helga's $69 film purchase to GDP, along with her sale of pictures for $700, GDP would rise by $769, which would count the value of the film twice. That would be fudging the books.

How about services? Can we tell the difference between a "final service" and an "intermediate service"?

There are also intermediate services and final services.

SERVICES OF THE CPA: Mort is a certified public accountant. Pat pays him $125 to fill out his personal income tax forms. This $125 fee is added to GDP because Mort performed a final service, which means it will not be used to make additional income for anyone. Later Mort fills out income tax forms for the Pincus Pines Funeral Home. The fee of $380 he receives from the home is not added to GDP because it is an intermediate service. The home uses the service to help it stay in business.

Mort's $125 fee for preparing personal income tax forms for Pat is added to GDP because his work is a final service; Pat is the final user of the service and its value is what Pat pays for it. But the funeral home's $380 fee is payment for an intermediate service, so it is not added directly to GDP. This fee adds value to the goods (caskets, etc.) and services the home sells. (The home provides "final services" in more ways than one.)

An intermediate service is one that is necessary to create a final good or service. To say that an intermediate service becomes part of a final product may seem like stretching a point, but the accountant's fee is part of the cost of being in business. Without the accountant's services the funeral home might not be able to stay in business to create the final goods and services it sells to its customers.

Is the cost of an intermediate good or service always included in GDP?

Because GDP numbers include only the money spent for final goods and services, intermediate goods and services are counted only to the extent they add monetary value to the final goods and services they are used to produce. However, don't expect that the value of final goods and services will always cover the costs of the intermediates used to produce them. *The contribution an intermediate good or service makes to GDP depends only on what it adds to the value of some final good or service.* That is actually a very fair way of measuring the value of what goes on in our economy. It means that the value of a final good that is added to GDP may be less than the cost of the intermediate goods used to make it. To see why, let's go back to Helga, who is trying to start that photography business.

VALUING HELGA'S PRODUCT: Helga spent $71 on the wrong film for her second job, photographing a wedding for Bruno and Doreen. That was a bummer because the pictures she took of the wedding were not acceptable (too grainy and yellowish), and her customers did not buy any of them. We already know that the $71 isn't counted as part of GDP because it's an intermediate good. Her final product, Bruno and Doreen's wedding pictures, had a market value of $0 (no sale), so the film and the pictures added nothing to GDP.

Helga had better not give up her weekday job just yet! (Fortunately the bride's uncle got some fair snapshots with a disposable camera he picked up before the ceremony.) Helga's product, which is a final good, had no market value, so it could not increase GDP. Unfortunately that meant that the film she used to make these pictures also had no value to any final user. Helga's experience shows us another facet of GDP: *GDP is not a measure of all the economic activity that goes on in the nation; GDP is only a measure of the value that economic activity has for end users* (the young couple). Helga's final good had a market value far below the costs of the intermediate goods that went into making it. We assess economic activity on the basis of its market value, not its cost.

This feature of GDP also means that something can have a value far above the cost of intermediate goods and services put into it, such as a basketball autographed by a superstar like Michael Jordan. The unadorned basketball may cost $10 to produce and have a market value of $20, which is what it would add to GDP when sold. However, a superstar player might get $50 for taking ten seconds to put his name on it (which is an intermediate service). With this signature added to the product, the basketball may have a market value of $100, and this is the amount its sale to a final user would contribute to GDP.

Is GDP always based on market values?

Over 80% of all of the goods and services created in the United States are sold in the market. When they are sold, we can find out their market value. However, some goods and services are given away because end users do not have to pay for them. Examples of this are distributions of food and clothing by governments and by charities, many services of religious organizations, and other work for which no payment is received. *Goods and services distributed without charge by governments and nonprofit groups are included in GDP at the cost of producing them* (☛ Art. 2: More on Gross Domestic Product, page 12). That also means anything you do without pay, such as mowing the lawn for your mother on Mother's Day, never gets into GDP at all. (If you charge her the rest of the year, that gets in.)

How large is the GDP of the U.S. and how important are services?

Now let's look at some numbers. Gross domestic product for a nation as large as the U.S. is an impressive sum. *In 1993 the total value of goods and services created in the U.S. was over 6,300 billion dollars.* That's more than $24,000 per person. Economists often like to measure GDP in trillions of dollars. One trillion dollars is one thousand billion, so that $6,000 billion is $6 trillion (which looks like a more manageable sum, I suppose).

The collection of companies and individuals in a nation that perform services are called the nation's **service sector**. We often hear that the U.S. is becoming a service economy. Is this true? The figures in Table 1A show that it is one now; *just over half of America's GDP now comes from the service sector.*[1] Less than 40% of GDP came from the production of the goods, from bulldozers to diapers, that come from the **manufacturing sector**.

The remainder of our nation's output, 8%, comes from the construction of houses and other buildings. Construction is put into a separate category because houses and buildings provide their users with "services" over the many years they are used, unlike other services that are consumed within the year (☛ Art. 16: Investment, page 197).

Table 1A

Types of Outputs That Made Up Real Gross Domestic Product of the U.S. in 1993

Sector	Value of Output ($ billions)	Percent of GDP
Goods	2,406	38
Services	3,405	54
Construction	532	8
GDP:	6,343	100

How does the GDP of the U.S. compare with the GDP of other nations?

GDP can be used to compare the sizes of economies. The 1992 GDPs of some nations are shown in Table 1B below. The table has leading industrialized nations and some poorer nations.[2]

The U.S. has a large economy. In fact, *in 1992 the economy of the United States was more than twice as large as that of Japan, the world's second-biggest economy*, and many times larger than the economies of lesser-developed nations, such as India, Mexico, Colombia, and Nigeria. The combined output of the U.S. and Japan is much larger than the combined output of the other nations in the table. India has a smaller economy than does Mexico, although India's population is much larger.

Table 1B

GDP of Selected Nations in 1992

NATION	GDP ($ BILLIONS)	GDP PER CAPITA
United States	5,951	$23,400
Japan	2,468	19,800
Germany	1,398	17,400
United Kingdom	921	15,900
Canada	537	19,600
Mexico	328	3,600
India (1993)	240	270
Taiwan	209	10,000
Saudi Arabia	111	6,500
Israel	57	12,100
Hungary	55	5,380
Colombia	51	1,500
Nigeria	35	300

Can GDP be used to compare the economic well-being of nations?

While GDP is a good indicator of the relative size of economies, we should recognize that economic activity is created by people and that the populations of nations differ. If we are interested in using GDP as an indicator of economic well-being, we must take population into account. This is done by calculating **GDP per capita**, which is GDP divided by the number of people in the nation. In other words, it is the average amount of economic output attributed to members of the population. Examples are shown in the right column of Table 1B.

GDP per capita is often used to represent the relative well-being of an economy's population. For example, since the GDP per capita in Japan is a lot higher than that in Mexico, we might conclude that the average resident of Japan enjoys a higher level of material well-being than does the average resident of Mexico. We might also conclude that the average resident of Israel has a higher income ($12,100) than does the average resident of Saudi Arabia ($6,500).

But we must be careful not to carry these comparisons too far. Many factors determine the average resident's living standard. For example, a nation's GDP per capita may be high, but if the nation's income is distributed unevenly, a few people might enjoy high living standards while the others may have little. GDP per capita is only an average. Just as my old statistics prof once pointed out, you could drown by crossing a river that has an average depth of eight inches if you step into a part with a depth of eight feet.

What was wrong with the old GNP?

For years **gross national product (GNP)** was the official measure of economic activity in the United States, and in some other countries as well. GNP is the total market value of all final goods and services that are produced within a year by citizens of a nation . . . no matter where they are produced. *Gross national product includes the value of goods and services on the basis of who produced them. Gross domestic product includes the value of goods and services on the basis of where they were produced.*

In January of 1992, GDP replaced GNP as the official measure of the value of the total economic output of the United States. Canada made the switch from GNP to GDP in 1986. Actually, the United Nations has been promoting the use of GDP for many years, and the U.S. was the last major holdout.

WHAT LOWELL DID FOR GDP AND FOR GNP: Lowell is a nightclub singer and comedian and a citizen of the United States. He works in supper clubs, lounges, and at special events along the eastern border of the United States and Canada. Last year Lowell was paid $15,000 for performances in the U.S. and was paid $22,000, in equivalent American dollars, for performances in Canada. Under rules for calculating GNP, his U.S. citizenship meant that all of his earnings of $37,000 were added to the GNP of the U.S. for that year, but his earnings added nothing to the GNP of Canada. Because GDP is based on location, his work added $15,000 to the GDP of the United States and $22,000 to the GDP of Canada.

The switch to GDP made a lot of sense. Now all major nations are using the same basic measurement of economic activity. Furthermore, under the GDP standard a nation's economic activity is measured by what takes place within its borders, not by what is being done by people around the world who claim residency in a nation.

ARTICLE 2:

MORE ON GROSS DOMESTIC PRODUCT

What's Left Out?

Reading Suggestion: You may wish to read or skim Article 1 before proceeding with this article.

Where are goods and services produced?

Economists usually put the producers of goods and services in our economy into one of three groups called sectors. Most goods and services are produced by the **business sector**. It is likely that all of your food, appliances, soap, nail polish, and most of the other things you buy are created by business firms. The same is true of most services that you purchase, such as air travel, haircuts, and shows.

The business sector consists of all profit-seeking firms and individuals (even those who do not succeed in making profits!). These firms include large companies like Exxon, Pepsi, and IBM, and small businesses such as the newsstand, your beauty salon or barbershop, and most lawyers and physicians.

But not all of the nation's output of goods and services comes from businesses. Some of our economy's production also originates in the **household sector**. Most of us rely on this sector for some of the services we use. This sector includes all nonprofit organizations. The Salvation Army, churches, volunteer firefighters, nonprofit hospitals, and other charitable institutions are all part of the household sector. So are most colleges and universities. Services of a for-profit hospital, however, are part of the production of the business sector. The services of health care professionals in private practice are also in the business sector, even if they do some of their work in nonprofit hospitals.

Don't be confused by the word *household;* it does not mean the same thing as a home business. Anyone who does work at home for profit is part of the business sector.

A lot of what the household sector creates is given away by charitable organizations. But some output of the household sector is sold. Some hospital services are sold when they can be billed to insurance companies or to patients. Even churches sell some of their services, as you will see below.

The **government sector** also produces goods and services. Governments provide services like national defense, education, social counseling, and police protection. Governments also build roads and munitions plants (☛ Art. 21: The Business of Government, page 285).

Governments also produce some goods and services that are sold. Increasingly, governments are imposing **user charges**, which are fees you must pay for some of the things government can do for you. For example, governments may produce and sell publications, and they charge for services like issuing housing permits and fishing licenses. Turnpike tolls are government user charges.

Although most of the goods and services we use are produced by businesses, we cannot ignore what goes on outside the business sector. *GDP includes the output of the business, household, and government sectors of the economy.*

How do we calculate the contribution that the business sector makes to GDP?

Remember that GDP is intended to measure the total value of the nation's economic activity. To get the total value of what is produced in the business sector, goods and services are counted at their **market value**. *Market value is what the end user of a product or service pays for it.* The best way we have of finding out what the output of the business sector is worth to people is to find out what they are willing to pay for it. That's market value.

GDP includes all the money people pay for the final goods and services they buy from the business sector; it's what people spend for flowers, cars, movies, desk diaries, socks, books, and the millions of other things that the business sector creates and that have value to the user.

> **ROBIN SELLS SHAREWARE:** Commercial computer programs (software) are copyrighted so they cannot be copied and sold by anyone other than the publishers. By comparison, shareware is computer software that its creator puts in the public domain so that anyone can legally copy and use it. Robin distributes a shareware game program (for home entertainment) through the mail for a price of $12 per copy. He claims that his computer game has the same features and the same look and feel as a popular commercial computer game that sells for $85 or more. But every sale of Robin's product adds only $12 to GDP.

Robin's customers may be getting a computer program worth $85 for only $12—a real bargain. Even though Robin's customers may be willing to pay up to $85 for it, GDP is increased only by what people actually pay. Robin's example shows that the government's approach to measuring the value of goods and services in the business sector may understate what they are really worth.

The book you are reading may be another example. If this book improves your economic literacy enough to make you more helpful to your boss and customers, or it enables you to be a more informed investor or voter or speaker, it will be worth far more to you than the modest price you paid for it (which is the amount that its sale contributed to GDP).

Are the values of the goods and services in the household and government sectors measured in the same way as those of the business sector?

How do we assess the value of things done in the household sector and in the government sector where most goods and services are distributed to end users without a price? We cannot simply ignore them when putting GDP figures together, but without a market value we cannot determine what they are really worth to their users. As a compromise we use the costs of producing them.

WHAT HILLARY'S CHURCH GIVES TO GDP: Hillary is a member of a church in her hometown that provides many benefits to the community such as worship services, counseling, youth and social activities, and distributions of food to needy persons. The church's minister gets the use of a house on church property, with some of its maintenance costs paid by the church. His salary and household allowance, the salaries of a secretary and custodian, church supplies, building upkeep, utilities, and related outlays come to $190,000 per year. The activities of this church, therefore, add $190,000 to GDP.

The government statisticians who compile GDP cannot put an actual monetary value on most of the services Hillary's church produced in a year because they are not "sold" (we will discuss the exception next). So the compilers of GDP *estimate* the value of the church's services by looking at what it paid to produce them. The church spent $190,000, so that is the value given to its output. (The church is regarded as the final user of what it bought because it did not resell any of these things.)

Churches are not the only part of the economy treated this way. Most government goods and services are also distributed without charge. So, as in the household sector, we must use costs to determine what they add to GDP. *Government statisticians use the costs of most goods and services created by the household and government sectors to determine their value because these goods and services are not sold; any output that is sold is valued at its price.*

The way market economies value the contributions of the government and household sectors is far less satisfactory than the way they value the contributions of the business sector. Admittedly, cost is not the same as market value. In fact, this approach probably *understates* the value of the output of the government and household sectors, but it's the best that the GDP number crunchers can do.

Some people may be tempted to think that they "pay" for government services by paying taxes. That is not the way government distributes its services, however. Your use of government services may be unrelated to your tax payments. In fact, many people who pay little or no taxes use more government services than those who do. Think of the beneficiaries of food stamps, welfare payments, unemployment compensation, disaster relief, and medicare. (Of course, if you don't pay the taxes you owe, you may be required to use another "free" government service: residence in a jail.)

The household sector, like the government sector, sells some of its output. Here is how Hillary bought one of the services of her church.

SELLING A CHURCH'S SERVICE: When Hillary married Dan, her wedding was held in the church. The minister received $100 from Dan. The church organist was paid $80, and the church received $400 for use of its chapel and social hall, where the reception was held. Therefore, the value of the church's services for the wedding added ($100 + $80 + $400 =) $580 to GDP.

Unlike most church services, weddings are "sold," so that the market gives us a value for it.

How large are the sectors of the U.S. economy?

Table 2A shows us how important each sector is.[3] More than four-fifths of the GDP of the U.S. originates in the business sector. That's not surprising when you look at the things and services you use every day; most of these come from businesses.

How does money that is earned abroad (foreign earnings) change our GDP?

Many American firms and individuals make investments in other nations. If they own facilities that produce goods and services outside the country, what happens to the GDP of the United States? If these investments make money, how do the profits affect GDP?

Table 2A

Sources of the Gross Domestic Product of the U.S. Economy in 1993

SOURCE OF OUTPUT	VALUE OF OUTPUT ($ BILLIONS)	PERCENT OF GDP
Businesses	5,371	85
Households	285	4
Governments	687	11
GDP:	6,343	100

GROWING PROFITS ABROAD: American Yellow Peel Co. is owned by U.S. residents. Its holdings include a wholly owned plant that processes fruit in the Central American nation of Belize. Output of the plant in 1994 was valued at $1,400,000 in U.S. money; this output was included in the GDP of Belize for 1994. The Belize plant earned a profit of $75,000 from its activity that year, which American Yellow Peel Co. distributed to its owners in the U.S. Therefore these profits were part of the company's earnings in Belize; they could not be added to the GDP of the United States, even if they are eventually sent to the American owners.

Goods and services produced abroad by U.S. firms and residents are only added to the GDPs of the nations where they are produced; ownership is not relevant. The profits earned abroad cannot be added to the GDPs of two nations; that would be double counting.

How do transfers of property affect GDP?

A lot of buying and selling of property goes on in our economy that never shows up in GDP, and for good reason; transfers of ownership do not add value. House sales are good examples, although not everything associated with a house purchase is excluded from GDP.

> **RUFUS'S "NEW" HOME:** In 1995, Rufus bought an eight-year-old house from Terry for $135,000. It was sold through a real estate broker to whom Terry paid a commission of 7%, which comes to $9,450. As a result of this transaction, GDP rose by only $9,450.

The GDP for 1995 includes only the value of final goods and services created during that year. The house was built eight years ago, and its value at that time (when Terry built it for $110,000) was included in the GDP for 1987. So Rufus's purchase in 1995 was only a transfer of ownership of an existing property. However, to complete this purchase a real estate agent performed services (showing the house to prospective buyers, running the negotiations, and closing the sale) that had a market value of $9,450, because that is what she was paid for them. The agent's commission became part of GDP in 1995.

Anytime people or businesses buy or sell property, such as stocks or bonds or land, the transaction is only a change of owners. *Transfers of property are not included in GDP because they do not add to the nation's output of goods and services.*

Are winnings and entitlement-program benefits part of GDP?

Take another look at Table 2A. Some people will be surprised that governments (local, state, and federal combined) create only 11% of the nation's output. After all, how many times have we heard about "big government"? Actually, the government is a large part of our economy, but it is not a large creator of goods and services. Most of what the government does is to redistribute goods and services that were created in the business sector (☛ Art. 21: The Business of Government, page 285). These are only transfers of ownership that add nothing to GDP.

Social security, medicare, and the distribution of food stamps are examples of government entitlement programs that involve distributions of money. These distributions of money are called **transfer payments**. Transfer payments are moneys given to individuals or to businesses when the recipients are not required to perform any service or to create any goods in exchange for these payments.

When a severe hurricane, such as Andrew in 1992, hits populated areas, the U.S. Army may distribute food, blankets, tents, and other items. Government budgets pay for most of these goods when the government purchases them from businesses. When these goods are sold to the government, they increase the business sector's share of GDP.

If you added up all local, state, and federal government budgets in the U.S., you would get a sum of money that is more than one-third the size of U.S. GDP, but that does not mean all this government money goes into GDP. The fact is that most government budgets are devoted to transfers of money; governments do not create lots of goods and services. That is why government budgets are larger than what governments contribute to GDP.

State and local governments also make transfer payments for welfare, unemployment compensation, and other purposes.

TANJA AND SAGE GET HELP: An earthquake destroyed the house where Tanja and Sage lived. Fortunately, they were not harmed. Government agencies provided temporary shelter for them in a motel and furnished food and clothing until they established a new home. This assistance cost these agencies a total of $8,000. The government agencies' help added $8,000 to GNP because this was its cost, regardless of what its value was to the couple.

The government agencies purchased services (shelter) and goods from the business sector, where they were created, so the $8,000 actually showed up as a contribution of the business sector to GDP. Government just paid the bills. On the government's books the $8,000 shows up as a transfer payment. The agencies merely transferred the services and goods from the business sector to people needing help.

Winnings are also transfer payments. Suppose you purchased a state lottery ticket and, as a result, won $350,000. Your winnings would add nothing to GDP because you were not required to do any work for the state to earn this prize; you would have created nothing that would go into GDP.

Governments are not the only sources of transfer payments. You might have won money from a drawing run by a store, found a winning sticker in a soda bottle cap, won a publishers' sweepstakes, received prizes on a television game show or other event for which you did not have to perform some service for your award. These are examples of events that result in transfer payments made by businesses to individuals. *Transfer payments, including those from governments, add nothing to GDP because they do not represent the creation of goods or services.*

Are any economic activities left out of GDP?

A lot goes on that is not counted in calculating GDP. An important example is illegal activity. A thief may work hard for his or her ill-gotten gains, but since the "services" of the thief are illegal, they are not considered to add value to the economy and they are not added to GDP.

But this leads to some strange practices by GDP accountants. Some economic activities are included or are left out of GDP depending on where they occur. For example, licensed gambling operations and prostitution are legal in Nevada, so the market values of gambling and prostitution activities in Nevada are added to GDP. So are revenues from gambling in Atlantic City, New Jersey, on Mississippi riverboats in Illinois, on some American Indian reservations, and other places where gambling is legal. But the value of similar gambling and prostitution in places where they are not legal, such as Nevada's neighbor Utah, are not included in GDP. (Does this mean that prostitution is valuable for folks in Nevada but does no good for people in neighboring Utah?) *The value of illegal goods and services is not added to GDP.*

After reading the above paragraph you would be quite correct if you concluded that our method of calculating GDP is controversial. It would be presumptuous to say that it is unflawed. The rules for measuring a nation's economic activity are judgmental and are subject to change. Government statisticians are always debating their methods and often make adjustments in them.

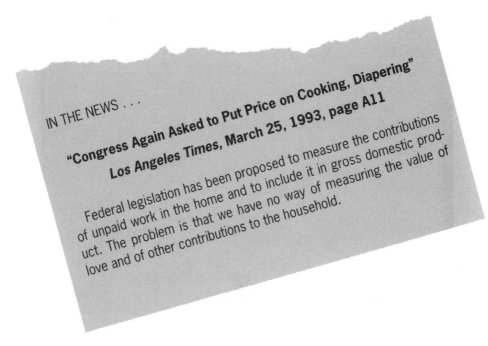

IN THE NEWS · · ·

"Congress Again Asked to Put Price on Cooking, Diapering"

Los Angeles Times, March 25, 1993, page A11

Federal legislation has been proposed to measure the contributions of unpaid work in the home and to include it in gross domestic product. The problem is that we have no way of measuring the value of love and of other contributions to the household.

Does GDP include the value of goods and services produced in the underground economy?

The U.S. government adds to GDP its own estimate of the value of activities in the so-called **underground economy**. When I was a college student working in New York City, I thought that the underground economy included just the vendors who sell pretzels and magazines in subway stations. But this economy really consists of illegal economic activities and of legal transactions that leave no paper trail, i.e., that do not involve a recorded transfer of money. The underground economy might include some (but certainly not all) flea market dealers, baby-sitters, moonlighting tradesmen, and other generally law-abiding persons who deal only in cash and who might not consider their income to be significant enough to report to the government. Less innocent members of the underground economy are drug dealers, prostitutes, thieves, and others who deal only in cash to avoid reporting their illegal activities.[4]

Legal activities in the underground economy should be counted in GDP because they contribute value to the economy. Some economists have estimated that the underground economy alone may be equivalent to about 25% of the measured GDP in the United States, but this figure is controversial. *GDP includes a rough estimate of the value of goods and services created in the underground economy.* The amount that the government adds to GDP for goods and services created in the underground economy is a guess, at best, but many economists believe it is too low.

GDP is an estimate of economic activity; it is not based on moral judgment about that activity. But we should recognize that it is difficult to measure accurately all that goes on in the economy.

Is GDP affected by activities that do not involve money?

Finally, we should note that goods and services distributed through **bartering** are not captured in GDP simply because no money changes hands, even though goods or services are created that have real market value.

> **BARTERING FOR HOME IMPROVEMENTS:** Alex and Nick are neighbors. Alex, who is handy at plumbing, installs some bathroom fixtures in Nick's home, but she charges him nothing for her work. In return Nick, who does good carpentry work, puts some cabinets in Alex's kitchen, without receiving any money from her for his labor. Neither project gets counted in GDP.

Nothing is added to GDP for either project because there was no market transaction. It is not that these two services had no value, it is that the government had no solid basis for measuring their value unless money changed hands. (Nick and Alex each bought materials for their projects from a building supply store. These purchases were added to GDP at the time they were made.)

Now, suppose Alex bought her cabinets from a building supply store and then paid Nick $500 for putting them in her kitchen. After this Nick, who bought the plumbing fixtures for his home, paid Alex $500 for putting them in his bathroom. As a result, GDP would go up by $1,000 to reflect the value of the two projects. Of course, neither Nick nor Alex would gain anything from exchanging equal amounts of money, but unless they went to this trouble of putting monetary value on their work, GDP could not pick it up. That is why our GDP figures really don't tell the whole story.

Economists often use the term **lesser developed countries (LDCs)** to refer to countries where living standards are relatively low. For example, the LDCs in central Africa have per capita incomes that are less than 1% as high as those in developed industrialized nations, such as the United States, Japan, and countries in Western Europe.[5]

Market transactions and use of money in LDCs are far less common than in developed nations. As a result, GDP figures from LDCs are even less reliable (and seriously understate real economic activity) than those from industrialized nations because smaller percentages of their economic activities result in recorded money transactions. Barter and unrecorded transactions are much more prevalent.

We can see that *GDP understates the size of the economy because it does not include many real economic activities, such as those in the underground economy and those that involve bartering.*

ARTICLE 3:

ECONOMIC GROWTH

How Fast Are We Getting Ahead?

How do economists measure a nation's economic progress?

If you want a quick read on how fast an economy is moving ahead, look at its **growth rate**. The growth rate is the percentage change in gross domestic product (GDP) from one year to the next. A vibrant, expanding economy will sustain a high positive growth rate over several years. Sometimes an economy's growth rate will be less than

Table 3A

Growth Rates of the Economy of the U.S. from 1991 to 1993

Year	Nominal GDP, Current Prices ($ billions)	Nominal Growth Rate	Real GDP, 1987 Prices ($ billions)	Real Growth Rate
1990	5,546		4,897	
1991	5,725	3.2%	4,868	−0.6%
1992	6,020	5.2	4,979	2.3
1993	6,343	5.4	5,135	3.1

---

zero; this economy is losing ground and may be in a recession—or worse.

One way of measuring economic progress is to look at the annual rate of growth of GDP, not counting inflation (see below). The U.S. government releases growth rates of GDP four times a year. This information is usually published in newspapers or in government reports.

From 1990 to 1991 the GDP of the United States grew by 3.2%, as shown by the third column of Table 3A.[6] That looks like fairly healthy growth for one year. However, inflation can distort growth rates. Because of such distortions we should understand (and look for) the difference between "nominal GDP" and "real GDP," as explained in the next question.

What is the "real" growth rate?

Economists are not content with just inventing words; they like to put their own meanings on words that everybody else uses. Two examples are the way they use the words *nominal* and *real* when they talk about anything that is measured in dollars. Here you are going to learn about nominal and real GDP. (Never mind that economists don't have anything called *"un*real GDP" or that "nominal GDP" does not mean paltry. Peculiarities like these add some mystique to the language of economics!)

GDP is the total dollar value of all final goods and services produced in the nation during a year (☞ Art. 1: Gross Domestic Product, page 3). When it is measured by adding up what people and businesses actually spend for things, economists call it **nominal GDP**. The prices used to calculate nominal GDP for a given year are the prices people actually paid during that year. Nominal GDP is given in the second column of Table 3A.

> **TAKASHI'S CD COLLECTION:** Takashi loves music and buys CDs and CD racks to store them. In 1993 he bought thirty CDs from a record club at $12.50 each. He also purchased two wooden CD racks from a local discount store at $25 apiece. These purchases added $425 to the nation's nominal GDP for that year. In 1994 he bought thirty-two CDs from the club, at the new price of $13 each, and two more wooden CD racks at the new price of $26.50 each. Takashi's purchases added $469 to nominal GDP in 1994.

Takashi's contribution to nominal GDP from his purchases grew at an annual rate of 10.4% (from $425 to $469). But does that mean that Takashi's share of the nation's economic activity (production of things) grew by 10.4%? No, because the 10.4% growth rate was only partly due to the increased number of products Takashi purchased for his use; the other part of the 10.4% growth rate was due to an increase in the *prices* of the things he bought. *Growth rate of nominal GDP is due to changes in quantities of goods and services purchased and is also due to changes in the prices consumers paid for these things.*

However, when economists talk about economic growth, they really mean changes in the *quantities* of goods and services that are produced. That is because people benefit from consuming larger quantities of things, not from paying higher prices for them. So when economists look at growth rates, they want to filter out the effects of price changes.

To see how they do it, let's go back to Takashi and his CDs.

> **TAKASHI HELPS REAL GROWTH:** Suppose that Takashi could buy CDs and racks in 1994 at the same prices charged for them in 1993. If so, he would have spent $450 in 1994 for the thirty-two CDs and two wooden racks he bought that year, compared with the $425 he shelled out in 1993 for thirty CDs and two racks. His spending would have increased by 5.9% ($450 compared with $425). This was Takashi's contribution to **real GDP** in 1994.

Real GDP is the money buyers would have spent on final goods and services in a certain year if they had been able to buy these same things at prices that were charged for them in some earlier year. Now, the particular earlier year you choose is not important as long as you always know what year that is. *Real GDP is used to compare the nation's outputs in two or more years.* The point is to make comparisons between years without being influenced by price changes; that is why economists pretend everything sold during those years was sold at the same prices.

Government statisticians computed the real GNP shown in Table 3A by dividing nominal GDP by a price index (☛ Art. 11: Inflation, page 128, for an explanation of price indexes). The price index showed how much prices changed between 1987 and the year for which real GDP was calculated.

In Table 3A we looked at the things people actually bought from 1990 to 1993 and saw what these things would have been worth if people had been able to buy these same things, in all years, at 1987 prices. (In these cases 1987 was the "earlier year.")

Perhaps economists' use of the word *real* seems to be strange, but it is an important part of the language of economics. Economists use the word *real* when they want to talk about changes in physical quantities of goods and services and they want to ignore price changes.

Real growth is the change in quantities of goods and services people buy. Looking again at Takashi's purchases, his share of real GDP grew 5.9% from 1993 to 1994. Thus, real growth was 5.9%; he actually got to enjoy 5.9% more things in 1994 than he did in 1993, although the amount of money he spent went up by 10.4% (the increase in his nominal spending).

Take another look at Table 3A. The fourth column shows what the U.S. GDP *would have been* in 1990, 1991, 1992, and 1993 if all goods and services were sold during these years at the prices that prevailed in 1987. (Remember, we are just pretending that prices were the same in all four years.) The figures in the fourth column are real GDP numbers. Using them, we see that real growth from 1990 to 1991 was a *negative* 0.6%, meaning the economy actually shrank. This is somewhat smaller than the positive 3.2% growth rate calculated from nominal GDP figures. The real growth rate tells us that the actual quantity of goods and services people got in 1991 was about one-half percent less than the quantities they received in 1990. By the same reasoning, notice that the real growth rates in later years were somewhat less than the nominal rates; there was a modest recovery in 1992 followed by more normal growth in 1993. The real growth rates give us a better picture of economic progress than do the nominal rates. *Real economic growth is the percentage change in real GDP from one year to the next; this shows how much progress the economy made in creating goods and services for end users.*

Incidentally, Table 3A shows us that prices rose about 2.3% from 1992 to 1993. That is because nominal growth equals real growth plus inflation; real growth of 3.1% plus inflation of 2.3% equals 5.4% nominal growth. *The difference between the real growth rate and the nominal growth rate is the rate of inflation.*

Graph 3A

Growth Rates of Real GDP

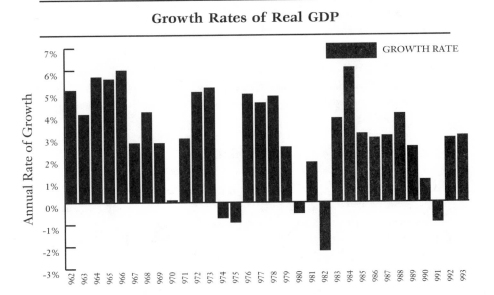

What is a normal real growth rate for the U.S. economy?

Graph 3A on page 27 shows how growth has varied over the past three decades.[7] The economy has not grown uniformly. In the "best" years the nation's real growth rate was better than 5% (1964–66, 1972–73, and 1984); during these years the economy took giant steps forward. In the "worst" years real growth was zero or negative (1970, 1974–75, 1980, 1982, and 1991). Part of these years there were recessions, when the economy took backward steps; fortunately the years when real GDP fell were far fewer than the number of years when real GDP rose. A **recession** is a period of general weakness in the economy; it is always true that during recessions real GDP declines for at least two consecutive quarter years (☞ Art. 4: Business Cycles, page 35).

Economies do not progress smoothly. They all go through periods of expansion, when real growth is positive, and through periods of contraction (or recession), when real growth is negative. All of the years listed in Graph 3A where growth was negative were recession years, at least in part. (Recessions spilled over into other years as well. For example, there was a recession in parts of both 1990 and 1991, but negative real growth in 1990 was not large enough to overshadow the positive growth that took place that year.)

Immediately following most recessions the economy snapped back sharply. But there were exceptions. The recovery in 1981 was so weak the economy slipped back into another recession in 1982, but growth after that was swift. The recovery from the 1990–91 recession was slow.

From 1959 to 1992 the real rate of growth in the United States averaged 3% per year, but annual real growth varied significantly from year to year.

When are growth rates published?

Calculating GDP is a monumental task. Using information on both incomes and spending in the economy, the U.S. Department of Commerce estimates and reports GDP, and the rate of growth of GDP, only four times per year. Despite their best efforts, government bean counters cannot hope to record all activity in a large and

Table 3B

Real GDP and Real Growth in 1993, by Quarter

Period	GDP (1987 $ billions)	Growth (%)
1st quarter	5,078	0.8
2nd quarter	5,105	2.4
3rd quarter	5,139	2.7
4th quarter	5,218	6.3
Full year:	5,135	3.1

complex economy. The best they can do is to derive estimates. But the elaborate accounting system and care used by the Commerce Department suggests that the numbers are valuable and probably not far off the mark.

Each time GDP is calculated, it is presented as an annual total. Similarly, *growth rates are always expressed on an annual basis.* That's important to remember. Furthermore, economists always calculate growth rates by using *real* GDP figures, which means figures based on prices in some earlier year. That way the growth rates they get represent actual changes in tangible goods and services; they are not inflated by price changes.

Examine the figures for the year 1993 in Table 3B.[8] The real growth rate varied somewhat over the year, from an anemic annual rate of change of 0.8% to a very robust 6.3%.

Here is an example of how these quarterly figures were calculated. The Commerce Department estimated that production of final goods and services during the second quarter of 1993 (April, May, June) had a value of just over $1,276 billion. If this rate were maintained for an entire year, GDP would be 4 × $1,276 billion, or $5,105 billion, after rounding off, which is the amount shown in Table 3B. The quarterly estimates released during 1993 were not bad; a few months into 1994, when all the data were in, the government reported that actual real GDP in 1993 was $5,135 billion.

Are all government figures on economic growth reliable?

Economists and others have such a keen interest in economic growth that they cannot wait for the quarterly figures to be fully tabulated. To accommodate their hunger for data the U.S. Department of Commerce publishes a **flash estimate of economic growth** at the end of each quarter year. This is nothing more than an early estimate. A few weeks later, when the final figures are in, the same agency publishes a **revised rate of growth**; this is the final figure. The flash and revised figures are usually close, but *sometimes the difference between flash and revised growth rates is large*. For example, the flash estimate of the rate of annual growth of real GDP for the first quarter of 1993 was 1.8%; the final figure showed growth during that quarter at an annual rate of a mere 0.8% (see Table 3B).[9] Many economists have questioned the value of flash estimates because they are sometimes way off the mark, but interest in flash estimates remains high enough to keep them in demand.

How fast should the economy grow?

A sea change in attitudes about government involvement in a market economy occurred during the Great Depression of the 1930s, when the national governments of the United States and the United Kingdom used fiscal policy to strengthen their economies (☛ Art. 24: Fiscal Policy and Government Debt, page 325). One of the most important articulations of this, although it came somewhat later, was the U.S. Employment Act of 1946. The act did not mandate that the government maintain *full* employment, but it gave the federal government responsibility for using its taxing and spending powers to maintain a high level of national employment and prosperity (☛ Art. 6: The Unemployment Rate, page 60).

The vehicle for maintaining high employment was economic growth. *An economy must grow as fast as its population just to stay even; it must grow faster than population to progress.* Given annual population growth in the U.S. of about 2%, a 3% rate of growth of real GDP is usually sufficient to create enough new jobs to absorb additional workers in the labor force and to allow for some modest improvement.

What makes an economy grow?

Although a political commitment to maintaining economic growth was made by the Employment Act of 1946, economic growth became a particularly faddish topic for academic economists in the 1960s. This was due to the slow growth of the U.S. economy in the late fifties and early sixties and the desire of politicians and economists to accelerate the nation's progress. There may have been some mercenary motives as well. Economists have to make a living, and they saw that at the time the government was willing to give them hefty research grants to study economic growth. However, these grants only added to economists' passionate interest in this important subject, just as perfume may be used in the bedroom.

Another reason for political interest in economic growth in the 1960s was the Cold War. Capitalist and Communist nations were vying for the allegiances of nonaligned developing nations (so-called Third World countries) by trying to promote their economies. Many academic careers were built on new growth theories, and one economist, Robert Solow of MIT, won a Nobel prize for his work on this subject.

While economists differ in their prescriptions for growth, most have more or less agreed on the sources of economic growth. A nation's real GDP depends on the size of its **workforce** and on the amount of **capital** it has accumulated. The workforce consists of the number of people ready and able to do productive work. To economists *capital* means the quantity of factories, machinery, and other man-made assets that can be used to create goods and services. (To noneconomists *capital* generally means money.) Finally, GDP depends on **technology**. This represents the skill and know-how people have to enable them to use the labor force and capital the economy possesses.

An economy can grow by increasing its stock of capital. This happens when people and companies put some of their income aside to invest in new plants and equipment (☛ Art. 16: Investment, page 197).

An economy can also grow by increasing the size of its labor force. This happens as a population's birthrate grows, as people immigrate to a nation, or as more people decide to work. For example, if "domestic executives" (housewives and househusbands) go to work for money, and as people postpone retirement, the labor force grows (☛ Art. 5: Employment, page 50).

Finally, an economy can grow by improving its technology. This happens if workers become better educated. It also happens when inventors, scientists, and managers discover better ways of doing work and design better machinery. These technological advances make labor and capital more productive.

Thus, *an economy grows by increasing the size of its labor force, by increasing its capital, and by improving the productivity of labor and capital with better technology.* Economists have discovered that a little more than half of the real economic growth of the United States since World War II resulted from building up the labor force and capital stock. The rest was due to improvements in technology.

Do all nations have the same real growth rate at any one time?

Nations differ in their ability or willingness to increase the amount and quality (productivity) of their workforces and their capital. After all, a nation cannot improve its labor force unless (1) its population grows, (2) it has schools and other means for training people, and (3) workers are willing and able to get education. It cannot increase its capital unless it has money to invest. It cannot improve technology unless it can put effort into research and development and has the initiative to change its ways of doing things.

Another reason that growth rates differ among nations is that, during any year, some nations may be experiencing recessions while others are growing. In our global economy nations are closely linked through international trade and investment, but they are not all in step; some lead and some lag, and others just march to the tune of a different drummer.

Table 3C shows the growth rates of several nations for 1989 or 1990.[10] (Lesser-developed nations take longer to report their economic data, so for these nations the most recent figures were for 1989, at the time of this writing. For advanced nations 1990 data were readily available. To compare growth rates among nations it is important to use data from the same or nearby years.)

Table 3C	
Real Growth Rates of Selected Nations in 1989 or 1990	
NATION	GROWTH
Canada	−1.1 %
Colombia	3.7
India	2.5
Japan	4.5
Mexico	4.0
Nigeria	5.2
Saudi Arabia	1.5
United Kingdom	−1.9
United States	−0.7

During the period covered by Table 3C the U.S. and some other industrialized nations were experiencing a recession, hence their growth rates were negative. Other nations, such as Japan, entered recessions later. Germany's growth was dragged down by the acquisition of East Germany by the Federal Republic of Germany; real growth in East Germany was somewhat lower than that in the West. *Real growth rates differ among nations because they do not have the same ability to achieve economic progress.* Nations differ in their wealth of labor, capital, and technology.

In addition, *at any one time nations experience different influences on growth.* Political factors, discoveries of resources, technological progress, and economic policies are not the same in every nation at one time. So some nations may grow at the same time others experience setbacks, and later these scenarios may reverse. For example, the United States experienced a recession in 1990 and 1991 while the Japanese economy was growing strongly; see the growth rates in Table 3C. However, shortly afterward, Japan had a recession (1992 and 1993) at the same time the U.S. economy was experiencing moderate growth.

Does growth tell us about improvements in standards of living?

Real growth measures only changes in the amount of goods and services that a nation produces for end users. It does not tell us how much better off people are as a result of this production.

NEDSTOWN GETS A NEW INDUSTRY: Nedstown is a small city that had a high unemployment rate. The city's development commission has succeeded in getting a large corporation to build a food-processing complex on some vacant property. As a result, the unemployment rate declined sharply, many local firms increased their sales, and incomes rose. But the new industry also brought traffic congestion, air and water pollution, demand for new facilities (roads, schools, and sewers), and higher crime rates.

The new economic activity in Nedstown has increased real growth, which measures only the change in the market value of goods and services. The new traffic congestion has lengthened travel times for everyone, not just for the new plant employees. The new pollution has bothered many people, harmed gardens, and restricted the use of a public lake that was popular with swimmers and fishermen. The city must now spend money on new sewers and other facilities instead of improving parks and providing other amenities. Many residents feel that quality of life in the city has declined.

Economic welfare is the term economists use to represent the utility or satisfaction that people get from their incomes. Quality of life is an important part of economic welfare. When a place such as Nedstown experiences real growth, there are gainers and losers. The gainers are those who are better off as a result of increased income. The losers are those who feel that their quality of life has suffered because of the greater air pollution, congestion, and crime that occur when income goes up. If we could add up the gains from real economic growth and the losses in quality of life resulting from that same growth, we could find out if, on balance, the city's economic welfare has risen or fallen. Unfortunately we cannot do this. Much of what a city gains is easy to measure because it consists mostly of new income and consumption; these can be expressed in dollars. But losses are not easily expressed in dollars because they involve deterioration in quality of life, for which we have no commonly accepted yardsticks.

Because we do not have a widely accepted way of calculating changes in economic well-being, it is likely that *real growth, measured in dollars, exaggerates the benefits people get from the production of more goods and services.* The way we measure growth does not capture some negative effects that a region's higher income might have on its quality of life.

ARTICLE 4:

BUSINESS CYCLES

Riding the Economy's Roller Coaster

What are business cycles?

Business cycles are common in market economies where decisions about hiring and producing are made by many separate firms and government agencies. *A **business cycle** consists of more or less simultaneous expansions in many types of economic activity, followed by more or less simultaneous contractions in activity (or vice versa).* Cycles result from unintended excesses or shortages that occur because decisions in a free economy are made by many persons who do not have to coordinate their actions.

The former Soviet economies claimed to have moderated cycles by centralizing all major economic decisions, although one of the prices they paid for this was a lack of significant economic growth. Another price was persistent shortages of goods and services. (Actually, the degree of success that Communist governments had in moderating cycles is open to question because government bureaucrats could cook up data to describe the conditions of their economies.)

While cycles recur, they are not uniform. Some cycles are long and others are short. A cycle may have a duration of from one to as many as twenty years before being followed by another cycle.

Business cycles are really deviations from **long-term economic growth**. For the past fifty years the economy of the United States has grown an average of 3% per year. The upward movement in cycles often consist of higher rates of growth, while the downward

---

HANK HAWKS MAGAZINES: Hank runs a subscription service that sells magazines, at discount rates, to students and professors on college campuses. Enrollments at the colleges he covers have grown an average of 2% a year for over twenty years, and so have his subscription sales. During lean years, when student earnings and financial aid shrink, Hank's sales frequently drop, giving him negative growth. But when jobs and aid are plentiful, sales may grow at 4% or 5%. Over the fat and the lean years, Hank's sales growth (and his profits) follows a business cycle with a long-run average of +2%.

---

movements consist of "negative growth" or backward movement. Cycles are like the upward and downward movements of a roller coaster, but a roller coaster that successively moves the rider to higher altitudes; each upward movement is a little larger than the dip that follows it.

What happens during the business cycle?

A business cycle consists of two consecutive phases: an **upturn** in economic activity that is followed by a general business **expansion**. During this phase of the cycle incomes rise and new jobs are created. Following this, the pace of upward movement slows and the economy reaches a **peak** of activity; this is the high point of a business cycle. The peak is followed by the second phase, a business **downturn** where the economy begins experiencing negative growth. Sales of many businesses decline, unemployment increases, and some incomes fall. What follows this downturn is an accelerated slump called a **recession**. Eventually the economy reaches its **trough**, the low point in the cycle, from which an upturn starts a new business cycle. Thus, *business cycles pass through successive phases of upturn, expansion, downturn, and recession.*

Economists have a rough rule of thumb for finding out about when an expansion or recession begins. *In general, a recession begins around the time when a downturn results in two or more consecutive quarter years of decline in real gross domestic product. In general, an expansion begins around the time when an upturn results in two or more quarters of increasing real GDP.* (See the question and answer below on "dating" business cycles.)

A rapid expansion is sometimes called a business **boom**. A long and deep recession is sometimes called a **depression**. Boom and depression are subjective terms. A timeworn bit of economic humor is that when your neighbor is unemployed, it's a recession; when you are out of work, it must be a depression. Economists often disagree on the severity of an economic downturn or of the strength of an upswing in the economy. Pictures of couples are now common in the society pages of many newspapers; when I look at some engagement and wedding photos, I am convinced that love is blind. In economics as in human relationships, it depends on your perspective.

Business-cycle phases affect individuals and businesses.

FELICIA ADJUSTS HER SALES STAFF: Felicia is responsible for catalog sales and for the order department of a mail-order club selling recorded music: audiocassettes and compact discs (they gave up LP records five years ago). Every six weeks she mails catalogs to the record club's thirty-eight thousand members. During the past three years each mailing brought in an average of $400,000 in sales. During the first half of this year average sales per mailing fell steadily and are now down to $268,000. She interprets this as a business downturn presaging a recession and responds by reducing her order-department staff by 40%. Furthermore, some remaining staff members with low seniority are put on notice.

Felicia recognizes that the record club's products are luxuries and that they are among the first things consumers may cut from their budgets when their incomes fall. She also recognizes the phases of a typical business cycle. Specifically, a mild downturn often comes before a sharp recessionary decline in economic activity. Knowing the phases of the business cycle, Felicia responded to a one-third drop in sales by laying off 40% of her staff, thereby preparing for leaner times.

Of course, if Felicia's decisions are copied by many other business managers, the recession may become a self-fulfilling prophecy. Consumer confidence also plays a role. When some of Felicia's workers lose their jobs, they will cut back on their own purchases; as a result, sales of other firms will suffer, and this will lead to job losses in those businesses. The resulting domino effect could create a recession.

How long are expansions and recessions?

For the past fifty years (since World War II) the U.S. economy has moved completely through nine cycles. During this time *U.S. recessions have lasted an average of eleven months and business expansions have had an average length of fifty months.* That means that the average length of business cycles has been (50 + 11 =) sixty-one months, or about five years.

But the length of recessions, and of cycles, varies. Take a look at the nine recessions listed in Table 4A.[11] The shortest recession was only six months and the longest was sixteen months. Furthermore, all expansions (the periods between recessions) were not alike; some were short and others were long.

Notice that recessions were much shorter than expansions. In fact, we might say that business expansions are the "normal" conditions of the economy and that recessions are brief interruptions of long-term economic growth.

Was the Great Depression of the 1930s really the "big one"?

There is a lot of folklore about recessions. Like most folklore, our images of past recessions are based on both fact and exaggeration.

The U.S. Department of Commerce has data on recessions all the way back to 1858. According to these records, the so-called Great Depression of the 1930s was a whopping forty-three months long, stretching from 1929 to 1933. Many of today's senior citizens can tell us how they struggled through this period. The difficulties of the 1930s are well documented; they were severe, and we have come to believe it was the granddaddy of all recessions. But in terms of length, it was not. The recession from 1873 to 1879 was a lot longer (sixty-five months). Although we do not have a reliable measure of the severity of the recession of the 1870s, it might have been more painful than the recession of the 1930s since the nation had no New Deal or other government programs to aid the weak economy; the patient had to care for itself.

Perhaps one reason folks don't talk about the "Great Depression of the 1870s" is that we don't have anyone with us who lived

Table 4A

U.S. Recessions over the Past Fifty Years

Peak	Trough	Length (Months)
Nov. 1948	Oct. 1949	11
July 1953	May 1954	10
Aug. 1957	Apr. 1958	8
Apr. 1960	Feb. 1961	10
Dec. 1969	Nov. 1970	11
Nov. 1973	Mar. 1975	16
Jan. 1980	July 1980	6
July 1981	Nov. 1982	16
July 1990	Mar. 1991	8

through it, nor do we have the elaborate oral histories and statistical data that were collected about the Depression of the 1930s.

Another bit of economic folklore concerns the "roaring twenties," which preceded the Great Depression. Overall, the 1920s was a period of dramatic growth for many American industries. But this growth was interrupted by three short recessions (1920–21, 1923–24, and 1926–27) before the severe recession that started in 1929. In fact, no other decade was so pockmarked by recession. The agricultural sector was in almost continuous recession throughout the 1920s and well into the 1930s. Those flickering black-and-white movies of flappers and top-hatted gentlemen that helped to shape our image of that era are like sundials; they recorded only the sunny hours.

Lengths of recessions are not the same as severity. The sixteen-month-long 1973–75 recession in the U.S. was the most severe since that of the 1930s in terms of job losses and falling incomes. The 1981–82 recession was comparatively mild, yet it also had a length of sixteen months.

Do all major economic indicators turn down during recessions? Do they move up together during expansions?

Business cycles are broad events that have an impact on many people and businesses. But we have no single yardstick for measuring cycles. This is because, during a recession, some economic indicators fall rapidly at the same time that others decline slowly or hardly fall at all. Yet other indicators are laggards that start their declines long after the others. Furthermore, during recessions some economic indicators even move up. The same is true during expansions; the various parts of our economy do not move together. The economy is always a mixed bag.

CLEM AND BETTY FIX OLD CARS: Clem and Betty run an auto repair and salvage business. Recently in their community a lot of people were out of work, and business owners complained of falling sales and profits. Car transportation was important in their rural area, but most folks could not afford to replace their aging vehicles. Betty was the local heroine because she could almost always find in the salvage yard a used replacement part to keep an old car running; she also found many repairable cars, which were in big demand by younger drivers. Clem, the mechanic, worked twelve hours a day fixing up cars that their owners could not afford to replace. During the recession Clem and Betty's income nearly doubled from what it was when the general economy was booming.

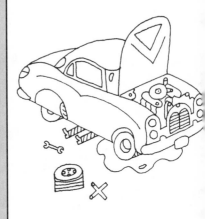

There are always small pockets of prosperity during recessions. Repair services, discount stores, used-furniture stores, and salvage operators often prosper; of course, so do bankruptcy lawyers. Some of these same businesses do not do well when the general economy is growing rapidly.

Gross domestic product, business profits, short-term interest rates, and some commodity prices move in sync with business cycles. Other economic indicators that conform closely to cycles are prices of steel, agricultural output, fuels, and sales of "big-ticket" consumer items. These big-ticket items include cars, pleasure boats, and furniture. The important fact to note about these items, called **durable goods**, is that buyers have some leeway in deciding when to buy them because they have potentially long useful lives. Other big-ticket items that are discretionary are services such as vacation packages and face-lifts (except, perhaps, for actors). Construction of houses is also highly correlated with cycles.

Cycles will have milder effects on the production of **nondurable goods** and of services. These are items that must be purchased frequently because they are used or consumed over short periods. Foods, utilities, and newspapers are nondurables. Services such as transportation, health care, and haircutting have the same weak response to cycles as do nondurables during the upward and downward phases of the cycle.

SIMON ADJUSTS TO UNEMPLOYMENT: Felicia's husband, Simon, was a supervisor in the order department of a record club until he was laid off as a result of "downsizing." While working, he took home $1,800 per month after taxes and other deductions. Unemployment compensation and money from his savings will enable him to contribute only $1,300 monthly to the household. He and Felicia, who retains her job at the club, have decided to make these changes in their monthly budget to cut expenses by $500:

- Reduce entertainment expenditures (including restaurant meals) by $150.
- Reduce vacation club contributions by $150.
- Decrease charge card usage by at least $100.
- Cut down grocery purchases by $40 (mostly dessert items).
- The household will cut charitable contributions, home improvements, and savings by $30 each (total of $90).
- Clothing purchases will drop by $25.
- By turning down the thermostat in winter, and up in summer, utilities will be cut by $25.
- Simon and Felicia will give themselves $50 less pocket money each month.
- Simon will take on an expenditure of $130 per month in additional costs to replace some of the insurance benefits formerly provided by his employer.

Many items in Simon's budget are probably inflexible over the next few months. Things like rent or mortgage payments, basic telephone and cable TV fees, life and home insurance premiums, and most light and heating costs are fixed; they cannot be changed quickly. It may be costly to refinance a mortgage. Removal and installation of telephone and cable services require payment of special fees, and depending on lifestyle and location, many people regard them as necessities. (The family agreed to lower thermostat settings in winter and to cut out some toll calls.) The major "give" in Simon's budget hits so-called discretionary items like new clothing, new appliances, vacations, and eating out.

The economy's response to a recession will mirror the adjustments in Simon's household. Sales of industries selling luxury goods and other discretionary items in Simon's budget will fall. This will include restaurants, movie theaters, and vacation resorts. Industries that sell necessities will notice lesser declines; these include utility companies, cable TV service, and health care providers. (Although some people consider basic cable TV a "necessity," premium and "pay as you view" cable services are a luxury.)

In general, *sales of industries that sell nondurable goods and essential services decline moderately during the downward phases (downturn and recession) of the business cycle; sales of industries that provide luxury goods and services decline sharply.* Sales of industries that decline sharply during recessions usually grow sharply during expansions. Employment in these industries generally rises and falls along with sales.

However, during recessions these conforming economic indicators will still be like raindrops on a windowpane in that they will not fall at the same rate nor will they begin their descents together. Some economic measurements are called **leading economic indicators** because they tend to start their declines before most others and/or they tend to start their expansions early. Here are some examples of leading indicators: initial claims for unemployment, stock market prices, issuance of building permits, and consumer expectations (sentiment).

Some other economic activities are **lagging economic indicators**. They tend to turn the corner after most others; they are among the last indicators to turn down in a recession and among the last to turn up in an expansion. Some lagging economic indicators are the prime interest rate, average length of unemployment, and changes in the prices of services.

Do economists have some favorite indicator to follow the course of business cycles?

The business cycle is not a measurement; it doesn't come with a number. That's because the business cycle is a notion about the more or less simultaneous movements of a large bunch of economic activities. In fact, there is no specific list of what all these activities are. This is frustrating to many economists because they have a passion for numerical indicators. Number crunching is in their bones.

Since there was no yardstick to measure the phases of a business cycle, economists had to invent one. It's called the **Index of**

Table 4B	
Index of Coincident Indicators for the U.S. Economy (Index = 100 in 1987)	
YEAR	AVG. VALUE
1989	114.5
1990	114.7
1991	108.7
1992	106.5
1993	109.1

Coincident Indicators and is used to help determine when business expansions and recessions begin and end. *The Index of Coincident Indicators is a useful, though imprecise, measure of the current condition of our economy.*

Meteorologists had the same problem. They could measure temperature, wind velocity, windchill, humidity, and atmospheric pressure, but they had no way of finding out if the weather was "good" or "bad." So they invented a Discomfort Index, made up of measurements of temperature and humidity. Of course, this index gives us a subjective assessment at best; there is no guarantee you will be comfortable when the Discomfort Index is low, and vice versa. No two persons may be equally comfortable (or miserable) when the index has a specific value. (Any church custodian knows that some members of the congregation will complain about the heat or cold no matter where the thermostat is set.)

By the same token, there is no reason to believe that every industry or sector of the economy will be prosperous when the Index of Coincident Indicators goes up, and not all parts of the economy will be hurting when the Index of Coincident Indicators plunges. The reason is that not all parts of our economy move in lockstep through an expansion or recession.

Some values of the index are shown in Table 4B.[12] The index is calculated monthly and compares current index components with their average value in 1987. The average monthly value of the Index of Coincident Indicators in 1992 was 106.5, which meant that economic activity was about 7% greater than it was in 1987. More important, however, was that the index value was lower in 1992 than it was in 1991. The index was somewhat below the peak it had reached in 1990. This showed us that the economy was still near the lows it hit during the 1990–91 recession.

Actually, the index reached its lowest monthly value at the end of 1991; it started to climb slowly about the middle of 1992.

How is the Index of Coincident Indicators put together?

The Index of Coincident Indicators is made up of four important economic yardsticks. The first component of the Coincident Index is **employees on nonagricultural payrolls**. This is the number of nonfarm workers who receive wages or salaries. Employment is an important indicator because it tells us how we are using the nation's labor force (people who are willing to work), which is our nation's most important economic resource.

The second component of the Coincident Index is **personal income less transfer payments**. Personal income consists of all the money people receive during a month or year. Transfer payments are those incomes received by persons who do not produce goods or services in exchange for them at the time these incomes are received; examples are social security benefits, unemployment compensation, welfare allowances, and lottery winnings. When you take transfer payments away from personal income, the remaining income consists only of what people receive for the work they do. The third component of the Coincident Index is **industrial production**. This is a measurement of the physical quantities of commodities and goods that our economy generates. It includes the production of factories, mines, oil and gas wells, and the output of electric utilities.

In the nineteenth century the famous American steel tycoon Andrew Carnegie would frequently stand on a hill overlooking a city and count the number of factory smokestacks that were in use. In the absence of more sophisticated statistical compilations, this was his measure of business activity. The Index of Coincident Indicators is today's more sophisticated way of "counting the smokestacks," and unlike Carnegie's indicator, it measures more than manufacturing activity.

The fourth component of the Coincident Index is **manufacturing and trade sales**. This component includes (1) sales of goods by manufacturers, (2) sales of wholesalers, and (3) retail sales of goods and services. Sales are not the same as production; a store may sell a toy doll that was produced months or even years ago, yet the sale is a measurement of current economic activity because it measures what the store is doing.

These measures only represent the huge variety of "doings" in the economy (to borrow the British jargon). They do not give us a complete picture of business cycles. But they include four of the broadest measures of economic activity that we have.

The Index of Coincident Indicators is not well known outside the economics profession. But it has a much more famous sibling called the Index of Leading Indicators, which is regularly reported by the media as a forecaster of economic conditions.

Is the Index of Coincident Indicators more useful than the nation's GDP when it comes to following the business cycle?

Real gross domestic product (meaning GDP with the effects of price changes filtered out) is a broad and important indicator of cycles. But real GDP does a poor job of tracking the economy closely. That is because GDP data is calculated and published only once every three months.

Each of the components of *the Index of Coincident Indicators is published monthly, so the index allows us to track the economy more closely than does GDP*, and it gives us earlier signs of important economic changes.

How do we know just when expansions and recessions start and finish?

Business cycles are not neat affairs; they represent advances and declines in a large number of activities, all of which seem to march to the beat of their own drummer. So picking a date when a cycle reaches its peak, or when it reaches its trough, is a tough call. This task is left to the deliberation of a small group of prominent economists who work for the National Bureau of Economic Research (NBER). The group calls itself the Business Cycle Dating Committee.

The NBER is a nonprofit research organization, supported by private donations, that back in the 1920s pioneered the study of business cycles. The NBER has examined hundreds of economic indicators, and most of what we know about cycles today comes from its work. The U.S. Department of Commerce, which publishes official economic data, recognizes the NBER's Dating Committee as our national authority for picking the tops and bottoms of cycles.

The Dating Committee determines the "official" month when an expansion or recession begins. Its authority comes from the recognition given to its dates by the Commerce Department and by most economists and business analysts. The committee bases its judgment on changes in real GDP, on the Index of Coincident Indicators, and on dozens of other important economic indicators. (Despite its name, the Dating Committee doesn't do anything for the social lives of economists.)

Most happy couples would find it hard to pinpoint the time when they fell in love (or, in some cases, when they fell out of love). That is because love develops, it does not just happen (except in the movies and several times in the lives of teenagers). Pinpointing the dates of the business cycle is just as difficult and subjective. It's a dirty job, but someone has to do it.

The Dating Committee is so thorough in its deliberations that its official pronouncements of the dates of cycle peaks and troughs are often made several months after the event. For example, the committee decided that the bottom of the 1990–91 recession in the U.S. was reached in March 1991. But this official date was not announced until December of 1992. Is it possible that the good professors on the Dating Committee are ever late for their classes?

2

Jobs and Wages of People at Work

No production takes place in an economy without the initiatives and efforts of people. The number of people employed in our economy, and the work they do, determine the goods and services that are created. But that is not the only reason employment is important. Employment generates most of the income people receive, and with this income they can buy the goods and services they need and want.

Article 5: Employment opens the chapter by discussing what determines how many people work. Employment is the number of people in the nation who are working for pay. You will see how employment is measured, what determines the number of people that employers hire (and fire), and where people work in our economy. But a mere counting of workers is only part of the employment picture. This article closes with a look at the "quality" of employment, the way in which the nation utilizes its workforce. Article 6 focuses on unused labor resources, or what is better known as unemployment. The article discusses the dynamic factors that cause the unemployment rate to rise and to fall. You will also see what high and low unemployment rates are and why the unemployment rate has gradually been drifting upward for over thirty years, even as the economy becomes more prosperous.

The unemployment rate is one of the most closely watched statistics in economics. However, there are actually three types of unemployment, and they differ in what they can show us about the condition of the economy. In this article you will see how to use them to gain insight into the nature of the problem of unemployment.

These articles on employment and unemployment are the most important of the chapter. They cover concepts basic to economic literacy. The next two articles are a little more technical.

Article 7: Changing the Workplace begins with an explanation of why people go in and out of the labor market. These entrances and exits are important because they determine the supply of workers the economy can use. This article explains how government legislation influences the workforce, as well as the incomes people receive for their work. Finally, the article analyzes the effect of labor unions on both jobs and wages. (Economists use the word *wage* when they mean any type of payment for a person's work, whether it be an hourly fee, weekly salary, bonus, or commission.) Unions exert more influence over the labor market than their sizes would suggest.

Employment and unemployment are familiar topics, although not ones that are widely understood. However, Article 8: Human Capital discusses a vital subject that has received comparatively scant attention outside the economics profession. Human capital is the productive capacity of the individual. It determines an individual's contribution to the economy, and as a result, it is closely related to income. In this article you will learn why people earn different incomes and what determines the value of their human capital. You will also learn how human capital can be increased and why it is important to the competitiveness and growth of the economy.

The articles in this chapter will give you an understanding and an appreciation of people at work.

ARTICLE 5:

EMPLOYMENT

How Many People Are Working?

How many people are working and where are they?

People working make things happen in an economy. **Employment** is defined as the total number of persons who are working for pay; it's a snapshot of what people are doing.

The total number of people employed is one of the most important and closely watched economic indicators for at least two reasons. First, people are the most important economic resource that a nation possesses; without employment of a skilled and ample labor force a nation cannot take advantage of its man-made assets and its natural resources. Second, employment is linked to income; the more people earn, the more they can buy. Therefore, employment goes a long way in determining the standard of living a nation's residents can enjoy.

Each month the U.S. Department of Labor reports the total number of people in the United States who are working for pay. This includes people who are self-employed and people who work for others. In this article you will learn about employment in the U.S. and how to analyze employment figures.

Table 5A gives you a quick look at employment in the United States.[1] First, notice the bottom of the table. On average, *over 120 million persons were employed in the United States in 1993.* (The number in the table is the average of monthly figures.) About 10 million of these people were self-employed, primarily in services.

The term *services* in Table 5A refers to all jobs in firms where the principal product is a service not listed elsewhere. Your barber or beautician, physician, plumber, and garbage collector are all in services. But service industries include retail stores, transportation, finance, and many other businesses. The government is also consid-

Table 5A

Persons Employed in the United States, 1993

INDUSTRY	WORKERS (THOUSANDS)	PERCENT
Services	32,445	27
Retail and wholesale trade	26,546	22
Government	22,875	19
Manufacturing	18,189	15
Finance	6,940	6
Transportation	5,896	5
Construction	4,813	4
Agriculture	1,915	2
Mining	610	1
Totals:	120,229	100

ered to be a service industry. Manufacturing includes all people working in places where the principal product is a tangible good. Manufacturing firms make furniture, appliances, machinery, foods, clothing, cosmetics, and other items.

Second, look at where people work. Certainly, *in terms of the industries people work for, America has become a service-oriented economy.* Manufacturing, once the dominant source of employment, now plays a minor role in providing employment.[2]

Workers are classified by the industry they work for, not by what they do. A secretary who works for a carmaker is employed in "manufacturing," and a secretary who works for a bank is employed in "finance," even if they do essentially the same type of work. In fact, they both perform services rather than make some item. The reason for classifying workers this way is that the automaker's secretary helps to facilitate the making of cars, even if he/she never gets onto the factory floor.

(Incidently, the term **workers** is used to refer to any people who receive pay for what they do. It does not refer to any particular group of employees, such as those who are near the bottom of the corporate ladder. Workers include people who wear coveralls and people who wear suits. Even college professors, whose workday apparel falls somewhere between coveralls and suits, are workers!)

Why do some workers get a small share of the value of what they produce, while others get a large share?

Just because 78% of employed persons work in service industries does not mean that three-fourths of the value of all the economic activity in the United States comes from services. In fact, currently services contribute only about half of the total value of the goods and services produced.

If services employ 78% of our workers, but produce only about half of what the economy turns out, are service workers less efficient than workers who manufacture goods? Not really. The services industry is more **labor-intensive** than manufacturing. That means that a larger percentage of the value obtained from selling services comes from the "sweat" of people who perform the services. By comparison, manufacturing is often **capital-intensive** because a large share of the value of many manufactured goods comes from nonhuman resources that are used to produce these goods: natural resources (e.g., wood, oil, foodstuff), machinery and equipment, and factories.

PHYLLIS AND DUANE AT WORK: Phyllis is a tour guide in a city. In a typical day her tours generate $300 in revenue for her employer. Her daily wage is $105, which is 35% of the revenue her work brings in; the remaining revenue pays for operating a bus, advertising, sales, the wages of other personnel, equipment, office overhead, and profit. Her husband, Duane, operates a steel press turning out car doors. In an average workday Duane produces doors worth $3,300 and he collects a wage of $165, which equals 5% of the value of the doors; the remaining 95% goes to pay for the costly machine and tools he uses, steel and other materials put into the product, power, administration, transportation, plant maintenance, and profits.

Phyllis's work is labor-intensive; her labor contributes most of the value of her product. Duane's work is important, but his efforts contribute a small share of the value of his product because there are important (and costly) contributions made by materials and machinery. Of course, without operatives like Duane no car doors would be produced at all.

Another reason that employment numbers alone do not tell us much about the value of output is that workers differ in their level of skill and in the demand people have for their work. For example, there is wide variation in the fees that professional violinists receive for a two-hour concert. *Because of differences in the labor-intensity of jobs, the skills people have, and the demand for their work, employment numbers do not tell us much about the value of the work people do.*

Differences in earnings received by Phyllis and Duane were influenced by the relative costs of the nonhuman resources they worked with. Now let's look at individual skills.

JENNY PUSHES BONDS: Jenny is a trader/salesperson for a financial firm that underwrites corporate bonds. Her job is to sell newly issued bonds to pension funds, banks, investment companies, insurance firms, and individuals. She is knowledgeable about her product and about her customers and sells nearly $100 million of bonds every year. Her major income is a share of the firm's underwriting profits. She receives $290,000 per year, which comes to about $5,600 per week, or $80 per hour for her typical seventy-hour week.

MIKE PUSHES PAPERS: Mike, like Jenny, sells paper. In Jenny's case, the paper is bonds. In Mike's case, it's newspapers, magazines, books, and greeting cards in the lobby of the building where Jenny works. The job does not require any special skills or training. He sells about $120,000 of publications per year and earns $24,000. That comes to about $10.25 per hour for his forty-five-hour week.

Jenny's and Mike's jobs each increase total employment by one. But they make quite different contributions to the economy, and their rewards reflect the difference in their skills. (Nonetheless, Mike earned enough to send his daughter Jenny to college, and he is proud of what she has done. Sometimes she takes him to dinner.)

What does employment tell us about the "quality" of work?

Employment figures such as those in Table 5A are nothing more than the number of persons working for pay. They say nothing about the **quality of work**. By quality of work I mean the degree to which a job utilizes a person's skills (including his/her time), its wages, and the job's potential for advancement in position, satisfaction, or rewards.

In our system of measuring employment we get little information about the quality of work. An important example of this is that a part-time job is counted as much as full-time work. Furthermore, the jobs count does not tell us anything about earnings. *Anytime someone gets a new job, the employment count changes by one, whether the job is full-time or part-time, and regardless of the pay received for it.*

Are there any statistics that tell us about employment conditions?

Economists usually do not look at employment counts alone. The U.S. Department of Labor gives us information about the extent of work activity and its rewards. Some of this information is in Table 5B.[3] The table reports information about persons who work on an hourly basis and are paid by the hour. Salaried workers who do not qualify for overtime pay are not included here. (The services category includes governments and all businesses that perform services, such as barbershops, auto repair facilities, and banks.)

The government reports the **average hours per week** worked by employees. Changes in hours worked per week are important indicators of future economic activity. When an individual worker is asked to work more hours, there is no change in the number of jobs, although individual income will go up. Generally, when hours per week increase consistently over several months, employers tend to hire more workers; employment goes up. After all, overtime is costly for employers. When they are convinced that increased demand for production is not temporary, it is cheaper to hire more people. Thus, *consistent increases in the total number of hours worked generally leads to an increase in employment.* The reverse is true when hours

Table 5B

Hours Worked and Earnings of Hourly Workers in the U.S., 1993

INDUSTRY	HOURS PER WEEK	AVERAGE HOURLY EARNINGS
All nonfarm employment	34.5	$10.83
Mining	44.2	14.60
Construction	38.4	14.35
Manufacturing	41.4	11.76
Retail trade	28.8	7.29
Services	32.5	10.81

worked decline consistently; sooner or later jobs will be eliminated and employment will go down.

Each month the government also reports **average hourly earnings of employees**. This is the average pay received by workers during that month. It is reported for a number of manufacturing and service industries, some of which are shown in Table 5B. Economists and human resources managers can use this figure to see the balance between the demand for workers (which is the focus of this article) and the supply of workers (the subject of the next article). *An increase in average hourly earnings generally means that the need (demand) for workers is growing faster than the number of people coming into the labor force.* Many employers regularly make "cost of living" adjustments to their wage scales to compensate for the effect of inflation on incomes. Therefore, if the need for workers grows faster than the supply, it is likely that increases in hourly earnings would be greater than the inflation rate.

Labor-market economists look at earnings figures together with employment figures. An economy is improving if both the employment count and the earnings figures go up.

What is underemployment?

The best jobs, for the worker and for the economy, are those that use all of the valuable skills that someone has.

> **ADRIAN STARTS A CAREER A LITTLE LATE:** Adrian received a master's degree in city planning, a highly specialized field. But when he graduated, there were no job openings in planning and he had no other training. To support his family he accepted work as a shoe salesman at a wage (salary) of $150 per week, plus commissions that averaged $35 weekly. After two and a half years he located a city planner's job in another state, moved his family, and started work at $32,000 per year (about three times his former income).

Adrian's job as shoe salesman can be regarded as **underemployment**. This occurs when people are working at jobs for which they are overqualified or that do not utilize their most valuable skills. Underemployment is widespread in lesser-developed nations. For example, American universities may educate foreign students for jobs that they cannot find when they return to their homeland, so they take work that does not require their education. Underemployment is also found in developed nations as well, especially when the economy is weak. *Employment statistics do not reveal underemployment.*

Adrian's underemployment (fortunately, temporary) also shows up another weakness in employment statistics; they do not tell us anything about a job's potential earnings growth or its permanency. A person may take a dead-end job or one that is subject to layoffs, but this kind of information is not available from the government's tabulations. As far as employment statistics are concerned, a job is a job.

How does the demand for goods and services affect decisions to hire people?

Employment increases when employers decide to hire more workers. Let's look at what leads to the hiring decision, and its opposite, the firing decision. That will give us some insight into the rises and falls in employment in our economy over time.

Employers hire workers when they have a need for them. The need, or demand, for workers is what is called by economists a **derived demand**. That means that the demand for workers to produce goods or services comes from the demand for the employer's product. Employers translate their customers' demand for what they sell into a demand for workers. *Employment will increase when the demand for goods and services rises.*

Demand for consumer goods and services will increase, as a rule, when consumers' incomes rise or when something increases their wealth (such as a boom in the stock market).

Government is also a big buyer; when governments spend more, they create new demand for what businesses produce.

New demand for consumer goods and services could create a triple whammy for employment. When businesses want to increase the amount of goods and services they turn out, they will hire more people. But demand for industrial goods and services (office products, freight hauling, plastic, etc.) will also rise, so suppliers will also increase employment. Furthermore, all newly employed workers will have the income to demand more consumer goods and services. They will buy more groceries, movie tickets, clothing, and so on, and the sellers of these things will have to hire more people. So new demand for goods creates a wonderful domino effect as new jobs create even more jobs.

Do wage rates influence employment?

The term **wage** is used by economists to represent any type of financial rewards someone gets from work. Wage does not simply mean an hourly rate of pay; it could be a salary, hourly fee, bonus, or commission.

In business, price means a lot. Employers will hire when it is profitable to do so; the profit they can make from new workers depends on the wages they must pay them.

HERMAN HELPS HIS PLANT GROW: Herman is manager of human resources for a manufacturer of weed trimmers used by homeowners with small lawns or gardens. His firm can sell its light-duty models to distributors for $50 wholesale. Each unit requires two hours of labor from factory floor workers (assemblers, packers, toolmakers, etc.) whose average wage is currently $15 per hour. At that wage level labor costs are $30 per trimmer. The remainder goes for materials, overhead, and profit. After consultation with the firm's production and sales managers, Herman decides to hire 125 more workers if he can get them for the current $15 wage, only 75 workers if average wages are as high as $17 per hour, and as many as 170 if the wage rate were to fall to $12.50.

Herman planned to hire 125 workers at $15 per hour because it would have been profitable to do so. If the wage were $17, the company would have to cut costs elsewhere by reducing equipment purchases, supervisors, and office staff, and this means the company could support fewer workers. If the wage rate were as low as $12.50, the company would save enough money to enable it to hire more supervisors and office staff so it can support up to 170 additional factory workers. It might also be able to lower its wholesale price and to sell more trimmers. That means that *employment increases when wages decline and employment falls when wages rise.*

How do product prices influence the number of jobs?

Suppose weed trimmers become really a hot item so that distributors who buy directly from the manufacturer (hardware wholesale jobbers or large store chains) can afford to pay $60 per unit, compared with the $50 per unit they paid previously. That means more profit can be made by Herman's firm, and it can hire more workers at the current wage rate. They would get enough new revenue from each trimmer to pay the costs of expanding the plant. When the plant hires more factory floor workers, it must also hire more office staff and supervisors as the firm gears up for higher volume. *Employment increases when prices go up, as long as wages do not rise and there are enough workers available to hire.*

How is the hiring or firing decision affected by the cost of machines?

There is one more consideration when studying demand for workers: the cost of replacing them with nonhumans. Economists call these the **costs of labor substitutes**. Few people cannot be replaced; at least, that is what I've been told whenever I demanded a raise. Factory workers can be replaced by machines, office workers can be replaced by computers, managers can be replaced by reorganizing a firm to cut out some middle layers, and so on. (College deans have even replaced some professors with television monitors so that one professor can teach students in several classrooms at the same time. But college deans haven't found machines to replace themselves or their staffs.)

SALLIE AND DON LOSE OUT: For the past six months Sallie and Don pumped gasoline, sold other car products, and collected money from customers of the town's last full-service gas station. They and four other attendants kept the station open ninety hours per week. At a wage of $6.75 per hour, plus fringe benefits, each attendant cost the owner $18,500 per year. Then the owner brought in self-service pumps, complete with credit card slots. Now the station operates with only four attendants covering the week; they stay inside to collect cash payments and to sell grocery items. Sallie and Don were laid off because they had no seniority. Employment fell by two.

By dismissing two workers the gas station's owner saved labor costs of $37,000, which was more than enough to cover the $32,000 to pay the mortgage and operating costs of the new pumps. These savings were not possible last year because interest rates were higher and the pumps had a higher price tag; the cost of having the same pumps would have been $45,000 per year. Only when the pumps became cheaper to own and run did it become profitable to replace Sallie and Don. *Employment falls when the costs of labor substitutes decline.*

Better machines often make it possible to drop people from the payroll. Take the ticket-dispensing machines that have replaced human token sellers in the subway stations of major cities. Someone found a way to take riders' money and to give them tickets without using a person in a glass-lined cashier's cage. This was a little breakthrough in technology, but a big saving in payroll. These improvements are what we call labor-saving, which is a genteel way of saying that someone found a way of giving a lot of other people the ax!

While some people may lose their jobs, these improvements in technology help others. When reliable ticket-selling machines are made, the demand for these machines goes up and so does the derived demand for workers who can make the machines. But the improvements were sought, and implemented, because the number of human ticket sellers whose jobs could be cut was greater than the few extra people being hired to make the machines. *Improvements in technology often result in losses in some types of jobs in the short run, but in the long run these improvements may create new employment opportunities for others and provide lower costs for the economy.*

ARTICLE 6:

THE UNEMPLOYMENT RATE

Who Is Not Working?

What does the unemployment rate tell us about the condition of our economy?

The **unemployment rate** is perhaps the most widely reported and closely watched indicator of economic health. Unemployment is a state of economic distress that rouses both fear and sympathy. The unemployment rate is generally high when economic conditions are poor, and the rate is generally low when economic conditions are good.

In the jargon of economics, **labor** is the term used to represent all types of human effort to produce goods and services; it includes both the intellectual energy and the physical energy (brains and brawn) that gets work done. Clearly, labor is a nation's most important resource. So another reason the unemployment rate gets so much attention is that it measures a critical unused resource in the economy.

Dramatic or persistent increases in the unemployment rate tell us that the condition of the economy is worsening. Similarly, *dramatic or persistent declines in the unemployment rate tell us that the economy is improving.* An improving economy usually means better job opportunities, rising incomes, broader prosperity, and higher standards of living. It also means higher returns on individual investments (pension funds, IRAs, stocks, mutual funds, etc.). A declining economy usually means the reverse.

How is the unemployment rate calculated?

The unemployment rate is the percentage of people in the civilian labor force who are not employed. Government statisticians find the unemployment rate by taking the number of unemployed persons and dividing it by the number of people in the labor force.

In the United States the unemployment rate has fluctuated considerably; over the past fifty years it has reached a low of about 3% and a high of 11%.

The total number of people employed is determined by employers' demand for labor. But the unemployment rate is determined by the demand for labor *and* by the supply of labor. The supply of labor is indicated by the nation's **civilian labor force.** The civilian labor force is the number of people who are working for pay or who are actively looking for work (☛ Art. 5: Employment, page 50). This is a large group: about 130 million people.

The labor force (most people drop the adjective *civilian*) is the number on the bottom part of the unemployment-rate equation. The number on top is the number of people in the labor force who are without work; this is the difference between the number of persons who are in demand by employers and the number of persons supplied by the labor force. In a recent year, for example, the labor force had 127 million persons, of whom 117.5 million were working; that left $(127 - 117.5 =)$ 9.5 million unemployed. The unemployment rate was about 7.5%.

Actually, the official unemployment rates, published each month by the federal government and by state governments, are only estimates. That is because they are based on a survey of the population. For example, each month the U.S. Department of Labor visits a carefully drawn sample of about 60,000 households.[4] A person in the sample is counted as unemployed only if the respondent says he or she did not work for pay and was looking for work during the past two weeks. Even though a sample of 60,000 seems small to find out about conditions of a nation with more than 120 million workers, it is very accurate, estimating the true unemployment rate with an error of less than one-tenth of 1%.

Under what circumstances will the unemployment rate rise, and when will it fall?

Unemployment occurs when the supply of labor exceeds the demand for labor; unemployment means there is a surplus of people in the labor force. Therefore, the unemployment rate will go up whenever there is either an increase in the supply of labor *or* a reduction in the demand for labor.

Now, let's spend a moment to take that in. When someone makes the personal decision to enter the labor force (that is, to look for work), but does not yet have a job, he or she is classified as being unemployed, and the unemployment rate goes up. Whenever an employer hires someone who is not working, the number of unemployed persons and the unemployment rate both go down.

VERA MAE WANTS TO WORK: Vera Mae worked as a guidance counselor in a high school until, at age thirty-one, she gave birth to her daughter. She then spent all her time caring for her daughter and husband (and their dog). But at age thirty-seven Vera Mae went out to find work. Because she started looking for a job, she made the labor force increase by one, the number of unemployed persons go up by one, and the unemployment rate rise (a tiny bit). After six months of looking (unemployment) she found a job as a guidance counselor. When she started work, the number of unemployed persons went down by one, the labor force stayed the same, and the unemployment rate declined (a tiny bit).

The unemployment rate rises whenever people decide to look for work because their decisions to do so increase the number of unemployed persons. Vera Mae made it happen when she started her job search. But that is not the only way the unemployment rate rises. Meet Allen.

ALLEN LOSES OUT: Allen wrote code for personal-computer word-processing software (code is the set of instructions that makes computers do their thing). Allen's software, and competitive products, have saturated the current market. His company did not come up with radically new word-processing software, and sales have plummeted. To cut costs, the firm laid off Allen and half of his fellow software writers. The unemployment rate rose.

When Allen lost his job, he switched from the employed group to the unemployed group. As long as he looked for a new job, the size of the labor force did not change. *The unemployment rate rises when people lose their jobs but remain in the labor force.*

Now, let us look at the other side. *The unemployment rate falls when unemployed persons take jobs.* That happened when Vera Mae took her job and will happen again when Allen finds a new position. Allen would lower the unemployment rate by working either for someone else or for himself. If Allen decides to start his own business, he becomes self-employed. In effect, Allen would take a job working for himself the moment he decides to become his own employer and takes definite steps to start his own business.

When does a drop in the unemployment rate mean the economy is getting worse?

Most people think that a lower unemployment rate means a healthier economy. But they could be fooled, sometimes. Let's look at the way the unemployment rate is calculated.

> **ALLEN TAKES A REST:** Allen is a good computer-software writer, but the software business is in a major slump. He searches hard and spends a lot of money on travel, long-distance telephone calls, résumé distribution, and lunches with contacts. After eight months without finding a job he decides to stop looking. He uses his free time to take some courses to improve his skills and waits for the job market to get better. The unemployment rate drops because Allen leaves the job market.

When Allen dropped out of the job market, the number of unemployed persons fell by one; that's because a person who is no longer actively looking for work is not considered to be unemployed. In addition, the size of the labor force fell by one because he withdrew from it. To see why the unemployment rate fell, we have to do some simple number crunching. (If you don't think you will enjoy this, skip to the next question.)

Suppose the labor force had 100 people in it and that 7 of these people were unemployed. The unemployment rate would be 7/100, or 7%. Next, one of these unemployed persons (Allen) quits looking; that means he drops out of both the unemployed group and the labor force. The number of unemployed becomes 6 and the labor force becomes 99. The unemployment rate would then be 6/99, or about 6%.

This example shows us that *the unemployment rate will fall if unemployed people quit looking for work*. When the unemployment rate drops for this reason, it's really bad news for the economy. The economy is so weak that unemployed people become discouraged and stop hunting for work. That is why the unemployment rate will sometimes fall in the middle of a serious recession. It happened early during the recession of 1973–75 (which was the worst in the U.S. since the 1930s), and it happened again during the brief recession of 1990–91.

How can you tell whether a falling unemployment rate is good or bad?

When using the unemployment rate as an economic indicator, you should find out *why* any change in the rate takes place. Here is a simple set of rules:

1. If the unemployment rate falls and the size of the labor force falls as well, the economy is not improving.

2. If the unemployment rate falls and the labor force does not fall, the economy is improving.

3. If the unemployment rate rises, the economy is getting weaker.

The unemployment rate rises either because people lose their jobs or because the labor force grows faster than employment. Either scenario is a negative sign for the economic environment.

IN THE NEWS . . .

"U.S. Economy Grows Despite Jobless Rate Rise"

Los Angeles Times, August 6, 1994, page A1

There was a vigorous gain in employment during the summer of 1994 as the economy grew. Nonetheless, the unemployment rate crept up from 6.0% to 6.1% in July of that year. The rate in California jumped more sharply, from 8.3% to 9.0%. Although new jobs were being filled, the labor force grew faster than the expanding economy could find places for the new workers.

How have unemployment rates behaved over the business cycle?

The unemployment rate is an "inverse economic indicator": a rising rate is bad news and a falling rate is good news.

The **business cycle** consists of (more or less simultaneous) improvement in a large number of important economic indicators, especially income and production, followed by a more or less simultaneous decline in a large number of important indicators. The business cycle represents the ups and downs of an economy. It's like a roller coaster, except that downswings tend to be shorter and milder (fortunately) than the upswings. The growth phase of the business cycle is called an **expansion** and the retrenchment phase is called a **recession** (☞ Art. 4: Business Cycles, page 35).

The unemployment rate always moves up sharply during recessions. In fact, it generally starts to move up even *before* a recession begins. That is why the unemployment rate is sometimes called a **leading indicator** for predicting recession.

The unemployment rate generally moves down during an expansion. But it generally starts moving down well after an expansion begins, which is why it is sometimes a **lagging indicator** for expansions.

While the unemployment rate moves in the opposite direction of the business cycle, it tends to be a leading *indicator of recessions and a* lagging *indicator of business cycle expansions.*

Why is the unemployment rate a leading indicator of recessions, but lags during expansions?

For many companies wages are the biggest cost of doing business. That is why *businesses lay off workers when sales fall or when they expect sales to decline.* Regardless of how much prosperity a business may have enjoyed, when things start to look bleak, the firm will often cut costs by reducing its payroll.

But that often brings a ripple effect. The newly unemployed workers have less income to spend. As they rein in their household budgets, retail sales drop so that total business sales are pushed down even more. As a result, rising unemployment accelerates the recession.

When sales begin to recover after a recession, firms often wait to hire new employees (or to call back old ones) until they are convinced business will continue to improve. *Businesses generally start hiring only after a business expansion is well established and they are convinced of the need for more workers.* That is because they do not want to commit themselves to new hires only to find it necessary to lay them off shortly thereafter if sales resume their decline. Firms do not want to incur the expense of training new employees only to lose them. They also want to avoid having to increase their contributions to their state's unemployment compensation fund when their laid-off workers collect unemployment benefits. This explains why the unemployment rate in the U.S. usually declines significantly several months after the end of a recession.

The 1990–91 recession in the U.S. gave us an example of the leading and lagging habits of the unemployment rate. The unemployment rate reached a low of 5% three months before the recession began. Later it continued to rise even after the economy had started to grow, climbing to a high of 7.8% about fifteen months following the official end of the recession.

But the unemployment rate is not an infallible forecaster of recessions. In 1973 the unemployment rate continued to decline moderately almost until the recession of 1973–74 began. No forecasting tool in economics works all the time. Nor is the lagging nature of the unemployment rate consistent during recoveries. In 1982 the rate began to fall sharply immediately after the 1981–82 recession came to an end.

Do all groups in the economy experience the same unemployment rate?

The average unemployment rates during 1993 give us a fairly typical picture of how unemployment hits different groups in the economy. The highest unemployment rate is experienced by teenagers, both men and women. In fact, like their ages, the unemployment rate of teens is usually in the upper teens. Unemployment rates also differ among racial groups. After teenagers, the highest unemployment rate is usually experienced by blacks, followed by persons of Hispanic origin, and then by whites. The lowest unemployment rate is for married men. The figures in Table 6A show us that *unemploy-*

Table 6A

Average Unemployment Rates of Groups of Workers in the U.S., 1989 and 1993

GROUP IN THE WORKFORCE	1989	1993
Men, over age 20	4.5%	6.4%
Women, over age 20	4.7	5.9
Teenagers	15.0	19.0
Whites	4.5	6.0
Blacks	11.4	12.9
Hispanic origin	8.0	10.6
Married men	3.0	4.4
Women supporting families	8.1	9.6

ment differs among age groups, among racial groups, and between married and unmarried persons.[5] The 1989 figures are from a year when the economy was weakening, prior to the recession that began the following year. The 1993 figures are from a year when the economy was expanding at a healthy rate. While the numbers change from one year to the next, the rankings of these groups are consistent.

Unfortunately, differences in unemployment rates among social groups may be partly due to **employment discrimination**; this is the use of race or gender by employers in making decisions about hiring or advancing people. For example, if an employer prefers to hire white employees rather than blacks among applicants with similar skills, the employer is practicing employment discrimination. This type of discrimination is illegal. While the existence of employment discrimination has been well documented by economists, it appears to be lessening.

The primary cause of unemployment is a lack of **human capital**. A person's human capital is her/his ability to be productive in the workplace based on talent, education, and experience. Human capital differs among social groups. Teenagers experience high unemployment because most of them have not yet developed salable skills; they lack human capital. Black adults experience high unemployment rates because they have less formal education and job experience than is found among other racial groups. Unfortunately, discrimination may be partly responsible for this lack of human capital if it affected the access of blacks to formal education (☞ Art. 8: Human Capital, page 88).

The swings of the business cycle bring about changes in unemployment rates. Take another look at Table 6A. The unemployment rates for 1989 were experienced near the top of a business cycle; the higher unemployment rates in 1993 occurred in the wake of the 1990–91 recession. The average unemployment rates in 1993 were higher than those in 1989. (The recession actually ended in 1991, but remember that unemployment is often a lagging indicator, so it typically moves down well after business expansions begin.)

For all workers the unemployment rate went from 5.3% to 7.4%. Women fared better in this recession than did men because a larger proportion of women managed to hold on to their jobs. This recession hit whites and married men rather hard. The relative increases in their unemployment rates exceeded those of other groups.

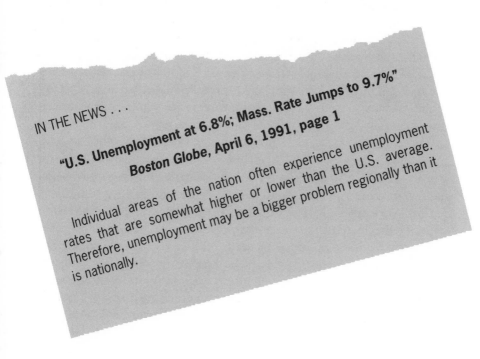

IN THE NEWS . . .

"U.S. Unemployment at 6.8%; Mass. Rate Jumps to 9.7%"
Boston Globe, April 6, 1991, page 1

Individual areas of the nation often experience unemployment rates that are somewhat higher or lower than the U.S. average. Therefore, unemployment may be a bigger problem regionally than it is nationally.

What are the major causes of unemployment?

Economists have identified three types of unemployment: frictional, cyclical, and structural. The first, **frictional unemployment**, occurs in the normal course of people changing jobs.

STILES MOVES ON: Stiles has an excellent record as a gourmet chef. Because of his special skills, and the shortage of gourmet chefs, he has found positions in three cities over the past twenty years with relatively short job searches. Two months ago he resigned from a position in Boston to move to Atlanta with his wife, who was transferred there by her employer. Now settled in Atlanta, he is busy making contacts and circulating his résumé. Until he finds a job, his unemployment adds to the unemployment rate.

Stiles will have no real problem with joblessness. There is a demand for his work; all that is needed is to make the right match. Stiles's temporary unemployment is an example of frictional unemployment.

While there is some debate as to how large it is, most economists are comfortable with estimates that frictional unemployment is around 5% of the labor force.[6] (Vera Mae's joblessness, while caring for her daughter, is not frictional unemployment because she voluntarily dropped out of the labor force; she was not counted as unemployed if she was not in the labor force.)

The second type of unemployment is **cyclical**. Cyclical unemployment occurs because of changes in the level of demand for workers. Allen, the computer-software designer we met a few pages earlier, gave us a perfect example. He had useful skills, but demand for his work went up and down with the fortunes of his industry. Most of the increase in the unemployment rate between 1989 and 1993 (see Table 6A) was due to cyclical causes. This weakness in the economy meant reduced demand for goods and services, and this reduced demand meant less need for workers. While cyclical unemployment is serious, it is often simpler to attack than are other types of unemployment. The way to reduce cyclical unemployment is to use economic policy to foster economic growth (☞ Art. 18: The

Federal Reserve, page 235, and Art. 24: Fiscal Policy and Government Debt, page 325).

The third type, **structural** unemployment, is a more serious and stubborn problem because it represents worker obsolescence. An unemployed worker is a victim of structural unemployment when employers do not demand the skills he or she offers. This occurs when technology or changes in products people want to buy cause employers to demand different types of workers. Economic growth does little to help this type of worker.

> **SHARYN FIGHTS PROGRESS:** Sharyn has worked as a secretary for many years. Her employer has ordered all secretaries in the firm to work with personal computers, in place of electric typewriters, by the start of next year. The younger secretaries sign up for a three-month course in word processing. However, Sharyn decides that she is too close to her planned retirement to make her investment in training pay off. After the first of the year she is terminated and immediately starts looking for a new job that will use her skills. All the promising openings for secretaries call for computer skills, so she remains unemployed despite the high demand for secretarial services in her community. The unemployment rate rises.

Sharyn's case is an example of structural unemployment, a mismatch between what she has to offer and what the workplace demands. For people like Sharyn, structural unemployment may last a long time, or it may be permanent.

Can the economy achieve zero unemployment? What is full employment?

Because of frictional unemployment, which is normal and is not unhealthy for the economy, *an unemployment rate of zero is not realistic*. In fact, the best that the economy can try to accomplish in the long run is to have an unemployment rate no bigger than the rate of frictional unemployment. For all practical purposes, we can say that such a happy situation is **full employment**.

In most regions the frictional rate of unemployment is perhaps as low as 4–6%, so we can say that an unemployment rate of about 5% is close to the **natural rate of unemployment**. (Economists differ about the exact way to compute this natural rate.) Furthermore, this figure probably varies from place to place. In some regions the unemployment rate can go as low as 3%, or even less, because there is little job shifting. For these regions the natural rate may be well under 5%; for practical purposes, this is "full employment."

How can the economy cope with cyclical and structural unemployment?

Cyclical unemployment comes about simply because business is bad; there is not enough demand for goods and services to keep people busy producing them. One remedy governments often try is **economic policy**. That is a broad term that covers any government activity designed to improve the condition of the economy; some policies may focus on increasing employment by businesses. A good example of this is an increase in government spending. When the government buys more airplanes or health services, when it builds highways and bridges, or when it increases aid to schools, more employment will follow in the wake of this government spending. Another example is for the government to reduce taxes; this gives people more money to spend, and that creates jobs (☞ Art. 18: The Federal Reserve, page 235, and Art. 24: Fiscal Policy and Government Debt, page 325).

Structural unemployment can be attacked only through job training, improved education, help in giving workers information about job openings that might exist outside their immediate area, or assistance in relocating workers. Government programs to promote training the unemployed for meaningful jobs that are in demand may help to reduce structural unemployment. But it is a hard thing to do. Sharyn gives us a case where even the offer of government training may not help. People's attitudes, and businesses' real needs, must be considered.

Since frictional unemployment is normal, it would be folly to try to eliminate it while maintaining a free society where people have the right to select their employment.

ARTICLE 7:

CHANGING THE WORKPLACE

Do Governments and Unions Make Work Better?

Who wants to work?

Let's start at the very beginning. Not everyone wants to work for pay. There are housewives and househusbands who have important full-time jobs to do at home. There are men and women over age sixteen who elect to stay in school to pursue an education (among other things). There are people who prefer leisure or charitable work and can afford to engage in it as a full-time occupation. Of course, there are also those who believe that, while hard work never killed anyone, why take chances?

Some people cannot work. Society has made important progress in making the workplace more accessible to productive people, but people requiring care may not be available to take employment. Others may be too young (except for the kids who make early fortunes by acting in television sitcoms). Finally, there are people paying their debt to society in penal institutions because they did the wrong kind of work!

Those who are employed or who are actively looking for work are members of the nation's **labor force**. The labor force includes full-time military personnel. When you take out the military (currently less than 1.5 million people and shrinking), you get the **civilian labor force**; this is our most important measure of the current supply of labor.

Economists employ the word **labor** to mean any human effort to create goods or services. Labor can involve brains or brawn; the

Table 7A

U.S. Civilian Labor Force, 1993	

CATEGORY	NUMBER (MILLIONS OF PERSONS)
Noninstitutionalized population	195.0
Labor force	129.5
Participation rate:	66.4%

operative who gets paid to haul trash and the executive who gets paid to plan and to write out orders for others are both members of the labor force.

The **labor market participation rate** is a "ten-dollar term" that means the percentage of persons sixteen years and older (legal working age) who are in the labor force. The participation rate is important because it, along with population, determines how much labor the nation can supply to produce things. Let's take a look at the current U.S. participation rate. From Table 7A we see that, of about 195 million persons in the U.S. who were old enough and free to work for pay in 1993, two-thirds decided to enter the civilian labor force.[7]

When the labor market participation rate rises or falls, it causes important changes in the workplace because the participation rate influences the size and the diversity of the labor force.

What causes changes in the labor market participation rate?

In part, people enter or leave the labor force in response to the wage level. If wages rise, people who decide to stay home sacrifice more potential income. The earnings they could get by working is called, in the jargon of economics, the **opportunity cost** of not working; in plain English, this is the money people give up by not entering the labor force. When wages go down, the opportunity cost of not working is lower and many people decide not to work.

(For most of us the term **wages** means the amount of money people earn per hour. Economists use the term wages to refer to any payment for work, whether it be hourly pay, weekly wage, bonus, or commission. The wage of a hamburger flipper at a fast-food joint may be $4.85 per hour. The wage of a stockbroker may be $190,000 per year.)

Demographics is also a factor. As the population ages (people live longer and/or birthrates go down), a larger percentage of the population will be retirement age and the participation rate will decline. The participation rate also falls when birthrates rise and more mothers stay at home. Immigration also influences the size of the labor force.

ASSUNTA LOOKS FOR A JOB: Assunta lives in a small town where the major employer is an aircraft assembly plant employing her father and husband. She did well in high school and earned an associate's degree in manufacturing at the local community college. For years the attitude of the plant managers was that well-paying factory floor jobs were too hard and dirty for females, so Assunta busied herself with fixing up her home and doing volunteer work for her church. But after a group of female applicants for factory jobs filed a lawsuit against the firm, alleging employment discrimination, Assunta decided to enter the labor force. She applied for one of several factory openings, and in doing this, she increased the labor market participation rate.

The relations between employer and employee are affected by numerous federal and state laws. During the last thirty years legal factors have been the most important influence on the participation rate. Beginning with the federal Civil Rights Act of 1964, a large body of legislation designed to reduce discrimination against women, minority group members, persons with disabilities, people over age forty and military veterans was produced. The result was that individuals were encouraged to enter the labor force who might not have done so otherwise. The result was an almost steady increase in the participation rate from the 1960s, when it was just over 50%, to the late 1980s, when the rate reached a high of nearly 67%.[8] In general, the participation rate responds positively to enforcement of laws against discrimination in the labor markets, the acceptance of diversity in the workplace, and the availability of child care services for working parents.

As antidiscrimination legislation reached into colleges and universities, more women and minorities sought advanced education. This also led to their entry into the labor force in increasing numbers.

Laws and wage rates are not alone in influencing the participation rate. The rate had been creeping upward over many years because of changes in society's attitudes about women and minorities in the labor force.

However, the participation rate began to fall slightly in the early 1990s, partly due to the recession that opened the decade, but also due to a lower rate of growth of wages. In addition, perhaps, many women (and some men) have decided to devote full time to child care.

Who is affected by minimum wage laws?

The **minimum wage** is the lowest hourly rate of pay an employer can give to workers. This wage is set by federal and state laws. In 1991 federal law set the U.S. minimum wage at $4.35, although state and local laws in many areas set higher minimums. The purpose of minimum wage legislation is to improve the living standards of workers in low-wage jobs. One argument in favor of higher minimum wages seems to be based on the assumption that unskilled workers at the bottom of the pay scale may be unfairly exploited by employers. Another argument, perhaps more appealing, is that we should try to provide all workers with a "living wage."

Actually, minimum wage laws influence everyone's pay, all the way up the ladder. When the minimum wage is increased (it has never gone down), the lowest-wage workers get an immediate raise in hourly pay. But people in higher positions expect to earn more than their subordinates. After all, that is the reward they get for being more experienced or more productive. So senior people will try to keep their wage advantage by asking for raises. In this way the raise given to the lowest-paid employee has a ripple effect on all other workers up the line.

PAY RAISES TRICKLE UP: Below is the former pay scale of some employees of Abfall Products Co., which supplies the trash-hauling industry. When the minimum wage in the state was raised recently to $4.65 per hour, the higher minimum wage caused all of Abfall's assistant clerks to receive the same wage, regardless of seniority or job performance. The firm thought this was unfair and that it would not give employees the incentive to increase the quality of their work or to stay with the company. So it decided to give all assistant clerks a 7% raise, which put the range from $4.65 to $4.98.

Table 7B

Abfall Products Co.
Former Pay Scale of the Credit Department

Position	Number of Persons	Wage Range
Assistant clerk	5	$4.35–4.65
Office clerk	8	4.95–6.10
Office manager	1	7.50

The new minimum wage only required the employer to raise the wages of those assistant clerks who were below $4.65. But it then had to change the wages of all assistant clerks to maintain equity and to provide incentives. The effect did not stop here. Notice that after changing the wage scale for the lowest level of employees, some assistant clerks earned more than full office clerks, who were at a higher grade and who had more responsibility (or relatives in senior management).

This meant the clerks had to get a raise to give them a wage that reflected their higher position. Later, after the clerks got their raises, the office manager bargained hard and also got a raise; after all, if she didn't stay as far above her employees, it would look as though she had gotten a demotion. And so it goes up the line. *An increase in the minimum wage pushes wages up for nearly all workers.*

IN THE NEWS . . .

"USA Snapshots: Tracking the Minimum Wage"

USA Today, August 31, 1993, page A1

The first minimum wage in the United States was 25¢ per hour, introduced in 1938. Allowing for inflation, this was equal to an hourly wage of $2.56 in 1993. But the minimum wage was $4.25 in 1993. Legislated advances in the basic wage rate have far outstripped inflation.

How far up the line do workers feel the effect of a boost in the minimum wage?

As you just saw, anytime the minimum wage is raised, there is a ripple effect up the wage ladder. When you toss a pebble into a still pond, the largest ripples will occur around where the pebble hit; farther away from the point of impact the ripples will be successively smaller. *The further up the wage scale, the smaller will be the impact of a raise in the minimum wage.*

EVELYN AND KARL ARE UNMOVED: Evelyn is the executive vice president of Abfall Products, earning $135,000 per year. (It is difficult to express this as an hourly wage since her workweek varies between thirty-eight and seventy hours, without a change in pay.) Her immediate subordinate is Karl, the vice president and comptroller, who has a wage (paid as a salary) of $95,000. They do not feel their statuses are threatened by the higher minimum raise and their wages are unchanged. The ripple effect doesn't create a splash in their part of the pond.

It is doubtful someone earning $135,000 would have a change in incentive if her or his wage was changed by a few hundred dollars per year. But *a change in the minimum wage might cause a wage compression.* That means the difference between the wages of the higher-paid workers (whose wages will change little or not at all) and the wages of lower-paid workers (whose wages will get a big boost) will be smaller. The danger of wage compression is that it might lower the morale of some employees.

How will a change in the minimum wage affect the overall economy?

Because of the ripple effect of changes in the minimum wage, wage rates are pushed up for many workers when the minimum wage is raised. These broad-based increases in wages inevitably raise employers' labor costs. These higher costs are passed on, at least partially, in the form of higher prices for products and services. That means a wide range of prices go up along with higher wages. Although minimum wage laws are not a major cause of inflation, *increases in the minimum wage may tend to increase inflation* (☞ Art. 11: Inflation, page 128).

GLEN IS SQUEEZED: Glen runs a messenger service in the city. He employs eight messengers at wages of from $5.50 to $7.75 per hour and a dispatcher at $9.40 per hour. These wages account for 70% of the costs of running his business. When the minimum wage rises, he gives his employees raises averaging 7%, which raises his total operating costs by 5%. Since he operates on a small profit margin, he raises his fees 5%. Other delivery services in the city follow suit.

Glen's case illustrates the point that *changes in the minimum wage have significant impacts on the costs of operating businesses that rely heavily on low-wage employees.* Delivery services, fast-food restaurants, custodial services, security-guard agencies, grocery stores, and amusement parks are other businesses that would be hard hit by a higher minimum wage. In fact, the minimum wage level has a significant impact on most **labor-intensive industries**; these are businesses in which wages are a large share of the total cost of doing business. Service businesses are generally labor-intensive.

Economists have often asked whether high minimum wages really provide long-term benefits for the economy. Those workers who are at the lower end of the pay scale will get higher incomes, but everyone in the economy will bear part of the cost of these raises because of the higher prices their employers will have to ask for the things they sell. In fact, since the wage change at the higher wage levels may be small or nonexistent, these people may suffer a real loss in their purchasing power.

Do increases in the minimum wage improve living standards for people at the lower end of the pay scale?

A minimum wage rate is intended to improve and to protect the living standards of the lowest-paid workers in society. The argument in favor of a minimum wage is that it provides an income sufficient to give a worker an acceptable standard of living. Whether or not a worker lives at the poverty level depends on her or his family size and on the income of the entire family.

HOW JOE AND BRAD GET BY: Joe and Brad are night security guards in an office building. This job pays each of them $4.55/hour for a thirty-hour week, which comes to $7,100 a year. This is their only job. Joe is the sole supporter of his wife and two young children. They share a house trailer Joe inherited from his uncle. Any increase in the minimum wage would help Joe a lot. Brad attends a city college part-time and lives with his family in an upper-middle-class neighborhood. Brad would add any pay raise he gets to his savings account so that he might replace his five-year-old car.

At the current minimum U.S. hourly wage rate of $4.35, a full-time worker would earn $174 per forty-hour workweek or $9,048 per year, before paying taxes. An increase in the minimum wage to $4.65 would raise full-time employment income to $9,672. This extra $600 may be helpful, even if some of the $600 is eaten away by inflation. But remember, workers who are far *above* the minimum wage will not be affected as much by a new minimum wage rate as they are harmed by inflation. Inflation affects everyone.

Since the effect of higher minimum wages on workers above the lowest wage level is small, and since higher minimum wages exert inflationary pressure on the economy, *there is no evidence that changes in minimum wages have, in the long run, significantly reduced the proportion of persons living below the poverty level.*

Would changes in the minimum wage affect nonwage benefits from employment?

Wages are not the only benefits most people get from working. So-called fringe benefits are important. These include paid vacation, sick days, health and/or life insurance, training or educational benefits, social security, and unemployment compensation. Many workers may also be provided with contributions to a pension fund. Although people at low-wage jobs may receive few fringe benefits, whatever they get is part of their compensation. *An employer, faced with the new costs of a higher minimum wage, may try to reduce fringe benefits.* Insurance coverage is the easiest to reduce, although companies could also increase job tenure required for vacations, reduce sick days, or make other adjustments. This is particularly likely if a business's customers are so price sensitive that cost increases cannot be passed on to them.

Higher minimum wages may also cause employers to change working conditions. They might increase workers' output quotas, reduce the number of work breaks to the minimum required by law, or even reduce the number of hours worked (see the next question). Minimum wage laws apply only to hourly income, not to total compensation.

Do minimum wage laws increase unemployment?

SERGE GETS MORE LEISURE: Serge is a porter/clerk in a small candy shop owned by Evelyn. He worked forty-two hours per week at $4.35/hour. When the minimum wage went up to $4.65, Evelyn realized she could not afford the extra $655 per year it would cost her to let Serge work forty-two hours. This was partly due to increases in other costs that Evelyn had to pay as a result of inflation. She asked her teenage daughter to help out some more and now does some of Serge's former jobs herself, even though it means she must spend more time in the shop. Serge was cut back to thirty-eight hours per week and his income fell by $312 per year.

Serge's experience is less painful than what many minimum-wage workers might experience. A worker generally gets a low wage because his or her productivity is low; by virtue of the nature of the job and/or the worker's lack of skills, he can contribute little to the business's revenues. If the wage goes up, the worker may be too expensive for an employer to hire profitably. The result is that employers will reduce the number of low-wage people employed. It could have been worse for Serge; he could have become a victim of unemployment rather than of underemployment.

Like other goods and services, the demand for labor depends in part on its price. The price of labor is the wage rate. *If the wage rate goes up, unemployment is likely to increase* because the demand for labor will fall. Minimum wage laws interfere with the normal mechanism of the marketplace by putting a floor on wage rates (☛ Art. 9: Prices and the Economy, page 102). When that happens, something has got to give. Some workers will gain income while others lose jobs. The laws guarantee a minimum hourly income for the employed; they do not guarantee a minimum yearly income, or even a job.

IN THE NEWS . . .

"Higher Wage Base Urged"

New York Times, August 21, 1993, page A43

U.S. secretary of labor Robert B. Reich is recommending that the minimum wage be raised from $4.25 to $4.50 per hour and that the base wage rate be raised automatically to adjust for inflation.

"The Persistent Folly of a Higher Minimum Wage"

Chicago Tribune, October 17, 1993, page 3

Fewer than 5 million Americans work at or below the minimum wage (the minimum wage does not cover all workers). It is estimated that a higher minimum will raise the incomes of some workers by only 6%. But it would reduce the incomes of those who lose their jobs by 100%.

How do labor unions affect wages?

Most people bargain with their employers one-on-one and must eventually either accept or decline the wage rate offered to them. Of course, that often puts workers at a disadvantage. There are fewer employers than there are workers, so employers have more choice of whom to hire than workers have of places to work.

There are exceptions, of course, and we all want to be one of them. When Paul Volcker stepped down as chairman of the Board of Governors of the Federal Reserve System, he lost little time in landing a job in private business that paid him (reportedly) over $2,000,000 per year. He had a wide choice of jobs, including college teaching (which he considered for a few minutes). But that is only because there are few Paul Volckers (☞ Art. 18: The Federal

Reserve, page 235). There are also few Lee Iacoccas, Sylvester Stallones, and Michael Jordans.

A **labor union** is a formal organization of workers who join together to engage in **collective bargaining** with employers. That means they try to form a kind of monopoly of labor to give themselves bargaining power. In most cases the employer bargains directly with a union negotiator who represents all of the workers and acts as their agent. The theory is that a big union stands on equal footing against a big employer.

The truth is that wages and employment are determined by the demand for workers and by the supply of workers. *The union is effective only to the extent that it can increase the demand for its members or reduce the supply of workers the employer can hire.* In practice, unions try to do both, and they meet with varying degrees of success.

How can unions increase the demand for their members?

If the demand for workers goes up, so do wages. The demand for workers is what economists call **derived demand**. That means that the need for workers is dependent upon the demand for the goods or services that the workers make.

Unions share a common interest with employers; they all want to see business grow. *Unions try to increase the sales of their employers.* To the businesses, growth in sales means more profits. To the unions, growth means that employers need more workers (who are union members). That is why unions spend money to urge the public to buy their employers' goods. Textile workers tell us to "look for the union label" in garments, or to "buy American" if foreign producers threaten union members' jobs. Teachers' unions advertise to promote interest in education, and automobile workers lobby legislators to reduce imports.

Unions sometimes try to increase demand by making their members more desirable for employers to hire. They could help to train workers, to provide educational benefits, or to recruit union members more selectively. All of these things, if successful, will make union members more productive. That is the only way to make workers cheaper for employers to hire without reducing wages. As workers increase their productivity, they are more profitable for employers to hire, and the demand for them goes up.

Can unions really control the supply of workers?

If the supply of workers goes down, wages tend to go up, provided that nothing else changes. The best way for a union to control supply (or *limit* supply) is to have a monopoly on the supply of workers.

The American Medical Association is a classic case of an organization that acts almost like a union in its efforts to control supply. It accredits medical colleges that turn out MDs and, in so doing, controls the number of new doctors put on the labor market. This may also maintain high standards of quality. The net effect is to limit supply, although in recent years the influx of physicians educated abroad has weakened this control a little.

A strike is a way of limiting the supply of workers to businesses, although temporarily. Employers may try to hire permanent replacements. But this often takes time, can be costly, and creates labor unrest. If businesses cannot readily get replacement workers, a strike can significantly increase a union's bargaining power.

A direct way of limiting supply is to succeed in getting employers to have a **union shop**. This is a workplace that hires only union members. Although some states make union shops illegal, a union that gets employers to hire most of its employees from among union members accomplishes almost the same objective. For many years the association of major league professional baseball players, which operated very much like a union, succeeded in steadily raising salaries of its members until the average player received over $1 million per year. By hiring only association members, major-league owners created what was equivalent to a union shop.

Wages tend to be higher when a union's monopoly power over workers is strong. A very successful (or lucky) union is one that bargains with employers who are faced with a shortage of workers (☞ Art. 9: Prices and the Economy, page 102).

Is the influence of unions declining?

Union membership grew rapidly during the 1930s and 1940s when laws were passed giving them important powers. Unions primarily recruited workers in manufacturing industries, in part because manufacturers could afford to pay more. That is particularly true of industries that are not labor-intensive, because in these industries each worker works with a large amount of capital (costly machinery or equipment) and is responsible for a high level of revenue.

Another reason for targeting manufacturers was that these employers often exercised a high degree of monopoly control in their product markets. If a producer has a monopoly, it can charge high prices for its output and that gives it more revenue to share with employees.

Union membership peaked in the 1970s. *Only about one in six workers in the U.S. is represented by a union.* Union membership may grow again as unions try to organize more service-industry employees, especially office and government workers. Right now union influence is great in those few areas of employment where unions represent the majority of workers, such as autos, steel, and textile

RANDY GETS A RAISE: Randy is one of fifty-five drivers employed by a charter bus company. He drives senior citizens, youth groups, convention delegates, and others on special one-day or overnight excursions. Drivers in his company are not unionized. The local scheduled bus lines have unionized drivers. Frequently, when these scheduled carriers advertise for new drivers, some of Randy's coworkers quit to work for them. Two months ago the union and the scheduled carriers agreed to a 14% pay hike spread over the next three years and overtime pay equal to 1.65 times the regular hourly wage. Last month Randy's employer announced that it will grant him and his coworkers a 12% pay raise over the next three years and that it will start paying overtime rates of 1.5 times hourly wage for overnight trips. Previous raises at the charter line averaged only about 2.5% per year, with no overtime pay rates.

manufacturing, and (in some states) public schools. *However, unions are a visible presence in the labor market, and many employers of nonunion workers are influenced by union agreements when bargaining with their employees.*

One of the ways unions can influence the economic conditions of nonunion labor is that they may be a potential threat to nonunion firms; the possibility that a firm's employees will join a union or leave for union employers plays a part in the relationship between employers and the hired help. Would Randy's employer have been as generous if it operated in a region where all other carriers were nonunion? Unions can certainly change the labor market.

IN THE NEWS . . .

"As Unions Decline, Labor Laws Constrain the Job Market"

Wall Street Journal, September 2, 1992, page A11

Until recently, the share of the U.S. labor force represented by unions has been shrinking. However, this does not mean that employers have more flexibility in hiring, paying, or firing workers. There has been a growing number of legal constraints on employers. These include minimum wage laws, the Davis-Bacon Act (which sets a floor on wages that can be paid to workers on federal projects), and antidiscrimination laws. In some ways these laws replace the roles played by unions.

ARTICLE 8:

HUMAN CAPITAL

The Value of Brains and Sweat

What is human capital?

Although it has been in the vocabulary of economists for over thirty years, **human capital** is still not a familiar term to many people who study economics. But you will hear about it as economists and policy makers become more concerned about the place of the U.S. in competitive global markets. Our economy's future growth will depend largely on its development of human capital. This is true because our economy is becoming more dependent on services and also because the increasingly sophisticated technology we are using to create goods and services demands a more capable workforce.

Human capital is the capability a person has to produce goods or services that have value. Human capital is the sum total of someone's talents, skills, energy, and motivation. It is what a worker is actually paid for in the labor market. By using human capital, a glassblower creates useful or beautiful products, a nurse promotes healing, and a plumber gets your home's water system to work.

Why do economists use a term like *capital* when talking about human beings?

The word *capital* means different things to different people. To make things clear, you should recognize that *there are actually two types of capital in economics: physical and human.* **Physical capital** is an asset that can actually create a product or service, for example, a backhoe, a printing press, or an apartment building (which provides shelter to its residents). Economists will tell you that the more physical capital a nation has, the more productive capacity it possesses, if investments are made in the right things (☞ Art. 16: Investment, page 197).

Many people consider **money** to be capital, but economists do not. Money may be used to try to make money, such as money invested in the stock market or in a bank account. Bankers will tell you that the more financial capital you have, the more profit you can earn, if you use it correctly. But *economists do not use the term* capital *when talking about money because money cannot produce anything.* Money may be able to produce more money by earning interest, but money does not itself satisfy human needs; it cannot be eaten, worn, slept on, and so on (we're talking about normal humans here). Money can be used to acquire things that meet human needs, but by itself, it is only pieces of paper. In many ways, human capital is similar to physical capital. The more an individual invests in education or practices to develop his useful skills, the more he contributes to society and, usually, the more income he will receive for himself. Human capital comes from investing in human beings.

For generations economists have analyzed the effects of investment in physical capital on a nation's economic growth and on standards of living. It was only in the 1960s that they began to fully realize that investment in human beings was just as important; in fact, in an increasingly technical and service-oriented economy, investment in human beings may be even more important than investment in things made of brick and steel.

At first glance it seems dehumanizing to equate physical capital and human capital. But the similarities are revealing. *If our economy is to grow, and we want to improve our standard of living, we should make intelligent investments in people as well as in things.* This means individuals like Steve.

> **STEVE WANTS TO DRILL:** Steve grew up with the desire to be a dentist. His neighborhood needs a dentist. Although few members of his minority race entered the profession, he had encouragement and support from his family, and these gave him added motivation. To set up a practice, he knows he will need two treatment cubicles, each equipped with drills, patient's chair, X-ray machine, cabinets, and instruments. He will also need a reception area, an office for consultations and study, and a small lab room. There will be outlays for supplies, insurance, hiring dental assistants, and old magazines for the waiting room. All this calls for investment in physical capital. But first, he has to get the necessary training. This will mean college for a BS degree, dental school for the DDS or DMD degree, and an internship; these call for an even larger investment in human capital.

Is one type of capital sufficient to make a worker productive?

Steve could have access to all the money he needs to make his investment in physical capital, but without a complementary investment in human capital he could not produce the services his neighborhood needs. He cannot go far in dentistry without his instruments and without his education. *Most occupations require workers to use a combination of human capital and physical capital.*

The more valuable a person's human capital is, the more use he or she can make of other types of capital. In other words, *human capital makes physical capital more productive, and physical capital makes human capital more productive.* An artisan or physician cannot get much out of the best tools of her profession without human capital. Conversely, the artisan or physician cannot render her services without the requisite physical capital (or "tools of the trade").

How does a worker get human capital?

Everyone has human capital, but we differ in the types and amounts of human capital we possess.

Like physical capital, *human capital is accumulated by making investments in it.* One way to accumulate human capital is by acquiring education, because education is often the most effective way of getting the knowledge and skills one needs. (Formal education also provides a "signaling" advantage, which you will learn about later.) It would have been hard for Steve to become a dentist without education, even if the law (licensing) did not require it.

Education does not just come from schools. On-the-job training and job experience also build up one's human capital. Apprenticeship is a form of on-the-job training. Innate talent is also part of one's human capital, and practice is needed to develop it. Society's most gifted musicians and artists spend many hours every day practicing their skills.

Investment in human capital actually begins by sustaining and developing the human being. Nutrition and health care are basic investments in human capital. Malnourishment and disease prevent people from being fully productive.

Social structure also plays a role. If access to education or experience is impeded by any type of discrimination (e.g., racial or sexual) or by lack of finances, society is prevented from developing human capital.

Some elements of human capital are more difficult to develop. These include attitudes, motivation, and entrepreneurship. Without the psychological support his family provided, Steve might not have been motivated to break through racial barriers to try to become a dentist. Entrepreneurship and leadership are important buzzwords in business schools today; they are part of human capital. However, our educational institutions have not yet learned how to make leaders and entrepreneurs; they can only help them along.

What are the returns to investment in human capital?

Let's talk real money. People invest in something when they see an opportunity to make a profit that is larger than what they can expect to make somewhere else. *The return to human capital is the income coming from investment in human capital.*

As an example, let us look at financial returns to investment in a college education for adults in our population who work for pay. In 1990 the average (median) income of adult male workers with no more than a high school education was $26,650. At the same time the average income of adult male workers with four years of college was $39,250, or 47% more. The difference between these two incomes was $12,600. That was the average return that year to an investment in a college education.

What about additional investments in education? In 1990 the average income of adult male workers with one or more years of graduate college education was $49,300, 26% more than the earnings of those with four years of college. Graduate education pays off.

Now let us look at adult women. The average income of the female high school graduate who worked was about $18,300; this average jumped 53% to $28,000 with four years of college and went up another 20% to $33,750 with a fifth year of college education.

Women received smaller incomes all around. Some of the income differences may be due to the fact that many women have interruptions in their careers (for child care), which gives them less lifetime job experience, or that women are likely to hold part-time jobs. Gender discrimination may also play a significant role, despite considerable progress in reducing discrimination since the 1960s. In terms of relative incomes, women seem to earn a greater payoff for four years of college than do men, although they get a smaller relative payoff for the fifth year of higher education.

The returns to higher education have been steadily increasing. In 1970 four years of college boosted men's income an average of 39%, compared with 47% (see above) twenty years later. In 1970 women's income was boosted 46% by college, compared with 53% in 1990. The job market is becoming more demanding with respect to the educational requirements of workers. The reason is that there are now fewer jobs for those with only a high school education as work becomes more complex and technology advances; the incomes of high school graduates are slipping. The college degree is becoming more important.

What we have seen here are only the financial benefits of investment in human capital. The other side of the issue is the cost of acquiring human capital.

When is investment in human capital worthwhile?

People will invest in human capital when they expect to get a good return on that investment. If people are motivated by money, they will invest when the income they will receive exceeds the cost of the investment.

SANDY GETS ANOTHER DEGREE: Sandy is twenty-five years old and teaches music in a public junior high school. She has a bachelor's degree in music. She has the chance to earn a master's degree in education at a local state university, taking evening and summer classes for two years, while keeping her teaching position. Once Sandy gets it, her income will increase by $800 per year. She plans to retire at age sixty-seven; the second degree would also boost her pension income by $269 per year. Sandy's life expectancy is age eighty-six. If she studies for the master's degree, tuition and other items would cost her $8,000 of her own money. This investment looks as though it will get a good return, so she signs up for the master's program.

Based on money income, Sandy made a good deal. How do we know? In this case it is almost intuitive; she will invest $8,000 up front and get an annual benefit of $800 for thirty years plus a higher pension; that is a better return than any bank account would give her right now.

But the way the economist would verify that this is a good investment would be to calculate the **present value of earnings** that she would get from the master's degree. If the present value of her added income is greater than the cost of getting the degree ($8,000), she would be better off having it.

Present value (or PV) has to be calculated using a computer, but the concept is simple. PV is the amount of money Sandy would have to put in a bank today to get the same income benefits the master's degree would bring. If the bank paid interest of 6%, she would have to start her account by depositing $11,650 now at age twenty-five. Then she could start drawing out $800 per year after she turns twenty-seven, always leaving the rest to earn interest. When Sandy turned sixty-seven, she would start drawing only $269 per year to age eighty-six; after that the account would be used up. The PV of the degree program is $11,650. If she did not want to invest this money in the bank, the only other way she could get the same income would be to invest $8,000 in education and to earn the degree.

People invest in human capital when the return is greater than the cost. If Sandy did not want to get the degree, she would have to come up with an extra $3,650 to get the same income benefits as the degree would have given her. She could save $3,650 by getting the master's degree. This makes the degree a better deal.

Can someone really make good decisions about human capital using the present value approach?

In looking at Sandy's decision, we ignored the matter of risk. The returns to investment in human capital are really not as certain as Sandy's case made them out to be. There were a lot of ifs.

First, Sandy assumed the tuition would stay at $4,000 per year. If the tuition were to go up dramatically, the degree might not be worth the investment. Specifically, if the tuition went to more than $11,650 for the two years, the cost would be greater than the PV of the added income; she would not take the degree. Second, she assumed the degree would bring extra income of not less than $800 per year. Third, she assumed a bank account would never give her more than 6% interest. (If the interest were 10% or more over her lifetime, the degree would not be worth the investment.) Fourth, she assumed she would not retire earlier than age sixty-seven nor live longer than age eighty-six.

All of these are examples of the risks involved in investing in human capital. If risks are really large, there will be less investment. *People will be reluctant to invest in human capital if the payoffs are uncertain.* (A divorce lawyer once observed that doctors often spend many years acquiring their education, with great sacrifices made, and few benefits received . . . by their first wives.)

Of course, we have only been looking at the cold, hard cash side of decisions about human capital. Economists are really warm people, and they can see there is more to it.

Are all the returns to human capital measured in dollars?

We could make cold calculations about Sandy's problem because, with a public school teacher's highly structured pay scale and little chance of advancement, money was the main issue. Her teaching job would not change much, if at all, with or without the degree. (Sandy was fortunate to have had the choice of continuing to teach with or without the degree. In some schools her employment would be terminated if, within a certain period of time, she failed to get the master's degree.)

Of course, not everyone works just for money. Economists say we get two kinds of rewards from work, **money income** and **psychic income**. Psychic income is the personal satisfaction, enrichment, and enjoyment we get from what we do. Money income is the dollars and cents we take from the job. *Most people work for a combination of money and psychic incomes.*

There are fortunate people who manage to maximize both types of reward. Highly paid actors, famous musicians, "best-seller" novelists, and billionaire captains of industry make more money in their jobs than they could earn anywhere else and often have a fun time doing their work. But most of us must strike a balance between money and psychic income.

LENORA LIKES PROFESSING: Lenora is an engineering professor at a state university. She is forty-three years old, likes studying materials engineering, and feels that her $52,000 annual wage is adequate. With her degrees and experience, she could make at least $75,000 per year as an engineer for a manufacturing firm. In fact, it is common for many of her students to make this much by the time they are in their forties. But working in business would not give her the freedom to select her own research projects, to run experiments, and to teach classes. She has more freedom to manage her time than she would in a business firm, where her schedule would be tightly controlled. Once the university granted her tenure, she had more job security than a business could promise her, even if she ran her own company. By opting for a lower wage, but higher nonmonetary benefits, she has struck a balance between money and psychic income.

The balance Lenora has made is similar to that made by most ministers, authors, teachers, and other professionals whose monetary incomes may not be high.

Are there returns to human capital that the individual worker does not get?

An important point in economics is that individuals are not the only ones affected by their decisions. What you or I decide to do about our education, for example, has an impact on society. In the lingo of the economist, investments in human capital create **externalities**. Externalities occur when a decision is made that is felt by others who had nothing to do with the decision.

Externalities occur all the time. Here is a simple example that does not involve education. Suppose your neighbor throws a big party to which you are not invited. The guests' cars take up all the parking spaces on the street, and the noise from their talking or loud music keeps you awake. These are externalities to you because you made no decision to hold or attend the party, but it still affected you (☞ Art. 21: The Business of Government, page 285). Fortunately, not all externalities are negative. If a neighbor plants a beautiful garden that you enjoy when you walk past his property, you are receiving an externality: you did not pay for the garden, but you benefit from what he did.

Investments in human capital usually create positive (beneficial) externalities that people who had no part in making the investment enjoy. When you acquire an education, you become a more informed citizen and can make greater contributions to your profession and to your community.

BENNY GIVES SOMETHING BACK: Benny is a financial planner who sells insurance, mutual funds, and other money-management products. He has a BS in business and was earning $23,000 three years out of college. He then decided to earn an MBA in a two-year program, specializing in finance. In his graduate program he learned about some new financial instruments that helped him to design innovative retirement programs when he returned to his job. These new programs attracted substantial new business and enabled many of his clients to retire earlier than planned, and with more income than they had anticipated. Benny's income as a financial planner grew to $80,000 per year soon after receiving the MBA. A short time later, he was elected to his community's school board, where, because of his expertise, he suggested a change in the financing scheme the school district was using for a new high school building; implementing his suggestion saved each taxpayer an average of $75 per year.

Benny paid for, and worked for, the MBA. His investment in his human capital had two benefits. First, his income increased because he became a more productive worker. This new income was his personal return on the investment. (Economists call this an internal benefit.) Second, many taxpayers benefited from his newly acquired skills, although Benny got no money for his service on the school board. His contribution to the community is an external benefit (externality) of his MBA.

Because society gets something out of individual investments in human capital, it contributes toward this investment by subsidizing schools and colleges. By subsiding schools, society gets more people to invest in their education than would otherwise do so. This is also why many employers pay for part of educational programs taken by employees. The employee gets more money in return for studying and the employer makes more profit in return for investing in the education. In Sandy's case, the school board believed her students and colleagues would benefit from her master's degree, which is why it offered her an incentive to get it.

Recently economists have been investigating the role that externalities play in promoting the growth of national economies. Society's returns from investment in human capital are so large that they are an important factor in economic growth (☞ Art. 3: Economic Growth, page 23).

What is the "signaling" effect of degrees and certificates?

A college degree, or a certificate from a training program, may open the doors to a desirable job. It becomes a **signaling device** if the employer makes it a condition for getting the job. In such cases, *evidence of formal education, as a signaling device, is used in place of more relevant indicators of competence.* With respect to teachers like Sandy, that relevant indicator might be her effectiveness as a teacher. But in many fields relevant indicators may be hard to discover, or they may not be available; it may be difficult for an employer to know exactly how productive a job applicant will be without costly testing or investigation of her/his background.

The problem with using formal education as a signaling device is that the education may not be relevant to subsequent job performance. When it is not, both employer and worker suffer.

> **OTIS LOSES OUT:** Otis is a research chemist for a manufacturer of fertilizers. He grew up on a farm, has a BS in agronomy and a master's degree in chemistry. During his twenty-five years in the lab he helped to develop successful new products for his employer and is now assistant director of research. Because of the rural location of the lab in Iowa, there are no local universities he could attend to further his formal education. But he knows farmers (the customers) and their problems and keeps himself current on work in fertilizer development. When the research director's position was open, he was passed over for the job because he lacked a doctorate. The company hired a young Ph.D. to be Otis's new boss because local management believed a Ph.D.'s name on research reports would give them more credibility at corporate headquarters in New York.

If he could have, Otis would have earned a doctorate, not to make himself more productive or competent as a researcher, but to get through his employer's screening process.

Employers sometimes mistakenly think that universities can certify the job performance of their graduates. Universities provide for, and certify, the acquisition of knowledge on their own turf. They do not provide warranties on the performance of their graduates in the workplace. Education is not the only way, or necessarily the best way, of investing in human capital.

3

Prices

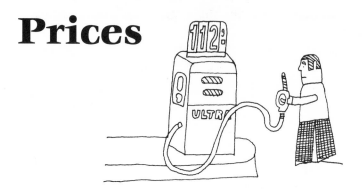

Prices are at the center of a market economy because they make things happen. Producers use prices to decide what to make, and sellers use prices to decide who gets what is made. Buyers use prices to help them decide what to buy.

The first article in this chapter, Article 9: Prices and the Economy, will give you basic lessons about prices and the work they do. Most people know that supply and demand determine prices, but few people (even college students) really understand how this happens. The information in Article 9 is essential to economic literacy. You will learn the way that the demand for, and the supply of, goods and services work together to set the prices people pay for things. Even if you are more interested in other parts of this chapter, you should at least skim over Article 9 first.

Prices are dynamic elements in a market economy because they are subject to change. Price changes are vital to maintaining a healthy economic environment because they make the frequent adjustments that keep an economy well tuned and working smoothly. Some prices, like the cost of a local call in a pay telephone, change rarely, but when they do, the change is significant. (When local pay-phone calls jumped from ten cents to a quarter, overnight they rose 150%.) On the other hand, the prices of fuel, stocks and bonds, farm products, and thousands of other important items are changing constantly, although usually by small amounts. Article 10: Price Changes explains how prices change in response to new events in the economy.

The third and fourth articles give you aerial views of price changes; they cover the elements of inflation. Article 11: Inflation introduces this important topic by explaining how inflation is measured and why some of our most popular inflation gauges sometimes give us a distorted picture of the effects of inflation on people and businesses. Article 12: More About Inflation begins with a quick review of the history of inflation in the United States. You might be surprised to learn that the inflation you have known in your lifetime, and that of your parents, has been more persistent and dramatic than that experienced by earlier American generations.

While we are on the subject of history, Article 12 also takes a look at the performance of many popular shelters people have run under to protect their wealth from the ravages of inflation. Some of these so-called inflation shelters have been rather leaky.

One of the most important prices we pay is the charge for using other people's money; this is the subject of Article 13: Interest Rates. Anyone with a mortgage or auto loan, and most folks who use credit cards, have paid interest, and the sums can be substantial. Interest rates often determine what we can afford to buy (and how long we must make payments for it); they also determine the value of investments. Article 13 explains what makes interest rates high or low and why all interest rates are not the same. This article will also tell you how and why interest rates and inflation are so closely linked.

This chapter on prices is a "must read" for developing economic literacy.

ARTICLE 9:

PRICES AND THE ECONOMY

Why Prices Make Things Happen

Reading Suggestion: This article explains how prices are determined and what they do. You should read or skim it before reading the following article on what makes prices change.

What do prices do for our economy?

Our economy has three basic functions that affect everyone. First, our economy has to decide *what* goods or services we need to produce. We cannot produce everything that everybody wants; we must make choices and compromises. Should we use our workers, natural resources, and factories to produce more electric drills or more handguns? Should we grow more orchids or more broccoli? Producers use prices to help them make these decisions.

Prices play the same role in producing services. Should we use schools and colleges to produce more engineers or more accountants? Do we need more elementary school teachers or more financial analysts? The earnings (the "price" received for her/his work) a person gets from a profession is an important consideration when selecting a career, although it is not the only one. While personal interests, satisfaction, and talents are always important, many people are attracted to high-paying professions and are less willing to take up low-paying work.

When we decide what to make or what service to perform, we have to decide *how* to make it. For example, bottles can be made by hand (and mouth) or by machine. Even services can be delivered in different ways. How should the job be done? Prices help us to decide.

When the good or service is produced, we must decide *who* will get it. Should that original painting by Pollock go to a museum in Texas or to a Japanese art collector? Who should drive the Mercedes and who should have the Chevy? Prices determine the outcome.

In a **command economy** most of these vital decisions are made by a central government authority. There are no pure command economies in the world today, but the Communist economies in Cuba and the People's Republic of China come close, and so did the economies of the former Soviet Union and Eastern Europe.

In a **market economy** *prices determine what is produced, how it is produced, and who will get the things we make.* A market economy uses prices as "signals" telling us how to use our resources. This may seem to be a cold way of doing things, but in most cases it is the most efficient (and, some would argue, the fairest) system of allocating resources that human beings have devised.

There are no pure market economies in the world because markets do not solve all economic problems (☞ Art. 21: The Business of Government, page 285). The world's most advanced industrialized nations, including the United States, have what can best be described as "mixed" economies, in which the vast majority of products are allocated by markets.

Does the market economy's pricing system always give us good results?

Prices are not always reliable guides to running our economy: there are a few cases of what economists call **market failure**, where prices lead buyers and sellers into making bad decisions. The reason is that society is not satisfied with the way prices alone would allocate some of our resources. For example, should health care be given only to those who can pay the price? Should people be permitted to smoke tobacco products anywhere if they are willing to pay the price of these products?

While the price system you will learn about in this article is fair and efficient most of the time, sometimes the system leads to socially unacceptable results. When this occurs, we say the market has failed. Market failure occurs whenever the results of the price system are unacceptable because the actions of buyers and sellers harm "third parties" (innocent persons). For example, the price of whiskey may be so low that some people will have a few drinks before driving home, endangering users of the highway. The price of ivory may be so high that elephants are killed, unsettling an important ecological balance.

When markets fail, society turns to its governments. *Government regulations restrict the workings of the price system when markets fail to produce results that benefit society.* (☞ Art. 21: The Business of Government, page 285, on why markets sometimes fail). Fortunately, the price system works well for most activities in the economy. So let's look at the successful uses of prices.

What is the demand for a product or service?

Most people know that prices result from the demand for, and the supply of, a product. To see how markets work we must look at both of these elements in the market. We start with demand because nothing would be supplied in a market economy unless we expected a demand for it.

Your **demand** for chewing gum is the quantities you are willing to buy at different prices, under a given set of conditions. Your demand depends on such factors as taste, income, the availability of other products you could use in place of chewing gum, and other circumstances that make chewing gum desirable to you.

The price of a product does not influence my demand (desire) for it. Either I enjoy chewing gum or I do not; the price does not determine how much enjoyment I can get from the product. The price just determines how much of it I can buy.

Economists call the benefits (enjoyment, usefulness, etc.) you get from a product its **utility**. In a way, utility is like happiness; you know what it is, and how it feels, but you cannot measure it in numbers. Nonetheless, what makes buyers put down their money is the utility they *expect* to get from their purchase. Of course, not all purchases give you the utility (satisfaction) you expect; but you usually do not know this until after you have made the purchase.

The demand for something comes from the desirability or necessity of the product. Price is important only because it influences the amount *of the product you are willing to buy.*

What determines your demand for a product?

What determines your demand for a product (good or service) is what you want and how well you expect it to satisfy this desire. Experience and knowledge about a product help to shape your expected utility from using it. But there is more to your demand: your ability to buy. I may want to buy a world cruise that includes a first-class suite, but if I cannot afford one, I cannot be part of the market's demand for that service. The things that will give you satisfaction depend on your circumstances. Let's look at these circumstances.

First of all, your demand for most consumer products, such as shoes, depends on your *income*, or more directly, on your **purchasing power**. Your purchasing power is your ability to purchase goods and services. The higher your income, the more shoes you are likely to buy during the year and the more you are likely to spend on each pair. Buyers with high incomes are also likely to be less sensitive to the price of shoes than are lower-income buyers. Not only does your income determine how many shoes you can buy (demand) at any given price, it also says something about your lifestyle and the wants that go with it.

Second, your demand depends on *taste*. Fashion plays a role in the type and quantity of shoes you buy. If shoes are important in your work (or in your social life), you are likely to buy more shoes than someone who is less concerned about footwear. If you want to be one up on Imelda Marcos, your demand for shoes will be different than if you hang around with Willie Nelson. Your lifestyle, and the people around you, help to develop your taste for shoes.

Third, demand is influenced by the *prices of related goods and services*. If you are content to chew on peppermint candies in place of gum, your demand for gum will be influenced by the price of peppermint candy. In this case we would say that peppermint candy is a **substitute** for chewing gum. Demand for chewing gum is likely to increase if the price of a substitute goes up.

Other prices are important, too. Consider your demand for dress shirts. Suppose you always buy a necktie when you buy a dress shirt. In that case a necktie is a **complement** to a dress shirt. If the price of neckties goes up, your demand for dress shirts will go down, and vice versa. Similarly, the demand for skirts depends (in part) on the price of blouses, the demand for cars depends on the price of gasoline, and so on.

So we see that your demand for *most* goods and services depends on your income, tastes, and on the prices of substitutes and complements. In addition, your demand for a *specific* good or service also depends on a number of special factors unique to that product. For example, your height might not have anything to do with your demand for hair curlers, but it influences your demand for high-heel shoes. Taller people might have less demand for high-heel shoes than do shorter persons.

Demand for a product or service is determined by income, tastes, prices of related goods, and other factors. Demand reflects the desirability of an item. The price of the product or service determines the quantity you will buy.

How do consumers use prices?

Prices play a major role in determining what we decide to buy. To express this important point economists have formulated the so-called **law of demand**. This law of economic behavior (which was never passed by a legislature) simply states that, *in general, people buy a larger quantity of a good or service when its price is low than they would buy when its price is high.*

REZA GOES FOR GRAPES: Reza is a careful shopper. Her family likes fresh grapes, which she purchases on her weekly trips to the grocery store. When grapes were 99¢ per pound, she bought two and a half pounds per week. When the store charged $1.39, she cut her purchases to one and a half pounds. Yesterday the price was up to $1.79; she thought this price was so high she bought only one pound and purchased some bananas with the money she did not use to buy grapes. She decided that if the price goes above $2, she will not buy any grapes and will buy more bananas instead. Reza does not regard grapes as an essential good, so she is sensitive to their price.

Reza's buying habits, recorded on the left side of Table 9A, illustrate the law of demand. As the price of grapes went up, the quantity

Table 9A

Two Shoppers Demand Grapes

WHEN THE PRICE IS . . .	REZA BUYS . . .	AND REZA SPENDS . . .	SUSAN BUYS . . .	AND SUSAN SPENDS . . .
$0.99/lb	2$^{1}/_{2}$ lbs	$2.48	3$^{3}/_{4}$ lbs	$3.71
1.39	1$^{1}/_{2}$	2.09	3	4.17
1.79	1	1.79	2$^{1}/_{2}$	4.48
2.09	0	0	2$^{1}/_{4}$	4.70

of grapes that she demanded went down. That is the law of demand in action.

Now let us look at the behavior of Susan, another consumer. Her buying habits are shown on the right side of Table 9A. She also obeyed the law of demand; as grape prices rose, the amount of grapes she bought went down. Even so, unlike Reza, she spent more money on grapes when the price was high. Susan's response to a price increase was milder than Reza's; grapes were more important to her.

What is true for these two shoppers is true for the entire economy. As prices rise, the amount buyers demand declines.

How do buyers change their budgets when prices rise or fall?

We see that Reza is so sensitive to the price of grapes that when the price rose, she not only purchased fewer grapes, she also cut the amount of money she spent on grapes. Economists have a special term they apply to such behavior; they say that this buyer has an **elastic demand** for the product. *The quantity that is demanded of a product or service is elastic (very sensitive to price change) when higher prices cause buyers to spend less money on that product or service.*

This information is important to sellers (such as the grocery store owner). The money spent by the buyer is the revenue received by the seller. Therefore, *when the quantity demanded of a product is elastic, then any increase in price will reduce the total revenue (dollar sales) of the seller.* As a result of raising the price of grapes, the seller got less money from Reza.

On the other hand, when the price of grapes went up, Susan spent more money on grapes, even though she bought a lesser amount. Susan has an **inelastic demand** for the product. Apparently grapes are a more important part of her family's diet. Their taste for grapes is such that she is willing to make only small sacrifices in quantity when prices rise. *The quantity demanded of a product or service is inelastic (not very sensitive to price change) when higher prices cause buyers to spend more money on that product or service.* Because of her inelastic demand, sellers receive more revenue from shoppers like Susan when they raise prices.

In what way does a change in the price of an item affect the demand for other goods or services?

When the price of something changes and buyers spend fewer or more dollars on that item, they must purchase more or less of something else to stay within their budget. In Reza's case, when the price was up to $1.79, she spent 69¢ less on grapes than she did when the price of grapes was 99¢ per pound, and she could use this 69¢ to buy more of something else, like bananas.

When buyers purchase more of another item because the price of something goes up, we say that other item is a **substitute good (or service)**. *An increase in the price of one good increases the demand for a substitute good.*

Sellers would certainly want to know what goods consumers think of as substitutes. If bananas and grapes are substitutes, people who sell bananas can expect their sales to go up when the price of grapes rises.

Susan's demand is inelastic, so that when the price of grapes went up, she had less money to spend on other things. When the price of an item rises, substitute goods are not the only things affected. Suppose Susan's family likes to eat cheese with grapes. When she bought a lesser quantity of grapes, she had a lesser demand for cheese. When buyers purchase less of another item because the price of something goes up, we say that other item is a **complementary good (or service)**. So when the price of grapes rises, cheese sellers beware! *An increase in the price of one good reduces the demand for a complementary good.*

(A particular good is not always a substitute or a complement for

another. Some goods, such as grapes and thumbtacks, may be unrelated.)

Reza's and Susan's decisions show us that the demands for different goods and services is often related. When the price of one good
changes, it might affect the demand for something else.

Of course, buyers' reactions to lower prices are the opposite of
reactions to higher prices. A lower price of an item generally
increases the quantity of that item that is demanded; it will also
reduce the demand for substitutes and increase the demand for complementary items. The law of demand works in both directions.

What determines the elasticity of demand when prices rise or fall?

Why was Reza so willing to cut down on buying grapes when the
price rose? Her demand was elastic because she was willing to
change her buying habits significantly when prices rose or fell.

A buyer's elasticity of demand depends on how necessary a good
or service is. If buyers think of grapes as a luxury, their demand will
be very elastic. Another factor is the availability of close substitutes.
If buyers are willing to turn to an alternative, demand will also be
elastic. Reza was quite ready to buy bananas in place of grapes when
grapes became more costly. Finally, there is the matter of how
expensive something is relative to one's budget. People are more
sensitive to the price of cars, because they take a big chunk from
one's income, than they are to the price of grapes. Demand for big-
ticket items is more elastic than is demand for inexpensive things.

*The quantity demanded of goods and services is elastic if they are easy to
replace and/or they claim a large part of one's budget.*

Is price the only major factor that determines the demand for goods and services?

Price is important, but price is not everything. *Income* is a significant determinant of how much people demand. When their incomes
rise, people demand more, even though prices may not change.
Income gives people the ability to buy things; it increases what economists call their **purchasing power**. We also saw in an earlier question that higher incomes make buyers less price sensitive.

TERRY STEPS OUT: Terry has a passion for grand opera and lives near a city where live opera is available. When he was an assistant bank manager earning $30,000 per year, he attended about three performances a season and paid $81 each for orchestra seats. He recently become manager of a bank office at $46,000 per year. Terry now attends at least six performances a season.

Demand responds to income; this response is called **income elasticity**. Terry's income elasticity was high because as his income went up by half, his demand for opera tickets doubled.

The income elasticity of luxuries, such as opera tickets, is very high. But for necessities the income elasticity may be very low. An example of a good with a low income elasticity is toothpaste; people are not likely to buy a lot more toothpaste when their incomes rise. Conversely, the income elasticity of demand for some goods is negative: when one's income rises, one demands less of it. Economists call these **inferior goods**, a term that would make a marketing executive shudder. (To me, one of the little joys of higher income is eating less frequently in places where I have to dispose of my tray and wrappers.)

In the language of economics, people's demand for a good or service depends on the *utility* they get from it. Utility means satisfaction or usefulness. We saw how utility affects demand when we compared the buying habits of Reza and Susan (Table 9A). When grape prices rose, Susan cut back less on her purchases because the utility to her was greater than to Reza. The demand you have for something will increase if its utility increases.

> **KEN DRESSES UP:** Ken is sales manager of an office supply firm. For years he did most of his work by letter and telephone, so his wardrobe was not important to his business. He had his business suits cleaned and pressed about twice a year. To get to know his customers better, Ken now goes out of his office frequently to call on them at their places of work. Because he is representing his firm in person, his clothing, and its maintenance, is now more important. He has his suits dry-cleaned four or five times a year.

Dry-cleaning services became more important to Ken after he changed his way of contacting customers. The price of dry cleaning did not change, but his demand for this service increased because the utility he got from it was greater.

Tastes (preferences) change. Anyone who has been on a high school or college campus recently knows that baseball caps (sometimes worn backward) are in for both sexes. That increases their utility. Baseball caps have been around for a long time, yet the demand for them rose when they became "cool."

Sometimes tastes change suddenly and so does the demand for goods or services, even though sellers may have no responsibility for these changes.

> **HUANG AND SUE TAKE A HIT:** A hardworking couple owned a Chinese restaurant that had been enjoying moderate, but steady, growth in sales for five years. Despite this growth, Huang and Sue kept prices low and did not skimp on portions or food quality. A government agency recently announced, with some fanfare, that some oriental foods had a higher fat and calorie content than some hamburger sandwiches. While this conclusion was controversial, sales revenue in Huang and Sue's restaurant plunged 25%.

Consumer tastes changed when buyers changed their views about the healthfulness of Chinese food, even if this change was not justified. *Prices are not everything; demand for a product or service also depends on its usefulness (utility) and on buyers' incomes and tastes.*

How do prices determine the supply of goods or services?

Demand is only half the picture. A service is not sold, even if buyer demand is strong, unless someone is willing and able to supply (sell) it. The price of a service is what the seller receives in return. Price is the main inducement for a seller to supply what the buyer wants.

In a market economy **profit** is the driving force behind sellers. Profit is the difference between the revenue a seller receives and the seller's costs of doing business. When the price of her product or service goes up, the seller has the opportunity to make more profit (if her costs do not also rise), so she is willing to sell more. This results in the "weak" **law of supply**: *sellers often increase the quantity supplied of goods and services when prices go up, and they often reduce the amount they supply when prices go down.*

HENRY PUSHES HEELS: Henry owns the only shoe store in a small town. He has an area for stocking and selling men's shoes and another area for women's shoes. Originally the two areas were equal in size. When the price of women's shoes increased, he found he could earn a larger markup on women's shoes than he could get on men's shoes. To increase his income, Henry increased the women's area to occupy 70% of the store and decreased the men's area. After this change, women's shoe sales provided him with 90% of his profit. Henry is thinking about enlarging the women's area again.

Henry supplies shoes to retail buyers. Driven to make more profits, he used his resources (his store space) to increase the supply of women's shoes in response to higher prices for women's shoes.

Why is the law of supply weak?

There are some exceptions to the law of supply. The law of supply is weaker than the law of demand because lower prices do not always result in lower supplies, and vice versa. *Sometimes sellers will supply larger quantities of a product when the price goes down.* One reason is that higher volume may make up for lower price.

DIANE AND HARRIET SHIP PECAN CANDIES: Diane and Harriet sell their unique pecan candy by mail. Currently they charge $15 for a sixteen-ounce shipment, $20.25 for twenty-four ounces, and $25.50 for a thirty-two-ounce order. All prices include shipping and handling. Because they realize scale economies in shipping and handling, their $20.25 price represents a discount of 10% per pound over the price of a sixteen-ounce order. The $25.50 price gives customers a 15% discount per pound compared with the smallest quantity.

This pricing means that Diane and Harriet sell their candy at $15 for one pound, at $13.50 per pound for a $1\frac{1}{2}$-pound order, and at only $12.75 per pound for a two-pound order. They charge lower prices for larger quantities sent at one time to one customer. The reason is that their cost of packaging and mailing a $1\frac{1}{2}$-pound shipment is less than 50% more than the cost of packaging and mailing a one-pound order, and the cost of packaging and mailing a two-pound order is hardly more than that of a $1\frac{1}{2}$-pound order. So they pass part of these savings on to customers to encourage them to give larger orders. Sellers of many goods and services offer customers quantity discounts like these, which have the effect of inverting the relationship between price and quantity.

Similarly, higher prices may motivate workers to decrease the quantity of the service they supply.

JOHN TAKES STOCK OF HIS TIME: John works on commission as a salesman for a stock brokerage firm. He spends working time contacting prospective clients, recommending investments, and processing his clients' orders to buy or to sell stock. Since becoming a broker ten years ago, his income has grown steadily. Last year he earned $290,000, but worked an average of eighty hours per week. With such a high income, John has decided he can afford to cut back to a sixty-hour week, even though he realizes his income may fall as much as 20% as a result.

John's case illustrates "backward" supply; as the price of his services (his income) rose, he reduced the supply of these services. He decided to replace some work with some leisure, perhaps giving his family a larger share of his time.

Sometimes higher prices will motivate sellers to reduce the quantity they supply. This inverse relationship between prices and the quantities sellers supply holds only up to a point. There is a limit to the discounts Diane and Harriet can give without cutting into their profits. For example, they may be unable to realize savings in shipping and handling costs for orders beyond five pounds; accordingly, they will not offer lower prices per pound for orders larger than five pounds. Similarly, John will cut back his working hours only until his income reaches some level he feels he must have to maintain his lifestyle.

How do sellers increase the supply of goods and services when prices rise?

If resources were inexhaustible, we could produce everything everyone wants. Because our earthly resources are not infinite, we have to make choices, just as Henry did. He increased the supply of women's shoes by decreasing the supply of men's shoes.

Sellers must make choices because our economy can often increase the supply of one item only by decreasing the supply of something else. This is even true of our own labor. We make money by working, but we can work more only by giving up leisure time; we have only twenty-four hours in the day. We all make choices between work and leisure. Decisions on how much work we do are often made by comparing the satisfaction of leisure with the benefits of the income we could get from additional work.

Is price the only major consideration that determines the supply of goods and services?

Remember that what a producer supplies is tied to the desire to make a profit. The profit a seller can make depends on two important considerations: the price she gets for her product *and* the cost of producing or acquiring it.

All goods and services cost something to produce. A store manager has to pay the cost of acquiring a product plus the costs of running the store. For a manufacturer the cost depends on the expense of labor, materials, and other items that are needed to create a good.

Even services have a cost. The accountant has to bear costs of maintaining an office, obtaining current information about her field (new tax laws, for example), purchasing equipment such as computers and software, and paying for her assistants.

These are all examples of **factors of production**, which economists simply call factors. A factor is any labor or material resource that is used to create a product or service. Every factor has a price. The prices of the factors used to run a business are called **factor costs**. When factor costs rise, profits go down and so does supply, because higher factor costs mean lower profits.

CHRIS DOWNSIZES: Last year Chris ran three clothing stores in a metropolitan region, employing seven full-time and five part-time workers. Then a law was passed that required him to provide health-care coverage for his part-time employees, who were not previously given this fringe benefit. This new labor cost (which felt, to Chris, like a wage increase) would have reduced his firm's profit 60%. To avoid these costs, Chris dismissed his part-time workers, forcing him to close one of his stores.

When his costs went up, Chris cut back the output of his business; he decreased the clothing he supplied to the market. This is an example of the law of supply; *when the cost of producing a good or service rises, the supply of the product goes down.*

Technology is the process used to produce something; it is the way a producer puts things together to create a product or service. There are usually many ways of producing anything. A car can be assembled by using robots or by using a large amount of human labor. An accountant can complete tax forms using reference books, a calculator, pens, and paper, or the accountant can use a personal computer with software. When technology changes, so do the costs of production. *If a seller uses a new technology that reduces costs of production, profits will rise and the supply will also increase.*

CYNTHIA GOES HIGH TECH: Cynthia is a public accountant with her own firm serving small businesses and individuals. About 60% of her billings come from income tax preparation, which she used to do with the help of two assistants, manuals, forms, pencils, and calculators. Recently she acquired a powerful computer and sophisticated tax software that prompts for information, performs calculations, and produces completed tax forms. By using this new computer and software she reduced her average cost per tax filing by 20%. She used these savings to boost her advertising, to gain new clients, and thereby to increase the amount of her services she supplied to the community.

Cynthia changed from a labor-intensive technology to one that relies heavily on the computer. This technological change allowed her to increase the supply of her services without increasing her fees.

How are prices determined in a free market?

We have seen that as the price of something rises, two things happen at the same time: less of it will be demanded, but more of it will be supplied. **Market** is the word economists use to describe any gathering of buyers and sellers where a price of something can be negotiated. The market can be a special place where buyers and sellers meet, or in our electronic age, it can be the interaction of buyers and sellers by telephones, computers, or other means.

Fresh-pressed apple cider is available in most areas of the United States. Suppose people in a small town are willing to buy cider at certain prices in amounts as shown in Table 9B. According to the law of demand, the lower the price, the more cider people would be willing to buy. But the amount of cider that suppliers (generally, local orchards) were willing to sell fell when the price went down, which is also shown in Table 9B, in accordance with the law of supply.

If the price of cider was as low as $2 per gallon in this town, buyers would ask for 450 gallons each week, but store managers would be able to get only 150 gallons from cider producers. At this price the demand would be greater than the supply, which would create a

Table 9B

The Market for Apple Cider in a Small Town

If Each Gallon Sold For . . .	Buyers Would Demand . . .	Sellers Would Provide . . .
$2.00	450 gallons	150 gallons
2.25	400	200
2.75	350	250
3.25	**300**	**300**
3.75	250	350
4.25	200	400

shortage of (450 − 150 =) 300 gallons of cider, and many buyers would be disappointed.

Now look at what would happen if cider went up to $4.25 per gallon. At this lofty price buyers would want 200 gallons less cider than sellers would be willing to supply. If $4.25 was the price, this imbalance between supply and demand would create a **surplus** of cider, and many sellers would be disappointed.

Once the price hits $3.25, any surplus or shortage would disappear. In the jargon of economics, the price where there are neither shortages nor surpluses is called the **equilibrium price**, after a Latin word indicating balance. (Economists have always had a thing for Latin.) At this price, $3.25, the market is in balance: supply and demand are equal and there is no incentive to increase or to decrease the price.

There is a beauty in the way markets work. If prices are free to change, the market will always come into balance. If no authorities interfere in the marketplace, *the free market price eventually settles at the level where there are no shortages or surpluses in the market.* But this does not always happen quickly. How long it takes for shortages or surpluses to disappear depends on how fast information travels in the market, and how quickly buyers or sellers can react to new information.

ARTICLE 10:

PRICE CHANGES

What Makes Prices Go Up or Down?

Reading Suggestion: You might wish to read or skim the preceding article before reading this one.

What causes the demand for a product to change?

In the previous article we saw that the *demand for a product (a good or a service) depends on buyers' tastes, incomes, the prices of other products, and special factors related to the product.* All of these factors determine the utility buyers can expect to receive from the product. *Utility* is a term economists use to mean usefulness or satisfaction people get from a product. Rational buyers are motivated to make purchases on the basis of this expected utility.

Price is important only because it determines how much of a product purchasers will buy. Generally, price does not affect the utility of a product. The ability of a can of soda to quench your thirst is the same whether you must put 50¢ or $1.25 into a vending machine for the can. The price adds nothing to the taste.

There are exceptions to the principle that price does not affect expected utility. For some products price is an indicator of quality. For example, consumers may be unable to determine the quality of a product such as a facial cream; the inexperienced buyer may prefer the more costly creams on the belief that they are more beneficial than the cheaper ones. Another situation where price is a determinant of demand is where the price becomes part of the product itself. In this case the product is so costly that owning it provides status, which then becomes part of its utility. Would real diamond tiaras be such a popular ornament for wealthy women to wear on formal occasions if they could be had at supermarket checkout counters?

The expected utility you can get from a product or service can change based on experience or based on new information.

CLAUDE CHEWS IT OVER: Claude purchases chewing gum from a vending machine outside his office. When a pack of gum cost 40¢, he purchased about five packs per week. Then the price shot up to 55¢ and he reacted by cutting back to three packs per week. However, later he read a magazine article that convinced him that gum chewing increases alertness and lessens stress. This made gum more attractive to Claude, and despite the 55¢ price, he returned to buying five packs a week.

When the price of a package of chewing gum rose, the amount of gum Claude bought initially decreased because the utility he expected to get from it, relative to the utility he could get for the same money spent on something else (such as peppermints), was not worth the higher price. He would not get as much for his money. The satisfaction he could get from a pack of gum did not change just because the price rose from 40¢ to 55¢.

But once he read that article, he felt that the extra 15¢ he would have to pay for a pack of gum should not discourage him from buying more of it. Claude's taste for gum changed because he saw more advantages to gum chewing; this made him value gum more highly. What was the result? His demand for gum increased because he was willing to buy more of it, at either 40¢ or 55¢, than he was previously willing to buy. *The demand for a product rises when buyers increase the value they place on the product.* Of course, demand falls if this value decreases.

Where does price come in?

Once your demand is in place, the *amount* of an item you will buy depends on its price. Before he read an article on the advantages of chewing gum, Claude had a fixed demand (desire) for gum that motivated him to buy five packs per week when its price was 40¢ and to buy three packs at 55¢. Once he read the article, his demand increased because gum became more desirable; he was willing to buy five packs at a price of 55¢ in place of only three packs. *Demand for a product increases when the satisfaction you expect from the product increases. The price of the product determines the quantity demanded.* The quantity of gum Claude demands at 55¢ per pack will remain fixed until such a time as his demand for gum changes again.

How do prices change when demand changes?

Price is a wonderful equalizer. Remember that the demand for a product depends on buyers' incomes, tastes, the prices of related things, and other factors. When any of these things change, demand changes. If the change raises the demand, but the price does not change, there will be a **shortage** of the item, at least temporarily, and some buyers will be disappointed. That means that the amount of the item that people demand is greater than the amount suppliers are willing or able to provide.

If the change lowers the demand, a **surplus** will develop, at least temporarily. Here the amount demanded is less than the amount supplied, and some sellers will be disappointed (☞ Art. 9: Prices and the Economy, page 102) for a discussion of the supply side of the market).

In either case, the price should be changed to bring demand and supply back into balance. That is because shortages make prices rise and surpluses make prices fall (if prices are allowed to change freely) until the amount that buyers demand is the same as the amount sellers supply.

A subtle, but important, lesson in economics is that changes in the price of a product do not change the demand for that product; price changes *result* from changes in the demand for the product or changes in the supply of a product. Changes in demand, or supply, cause shortages or surpluses. Why this happens is explained shortly. Meanwhile, it is important to point out that *prices will fall anytime there is a surplus of a product or service; prices will rise anytime there is a shortage.* A surplus will push prices lower, whether the surplus came from a decrease in demand or from an increase in supply. By the same token, shortages push prices up, regardless of whether the shortage came about from a change in demand or from a change in supply. *Prices move up and down until they find the level where demand and supply are equal, i.e., where there are no shortages or surpluses.*

CHANGING THE PRICE OF BREAD: Julio is the bakery manager in a supermarket. For the past few months his bread baker has been baking and selling 150 loaves of fresh bread per day, which are priced at $1.35 each. This seems to be the "right" price because rarely are any loaves unsold at the end of the day (which would be a surplus) and rarely does a customer complain of not getting the fresh bread he/she wants (a shortage). But when other stores started selling pita bread, sales of loaves of fresh bread dropped about one-third. Julio was forced to sell leftover loaves on the day-old bread rack at a large markdown. To keep his bread baker busy he lowered the bread price to $1.05, which was low enough so that customers once again bought 150 loaves per day.

Julio found that *prices fall when demand declines.* Buyers found that the new low price was attractive enough to overcome any advantages they might have seen in pita bread. It's like marrying for money: the financial advantages may be enough to make you ignore other considerations!

Julio had another choice, if he did not want to lower the price. He could have kept the price at $1.35, but cut the amount of bread he supplied by one-third, because that is the most he could have sold at the price and still made a profit. (He would have to hire more help or pay overtime wages to produce more than 150 loaves per day.) *When demand declines, sellers can avoid a price reduction, or a surplus, only by lessening the quantity supplied.* Julio decided not to do this because he wanted to keep his baker busy.

How do prices change when supply changes?

Prices also change when the supply changes. Let's go back to Julio's bakery department before pita bread hit the market. One of the bread bakers in town retired. This reduced the amount of bread available in the town by one-third; the supply of bread went down. One result was that some customers of the retired baker came to

Julio's store and purchased their bread there. The result was a shortage: many of Julio's old customers were disappointed by not getting fresh bread. Reluctantly, Julio raised prices to $1.60 per loaf, from the old price of $1.35. At the higher price some customers switched to other products, and the amounts supplied and demanded were equal. *When the supply of a good or service declines, sellers raise the price until the shortage disappears. The reverse is true when supply goes up.* Here price performed an important role. The price rose as a means of eliminating the shortage.

Alternatively, Julio (or one of his competitors) could hire a new baker to meet the bread shortage, without changing the price from $1.35. In this case *the existence of a shortage could cause the supply of bread to go up but only if it is profitable to produce more at the prevailing price.*

Why do shortages occur?

Shortages are often a problem in a market economy. They occur when the quantity of something that is demanded is greater than the quantity sellers will supply. Shortages of electricity might occur during very hot days in summer. Sometimes there are shortages of tomatoes, mathematics teachers, computer memory chips, or physicians in rural areas. However, keep in mind that the quantities that sellers supply, and the quantities that buyers demand, both depend on price. The quantity supplied can be increased, and (at the same time) the quantity demanded can be reduced, by raising prices.

For most people, one of the hardest lessons in economics is that shortages occur because prices are wrong. *Shortages occur because prices are too low. So most shortages can be eliminated by raising prices.* If we have a shortage of fresh fruit in New England in January, we can eliminate it by having higher prices. These higher prices will reduce the quantity demanded. At the same time, higher prices will increase the quantity supplied as sellers are encouraged to get fresh fruit from distant places (perhaps flying it in from the Caribbean) at higher cost.

Of course, lovers of fresh fruit will have to make compromises, either by enjoying less fruit or by cutting back on something else, such as meat or fish. These compromises hurt. *When shortages occur, prices go up and living standards of consumers go down.* That is because buyers can afford less fruit at the higher prices. When fruit prices go up, people will no longer have a shortage of fruit, but they will have a shortage of *cheap* fruit. (If they are willing to pay higher prices without cutting back on their fruit purchases, they will have to compromise by having less of something else they once enjoyed.)

Of course, higher fruit prices will improve the living standards of those fruit growers who have fruit to sell. Others, such as the airlines that ship the product, will also benefit from new business. *Shortages create both winners and losers.*

Is there an alternative to high prices when we have a shortage?

Whenever the number of products buyers want is greater than what sellers have available, the available supply has to be rationed among the buyers. One way of rationing is waiting; potential buyers just queue up in a long line, the earliest arrivals at the line taking the front positions. Supplies are sold to people in the order they are in the line, with people in the back of the line getting nothing. This was true of gasoline buyers in the early 1970s (before prices were decontrolled) and is true of ticket buyers at many rock concerts. This method was familiar in Soviet economies where output and prices were set by government agencies.

The second alternative is discrimination. The seller chooses the buyers to receive her product. The choice may be made on the basis of prior relations (for example, favoring old customers). It could also be based on a potential customer's racial group, age, or other bases of selection; discrimination on these grounds may be illegal. Discrimination on any grounds is economically unjustified, in addition to being socially objectionable, because it means buyers are not being selected on the basis of their willingness to pay.

The third alternative is violence. The strongest, or best-armed, "buyer" takes the available supply (often with no money changing hands).

The price is the device the free market economy uses for rationing short supplies among potential buyers. That is one reason a market economy's method of handling shortages and surpluses is often called the "price system."

How do surpluses occur in a market economy?

The beauty of a market economy is that no central authority makes all the decisions about who will produce what item and how much he or she can make. Independent sellers are free to set their own prices and to decide how much they want to produce. But as a result, surpluses occasionally occur in the market. It is quite possible that sellers price their products so high that the amount demanded at that price is less than the amount supplied. Farmers sometimes have a surplus of cabbage, dress shops may have a surplus of halter tops, and a town may have a surplus of dentists. Regardless of who is responsible for a surplus, *surpluses can be eliminated by lowering prices.*

> **SELLERS SCRAMBLE IN THE EGG MARKET:** The egg business is easy to enter. Sellers only need some laying hens, a place for them to roost, a little feed, and at least one rooster. When the retail price of Grade A eggs reached $1.70 per dozen, several entrepreneurs, each on his own, decided to increase the supply by entering the egg business. However, with no coordination among them, too many sellers came in and swamped the market. To get rid of unsold eggs, the price soon dropped to $1.05 per dozen. At this price many sellers could not make a profit and decided to stop producing eggs, which was not good for the chickens, either!

Here, too, the price adjustment means that sellers must make compromises; they will usually receive less revenue (that means less income) than they expected. Some sellers will drop out of the market because lower prices will not give them the incomes they want; that will cut down the quantity of product that is supplied. That is how lower prices eliminate surpluses. But let's not forget that not everyone will be unhappy; buyers will benefit from the lower prices for eggs (and, at least temporarily, former laying chickens will be plentifully available to butchers).

Do price ceilings help buyers?

If a market economy's price system is to work well, prices must be free to rise or fall. However, sometimes society (or rather, the legislature that represents society) decides that a product or service is so critical to our well-being that its price should be held down so most people can afford to buy it.

A **price ceiling** is the highest price sellers are permitted to charge for a good or service. Most price ceilings are set by government agencies. For example, New York City sets limits on the rent that can be charged for certain older apartments. Some state governments set limits on the maximum interest rate that can be charged on credit card debt. These maximum prices are intended to protect consumers from being ripped off. But economists have shown that price ceilings have an important downside: they sometimes lower the quantity that sellers are willing to supply to the market, thereby creating shortages.

> **THE BANK THAT SAYS NO:** A bank sells its credit card in its home state and in a neighboring state. Its home state limits the interest rate it can charge state residents to 12%; the other state has no interest-rate ceiling. Because of the lower return the bank gets from providing credit to residents of its home state, the bank limits cardholders there to a line of credit equal to 10% of annual income, and it refuses to issue cards to persons with incomes under $40,000. In the neighboring state where it currently charges 19% interest, the bank sets credit lines at a liberal 25% of annual income, and it requires a minimum income of only $18,000.

In the state where it is subject to a ceiling interest rate (the interest rate is the "price" of borrowing money), the bank has cut back on its supply of credit; some potential borrowers will be unable to get credit. In the state where there is no ceiling, the bank is willing to supply more credit by issuing cards to what bankers might consider higher-risk borrowers. It is more profitable to issue cards in the state where the interest rate is higher; this higher interest rate gives the bank enough income that it can afford to occasionally make (what turn out to be) bad loans to riskier borrowers.

Some price ceilings may have no effect on buyers. *Price ceilings lead sellers of goods and services to reduce the supply that buyers can get* only *when the ceiling price is lower than the free market price.* That means that if, in the home state, the bank's supply of credit were to equal the demand for credit at an interest rate of 14%, a ceiling rate of 15% or more would have no effect because the free market price would not get that high. On the other hand, a price ceiling of 12% would create a shortage of credit; some potential cardholders and borrowers would lose out.

Price ceilings are intended to help people buy goods or services that society believes are important for everyone to have, such as affordable housing. They are intended to safeguard buyers from having to pay prices for essentials that are so high that many people cannot buy them.

But unless you are one of the few lucky buyers who gets the advantage of a lower price than would otherwise be charged, price ceilings are generally a bad idea. At best they help some people, but almost inevitably they create shortages that leave some buyers disappointed. Alternatively, if the price ceiling is above the free market price, it will have no effect at all!

Do price floors help sellers?

Price floors are sometimes set by government agencies and, occasionally, by groups of sellers themselves. A **price floor** is the lowest price that sellers are permitted to charge for their product. The minimum wage is a price floor because an employer cannot pay less for workers. The Organization of Petroleum Exporting Countries (OPEC) is a sellers' group that sets minimum prices at which its member nations can sell petroleum (although some members might cheat).

Some states set price floors on their agricultural products; for example, Pennsylvania sets the minimum retail price of milk sold in the state. Price floors will generate surpluses if they cause the quantity of an item that is demanded to be less than the quantity supplied.

GRACE'S GLUT OF DANISH: Grace works in one store of a regional chain of supermarkets. She estimates that she could sell out her regular shipment of Osric brand of Danish pastries at $2.89 a box. But in return for special (wholesale) price concessions from Osric's bakery, the chain agrees not to sell its boxed Danish pastries in any of its stores at less than the $3.49 a box charged by other sellers of this good. Grace's store is in a low-income neighborhood where few customers are willing to pay that much. As a result, about a fourth of each shipment usually goes unsold by the expiration date on the boxes.

The commercial bakery apparently did not want the supermarket chain to sell its product at less than the price charged by smaller stores to which it supplies its products. The surplus occurred because the price floor of $3.49 was above what the local customers would pay to buy the store's stock of the product. *Price floors cause surpluses when the floor price is above the price at which the quantity supplied and quantity demanded would be equal; otherwise, price floors have no effect.*

If the floor price for the Danish had been under $2.89, the floor would have been unnecessary. If floors are too high, buyers are deprived of good prices and will have to buy less product than they desire; sellers lose customers and may lose the possibility of making more profit out of higher sales volume.

Price floors are justified, by those who set them, as a way of giving sellers a "fair price." In this way it assures a minimal supply of a product by keeping suppliers (sellers) from leaving what might otherwise be an unprofitable business. Like ceiling prices, price floors are generally a bad idea, except for the few lucky sellers who are able to get them. That is because they make buyers pay more for a product than they would otherwise. They also discourage suppliers from looking for more valuable uses of their resources. Of course, if the price floor is below the free market price, the floor would have no effect on the market.

ARTICLE 11:

INFLATION

Examining the Effects of Price Changes

Reading Suggestion: Please read or skim this article before you read the next article on the history and causes of inflation.

What is inflation?

Inflation makes dollars like ice cubes; their value slowly melts with the passage of time. Inflation means $10 buys less today than it could buy last year, and last year $10 could buy less than it could buy the year before.

Not all prices move in the same direction: over time some go up, some stay the same, and others go down. As recently as 1979 a candy bar was about 20¢, a local call at a pay phone was a dime, and a gallon of regular gasoline was just over $1. Today that candy bar sells for 50¢ or more in most places and the telephone call is a quarter, but gasoline is still just over $1 a gallon. Some of today's popular gadgets, like cellular telephones, fax machines, and personal computers, are getting cheaper every year at the same time that clothing, health care, and haircuts are getting more expensive. So with this mix of price rises and declines, what is inflation? *Inflation is the general upward movement of prices of most goods and services.*

How do we measure inflation?

It sounds like a simple thing, but inflation is not easy to measure. To get a measure of inflation we have to answer questions on what, how, and when. What prices should we look at to get a fair measure of inflation? How do we decide whether price increases are inflationary? Over what time period should we measure price changes?

What prices should we look at when we measure inflation?

Should we look at changes in the price of kiwi fruit, even if most people don't eat kiwi fruit? If we think changes in the price of motor oil should be used to measure inflation, what grade of motor oil should we consider?

To get a true measure of inflation, we must find out what goods and services are in what economists call the buyer's **market basket**. The market basket tells us what he buys and how much of his budget is spent on each item. *A measure of inflation must show changes in the average price of those goods and services that people actually buy: the cost of things in their market basket.* When we measure inflation of the nation, or of a region, we look at the market basket of the average consumer. That means we include kiwifruit if it is in the average market basket, but we ignore its price if it is not.

Are all price changes inflationary?

How to measure price changes is important. Take the matter of quality; few things we buy today are exactly what they were before. When the price of a bottle of hair conditioner goes up, how much of the price increase is due to the fact that the product may be "new and improved" (as the label states)? It would be a mistake to think that the whole price increase is inflationary if today's product is really different; we must make **quality adjustments** when comparing today's prices with earlier ones. You cannot count every price increase as being due to inflation. *Inflation results from price increases that do not correspond to improvements in quality.*

CABLE TELEVISION SERVICE: Residents of a semirural area subscribed to a basic cable television service last year that gave them twelve stations for $14 per month. This year the basic service costs them $18.90 per month, which is a price increase of 35%. However, the basic service now delivers fifteen channels, 25% more than before. After considering this quality improvement, the inflation rate for cable TV service was 10% (35% price increase less 25% improvement in quality). This 10% rise is the amount of the price increase government statisticians use to calculate the region's inflation rate.

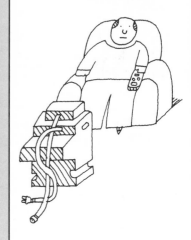

Personal computers give us a clear example of quality change. How do you compare the price of a personal computer today with one you bought ten years ago when today's PC has so many new features?

Services also change. A visit to the dentist today costs more than it did ten years ago, but are the benefits the same? Are you getting better treatment at today's visit because of new dental techniques and the larger body of information practitioners now have about their field? How much of the higher prices you pay can be linked to improvements in the quality of dental care? Remember, inflation can be blamed for only that part of the increased price of care that is not due to better care.

In the case of the cable TV service, it was easy to make quality adjustments to find out how much of the price increase was due to inflation. In most cases, this adjustment is far more difficult and subjective. Government price statisticians who calculate inflation rates must constantly make judgments about quality adjustments when they calculate inflation figures. Because of this, most measures of inflation are partially subjective.

BURT'S BLUE PLATE MEAL: Burt runs a small chain of 1950s-style diners that features a blue plate meal for $5.99. For the past two years each meal was carefully prepared with measured amounts of salad, potatoes, and green beans, four ounces of chopped sirloin steak, and a four-ounce slice of apple pie. This year Burt cut the meat to three and a half ounces and reduced the pie serving to three ounces. But he held the price at the widely advertised level of $5.99. Even though his price did not rise, Burt's changes added to the nation's inflation rate.

Sometimes inflation watchers find that quality changes may lead to inflation even when prices do not change.

If Burt was sharp at marketing, he may have boasted that the new meal reduced the calorie count for weight watchers. But no matter how you cut it, his change was inflationary even though there was no price increase. The quality of his product changed when the content was reduced, just as the quality of the TV cable service increased when stations were added. If Burt did not reduce the size of his servings, he would probably have increased the price of the meal, and the inflationary effect would have been more obvious. Government statisticians must calculate the increased price Burt would have charged for the original meal and use this hypothetical price increase to calculate inflation. For example, suppose the original-size portions in the meal would have been sold for $6.75. We could then say that the price of the meal went up by 12.7%. Burt's cutback in the size of the meal was equivalent to a 12.7% price hike, and this figure would be used to calculate inflation. So *prices do not have to rise to cause inflation, if quality declines.* As you can see, finding the inflation rate is not a simple job.

Over what time period should you measure inflation?

Finally, there is the *when* question. Inflation is measured by comparing today's prices to those we paid at some earlier time. But when was that? If someone told you that the price of hand soap went up 15%, you would want to know if that increase occurred in one month, in one year, or over five years, because inflation is relative to time. *The convention is to express price increases over a one-year period,* even if they occur over shorter time periods.

Because inflation is stated on an annual basis, you must be careful of what you read. If a market basket of goods costs 3% more in March of 1995 than it did in March of 1994, we say the **actual inflation rate** is 3% because prices really did go up 3% over a year's time. If the market basket cost 1% more in March than it did three months before, we say that prices rose during the quarter year at an **annual rate of inflation** of 4%. An actual rate is one that occurred over twelve months. An annual rate is a projection of what *would* occur over twelve months if the current trend were to continue; this is not really a forecast, but a statement about a short-term inflation rate that people can compare to annual rates.

How do economists prefer to measure inflation?

Economists use a variety of inflation measures, and each one answers the what, how, and when questions in a different way. Fortunately, they all tell about the same story, but with different twists. But for most of us, only two measures of inflation are really important, the **Consumer Price Index (CPI)** and the **Producer Price Index (PPI)**. The most closely followed and most widely used measurement is the CPI, so we will turn to that first.

How is the Consumer Price Index (CPI) put together?

There are two CPIs. One is the **CPI-U**, or CPI for all urban consumers. It measures price changes for the typical market basket of things purchased by consumers in nonrural areas. The second is the **CPI-W**, the CPI for all wage and clerical workers. This focuses on the market basket purchased by people who are employed in a broad occupational category. In 1992 the mean value of the CPI-U and CPI-W stood at 140.3% and 138.2%, respectively, of their 1982–84 average. *The CPI-U is the most widely used consumer price index*, although these two inflation measures differ little. In the rest of this article CPI data shown will be values of the CPI-U.

Both CPIs are percentages that show us the total cost of a market basket of goods and services today compared with the cost of the same basket at some earlier time. Every decade or so the U.S. Department of Labor (DOL) takes a survey of consumers to find out how they spend their money. The DOL finds out what they buy and what share of their incomes they spend on each item. The time the survey is taken becomes the **base period**. What consumers bought during the base period becomes the market basket used to construct the CPI. Then, every month, the DOL finds out how much money this market basket would cost at current prices. *The CPI is based on changes in the cost of buying the market basket of goods and services purchased by a typical consumer during the base period. The current value of the government's CPI is the present cost of this market basket, expressed as a percentage of the cost of the same basket in the base period.*

Look at Table 11A to see some recent values of the CPI.[1] During 1989 the average value of the CPI was 124; this means that the market basket of things people bought in the 1982–84 base period, if purchased in 1989, would have cost 24% more than it did in the base period.

The CPI is primarily used to calculate the annual inflation rate each year. Here is how it is done. Look at the last column in Table 11A. In 1990 the market basket cost 5.4% more than it did a year before because the CPI was 5.4% higher than it was in 1989; so 5.4% was the inflation rate that year.

Now look at the CPI value for 1992. While prices kept going up each year, notice that the **inflation rate** (the yearly rate at which the cost of the market basket rose) declined to about 3% per year. When

Table 11A

The Consumer Price Index (CPI) for Urban Consumers in the U.S. (Based on 1982–84 prices)

Date	CPI (Average)	Annual Change
1982–84	100.0	—
1989	124.0	4.8%
1990	130.7	5.4
1991	136.2	4.2
1992	140.3	3.0
1993	144.5	3.0

you use the CPI to learn about inflation, the change in the inflation rate is important to examine.

What does the CPI market basket look like?

How people spent their money during the 1982–84 survey period is important because the CPI figures are based on the brave assumption that people continued to spend their money in about the same way every month after the survey. (It seems these people would be in quite a rut!)

How the respondents to the 1982–84 surveys spent their income is shown in Table 11B.[2] A whopping 39% was spent on housing. This includes mortgage payments, rents, real estate taxes, home insurance, improvements, and related items. About as much was spent on all types of transportation as on food. Americans sure love to move around, and they are willing to pay for it. But they do not spend as much on clothing or on health care: these took only 6% and 5% of the cost of the market basket, respectively. *About 40% of the CPI is based on housing costs, whereas food and transportation each claim about 20% of the original cost of the market basket.*

Are you surprised to see that only 5% of the money spent on the market basket in the base period went to health care? Back in the early 1980s, when the market basket the government currently uses was put together, health care was less costly and claimed a smaller share of consumers' budgets than it does today. Besides, a lot of the cost of health care came out of insurance payments that are not part of the household budget; in many cases these insurance costs were picked up by employers as fringe benefits. (Fringe benefits are generally not counted as

Table 11B	
The CPI Market Basket During the 1982–84 Period	
Type of Spending	Percent of Budget
Housing	39
Food and beverages	20
Transportation	20
Clothing	6
Health care	5
Entertainment	4
Other	6
Total:	100

taxable income.) As health care costs went up faster than other costs, and as employers shifted more of these costs to employees, the 5% became out-of-date and no longer represents actual cost of living.

Does the Consumer Price Index measure changes in the cost of living?

The cost of living is the money we spend for the market basket of goods and services we are currently buying. Over time tastes change, new products come on the market, new services are required, and we alter our lifestyles. Think of the things you buy today that were not around a few years ago. For example, telephone answering machines, home computers, microwave ovens, videocassette recorders, camcorders, CD players, and other electronic gadgets claim a significant share of today's market basket, yet they are all relatively new items in that basket.

Many products and services that have been on the market for a long time are claiming larger shares of today's household budget. Pay television, health care, credit card interest payments, fast food, and home maid services for dual-career couples are some examples. They are replacing other goods and services. Changes in the cost of living depend on two things: changes in the *prices* of what we buy and changes in the *things* we put into our market basket.

The CPI is based only on price changes. The CPI market basket does not change for long periods. *Because consumers change what they buy over time, increases or decreases in the CPI do not measure changes in cost of living.* A cost-of-living index would measure changes in the prices of what people actually buy. The CPI is not a "cost of living" inflation index because it measures changes in the prices of the things people bought in the past (when the index was put together).

How much inflation do consumers actually experience?

When we change our lifestyles by buying different things from one year to the next, *the inflation rate you and I experience may be higher or lower than the inflation rate measured by the CPI.* It all depends on what is in our own market baskets. If the things we buy are rising in price faster than the things in the official CPI basket,

Table 11C	
1993 Prices of Selected Items in the CPI Market Basket as a Percent of Prices in 1982–84	
CATEGORY	PERCENT
Household fuel	90.3%
Motor fuel	98.0
New cars	131.5
Food and beverages	141.6
All items	**144.5**
Entertainment	145.8
Renters' costs	165.0
Public transportation	167.0
Medical care	201.4

the widely publicized CPI inflation rate *understates* the inflation we experience. When we buy things whose prices rise less than the inflation rate measured by the CPI, the CPI *overstates* the inflation we experience.

Take a look at Table 11C.[3] In 1993 the Consumer Price Index had an average value of 144.5. This means that from the last time the CPI market basket was surveyed (1982–84) until 1993 the CPI rose about 45%. Food rose by a lesser percentage, 41%, and medical care rose by 101%.

People whose market baskets showed that they spend more than 20% on food (the food portion of the CPI basket is shown in Table 11B) and less on medical care (which was 5% of the CPI basket) actually experienced less than 45% inflation over the period. Others, like Harold and Diane, were not as well off.

Harold and Diane suffered because their particular market basket was quite different from the CPI basket. Because they owned their home, which was bought many years before, and had no mortgage, they spend somewhat less than 39% on housing (the CPI basket's housing component), so that they did not benefit from the low housing inflation rate. The average price of what they had to buy, especially health care and public transportation, rose far more than the overall CPI. Inflation hit them much harder than the official inflation figures showed us. Their cost of living rose more than the official inflation rate.

HAROLD AND DIANE FEEL THE PINCH: Harold and Diane are a married couple. They both retired in 1983. Their combined pensions and social security benefits (SS) initially gave them a comfortable income that permitted travel. Furthermore, their pensions and SS benefits were pegged to the CPI so that their income would rise with inflation, as it is measured by that index. By 1993 the CPI had risen 45% from its level in the 1982–84 period and so had their income. (Harold and Diane retired in the middle of this period.) But health care costs, which took a large share of their budget, rose 101%. The cost of public transportation (which they relied upon heavily for local shopping trips and travel) rose 67%. They had to cut down on entertainment, clothing, and food purchases (especially eating out) to make ends meet. Inflation caused them to reduce their standard of living despite increases in their income.

What is the Producer Price Index (PPI)?

A more specialized, but very useful, inflation measure is the PPI. Most of the PPI is based on the costs that manufacturers pay for industrial commodities they use to make things, such as chemicals, fuel, lumber, rubber, and plastic. Other items are transportation equipment (forklifts, buses, etc.), agricultural supplies (seed and fertilizer), and furniture. The PPI also includes wholesale prices of many finished, and partially finished, goods that have not yet been sold to consumers.

How do the major inflation indicators compare? From 1992 to 1993 the CPI grew by 3.0% (see Table 11A), while the PPI grew by only 1.2%.[4] In fact, during the 1980s and early 1990s the CPI rose more rapidly than did the PPI. The CPI includes both goods and services, whereas the PPI includes only types of goods: raw materials (commodities), semifinished items, and unsold products. The inflation rate for services during this time was greater than the inflation rate for goods, which is why the CPI rose faster.

What is the core rate of inflation?

One of the most useful special indexes is a version of the CPI that is measured *without* food and energy costs. This important but lesser known index follows changes in the cost of only part of the average consumer's market basket. The CPI, less food and energy costs, is published by the Department of Labor each month along with its famous parent, the full CPI. This special index is used to measure the **core rate of inflation**, or "core rate," as most economists call it. The core rate of inflation is a measure of the average change in all prices except the prices of food and energy.

Food and energy costs, of course, are important parts of the consumer's market basket. But the prices of food and energy fluctuate more widely than do most other consumer prices. They move up and down more erratically over short periods of time because these prices are heavily influenced by events that are difficult to predict. For example, weather plays an important role in pricing foods. Political events and discoveries of natural resources significantly influence energy prices.

Because food and energy prices are so erratic, month-to-month changes in these prices can be misleading; over short periods of time changes in food and energy prices can give false signals about basic price trends. Erratic short-term price swings in food and energy add volatility to the full CPI. When food and energy costs are taken out of the CPI, the resulting inflation measure is smoother; that is, it moves more uniformly and is less likely to be distorted by short-term factors.

Over short periods of time the core rate usually gives us a clearer picture of inflation than does the full inflation rate. For example, in July of 1994 the full CPI rose at an annual rate of 4.1%, but the core rate was 2.3%.[5] Food and energy prices rose sharply that month and this pulled the overall inflation rate upward.

But for the twelve-month period ending in July 1994, the core rate was 2.9% and the full CPI rose by 2.8%. For the five-year period 1989–94 the average annual core rate was 3.9%, while the average annual full rate was 3.6%. Thus, over long periods the two inflation rates tend to be similar. So a core rate of about 3% is low by historical standards.[6]

How are specialized price indexes used?

The CPI and the PPI are broad measures of inflation because they include large numbers of prices. The U.S. Department of Labor also maintains dozens of specialized price indexes. The values of some of these specialized indexes are shown in Table 11C. *Special price indexes measure inflation for specific categories of goods or services that are included in the broader price indexes.*

One use of specialized indexes is to compare inflation rates among different groups of things. For example, notice from the figures in Table 11C that the cost of medical care and rental housing (both are components of the CPI) rose somewhat faster than did the overall CPI, while the cost of new cars and fuel rose by lesser amounts.

Businesses can often use specialized price indexes in determining the costs of specific goods or services.

BARNEY'S HOMES: Barney constructs about eighty single-family houses per year on land he is developing within commuting distance of two small cities. To control his costs, he has contracts with local lumber suppliers. The suppliers guarantee a price per board foot that will not rise by more than the PPI Lumber and Wood Products Index (a specialized price index) increases from the time the lumber is ordered until it is delivered. Barney placed a large order in October 1993 for wood that would have cost $130,000 at that time, when the index was at 177.7.[7] (That means the cost of wood was about 78% above its price during the 1982 base year used for the PPI.) When this lumber was delivered in January, the index was 186.5, or 5% higher, so Barney was guaranteed a price of not more than $136,500. Barney used the specialized price index in his contracts with suppliers to put a cap, or ceiling, on the price he would have to pay for lumber.

Barney's supplier used the specialized PPI index to set its prices. That gave Barney a little price protection by guaranteeing that he would not suffer from any greater inflation rate than that experienced by the lumber industry as a whole. That was some comfort.

How are price indexes used to measure the nation's growth?

Price indexes can be used to measure changes in economic activity. Just as the CPI was used to find changes in consumers' purchasing power, real GDP is found by using the **Implicit GDP Price**

Deflator (Art. 9: Prices and the Economy, page 102). The GDP Price Deflator is a price index that shows changes in the level of prices of *all* goods and services that are part of GDP (which is really everything that the economy produces). The GDP Deflator is much more comprehensive than the CPI or the PPI.

Take a look at Table 11D, which includes some of the data in Table 3A in article 3, in addition to values of the GDP Price Deflator.[8] The **Real GDP** is the value of goods and services when the effect of inflation is taken out. As you can see from Table 11D, when GDP in 1993 is expressed in 1987 prices (that is, when we ignore inflation from 1987 on), it is only $5,135 instead of $6,343 (Art. 3: Economic Growth, page 23).

Economists are more interested in real GDP numbers than in nominal GDP because changes in real GDP from one year to the next show the **real rate of growth** of the economy. This real rate is the actual increase in output of goods and services and is our most meaningful measure of economic progress.

The most precise way to find the nation's real growth rate is to divide nominal GDP figures by values of the GDP deflator to get real GDP. This method is illustrated in Table 11D. (For example, for 1992 the nominal GDP of $6,020 billion was divided by the GDP deflator 1.209 to get the real GDP of $4,979 billion.) The real rate of growth is equal to the change in real GDP from one year to the other.

However, a quick way to estimate the real growth rate is to find the percentage change in nominal GDP from one year to the next

Table 11D

Growth Rates of the Economy of the United States from 1992 to 1993

YEAR	NOMINAL GDP AT CURRENT PRICES ($ BILLIONS)	GDP PRICE DEFLATOR (1987 DOLLARS)	REAL GDP, 1987 PRICES ($ BILLIONS)
1992	$6,020	1.209	$4,979
1993	6,343	1.235	5,135
Growth:	+ 5%	+ 2%	+ 3%

and then to subtract the inflation rate; inflation for the whole economy is found by calculating the change in the GDP deflator. *The nation's real growth rate is about equal to its nominal growth rate less inflation.* Take a look at the bottom row of Table 11D. From 1992 to 1993 nominal GDP grew 5%; taking away an inflation rate of 2% leaves a real rate of growth of 3% (☛ Art. 3: Economic Growth, page 23, for another discussion of real GDP and nominal GDP).

ARTICLE 12:

MORE ABOUT INFLATION

Facts and Fallacies

Reading Suggestion: You should read or skim through the previous article on inflation before reading this one.

What is the history of inflation in the United States?

We tend to think of inflation as something that was always a part of economic life. But persistent *inflation is largely a phenomenon of the last fifty years or so.*[9] Unfortunately, we do not have reliable gauges of inflation prior to the 1930s, but economists have gathered enough price history about earlier years to sketch our nation's experience with inflation.

The value of some inflation barometers, such as the CPI or PPI, is often called the nation's **price level**. During the nineteenth century the price level in the United States moved up and down in great waves. The price level actually declined from about 1800 to 1850. Inflation only became a problem around the time of the Civil War, when prices shot up. Prices then declined sharply until the 1890s. The nineteenth century was a period of great price instability. The century actually closed with a lower price level than it had in the beginning.

The twentieth century was a different story. Because of shortages caused by the First World War, prices rose almost without interruption until the early 1920s. Even though the roaring twenties was a decade of growth for the economy, progress was not uniform. Prices (especially farm prices) actually drifted downward during most of the period and then plunged sharply during the Great Depression of the 1930s (☛ Art. 4: Business Cycles, page 35, for a discussion of the roaring twenties and the Great Depression).

Inflation became a real problem following the Second World War and has stayed with us, in varying degrees, ever since. (Inflation was held in check during the war by government price controls.) See Graph 12A. The 1950s began with high inflation due to the Korean War, but the inflation rate shrank for most of the next twenty years; in fact, the U.S. briefly experienced **disinflation**, or a general decline in prices, in the mid-1950s. By contrast, the 1970s was a decade of particularly serious inflation, with the price level rising at double-digit rates that had not been experienced in the U.S. since the Civil War, over a hundred years earlier. Inflation since the 1970s has been less, but persistent.

Graph 12A

Inflation Rates in the U.S., 1951–1993

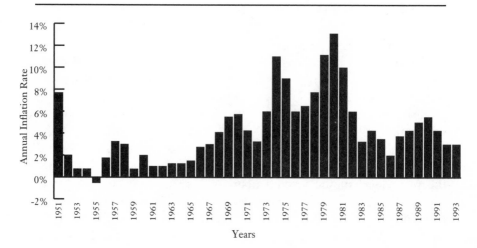

What causes inflation?

Sometimes a nation experiences **demand-pull inflation**. This will happen when a nation's income grows faster than its ability to produce new goods and services. As people use their new income to demand products, some shortages may occur. To get producers to create more, prices rise.

Demand-pull inflation may also result from a rapid growth in the supply of money and credit in the economy, which gives consumers more buying power. The effect is the same as rapid growth of income. As consumers use this new credit, they increase demand for goods and services; this could create shortages that push prices upward.

An increase in government debt may cause shortages as government goes on a shopping spree with borrowed money. For example, a sudden increase in demand might result from a military conflict that creates an urgent need for war-related products. *Demand-pull inflation results when the nation's producers cannot immediately satisfy an increased demand for goods and services.*

At other times a nation experiences **cost-push inflation**. This occurs because of spot shortages of raw materials or essential services that are needed to make things people need. For example, a shortage of crude petroleum in 1974 led to rapid increases in oil prices; some of this shortage was contrived by a group of small oil-producing nations that formed the Organization of Petroleum Exporting Countries, or OPEC. Since oil is used for so many purposes in our economy (petrochemicals and fuels, among others), costs of producing many things went up. Coincidentally, there was an unexpected shortage of agricultural products in the mid-seventies that resulted from crop failures in the U.S. and commitments to sell huge amounts of food to the former Soviet Union. This shortage aggravated inflationary pressures. *Cost-push inflation results from reductions in the supply of raw materials or services needed to produce other goods and services.* It seems that any five economists can probably give you six reasons for any particular period of inflation. But in general, inflation occurs because of an increase in demand for goods and services or because of a shortage in the supply of important resources.

Why do prices rise more than they fall?

As we saw in the beginning of this article, inflation is mainly a twentieth-century event. But throughout human history war has caused sharp inflation because war creates shortages. We had several wars in this century. But why did inflation persist in this century even during peacetime? One important reason is that inflation often accompanies rapid economic growth. To get more people to work, to get more machinery produced, and to get more resources extracted from the earth, businesses need an incentive. The incentive is higher prices. *Higher prices stimulate economic growth* if they get people and businesses to produce more.

The wage and price increases at the salad factory were needed to help the firm to grow.

THE SALAD FACTORY NEEDS WORKERS: A local firm makes tubs of salads that it sells to supermarkets for distribution at their delicatessen counters. It employs about 60% of the workers who live in the small, semirural community where it is located. The average wage in the factory was $65 per day last year. The market for salads is changing as Americans' concern with low-fat, lighter foods seems to be growing. So demand for prepared salads is growing significantly, and the factory needs to expand its employment by 30%. However, the major sources of new labor are communities some thirty to sixty minutes away by car. To recruit these workers the factory has to offer them a wage of at least $72 a day to cover the commuting costs and to provide incentives for them to leave their current employers. Therefore, the salad factory just raised the average wage of all its production employees to $72, both to attract new employees and to maintain harmony in the plant. (It would have been difficult to pay new workers more than it gives the older ones.) To maintain its profit margin while paying everyone higher wages, the factory also just increased the prices of its salads an average of 10%. These wage and price changes are contributing to inflation.

Upward price movements predominated in this century in part because there were several military conflicts; more important were the growth of labor unions (stimulated by important new labor laws) and minimum wage laws, both introduced during the 1930s. The influence of labor unions has been broader than their membership, which actually peaked about 1970.

Although some wage concessions were made by unions in recent years, labor unions have generally fought wage decreases. *Unions and wage legislation have made wages "sticky downward,"* in the words of the great British economist John Maynard Keynes. That quaint term means that wages can move up more freely than they can move down. Since unions made it difficult to reduce wages and prices (that is, they made wages sticky), there is a stronger tendency for inflation to occur now than there was in the previous century, when wages could move up *and* down more freely.

Is inflation always linked to economic growth?

When people demand more goods and services than are available at the moment, shortages occur. The way the economy eliminates shortages is to increase production, and this additional production is attracted by increasing prices. Higher prices give producers the incentive to supply more goods and services. This means that higher prices (inflation) often go hand in hand with economic growth.

While higher prices often spur the economy to grow, a partnership between inflation and prices does not always exist. Sometimes prices heat up, but the economy gets worse. That unhappy condition is called **stagflation**. This original term is a combination of the words *stagnation* and *inflation*. We experienced stagflation in the 1970s when critical shortages of raw materials, especially oil, raised production costs sharply. Many consumers could not afford the resulting higher prices for goods and services, so they bought less.

THE TOWN CUTS BACK: Nearly half the workers in a rural American town are employed in a textile factory. Because of fierce competition from foreign factories that employ low-wage workers, the town's factory will not be able to give workers raises for the next few years. However, state taxes and fuel costs, which are determined outside this rural community, increased 15%. To meet these higher expenses, the town's residents cut back on purchases of new clothing and restaurant meals. One clothing store and two restaurants in town were forced to close, creating unemployment.

Although total factory payroll did not decline, when prices rose and people bought fewer things, unemployment went up. *Cost-push inflation can sometimes lead to stagflation, when both prices and unemployment go up.*

Does the general price level ever decline?

The rate at which prices change varies from year to year, and even from month to month. The word *inflation* means that average prices rise. But on occasion the price level declines. Economists call this **deflation**. Deflation occurred frequently in the 1800s. It happened in this century, too, notably during the Great Depression of the 1930s before the introduction of minimum wage laws. The most recent period of deflation of consumer prices, though brief, occurred in the late 1950s.

Prices of producers' goods are more volatile than are prices of consumer goods and services. *The Producer Price Index occasionally declines;* annual rates of change fell into negative territory in 1987 and, briefly, in late 1991 and early 1992 as the U.S. economy was slowly recovering from recession. By contrast, *the CPI rarely declines,* and when it does, it is merely a blip in the statistics. For example, the CPI fell from 142.0 in November 1992 to 141.9 in December of that year.

Since inflation predominates, economists look for decreases in the rate of inflation and have coined a word for it, **disinflation**. Disinflation occurs when prices rise less in one period than they did in the previous period. Flip back to Graph 12A. Notice that disinflation occurred when the consumer inflation rate, as measured by the CPI, dropped from 4.2% in 1991 to 3.0% in 1992.

Who is harmed by inflation?

Inflation is a hidden "tax" on just about everyone. Inflation causes dollars to lose value because, as prices rise, the **purchasing power** of money declines. For example, when the CPI hit 144.5 in 1993, average prices of consumer goods and services had risen 44% from their 1982–84 level. Turning this around, it meant that a dollar you had in 1982 was worth only 69¢ in 1993. *Inflation harms those who hold money as a store of wealth* (that is, as savings).

The greatest deterioration of purchasing power is felt by those who keep money outside of banks, where it earns no interest. The next greatest losers are those who hold money in bank accounts or in bonds if the bank accounts or bonds pay interest rates below the rate of inflation.

Inflation harms lenders only if the interest rate they receive for their money is less than the inflation rate.

ROBIN'S DEAL TURNS SOUR: Robin is a member of a public school teachers' union and was its chief negotiator a few years ago when they negotiated a five-year contract. The contract called for annual salary increases of 3.75% for each of five years, which comes to 20% over the period. Back then, Robin looked like a hero. But one year after the contract began, the inflation rate jumped from 3% to 5% and stayed there for the remaining years of the contract. Prices rose 25% in the period, so the teachers' salary dollars lost purchasing power of 5% by the end of the contract. After that, Robin looked like a goat.

Another group of losers are wage earners whose incomes do not rise as rapidly as inflation. This includes pensioners whose income is not automatically adjusted for inflation and workers who were locked into fixed wage rates.

The members of Robin's union gambled on the inflation rate and lost because the inflation rate exceeded their raises. Robin, the chief union negotiator, expected inflation rates to stay under 3.75%. Of course, *a loss in purchasing power will be experienced by anyone,* union member or not, *whose annual income increases by less than the inflation rate.*

Is it good to borrow money during periods of inflation?

There is a pernicious fallacy about inflation that often parades under the rubric of "common knowledge." Most people believe that it is good to be in debt during a period of high inflation because you can pay back your debt with cheaper dollars. Similarly, it is believed that inflation is bad for creditors. This is true only under one special condition that occurs rarely nowadays.

MUHAMMAD AND TINA GET "LAND RICH": In 1988, Muhammad and Tina purchased a house for $200,000, taking out a $140,000 mortgage at 9% interest. Because of new businesses coming into their community, the town's population and housing values grew. By 1994 their house was worth $325,000. That meant that their equity grew from $60,000 to $185,000 in six years, beside the reduction in their debt due to mortgage payments they made during the period. This gain far exceeded the interest costs of the mortgage during these years (about $67,000) and the $15,000 in interest they could have earned on their $40,000 down payment. They benefited substantially from inflation.

The couple's equity grew more than 20% per year while their mortgage debt cost them 9% per year. Their wealth grew. *Inflation will benefit borrowers only if the inflation rate on what they own is greater than the cost of borrowing.* But now let's see what happens when the inflation rate is only 4%, which is closer to the actual real estate inflation rate in the 1990s.

TERRY GETS BEATEN BY INFLATION: Terry was told by his parents that a house is a great investment because the growth in real estate values will more than pay for even a large mortgage. In 1988 he bought a $200,000 house with a $140,000 9% mortgage. (It was a big place for a man alone, but there was room for his two sons, who visited on alternate weekends.) There was a building boom in his area and houses became plentiful. His house grew in value only 4% per year, so in 1994 it was worth $253,000 for a gain of $53,000. Meanwhile he paid nearly $67,000 in interest and he lost out on about $15,000 in interest he could have earned on his $40,000 down payment between 1988 and 1994. Putting these together, Terry came out with $29,000 less than he had before buying the house. (The property gained $53,000 in value, but Terry paid out $67,000 in actual interest and lost $15,000 in potential interest. Both of these, which came to $82,000, have to be considered as his costs for having the house.) He was a loser, even considering that he saved some rent by owning his own home. His parents couldn't understand it. His former wife said it was typical of Terry.

What went wrong was that Terry's debt cost him more in interest than he got back from the appreciation of his house. Terry's parents bought their house in the 1960s, when mortgages were about 4% and housing values galloped upward at 5–10% per year; back then houses appreciated at a rate far above inflation. But this era is over in America. The U.S. real estate boom that began in the late 1940s ended in the 1980s, as many savings and loan executives now know. *Inflation will hurt borrowers if borrowing costs (interest rates) are higher than inflation rates on what they own.* Terry's debt cost him 9% while the property he bought with the debt increased in value by only 4% each year.

The good times that real estate investors had during the long real estate boom taught some bankers a lesson. The lesson was driven home painfully in the 1970s when inflation often was far above interest rates. Bankers soon tired of being repaid their loan in cheaper dollars. Lenders today are sensitive to inflation and try to set their mortgage and other lending rates above the rate of inflation to protect themselves. Furthermore, it is getting increasingly difficult to find real estate, or other investments, that can be counted on to give returns that exceed the inflation rate. The easy real estate wealth accumulated by people like Terry's parents is harder to come by now in most parts of the nation (☞ Art. 13: Interest Rates, page 153).

How can someone protect his or her purchasing power during a time of inflation?

A **Cost of Living Adjustment (COLA)** has been built into many union contracts, wage agreements, some pension plans, and government programs. COLAs guarantee a person that he or she will receive annual increases in income equal to the inflation rate.

After a series of high inflation rates in the 1970s that created hardship for retirees living on fixed incomes, the U.S. federal government added a COLA to the social security program. *COLAs are the best protection against inflation,* but they are not always available. That is because whoever guarantees the COLA, whether it is a government or an employer, runs the risk of suffering losses due to inflation.

The next-best shield against a loss of purchasing power is to own assets

PAULINE GOES FOR GOLD: When Pauline, a fashion model, was thirty-eight years old, she had accumulated a nest egg of $350,000. She wanted to maintain its purchasing power until she could use it to start her own business in a few years. She used the money to buy gold coins, which she placed in a safe-deposit box. With an average annual inflation rate of 3.5% over four years, the dollar lost 15% in purchasing power. But the gold coins appreciated by 20% over this period. Pauline maintained the purchasing power of her nest egg and even turned a profit.

whose dollar value increases with inflation. At various times people have turned to gold, diamonds, artworks, collectibles, real estate, and stocks as hedges against inflation. Let's see how this works.

Pauline was lucky. Owning assets like this does not always protect you from inflation. A widely held fallacy in economic thinking is that gold is a good hedge against inflation. For centuries investors have bought gold to protect the purchasing power of their wealth. The truth is that the price of gold is determined by the demand for gold *and* by its supply. But only part of the demand for gold and little of the supply of gold are linked to inflation.

Demand for gold is partly due to its commercial uses in jewelry, electronics, dental material, and so on and is not just dependent on its use as an investment. If the demand for gold for commercial purposes declines, the price of gold may go down despite inflation.

Changes in supply influence gold prices. If major suppliers in South Africa or Russia want to raise money or have excess inventories, they will sell gold, and these sales may depress gold prices, regardless of the inflation rate. Discoveries of gold will also push gold prices downward.

Gold sold for over $800 per ounce in the late 1970s, but as of 1993 its price had fallen by half. During this time consumer prices rose over 50%. Woe to those who put their wealth into gold as a hedge against inflation during this long period! They were hit with a double whammy; they lost when prices fell and they lost more when inflation eroded the value of their remaining dollars. *Gold does not automatically shelter investors from inflation.*

It is not easy to pick an asset whose value will increase along with inflation. *Unfortunately, there are no popular investments you can count on to always increase along with the rate of inflation.* Diamonds may be a girl's best friend, but diamonds, collectibles, works of art, and other assets are not automatic hedges against inflation because their prices are also influenced by both demand and supply. Like gold, they are not always good investments.

Do the stock and bond markets protect investors from inflation?

Another popular fallacy is that stocks protect investors from inflation. The highest inflation rates of the twentieth century occurred during the 1970s, but stock prices plunged during most of the decade. As a protection from inflation, stocks were a medicine that killed the patient.

Why don't stock prices always rise along with other prices? The price of a stock goes up when investors expect a corporation's profits to grow. But profits depend on a firm's revenue and on its costs. Inflation will raise the corporation's costs of doing business, and that will shrink its profits and the value (price) of its stock. Inflation may enable the corporation to raise the prices of its products and thereby raise its revenue. But a corporation's profits (and stock price) will increase only if it can raise the prices of its products faster than its costs rise; some corporations may be able to do it, but others will not be in such a fortunate position. Therefore, *inflation may lead to either an increase or a decrease in a corporation's profits and stock price.* So there is no reason to expect the price of its stock to go up when inflation accelerates.

However, over the *long run* (if you are patient enough) profits from the stock market may offset inflation. That is because corporations' profits, and the price of stocks, go up when the economy grows, and the long-term trend of our economy is up. *Over the long run, stock prices rise because of economic growth, not because of inflation.*

How long is the long run? Investors running into the stock market to seek shelter from inflation may be disappointed if they hold stocks for just a few years, as they were during a lengthy stock market decline in the 1970s. But over a period of five or ten years or more, the stock market generally pays off.

Bonds are a poor hedge against inflation if they give their owners a fixed income. That is because inflation causes interest rates to rise. Remember that the interest rate is the price of borrowed money, so it goes up during inflation, as do other prices. However, rising interest rates cause the prices of bonds to fall. In fact, often just the *fear* of higher inflation sends bond prices tumbling. So when the inflation rate rises or is expected to rise, bond owners often see their bonds drop in value (☞ Art. 13: Interest Rates, page 153).

Unlike stocks, bonds do not tend to rise in value over long periods, unless interest rates fall (and that is not likely during inflationary times).

Some bonds, such as U.S. savings bonds, pay variable interest rates. These bonds make higher annual or semiannual payments to their owners when rates of inflation and interest rise. Interest payments that go up and down with the inflation rate offer some protection from inflation.

IN THE NEWS . . .

"Jobless Rate Falls to 6.4%, Igniting Fears of Inflation"
Los Angeles Times, May 7, 1994, page A1

The national jobless rate fell as the economy created more than a quarter million new jobs during April. However, this good news made investors fearful that rapid growth would generate higher inflation rates. These higher rates would then cause interest rates to rise. When the news was released, stock and bond prices on Wall Street tumbled. Good news is bad for investments if it might lead to inflation because of shortages in the economy. That is why investors prefer slow growth to rapid growth.

ARTICLE 13:

INTEREST RATES

The Cost of Renting Money

What is "the" interest rate?

Interest is the "rental" we pay for using someone else's money. It is the price of borrowed money, or credit. The **rate of interest** is the annual percentage return a lender can get for the use of his or her money.

There are many interest rates. Which interest rate is "the" rate depends on what business you are in. Recently the interest rate on a credit card advance was 18.9%, the interest rate on a home mortgage was 8.5%, and a one-year certificate of deposit (CD) paid 4.25%. Although the differences between interest rates will vary, *most interest rates move up or down together.*

Some interest rates get more attention than others. Businesspeople watch the **prime rate**. The "prime" is the interest rate banks charge on **floating rate** loans to the most creditworthy business firms. A floating rate loan is one in which the monthly interest charge moves up or down over the life of the loan, in accordance with conditions in the credit market. When credit was "tight" in 1989, the prime was up to 11.5%; when money was "easy" (cheaper to borrow, although not necessarily easier to get) in 1993, the prime was down to 6%. Very few businesses can borrow at the prime, but it is an important rate because most business loan rates, and many credit card rates, are pegged to it. For example, a small business might be able to borrow bank money at "prime plus 3%"; that would come to 9% if the prime was 6%. If the prime rose to 8%, the small business would be charged 11%.

The prime moves like a snail, sometimes not changing for a year or more. But when it does, something important is happening in the credit markets. That is because *many loan rates will move up when the prime interest rate rises* or fall when the prime is reduced by banks.

People who watch interest rates closely follow the **federal funds rate**. This interest rate is what banks charge each other for large (million-dollar-plus) overnight loans. (The term is misleading because the federal government does not set this rate. The name comes from the fact that banks transfer money to each other through the Federal Reserve Banks.) Because the rate is negotiated among banks daily, it is a sensitive indicator of developing trends in the money market. *Persistent declines in the federal funds rate often foreshadow declines in other interest rates,* and vice versa. For example, the federal funds rate dropped slowly, but steadily, from 8.25% to 7% during the last few months of 1990; the other shoe dropped when the sleepy prime rate was cut at the start of 1991, with other interest rates following.

Another important interest rate, especially for savers, is the **U.S. Treasury bill rate**. Treasury bills are short-term IOUs sold by the federal government in denominations of $10,000 or more. T-bills are used by banks, pension funds, money market mutual funds, and wealthy investors as short-term, interest-earning "parking places" for large sums of money. The well-known "T-bill rate" is the return investors get on three-month treasury bills. Many banks peg their CD rates to the T-bill rate. The interest rates on some credit cards and on many floating mortgage loans (called **adjustable rate mortgages** or **ARMs**) are also pegged to the T-bill rate. While few individuals invest directly in T-bills, the T-bill rate affects a lot of savers and borrowers (☛ Art. 19: Financial Markets, page 252, to read about government bonds).

All interest rates are expressed as annual rates, even for loans of less than one year. If you invested in a T-bill for three months and received an interest payment equal to 1% of your investment, we say you earned a 4% rate of interest because that is what you would get if the interest payments continued for a full year.

Why do lenders charge interest?

When someone has money, she can either spend it on goods and services or she can lend it to others. A fundamental tenet of economic life is that having something today is better than having the same thing tomorrow. If you want someone with money to postpone spending it and to lend the money to you instead, you have to give the lender a reward. That reward is interest. *Interest is the fee a lender receives for postponing her own consumption.*

What is the time value of money?

By collecting interest the lender may be able to buy more next year than she could by using her money to buy something today.

> **ANDREA PUTS HER MONEY TO WORK:** Andrea saved $12,000 that she intended to use to buy a compact car this month. However, she just decided to invest the money by buying a two-year certificate of deposit in a savings and loan association (S&L) that will pay 7.5% interest, compounded quarterly. After two years she will get back $13,923, which she expects will enable her to step up to a midsize car with more features than the car she could buy today. The interest she will collect is enough of an incentive to make her willing to put off her car purchase.

Andrea had a choice of spending $1 today or $1.16 in two years because that is what each of today's dollars will be worth then. *A dollar today is equal in value to more than one dollar tomorrow.* That is the **time value of money**. Unless money had a time value, people with money would not lend it.

How do lenders and borrowers respond to interest rates?

Like all other prices, *the rate of interest is determined by supply and demand:* the amount of money lenders are willing to lend (supply) and the amount of money borrowers are willing to pay for (demand). *When the interest rate goes up, the amount of money lenders supply increases. When the interest rate goes down, the reverse happens.* Andrea was willing to lend her money at a rate of interest of 7% or more. But she may have decided to pass up the bank CD, and to buy a car right away, if the interest rate her bank offered were, say, only 6%. Her fiancé, Guy, had a different set of priorities.

GUY'S TIME VALUE OF MONEY: Guy saved $12,000 at the same time and intended to buy a car to match Andrea's. He was more eager for a car than she was and felt that he needed at least 9% interest from a CD before he would postpone his car purchase. When the S&L offered him only 7.5% for a two-year CD, he turned it down and bought a compact car.

Everyone has his/her own "price" for postponing consumption. Mike and Beverly are different from Guy.

On the demand side, borrowers prefer lower rates of interest.

MIKE AND BEVERLY GO AFTER A HOUSE: A couple in their thirties has an income of about $41,000, or $3,396 per month. Their bank will provide them with a mortgage whose monthly payments do not exceed 25% of their pretax income, so they can get a mortgage requiring payments of $849 per month (that is, 25% of their monthly income of $3,396). The size of the mortgage they can carry depends on the fixed interest rate on the mortgage loan, as shown in Table 13A. If the lender sets the rate at 8%, they can borrow up to $100,000. But if the interest rate is as high as 12%, their bank will not lend them more than $76,000.

The figures in Table 13A essentially represent Mike and Beverly's demand for borrowed money if they hold to their budget of $849 per month, which is what their bank thinks they can safely handle. (Therefore, it is also what the bank is willing to supply.) The interest rate will determine how much they can borrow from their favorite bank. This will determine the type of house they buy or the down payment they have to provide. *The lower the rate of interest, the more money borrowers will be able to borrow.* If the couple's income grows,

Table 13A

Maximum Twenty-Year Mortgage Available from Mike and Beverly's Bank for a Monthly Payment of $849	
IF THE INTEREST RATE IS . . .	THEY CAN BORROW UP TO . . .
6%	$116,856
7	107,932
8	100,027
9	93,002
10	86,736
11	81,130
12	76,099
13	71,568
14	67,476
15	63,770
16	60,403

their monthly payments will be easier to make, but the bank probably wants to base its lending on what Mike and Beverly can afford *now*. Good thing, too. Mike is a university instructor (Beverly stays home with their baby), and universities are "anti-inflationary" employers! His income will grow at a glacial pace.

(Note to reader: Do not expect that every bank will set the same lending limits for people like Mike and Beverly. Some banks, S&L's, and other lenders may be more conservative or more generous. But all lenders follow the same principle: as interest rates rise, they will lend less money to customers with a given income. This is also true if the borrower wants a variable rate mortgage.)

How does inflation affect interest rates?

Andrea (see above) was willing to postpone using her $12,000 to buy a car because she expected the interest she would get from the S&L would enable her to buy a *better* vehicle later for about

$14,000. But her plans could be foiled if the price of cars goes up while her money is in the S&L. The culprit would be inflation.

A saver's real reward for postponing her purchases is an increase in her **purchasing power** (the quantity of things she can buy). To get that, the interest rate she earns must be larger than the rate of inflation. In the language of economics, we say that the **real interest rate** must be positive. The real interest rate is the interest received *minus* the inflation rate. If the interest rate the saver gets is 6% and the inflation rate is 4%, the *real* rate of interest she earns is 2%. That is how much her purchasing power would increase when the loan is paid off.

Suppose the price of the compact car Andrea could have bought went up to $14,000 by the time her two-year CD expired. Then she would not have gained any purchasing power. If the car price had risen to $15,000, Andrea would have lost purchasing power and earned a *negative* real interest rate.

Lenders, such S&L's, and savers, like Andrea, share the same desire for a return on their money that beats inflation. *Lenders and savers need an interest rate that is larger than the inflation rate to make lending and saving profitable.* Both interest rates and inflation rates declined in the early 1990s. From a peak of 10%, the average large deposit ($100,000+) three-month bank CD in early 1993 offered a rate of only 3%. Sophisticated savers turned away from them in droves. Why? Because inflation rates were expected to be more than 3% by the end of that year, so that the CDs would yield a real interest rate of 0% or less; that was a turnoff.

How do lenders and savers decide on what interest rate to ask for?

Suppose Andrea, the saver, expected the inflation rate to be 4% for each of the two years she would have her money tied up in the CD. If she wanted to increase her purchasing power 3% per year, as a reward for postponing her consumption, she would demand at least a 7% rate of return because 4% + 3% = 7%. She made the investment in the CD because the S&L offered her 7.5%. *At the very least, sophisticated lenders and savers demand an interest rate equal to their desired real rate of return* plus *the expected inflation rate.*

As simple as it sounds, this is not easy to do because it means that people with money to invest have to forecast inflation. This forecast is called the **expected rate of inflation**. *Interest rates that lenders and savers ask for depend heavily on the* expected *rate of inflation,* not on the actual inflation rate, because lenders and savers will not know what the actual inflation rate is until after they have made their investment.

If the actual inflation rate turns out to be higher than the expected inflation rate, then lenders and savers could wind up getting a smaller real rate of return than they had wanted. They may even lose purchasing power by getting a negative real rate of return. That happened in 1974 and 1975 when the interest rate on U.S. treasury bills was 8%, but the inflation rate shot up to more than 12%. To the surprise of lenders, the real rate of interest was a *minus* 4%. Lenders got zonked again in 1978 when the treasury bill interest rate was 11% and the inflation rate zoomed to 13%, producing another negative real interest rate.

Negative real interest rates rarely happen. But after the double punch they got in the 1970s, lenders stayed scared enough to keep real interest rates high for several years thereafter. Real rates even got up to a whopping 5% during the boom years of the mid-1980s. However, *over the long run, real rates of interest have been between 2 and 3 percent.*

What happens to the borrowers when real interest rates are above 0%?

Let us suppose Andrea lent her $12,000 directly to a friend instead of to an S&L.

ANDREA WINS AND CLIFFORD LOSES: Andrea loaned $12,000 to her friend Clifford, whom she trusts. Clifford agreed to pay her 7.5% interest annually over two years. He used the money to buy a plot of land for $12,000 on which he intends to build a house someday. Over the two years the annual inflation rate was 3%, and this is also the rate at which the value of Clifford's lot grew. Clifford gave Andrea $1,868 in interest for the use of her money. Clifford's lot went up in value by $731, so he lost $1,137 ($1,868 less $731) in purchasing power. Andrea gained 4.5% per year in purchasing power since the value of her money declined by only 3% per year, or $709, while she got $1,868 in interest, for a net gain of $1,159. Clifford lost, Andrea gained.

Here Andrea became the lender; she acted like a bank. This example shows us that *purchasing power shifts from the borrower to the lender when the interest rate exceeds the inflation rate.* A lot of people think that it is good to be in debt when there is inflation because you repay the debt with cheaper dollars. The borrower does repay with cheaper dollars, but these "discounted dollars" may be eaten up by higher borrowing costs. Just ask Clifford.

Had the opposite occurred, Clifford would have taken purchasing power from Andrea. *Only when the interest rate is smaller than the inflation rate do borrowers gain purchasing power.*

How do real interest rates affect the economy?

Most big lenders (banks, savings and loans, wealthy investors, insurance companies, etc.) and big borrowers (for example, major corporations) are sharp. They are more concerned with the real interest rate than with the **nominal interest rate** (the rate on paper) because they want to increase the purchasing power of their money. That is why loans may not be easy to get even when nominal interest rates are high.

HARVEY HOLDS OUT: Harvey inherited $300,000 three years ago that he gladly invested in a three-year bank CD paying an annual rate of 6%. This year his bank invited him to reinvest his money in a five-year CD at a nominal interest rate of 8.5%. He declined to supply his funds because he expects the inflation rate to equal or to top this rate. Instead, he invested money in the stock market and in land he expects to appreciate at more than the inflation rate.

If Harvey had expected a normal inflation rate of 2–3% (that is, an inflation rate close to the average rate that the U.S. has experienced over the past few decades), he would have jumped at the bank's offer and eagerly lent all of his money so that the bank could have lent it out to its customers. But he believed the five-year CD would give him a negative real interest rate. *The supply of credit will not increase even if* nominal *interest rates rise if lenders expect to end up with low* real *interest rates.*

On the loan demand side, many people and businesses may be willing to borrow money at very high nominal interest rates if they expect inflation rates to be high or they expect business investments, which they would make with the borrowed money, to be very profitable. This is why we sometimes see the demand for loans rising even though nominal interest rates are going up. From 1986 to 1989 the prime rate rose from 6.5% to 11.5%; nonetheless, bank loans increased more than 25%.

If real interest rates are high, low nominal rates will not stimulate demand for loans. The U.S. passed through a mild recession in 1990 and 1991. During this time interest rates fell sharply; the prime plunged from 10% to 6% in eighteen months, and mortgage rates fell to their lowest point in over twenty years. However, in the two years after the recession bank lending declined slightly, in contrast to its normal long-term growth. The demand for credit did not increase, in part because the real interest rate was still high. With inflation expected to be around 3%, the real rate of interest on most loans (which have interest rates above the prime) was well over 3% (6% prime less 3% inflation). The economy needed a lower real interest rate to stimulate borrowing.

The supply of, and demand for, credit depends more on real interest rates than on nominal interest rates. Had Harvey not considered the real interest rate, he might have jumped at the bank's 8.5% offer and regretted it later.

How are interest rates affected by uncertainty about inflation?

Forecasting is a tricky business. Setting interest rates on the basis of the expected inflation rate is a little bit like shooting dice. Lenders take a risk by betting against inflation. If actual inflation rises above the expected rate of inflation, they lose.

When the inflation rate moves up and down a lot, it becomes more difficult to decide on the expected rate of inflation, and lenders become nervous. To help them sleep at night, they add a **risk premium** to the interest rate they demand from borrowers. This risk premium is a cushion to shield themselves against unexpected jumps in inflation.

EDWIN PLAYS IT SAFE: Edwin is the chairman of a bank's loan committee. He expects the inflation rate for next year to be 4.5%. He wants the bank to earn a 3% real interest rate. But because inflation has jumped between 3% and 7% over the past couple of years, he decides to add a 1% risk premium. Therefore, he recommends that the bank's lowest (prime) interest rate for loans be 8.5% (4.5% + 3% + 1% = 8.5%).

Because of the risk premium, *interest rates tend to be especially high when the inflation rate is hard to forecast.* This is one reason interest rates were unusually high right after the turbulent inflation rates of the 1970s.

As you will see in the next question and answer, there are other reasons why lenders sometimes add risk premiums. But lenders cannot be too liberal in setting risk premiums because the higher they set interest rates, the less money people will borrow. Bankers and other professional lenders don't want to shoot themselves in the foot.

How does risk affect interest rates?

Bankers don't like to tell you this, but the fact is that not all the loans they make are paid off. Sometimes a lender makes a bad choice of borrowers. When a borrower fails to repay all of a loan, the loan is said to be in **default**. In addition, not all loans that *are* paid are paid on time. When payments are more than thirty days late, the loan is said to be **delinquent**. Both types of problem loans cost the lender money.

Lenders have to be willing to take some risks. They may know that a certain percentage of their lenders will not repay loans on time or at all, but they don't know which individual borrowers will be disappointments.

Lending is similar to selling life insurance. A life insurance company knows what percentage of its policyholders are likely to die each year, but it cannot pinpoint which ones. It knows that the older the policyholder is, the more risk the insurance company takes of having to pay out death benefits, so it charges higher rates to older persons. For example, one insurance company currently offers a $100,000 term life insurance policy to a thirty-year-old person for a premium of $310 per year. A forty-year-old must pay $589, a sixty-year-old must pay $3,197, and anyone older could not buy insurance at all.

> **JOE'S CREDIT CARD:** Joe is an internal auditor for a department store, earning about $62,000 a year. He thought he was on the fast track. He spent about $75,000 per year, including payments for a heavily mortgaged home he'd bought in a posh neighborhood where the store's vice presidents lived. He didn't worry about debt because he expected a promotion to the position of comptroller, with a salary of at least $90,000. The advancement never came, and after a while, Joe was forced to declare bankruptcy. He lost overdraft privileges at his bank and all the no-fee, 12–14% credit cards he had used before bankruptcy. After painfully adjusting to a more moderate standard of living, the only credit card he could obtain had an annual fee of $50, required him to maintain a $500 bank deposit, and charged 21% interest. Because of his record, Joe was considered a high-risk borrower and his cost of credit was high.

Lenders charge higher interest rates to borrowers in higher-risk categories, just as insurance companies charge higher rates to people in higher age categories. *The higher the risk of default or delinquency, the higher the interest rate will be.*

How does risk affect interest paid by bonds?

A bond issued by a government or by a corporation is a way of borrowing money. The default risk of bonds is graded by bond-rating agencies such as Moody's and Standard & Poor's Corp. The bonds with the highest grades are those considered least likely to default.

The interest investors receive from a bond is called the bond's **yield** (☞ Art. 19: Financial Markets, page 252, to learn more about bonds).

Because bonds are rated according to their riskiness, and because bond yields are published, it is easy to find the risk premiums received by lenders. *The riskier the bond, the higher is its yield.* To prove this, let's look at some actual risk premiums on bonds that all had about ten years until maturity.

The U.S. Treasury bond is free of default and delinquency risk because it is backed by the federal government. Therefore, the interest rate it returns is the **risk-free interest rate**. Table 13B shows that on one day in October 1994 this was 7%.[10] At the same time the highest-quality corporate bonds yielded just under 8%. This yield represented a risk premium of about 1%. That is because there is a chance that even the biggest and most profitable corporations might default. Lenders (investors) were willing to accept an extra yield of 1% to compensate them for this risk.

Slightly less creditworthy corporations paid lenders 8.1%. The risk premium for these medium-quality bonds was 1.1% (8.1% less the government bond rate of 7.0%).

The corporate bonds with the lowest-quality rating are genteelly referred to in financial circles as **high yield bonds**. However, you might know of them by their common nickname, **junk bonds**. Table 13B shows rates paid on intermediate-term bonds, which have maturities of about ten years. The average junk bond in Table 13B yielded about 11%, which represented a sizable risk premium of 4%. A corporate-bond interest rate of 11% might have been seductive to

Table 13B

Riskiness and Yields of Intermediate-Term Bonds— October 1994

Bond and Grade	Yield
U.S. Treasury	7.0%
Corporate, high quality	7.9
Corporate, medium quality	8.1
Corporate, low quality	10.9
Tax exempt (nonfederal)	5.7

some investors in the fall of 1994. But these bonds are not for widows and orphans.

Are high-interest investments, such as junk bonds, really more profitable than safer ones?

Junk bonds pay higher interest rates because there is a higher risk that they will default. But the promise of higher interest does not mean much if a corporation goes belly-up and you lose your money.

> **TROY'S AND RICHELLE'S BOND FUNDS:** Troy and Richelle work on Wall Street and manage separate bond market mutual funds. Troy invests in a portfolio of "high yield" (junk) bonds. His bonds had an average promised yield of 10.0% last year. But during the year 3% of these bonds defaulted, so his portfolio lost 3% of its capital; this gave the portfolio a net yield of 7%. (That is, he earned 10.3% from interest payments on the good bonds but then lost 3% of his capital because of defaults. That gave his fund a net return of 7%.) Richelle is responsible for managing a conservative mutual fund that invests in high-quality corporate bonds, with an average yield of 7%. None of these bonds defaulted, so her fund's net interest was also 7%.

Troy's experience shows us that higher interest rates do not necessarily give the lender more profit if borrowers fail to repay loans. In this illustration the net return from safe loans and from riskier loans was about the same. Actually, that is not the result of mere chance. Economists have shown that, in many investment markets, *over a long period of time, the net results from risky investments will be about the same as those from safe investments when you take into account defaults of riskier loans.* They call such markets **efficient markets** because the risk premiums are just large enough to compensate lenders for losses. Troy received a risk premium of 3.3%, which, in this year, just covered his losses.

Over short periods high-risk investors like Troy may prosper, but that is because they may be temporarily lucky. If good fortune had smiled on Troy, none of his bonds would have gone sour during the year and his net return would have been larger than Richelle's. (That is the year he should ask for a raise!) Eventually the law of averages is likely to catch up with Troy and give him a few bad years.

Do taxes influence interest rates?

The interest a lender gets to keep is what is left after he pays income taxes. The highest individual federal income tax rate, as this is being written, is 39%. If a wealthy investor owned the risk-free U.S. Treasury bond listed in Table 13B, he would be left with a yield of 4.3% after paying the top tax rate. (The interest paid by U.S. Treasury bonds is exempt from most state and local taxes.) A tax bite that could really cut into those shopping trips to Tiffany!

However, the interest paid by nonfederal government bonds is exempt from federal income taxes. These bonds are issued by states, counties, school districts, cities, and other government authorities. Because investors in these get to keep all the interest they receive (except for local taxes), these bonds are attractive, and lenders are willing to accept yields that are even lower than those they demand from the safer U.S. government bonds. That is why these **tax-exempt bonds** paid an average yield of only 5.7% in October 1994 (see Table 13B). An investor in the top tax bracket would get to keep more interest from tax-exempt bonds than he would by owning U.S. government bonds.

Of course, these nonfederal government bonds carried with them some small risk of default or delinquency. (Defaults of nonfederal government bonds are rare, but they do happen.) The after-tax yield on U.S. bonds was 4.3% and it was 5.7% for tax exempts. This difference of 1.4% in after-tax yield can be regarded as a risk premium.

The difference between the yield on tax-exempt bonds and that on U.S. government bonds shows us that *lenders (investors) whose interest is exempt from federal income taxes will accept lower interest rates than will lenders whose interest is fully taxed.*

Do tax exempt bonds give everyone an attractive interest rate?

We saw that tax exempts may give wealthy investors an attractive interest rate with a healthy risk premium. But are tax exempts as profitable for lower-income investors?

For folks in a 28% tax bracket, the after-tax yield on U.S. Treasury bonds was 5%, compared with the 5.7% available from tax exempts, using the rates in Table 13B. This means that these lower-income investors have to settle for a risk premium of only about 0.7% when lending to nonfederal governments. Consequently, the lower your tax rate is, the less attractive tax-exempt bonds are as investments. *Low-income investors receive smaller risk premiums from tax-exempt bonds than do high-income investors.*

How do long-term interest rates differ from short-term interest rates?

Your ability to make changes in the way you invest your money is referred to as **liquidity**. Short-term investments give investors more liquidity, which investors prefer. Other things being the same, that is why long-term loans and investments are less attractive than short-term ones.

> **JOSHUA IS SAFE, BUT SORRY:** When Joshua retired, he invested the entire lump-sum payment he received from his company's pension fund, $550,000, in twenty-year U.S. Treasury bonds that paid him an interest rate of 6% per year. He felt confident he could live on this interest income of $33,000, plus his social security benefits. But six years later the T-bond interest rate on new bonds was 11%, which would have paid him a much needed $60,500 per year, considering the inflation that occurred during these years and ate away some of his purchasing power. But his money was tied up and he could not take advantage of this opportunity.

When interest rates went up, the value of Joshua's old bonds went down, so he would have lost a lot of money by selling them. He was locked in. Lenders are not comfortable tying up their money for long periods because they do not know what other investment opportunities will present themselves (☛ Art. 20: Prices in Financial Markets, page 265, for a discussion of bond prices).

Finally, a lot can happen in the economy over five or ten years. A borrower may look secure for the next year or two, but unexpected (and unpleasant) things can happen that can take away an investor's peace of mind. The further ahead you look, the cloudier your vision will be.

Borrowers (such as governments and corporations that issue bonds) have to give lenders (investors) an incentive to make them commit their money for long periods and to give up their liquidity. This incentive is like a risk premium that comes in the form of added interest. That is why *interest rates for long-term loans are usually larger than those for short-term loans.*

Graph 13A gives you examples of the spreads (differences) between rates for U.S. government securities at two points in time.[11] As you can see, the longer the term of a bond, the larger the interest rate. The relationship between interest rates and maturity is called the **term structure of interest rates**. (If you plotted it on a graph, you would have a figure called a **yield curve**.)

Graph 13A

Yields on U.S. Treasury

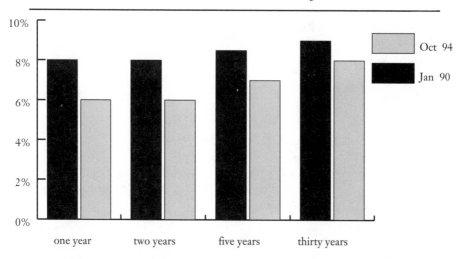

What determines the spread between long-term and short-term rates?

Remember, the expected inflation rate is an important determinant of the interest rate. If the expected inflation rate is high, interest rates will be high.

Before lenders can make decisions about long-term commitments of their money, they have to form expectations about future inflation rates, and the effects of this inflation on interest rates. That is how they know what interest rates they should demand.

Potential borrowers also must form expectations about future inflation rates and interest rates. Based on this, they can decide what interest rate they are willing to pay.

Spreads can be revealing if you know how to "read" them. *Spreads between long-term and short-term interest rates tell you what players in financial markets expect future interest rates to be.*

But the spread tells us even more than what people expect interest rates to be. Inflation rates and interest rates are heavily influenced by the state of the economy. Therefore, expectations (forecasts) about inflation and interest rates are often based on expectations about the economy. A growing economy often generates higher inflation rates. Higher inflation rates lead to higher interest rates. Therefore, *interest rate spreads often reveal what financial-market players expect the condition of the economy to be.*

If long-term interest rates are only *slightly larger* than short-term interest rates, what are financial-market traders saying about future interest rates?

If spreads are positive, but small, lenders are expecting future interest rates to be the same as present interest rates.

ALI MAKES HIS CONDITIONS: Ali is responsible for investing the policyholder premiums received by a life insurance company. The company's economists expect the economy to grow slowly, so inflation and interest rates will remain the same over the next three to five years. Right now Ali must decide whether to invest $25 million of the firm's cash in one-year T-bills that yield 6% or in five-year U.S. Treasury bonds. He will tie up the funds in the bonds only if they yield at least 6.25%; otherwise he will keep the funds liquid by investing in one-year T-bills.

If Ali expects the interest rate on one-year T-bills to be 6% for the next three years, he can keep his funds liquid by just investing, and reinvesting, in one-year bills for the next three years. Then, if interest rates rise during the five-year period (which would be a pleasant surprise to him), he will be able to take advantage of it. But to get him to commit himself to five-year bonds and give up liquidity, he would have to get at least a small premium (.25% or so) as an incentive.

This is similar to what existed in early 1990, as you can see in Graph 13A. Economic forecasters were expecting the economy to grow slowly or to soften, which would bring inflation and interest rates down slightly. As they soon found out, a recession started later that year, interest rates declined, and they stayed low for more than three years until rising in 1994.

If long-term interest rates are *smaller* than short-term interest rates, what are financial-market traders saying about future interest rates?

On rare occasions, perhaps once every ten years or so, interest rate spreads are negative. This means that lenders are expecting inflation and interest rates to fall significantly.

> **RICHELLE LOCKS DOWN HER RETURN:** Richelle, the bond-fund manager, is able to invest in bonds with one-year maturity at 9% or in five-year bonds at 8%. Lenders need to get a risk premium of at least .5% before they are willing to commit their money to five-year investments (as an incentive to give up liquidity). But Richelle expects one-year bond rates to decline to yields that will perhaps be as low as 7.5%, so she settles for 8% on the longer-term bonds because she does not want to have to reinvest her money in a couple of years at what might turn out to be a lower rate.

These *negative spreads, which the pros call an inverted yield curve, often come before a recession.* Keep in mind that negative spreads like this indicate only that the experts are generally pessimistic about the economy. That does not mean a recession is bound to follow, but the experts have a good batting average.

If long-term interest rates are much larger than short-term interest rates, what are financial-market traders saying about future interest rates?

When interest rate spreads are large, market experts are predicting higher inflation and higher interest rates. This often occurs when the economy is expected to increase its rate of growth. The experts may be wrong. Meanwhile, if corporations and governments (borrowers) want to sell long-term bonds under such a circumstance, they will have to offer relatively high yields to get investors to make long-term commitments of their funds.

Take another look at Graph 13A. In January 1990 the interest rate spread was small; investors in five-year bonds were willing to accept a small premium (0.2 of a percentage point) over the yield they could get on one-year investments. The economy was weak and investors expected low growth in the next few years. They were fairly prescient; a recession began later that year.

In the fall of 1994 the picture was different. The U.S. economy had recovered from the recession and was growing slowly. Investors were fearful that this growth would bring increased inflation and higher interest rates. To protect themselves from losing purchasing power, they demanded a larger interest rate spread (1.3 percentage points) than they did more than four years earlier.

4

Households and Businesses

conomists divide the economy into three parts that they
call sectors: household, business, and government. This
makes it easier to analyze economic activity because each
sector has a unique role. In a market economy the household sector is the largest and the government sector is the smallest.
But economists group these into another division of the economy,
the private and the public sectors.

Household and business make up the private sector because it
includes property owned by individuals and corporations. This
chapter explains this private sector. Government is in the public sector because its property is "owned" by all of its citizens. The public
sector is discussed in its own chapter (☛ Chapter 6: Government
and the Economy, page 283).

The household sector is where you and I live. Everyone is a member of a household. One person living independently is a household;
two or more people living together also make up a household,

regardless of whether they are legally related or where or how they live. (Even the homeless person is, technically, a household.)

The fuel that our economy runs on is the income received by individuals in the household sector. This is the subject of Article 14: Personal Income. Personal income makes up 85% of all of the income received in the United States and is equally important in the economies of other industrialized nations. The first part of the article gives you a snapshot of personal income in the U.S., showing you how big it is and where people get it. Personal income is always changing, and when it does, it affects the economic environment; the remainder of Article 14 tells you why personal income moves up or down over time.

Article 15: Consumer Spending and Saving discusses what households do with their income. When people spend, they create jobs and income for others. These jobs create goods and services. Consumer spending is the economy's major source of business sales.

Not all household income is spent. Whatever is left over after the bills are paid is saved. Article 15 also explains how and why households save some of their incomes. You will see that savings mean a lot for the market economy because savings provide the money for investing for future production. A nation that saves is a nation that grows.

The last part of this chapter, Article 16: Investment, explains why people and businesses invest and how that helps to shape our economic environment. This is not an article about stocks and bonds (that type of investment is covered in Chapter 5: Money and Credit). This is an article about factories, machinery, and buildings: the things used to make the goods and services that meet our material needs, and some of our other needs as well (consider the computer used by a dating service). How much real investment, and what type of investments, a nation makes are critical to its growth.

ARTICLE 14:

PERSONAL INCOME

Our Nation's Primary Fuel

What is personal income?

Personal income is all the money that people receive in a year, no matter what the source or the reason they received it. Most of the money paid for the goods and services produced in the economy winds up in the pockets of individuals. For example, in 1993 the value of goods and services created in the United States was just over $6.3 trillion (that is $6,300 billion). Eighty-five percent of this amount, $5,374 billion, came back to individuals as income of one kind or another; the rest went to governments and corporations.

Personal income is the fuel our economy runs on. Most of the money people spend comes from the income they receive. If income goes up, so does spending, and vice versa. This spending determines the nation's sales, production, and employment. Because so much depends on personal income, it is important to know where personal income comes from and how it changes.

Personal income is any money people receive during a year. There are several sources of personal income. Let's look at them.

What is the largest source of personal income?

Most personal income comes from the pay people get for the work they do for an employer. Take a look at Table 14A.[1] In 1993 nearly two-thirds of personal income was received from wages, salaries, and "other labor income" (e.g., commissions and fees) received by employees.

Another 8% of personal income that year consisted of profits of self-employed people. Anyone who works for herself or himself is called a proprietor, as long as the business is not a corporation. Prof-

Table 14A

Personal Income by Source, 1963 and 1993 (billions of current dollars)

Income Source	1963 Amount	1963 Percent	1993 Amount	1993 Percent
Wages, salaries, and other labor income	$329	69%	$3,435	64%
Proprietors' income	58	12	442	8
Interest, dividends, and rents	66	14	843	16
Transfer payments	36	8	915	17
Less social insurance payments	−12	−3	−261	−5
Totals:	477	100	5,374	100

its of self-employed persons are called **proprietors' income**. A proprietor may be a store owner, lawyer, private detective, or any other worker. Partners in a nonincorporated business are also proprietors.

How about income earned by corporations?

Corporations are legal beings; they exist on paper, not as flesh and bones. Since they are not persons (human beings), *income kept by corporations is not counted as personal income.* Personal income includes only money people get for themselves.

However, a big part of personal income comes from money corporations pay out to persons. This personal income can come from wages, salaries, commissions, fees, bonuses, interest payments, or dividends paid to stockholders. Income received by corporations becomes personal income only when, and if, it is turned over to people.

Is a corporation's income considered to be personal income if the corporation is owned by the people who work for it?

A lot of people work for corporations that they own. Many professionals, such as physicians, accountants, and lawyers, form personal corporations to run their private practices. That is because corporations have limited liability. This means that clients or customers who successfully sue corporations can get only the assets owned by the corporation; they cannot get other assets owned by owners of the corporation. These special corporations often include the term *personal corporation* (P.C.) in their title, such as Jones & Fuentes, P.C.

More people work for regular corporations that are not personal corporations. These businesses typically include the terms *corporation* (corp.) or *incorporated* (inc.) in their title, such as General Tools Corporation or Office Software, Inc.

Corporations are not human, so anyone who works for a corporation is not classified as a proprietor, even if she owns all of the corporation's stock. Let's see how working for her own corporation determines Anita's share of the nation's personal income.

> **ANITA'S INCORPORATED SALON:** Anita runs a hairstyling salon. She made her business into a legal corporation to limit her legal liability. She drew a salary of $35,000 from the corporation in 1993, which shows up in Table 14A in the wages and salaries row. After paying this salary and other expenses of the business, the corporation had a profit of $7,500 and it paid this to Anita as a stock dividend. This $7,500 was included in Table 14A in the interest, dividends, and rents row.

Anita's $35,000 salary, plus the $7,500 she took from the corporation as a dividend, together add $42,500 to the nation's personal income because they represent money she got as a person.

The division of Anita's income between salary and dividends is arbitrary, as far as personal income is concerned. As the head of her corporation she could have given herself, for example, $10,000 less in salary and $10,000 more in dividends. Her total personal income, and that of the nation, would not have changed if she had done so.

However, one decision Anita could have made would have changed personal income. Suppose Anita decided to let the corporation keep the $7,500 profit for future use. If this income were kept by the corporation, it would not have been part of personal income, and the nation's total personal income would have been $7,500 smaller. In any given year, *the more income that corporations keep, the smaller personal income will be;* personal income does not include income kept by corporations until that money is paid out to human beings (which it eventually will be in later years).

Any income a corporation receives, and that it decides not to pay out as dividends, is called **retained earnings**. Retained earnings are part of the nation's **national income** (and its gross domestic product), but they are not part of personal income. That is because national income includes any money that is earned, whether it is received by human beings or by corporations.

Do property and wealth contribute to personal income?

The largest share of a nation's personal income comes from the wages and salaries people earn. But a significant amount of personal income comes from people's investments. Economists distinguish between two types: financial investments and real investments. **Financial investments** are pieces of paper (or even just computer entries) such as stocks, bonds, and bank certificates of deposit. These assets do not produce goods and services, they produce only income (if they are successful).

Real investments are machines, factories, or other tangible property that produces goods and services. Owners of real investments get income from selling the things that they produce.

The income produced by investments consists of payments that people get for the use of their property. Anita got a dividend of $7,500 because she owned stock, and the corporation paid her this as a reward for the use of the money she gave the corporation when she bought the stock. Most income from financial investments consists of stock dividends, interest payments from bank accounts or bonds, and rents on real estate.

Other investment income consists of **capital gains**. An investor earns capital gains when she sells a (real or financial) investment for more than she paid for it. If Anita paid $60,000 for her stock in 1985 and sold it for $230,000 in 1995, she would earn a capital gain of $170,000, which would become part of the personal income of the nation in 1995, the year she received this capital gain.

Be careful not to conclude that investment income is unearned. Of course, we have all heard about people who inherit property that they leave to the management of others; they enjoy the income from this property with no effort on their part. But these are the exceptions. Most investors make an effort to select and to watch over their investments. They may also work hard to improve or to maintain their property, such as the apartment landlord who fixes the plumbing and paints the rooms or pays others to do this. *Personal income includes the money people receive for the use of their property*, regardless of how active they are in caring for it.

One-sixth of all personal income received in 1993 came from investments in bank accounts, stocks, bonds, real estate, and other investments. This included capital gains.

Is all personal income earned?

Finally, a small part of personal income people receive comes in the form of what economists call **transfer payments**. The distinctive feature of transfer payments is that the people receiving them do not have to perform any service in return for this money, nor is this income paid for the use of their property.

Social security benefits, unemployment compensation, welfare allowances, and health care allowances are important "transfers" (that is the short term for transfer payments). Lottery winnings and gifts are also transfers. Even though they are not earnings, they are part of the income people receive, so they are included in personal income.

ANGELA'S SCHOLARSHIP: Angela is a college student in the United States. Her aunt in Switzerland, along with a Swiss civic organization, together send her $25,000 per year to pay for her college and living expenses. Since this money is a gift, the U.S. government number crunchers consider it a transfer payment from abroad, and that is how it is included in personal income.

While transfer income is included in personal income, since it is part of the money people receive, it is conventional to *subtract* from personal income **social insurance contributions**. They are what workers must pay to qualify for benefits from certain government transfer programs.

In the United States most social insurance transfers consist of social security, medicare, and unemployment compensation benefits. Social insurance "contributions" are not voluntary; people who work must make payments for social security, medicare, and unemployment compensation programs. These contributions are called **payroll taxes**. Take a look at your payroll stub next payday and add them up; they may be larger than you think. (Payroll taxes, however, do not include income tax withholdings. That is because income taxes are not linked to specific government benefit programs. What is more, payroll taxes are only required to be taken out of income received from employment. Income taxes must be paid on both employment and [most] nonemployment income.)

In 1993 transfer payments were 17% of personal income, as you can see from Table 14A. However, 5% of personal income was taken out for mandatory social insurance contributions, so net transfers contributed about 12% of personal income.

Transfer payments, less social insurance contributions, are included in personal income because they are part of the money people receive and this money contributes to their spending power.

Not all transfer payments come from governments. Transfers may include gifts people give one another, such as the money you might send to your niece or nephew for a birthday. Some transfers are taxed, while others are not.

Has the mix of personal incomes changed over the last thirty years?

The shares of personal income that come from the sources we just discussed have remained relatively constant for the last few decades. However, some small, but significant, changes have occurred, as you can see from Table 14A. *The share of personal income that people in the United States get from transfer payments has more than doubled.* At the same time, the shares of personal income received from work (wages, salaries, and proprietors' income) have declined.

The growth in transfer payments resulted from dramatic increases in entitlement programs during the 1960s and 1970s, starting with the War on Poverty program of President Lyndon Johnson. During this period social security was extended to cover more people, social security benefits were enhanced by cost of living adjustments, medicare was introduced, and the U.S. Department of Housing and Urban Development was created to take several initiatives to improve housing and transportation. Other government programs were also started during this quarter century in what was perhaps the largest expansion of the public sector since the 1930s (except for World War II).

How much money do people have to spend?

While personal income is the total sum of money people receive, it is not all spendable. That is because the government requires you to use some of your income to pay taxes. After paying them, what you have left is called **disposable income**.

Disposable income is one of the most important economic measurements in the economy because it tells us how much money people have to spend. Remember, spending is what drives our economy.

DICK LOOKS AT HIS PAYCHECK: Dick earns $345 per week entering charge-account data into a computer for the credit department of a department store chain. His federal, state, and local government income tax payments come to $62.10 per week, leaving him with $282.90 as after-tax disposable income. His employer also deducts a contribution of $11.32 per week to his pension plan, $6.70 for life insurance, and $15 for the use of his employer's day care center by his three-year-old daughter. His take-home pay is, therefore, $249.88 per week.

Dick's weekly disposable income of $282.90 is what he has after paying fixed obligations, such as taxes, over which he has no control. All of the other deductions his employer made were part of his *spending,* and he had some control over them; he used these deductions to buy life insurance, a pension, and day-care services. Even if his employer required him to contribute to a pension or to buy life insurance as a condition for keeping his job, he did (or will) receive personal benefits, specifically in return for these payments, that he would not have received otherwise.

Disposable income is what people can spend. That means that disposable income figures are important to watch if you are interested in forecasting retail sales, housing purchases, or almost any other type of spending. Of course, not all of a person's disposable income is spent; some of it may be used for savings (see below), but unlike taxes, that is a matter of choice.

Because disposable income influences consumer spending more than personal income does, you can see how changes in income tax rates can influence spending in the economy. *When income tax rates rise, disposable income falls and spending declines.* That is why higher taxes can hurt the economy and lower taxes can stimulate consumer spending.

ARTICLE 15:

CONSUMER SPENDING AND SAVING

Power of the Purse

How do people spend their income?

Look at Table 15A.[2] People spend most of the income they receive (and some spend even more). In 1993, a typical year, a little more than one-tenth of disposable income was spent on **durable goods**. These are big-ticket items with a useful life of three years or more, such as furniture, cars, and appliances. A distinctive feature of "durables" is that consumers have some discretion about when to buy them. For example, there is usually no specific time when a sofa or a car has to be replaced. People are more flexible about when they buy cars or television sets than they are about when they buy food or comic books.

Table 15A

Uses of Personal Income in 1963 and 1993
(billions of current dollars)

Disposable Income Used for . . .	1963 Amount	1963 Percent	1993 Amount	1993 Percent
Durable goods	$52	12%	$538	11%
Nondurable goods	169	40	1,339	29
Services	163	39	2,501	53
Payment of interest	9	2	108	2
Personal transfers	1	0	10	0
Savings	25	6	193	4
Adds up to disposable income of . . .	419	100	4,689	100
Which comes out of personal income of . . .	476	—	5,375	—

About 30% of disposable income was spent on nondurable goods such as fuel, food, newspapers, and other items with a short useful life. *The lion's share (over 50%) of disposable income was spent on services,* including auto repair, health care, insurance, and entertainment. A tiny percentage was spent on nonmortgage interest and on gifts to others (personal transfers).

Not all money people received was spent. *Income receivers in 1993 chose to save an average of 4% of their disposable incomes.* These savings included money put into bank accounts, pension plans, and financial assets (stocks, bonds, etc.).

Have spending patterns changed over the past three decades?

People spend part of their income and save part of it. **Consumer spending** is what we call the income used to purchase things. What people buy is often divided into three broad categories: durables, nondurables, and services. **Consumer durables** are big-ticket items that have a useful life of three years or more. They include automobiles and vans, appliances, some types of clothing, furniture, watches, pleasure boats, home computers, and similar items. **Consumer nondurables** include the rest of the tangible things people buy for their use: food, paper products, publications, CDs (the musical kind), cleaning supplies, gasoline and oil, cosmetics and toiletries, drugs (legal and illegal), etc. **Consumer services** consist of the things others do for us that provide repairs, entertainment, transportation, personal care, utilities, and so on.

During the thirty years from 1963 to 1993 consumers made some major changes in the way they disposed of their incomes. The most notable change was that *consumers reduced spending on nondurable goods and increased spending on services.* This is the major reason many advanced nations are developing into service economies. This means that our incomes have grown faster than our appetite for manufactured goods.

Have savings habits changed?

The second notable shift in consumers' use of money is the reduction in the **savings rate** that occurred during the last couple of decades. The savings rate is the percentage of disposable income that is *not* spent. This is an important figure for economists to study.

A farmer needs to use some of his or her crop to get new seeds for future production. Similarly, the savings rate is important because real **savings** are the economy's "seeds" that it uses to produce things in the future. Savings are used to give banks the funds that they lend out to individuals who build houses and to businesses that build factories. Savings are also used to purchase newly issued stocks and bonds from corporations. (We do not count purchases of "old" stocks and bonds as savings. These purchases are only transfers of property from one saver to another; they do not result in the production of "new seeds.")

Businesses use the money they get from bank loans, and from selling stocks and bonds, to buy inventory, to construct new production facilities, and to purchase machinery and equipment. Consumers borrow savings to build houses, to buy new cars, to finance education, and for other purposes (☞ Art. 16: Investment, page 197).

Sooner or later these uses of savings all lead to creation of new goods and services, to new jobs, and to the incomes of those who get these new jobs. In addition, as businesses accumulate productive assets, they replace worn-out equipment and they maintain or increase their capacity to produce goods and services in the future.

A second reason the savings rate is important is that it increases the amount of goods and services that consumers who save can purchase in later years, which promotes continued growth of the economy. The more people put aside today, the more they will have available to spend later. An important component of consumer savings is investment in pension plans. These plans give people purchasing power during the retirement years, when the earnings they get from work may be lower or nonexistent.

Unfortunately, *the savings rate declined significantly during the 1963–93 period*, which began with a rate of 6% and ended with a rate of 4%; during this time the savings rate was as high as 8% and as low as 4%. Although economists debate over the best way to measure the savings rate, most will agree that the savings rate in the United States is now somewhat lower than the rate in most other industrialized nations, such as Japan and Germany.

The amount of disposable income consumers allocate to savings is important because *the savings rate is an important determinant of our nation's future economic growth.*

IN THE NEWS . . .

"Our Savings Rate Doesn't Rate"

SACRAMENTO BEE, November 6, 1994, METRO FINAL, page E1

Americans save, on average, less than 4% of their incomes. This is less than half the rate of workers in many other industrialized nations. Although they can rely on some "safety nets" to supplement retirement income, such as Social Security and Medicare, 4% is still too little. A recent study showed that American workers currently put away only about a third of what they will need for retirement to maintain their living standards.

Are savings really good or bad for the economy?

Economists long ago recognized what they call the **paradox of thrift**. The paradox is that saving is good for the individual, but it is bad for the economy. Here is why. If I save part of my income, I will be better off in the long run because I will have more wealth and greater purchasing power in the future. This is especially true if I invest my savings so that they will grow.

However, the money I decide not to spend cuts into the current sales of stores, service people, and manufacturers. If lots of people saved money, the sales of businesses in the economy would be lower than they would have been if their customers spent money more freely. Saving may be a private virtue, but it can be a public vice.

There is some truth to the paradox of thrift. *If people save more money, businesses will sell less, and jobs and income will be lost, in the short run.*

However, in the long run, thrift pays off for the entire economy. That is because the money that is saved will be used to make investments. These investments will modernize equipment, build homes and factories, and finance research and development of new products and methods.

BURT BUILDS A BETTER BAG: The luggage industry is generally not very innovative, which is one reason most luggage owners replace their bags only when they wear out. Burt, a pilot, travels frequently, and he is also an independent inventor. Working in the basement of his home, he developed a new design for making luggage that was lighter, stronger, and more manageable than conventional bags. When it was perfected, he obtained financing to produce and market his new product. He did this by selling stock to investors and by getting bank loans. Sales of his new product were brisk because he offered an innovative product that met a need. With his financing he built a prosperous business that created jobs for many people.

Burt's activities created new jobs and new incomes for the people who took these jobs. He got his money from savers. If people had not saved money, the banks would not have had the funds to lend and investors would have had no money to buy stock. Burt's experience illustrates the way personal savings can be used to create growth in the economy.

When the savings rate rises, it has the immediate effect of depressing sales, employment, and income as people switch from consumption to saving. However, afterward these savings will be used to create new jobs and incomes. *In the long run higher savings rates lead to higher economic growth.*

What determines how much money consumers spend?

People in the retail trades want to know how much consumers will spend because that determines their business activity and profits. Government policy makers want to know, too, because consumer spending is the major driving force of our economy; the nation cannot be prosperous if consumers do not spend money.

Economists have helped them both by coming up with explanations of how much people will spend. (Don't ever expect economists to come up with *one* explanation for something. It has been truly said that four economists will have five answers to any question!) Most current explanations come under the heading of what are called forward-looking theories of consumption.

Forward-looking theories of consumption say that the amount of money consumers spend depends on their current disposable income, their expected income, their total wealth, and interest rates. *Expected and current incomes are the most important determinants of consumer spending.*

In what way does expected income influence consumer spending?

More and more, economists are focusing on **expected income** as the key for explaining how consumers behave.[3] To see why, think about how we spend our money. What we spend every month or year largely depends on the lifestyle we select. In fact, most of our spending is determined by our choice of lifestyle because of long-term commitments we make (mortgage or rent, insurance, transportation, etc.) or formation of buying habits (for example, diet, clothing, and entertainment). We may splurge one month, for a holiday or vacation, but then we may tighten our belts the next month to make up for it.

How do we select our consumer lifestyle? That is, how do we settle on our monthly budget? The answer is that our budget is set by our expected income. Every responsible consumer has to form a notion of his expected income before settling on a budget; some of us are more realistic about it than others.

A consumer bases her estimate of *expected income on her past income and her forecast of future income.* This is tricky, especially for inexperienced consumers starting to keep their own households. With experience, most folks tend to get it right. See how Fay did it.

FAY SPENDS FUTURE INCOME: At age thirty-two Fay has worked as a salaried insurance claims adjuster for six years. During this time her salary has risen about 6% per year, as a result of merit increases and promotions, and is now $36,000; this gives her about $2,200 per month after taxes. She expects this income progression to continue for the next several years. Her average monthly expenditures are $2,500, which is what she can expect to make in two years. She finances her current "deficit spending" with a mortgage on her condo, a car loan, overdraft loans from her checking account, and credit card loans.

If Fay's expectations are realistic, her current spending is not irresponsible. She is basing her current spending on her expected income. Current income plays only a part in helping her to guess at her expected income; expected income is also based on her past earnings experiences and on her forecasts of her future earnings.

People get into trouble when they formulate an expected income that is unrealistic and then base their spending on it. If Fay were to spend $4,000 per month because she expects to win a large lottery within the next year or so, her consumer spending may soon decline dramatically if her dreams are not realized. (She may get a healthy nudge from her banker if she finds she cannot continue borrowing so much money.)

The forward-looking theory of consumer expenditures says *consumers base spending decisions largely on expected income.* This theory is used by economists to explain why the nation's consumer expenditures, which result in retail sales and purchases of services, grow at a fairly even rate over time and fluctuate much less than income.

The theory is also used to explain why *consumer expenditures decline less than income during recessions, and vice versa.* After all, it takes time for consumers to make significant changes in their budgets, which are tied to their lifestyle.

Lifestyle alone does not account for the relative stability of consumer spending in the economy. During recessions, when incomes decline and unemployment rises, government takes a smaller tax bite out of income. In addition, unemployment compensation, welfare payments, food stamps, and other assistance give consumers the ability to maintain a level of spending that otherwise would not be feasible. Lower taxes and assistance programs are safety nets that hold up consumption. That is why they are also called **automatic stabilizers**; they help to stabilize spending.

How do consumers calculate their expected income?

Expected income depends on past incomes, on current income, and on our forecast of future incomes. Certainly our past experiences play a heavy role in formulating our expectations. If a forty-year-old internal auditor never earned more than $70,000 per year during his career, it is not likely he would expect his future income to vary far above this figure, allowing for inflation. An expected income of $330,000 by age fifty might be unrealistic, but an expected income of $110,000 would be in-line. (An income of $70,000 at age forty would grow to $110,000 by age fifty with an annual average increase of just under 5%.)

Forecasts of future income are unavoidable; we all must make one before we settle into a budget-based lifestyle. As we saw in the paragraph you just read, our past incomes give us a huge head start in making this forecast. Beyond that, however, our forecasts are shaped by our outlook about the future, and this outlook is based on our optimism or pessimism. Economists often refer to this optimism or pessimism as **consumer confidence**.

Economic forecasters are very concerned about consumer confidence. Because of this, surveys of consumer expectations (or consumer "sentiment") are made regularly. If consumers expect their incomes to grow and they feel secure in their jobs, their confidence level will be high. Economists would conclude that *a rise in confidence means that consumers will raise their expected income.*

Why are economists so concerned about expected income? Because purchasing decisions are based on it, *increasing expected income often means that consumers are preparing to spend more money.* If consumers get economic news that they think is bad, consumer confidence and expected income will decline. That is why it is quite common for consumer confidence to be low in the latter part of a recession when the nation's unemployment rate is high.

Consumer confidence is mercurial; it may rise or fall significantly over short periods. Expected income depends on both past income, which is set in stone, and on consumer confidence, which can quickly change. Of these two factors, past income is the most important for shaping our buying habits. Because of the drag of past income, expected income changes slowly.

Many economists make forecasts with a forward-looking theory (explanation) of consumer spending called the **permanent income hypothesis**. This theory states that consumers tie their spending to a measure of expected income and to their wealth. Since expected income changes slowly, the permanent income theory is used to explain the fact that over time consumer spending (both for individuals and for the nation) changes less than changes in income.

Actually, the term *permanent income* is a bit of an exaggeration; since consumers are always fine-tuning their outlook for their income, no expected-income figure is "permanent." Whenever a consumer gets an unexpected raise or promotion, is shocked by a layoff, or sees opportunities for advancement fade, he readjusts his permanent income. Remember, someone's expected or permanent income is only a guess; it is not written in some official record book. But it is important because people make important buying decisions based on that guess.

How do economists explain the way current income affects spending?

If people have more disposable income, they will spend more money because current income gives them purchasing power. Remember, disposable income depends on both total income and taxes. As income rises or as taxes fall, disposable income goes up and people spend more money. That is why *higher current incomes or lower taxes increase consumption.*

Most economists once believed that consumer spending went up or down almost entirely as a result of changes in current income. Therefore, makers of economic policy believed the way to get someone to spend more was to increase his or her income. Likewise, they believed that when someone's income dropped suddenly, perhaps due to loss of a job, consumer spending would plunge.

With the aid of consumer surveys and good statistics on spending, modern economists have modified their views about the importance of current income as a motivator of spending. We now know that *most people's monthly spending changes less than their monthly income.* This is illustrated by Hector's living expenses.

HECTOR'S LIFESTYLE: Hector is a physician in a private family practice. His income depends on his patient traffic and demands for his services, and these change constantly. During any given month, after paying the expenses of his office, his net income may be as low as $3,000 or as high as $20,000. However, his monthly living expenses are about $9,000, which is about equal to his average monthly income. His monthly expenses are fairly constant because payments for his house mortgage, groceries, children's private school tuition, domestic help, club dues, alimony, and other expenses do not change much. In months when income is high, he puts money into savings; when income is low, he uses some savings to pay bills.

Hector's net income (which is really his business "profit" as a proprietor, although medical professionals don't use commercial language like that) changes more sharply, and more frequently, than the changes he could make in his monthly cost of living. Hector's situation is shared, on different scales, by many earners in our economy such as business owners and commissioned salespersons. The more variable current income is, the less it influences changes in consumption. That is why, over short periods, *consumer spending changes less than income.*

In what way is spending affected by temporary changes in income?

Many people experience temporary swings in income. For many business owners and practitioners, such as Hector, these swings become a way of life. For others, swings are rare, but they happen. For example, some people have windfalls that momentarily boost income, and some experience temporary layoffs that pull income down for a while.

Of course, one cannot live beyond his or her means indefinitely. Over the long term current income must constrain our spending. In general, small *changes* in current income are not much help in explaining changes in consumer spending. However, large temporary changes in current income can have significant short-run effects.

> **GLENN AND JENNY'S BIG FIND:** Glenn and Jenny are a married couple in their mid-fifties with a salary income of about $4,400 per month after taxes, pension contribution, and other payroll deductions. They generally stick close to their budget, which calls for spending $3,800 per month. They place the remainder in savings. Two months ago they found an old postcard collection in their attic that had belonged to a deceased relative. Having no interest in postcards, they sold the collection and were amazed to get $6,500 for it. The following month they used this windfall to spend $6,000 on new furniture; their total spending that month was, therefore, $9,800. This was only a temporary one-time increase in their spending.

While expected income is the major factor in determining what people spend, *consumer spending may be temporarily increased or decreased in response to significant random changes in current income.* Like the surface of a lake, consumer spending is never smooth for long.

Where does wealth come into the picture?

The forward-looking theory of consumer expenditures does not ignore wealth as an influence on purchasing decisions. People possess varying amounts of wealth in the form of real estate, stocks, bonds, bank CDs, collectibles, and so on. This wealth often influences the amount of current income that people spend. A person with an income of $40,000 per year and with a money market account of $700,000 may feel free to spend a large percentage of this income on consumption, perhaps as much as 100%. Another person with the same income might spend a smaller portion of that income if his savings totaled only $12,000.

This illustration points to an important characteristic of consumer behavior. *An increase in wealth generally increases consumer spending.* This is sometimes referred to by economists as the **wealth effect** on consumption. When people feel wealthier, they feel freer to increase spending, even if their income does not change. The opposite is also true.

STACEY'S NEST EGG CRACKS: By her forty-third birthday Stacey had accumulated an individual retirement account (IRA) worth $175,000. Most of this was invested in blue-chip stocks. Shortly after her birthday, however, stock prices declined sharply for three weeks, reducing the value of her IRA to about $135,000. Although she was many years away from the time she would draw on this account, her stock market losses made her feel poorer. She postponed her plans to buy a new car, canceled a two-week cruise, and cut back on contributions to her church, even though her job and salary were not affected by the drop in stock values.

Stacey's decisions illustrate the way economists expect changes in the value of assets to affect spending. A fact of economic life is that *wealth, as well as income, determines spending.*

What types of wealth influence spending?

There are two kinds of wealth: human and nonhuman. Human wealth is not tangible. Economists call this nontangible wealth **human capital**, and we all have it, in varying amounts. Human capital refers to the salable skills someone has that are based on her or his education, experience, and talent. A chemical engineer has more human capital than does a data entry clerk. A physician has more human capital than does a nurse.

Human capital has a market value; it can be turned into income. The value of a lawyer's human capital depends on what legal clients are willing to pay for her services. A musician has human capital that can be valued by what audiences are willing to pay to hear him perform.

JUDY AND RUPERT AS SAVERS: Judy received her MBA from a prestigious university and has enjoyed eight years of rapid advancements in retail merchandising. Now, at age thirty-two, she is an associate with a major consulting firm, earning $75,000 plus bonuses. With prospects for a long and profitable career, she has adopted a comfortable lifestyle with little savings. Rupert, at age fifty-one, earned $75,000 last year as a union ironworker on construction projects that provided generous overtime work. His job is physically taxing and stressful, so he plans on retiring at age fifty-nine. Because of the uncertainty of his project assignments and earnings, and the need for early retirement, he saves about 35% of his income.

Judy possesses considerable wealth in the form of her human capital, which she expects will contribute to her income as long as she wishes to work. She spends nearly all of her current income because her wealth effect is high. Rupert has little human capital, so he must rely on accumulating more nonhuman wealth to secure his future income. Consequently, he is careful not to spend a large share of his income; his wealth effect is small.

Human capital has an effect on spending, just as tangible wealth does. *The more human capital someone possesses the more of his income he is likely to spend.* That is because a large stock of human capital gives the consumer the same sense of security tangible wealth provides. Marketable skills are like money in the bank.

A consumer's spending is influenced by both human wealth (human capital) and by nonhuman wealth (tangible assets) (☞ Art. 8: Human Capital, page 88).

Do changes in wealth affect expected income?

An important event occurred in the summer and fall of 1987. Over a period of a few months American stock prices fell dramatically. Some major stock averages declined as much as 50%. In fact, on one climactic day, October 19, the Dow Jones Industrial Stock Average declined a whopping 25%. To date, this is the largest one-day decline in the history of the stock market in the United States. On that day alone investors lost $500 billion in wealth. Altogether, nearly a trillion dollars of wealth vanished during the last half of 1987.

Many economists expected that this huge loss in wealth would have a significant negative effect on consumer spending.[4] In fact, many felt that the expected drop in spending would set off a recession. But what followed was a small downward slip in retail sales and a brief downturn in consumer confidence. After that, stock prices recovered quickly and the economy continued to grow.

The reason we got over this event with little pain was that the stock market crash in 1987 did not move consumers to reduce their forecasts of personal income. They held to the same level of expected incomes they had formulated before the crash; that is why consumer spending did not fall.

The valuable lesson we learned from the crash of '87 was that *losses in wealth lead to a fall in consumer spending only if they reduce consumers' expectations of their future incomes.*

The magnitude of the crash of 1987 was *double* the more famous stock market crash of 1929. The crash of '29, however, will continue to have greater fame because it was a symbolic overture to the Great Depression of the 1930s. By contrast, the crash of '87 did not usher in any changes in the fundamental condition of the nation's economy, thanks to sounder business fundamentals and quicker remediation by the Federal Reserve Banks (☛ Art. 18: The Federal Reserve, page 235). If consumers had panicked and not maintained their spending, the crash of '87 would have been far more than a footnote in U.S. financial history.

Does age make a difference?

The biggest role in determining what consumers spend is played by expected income. Lesser roles are played by temporary swings in income and by changes in (human and nonhuman) wealth.

There is good reason to believe that age has a role as well. *Young consumers frequently spend more than their immediate incomes.* When people set up their own households, they often go into debt to buy a house, cars, furniture, appliances, etc. Also, young people often experience significant progressions in income as they earn college degrees, acquire new skills, and enter new professions.

Middle-age consumers are generally the economy's biggest savers. With debts largely paid off, and the need to save for retirement, they have more free income and incentives for putting money aside. Thus, *middle-age consumers generally spend a smaller portion of their incomes than do people in other age groups.*

Older people, particularly those who are retired, are spenders. For these consumers, savings are to be spent, not accumulated. Their spending often exceeds their immediate income. (They sometimes wear caps, or have car bumper stickers, that announce, "I am spending my children's inheritance.")

These observations are the basis of what economists call the **life-cycle theory of consumption**, which relates spending patterns to age. An important conclusion from this theory is that the nation's spending and saving habits are linked to the average age of the population. This partly explains why the nation's savings rate declined from the 1960s to the 1980s, when the baby boomers hit their spending stride. As the U.S. population ages, so that the share of the population in the middle-age range increases, we can expect savings rates to rise; that is because middle-agers save more.

ARTICLE 16:

INVESTMENT

Building Our Nation's Wealth

What are *real* investments?

In economics, **investments** aren't what you might think they are. If you are like most people, you think of yourself as making an investment when you buy pieces of paper that earn money: savings accounts, stocks, and bonds. However, to an economist, *businesses make investments when they acquire new things that can be used to produce goods and services.* For example, a dairy farmer's new milking machine by itself does not meet any human need, but has value as an investment when it is used to collect milk that people drink. These things that businesses invest in are **capital goods**, or simply **capital**.

Economists' use of the term *capital* is frequently misunderstood. In financial markets *capital* means the money or funds that people use to earn interest or profits; to some extent this has also become common usage. But with respect to economics, capital means any man-made asset used to create goods or services.

To keep things straight when talking to general audiences, economists may use the term **real investment** to mean the acquisition of productive assets that can be used to make the goods and services. When people buy pieces of paper that earn interest, they are making a **financial investment**.

Real investments (capital goods) are essential to an economy because they are what we use to help us to *create* useful goods and services. Financial investments make money, but money does not meet human needs; it only helps to determine who gets the goods and services coming from real investment.

What is the connection between financial investments and real investments?

Financial investments often lead to real investments. Suppose you save $1,000 from your salary and put it into a bank certificate of deposit (a financial investment). The bank that sold you the CD might then take $900 or so of your money and loan it to a supermarket, which uses it to buy a new computer-linked cash register (a real investment). Your financial investment financed the real investment.

However, *financial investments turn into real investments only when your money is used to buy* new *productive assets.* The term *new* is important.

ARETHA GOES HIGH TECH: Aretha is a manufacturer's representative for a cosmetics firm that makes and distributes over two hundred products. As she visits retailers, she determines their needs for merchandise, suggests promotional activities, and coordinates delivery schedules. In 1995 her firm invested $4,000 to install in her car a new cellular telephone, fax machine, and copier. In addition, they gave her a $3,000 laptop computer that was purchased for the company's president in 1993. These were intended to improve her communications with her customers and with the firm. With them, she increased her average sales from $21,000 to $34,000 per month.

The $4,000 the company used to acquire new equipment was counted as a real investment in the economy in 1995. This is because it increased the nation's stockpile of productive assets (see *capital stock*, discussed later). However, the $3,000 used laptop computer was not part of the economy's real investment. The computer had already been counted as a real investment in 1993. *Real investment takes place in the economy only if the economy's stock of capital is increased.*

Incidentally, the increase in Aretha's business showed us that this real investment was productive. It contributed to the nation's output in 1995 and will probably continue to do so as long as it is used.

Why are real investments important?

Real investments make the economy grow. That is because machinery, equipment, factories, etc., make human labor and natural resources more productive. An accountant can turn out more work after investing in a computer, a computer distributor increases productivity by investing in forklift trucks, and a manufacturer of computers invests in conveyor belts to speed assembly of its products.

Economists have shown conclusively that *the more real investments an economy makes, the more rapidly it will grow.* (Economists highlighted the role of investment when they developed theories of economic growth in the middle of this century.) The more people invest, the more things they can produce. When production goes up, so do incomes and, frequently, so do standards of living. The link between investment and output holds true for individual companies as well as for the economy.

By making a real investment of $4,000, Aretha's firm increased sales more than 60%. That is because the new equipment, which made her car a complete mobile office, increased her productivity; she could get more work done.

Investments might also enable us to get more out of the material resources used to make goods and services. For example, an investment in a computerized pattern-cutting machine will cut down on waste in cutting out dress and suit material.

Do all investments make our economy better off?

How much a business investment improves our well-being depends on what the investment does. If someone builds a machine to make furry nose rings, but there is little demand for this product and the machine has no other use, this investment will not contribute much to our nation's production of useful goods and services. That is because the machine's output would have little value; few might be willing to pay for furry nose rings.

Unproductive investments use our nation's resources, but they do not improve our standard of living. Many years ago some economists referred to unproductive investments as "pyramid building." The term comes from the practice of some pharaohs in ancient Egypt who used valuable labor and materials to construct government monuments that did nothing to feed or to clothe the nation's population.

(Eventually the investment in Egyptian pyramids paid off when they became revenue-generating tourist attractions nearly five thousand years after their construction. But considering the long years in which the nation received no income from these projects, the pyramids probably proved to be a poor investment. I don't think any economist has evaluated the returns to the investment in pyramids; most of what economists know about Egypt they learned from the opera *Aida*.)

Investments improve our economy only if they increase production of the nation's goods and services. However, government figures on investment spending, which we will see later, make no distinction between good and bad investments. In addition, government accounts in the U.S. do not make a distinction between government investment and government consumption of goods and services. Everything is lumped into government spending, whether it be money spent on army rations, space stations, or the modern equivalent of pyramids.

In what way does real investment affect capital stock?

The total quantity of productive assets a nation has at one time is called its **capital stock**. Capital stock is important because it is what people have to work with for producing goods and services. Capital stock results from past investments.

CECIL MAKES AN INVESTMENT: Cecil started a taxi service in a small city. He purchased seven new cars, had the cars customized to serve as taxis, bought the necessary government licenses for each cab, set up a dispatching office, hired drivers, and advertised in local media. Cecil spent $180,000 on new cars and office equipment, and these became his firm's capital stock; they also became part of the nation's capital stock. Three years later, as his business grew, he purchased two more new customized cars for $45,000, which *increased* his firm's (and the nation's) capital stock. Five years later he sold his business to his third cousin for $260,000 because his wife wanted to move to a warmer climate.

Investment is the activity of increasing the capital stock. Cecil initially made a (real) investment of $180,000, which became capital stock. Later he made an additional investment of $45,000, which increased his capital stock. But his cousin's investment of $260,000 in the business did *not* increase capital stock because it was only a financial investment.

What is included in investment spending?

Investment spending is the term economists use to refer to the actual amount of money spent on investment. Cecil's investment spending was the cost of his new equipment. So far we have just talked about investment as an increase in the nation's (or in a firm's) capital stock. But investment is really much more. Investment is spending on *anything* that increases productivity.

Unfortunately, the practice in most nations is to define investment spending in a narrow way. Government number crunchers provide us with data on just three types of investment:

- business fixed investment
- business inventories
- residential construction

Real investment in the United States is shown in Table 16A.[5] The lion's share of our measured investment is **business fixed investment**, which consists of "hard goods" such as buildings and equipment. In 1993, for example, business fixed investment, measured in constant dollars (that is, using 1987 prices), amounted to $592 billion, which was about 12% of the value of all goods and services turned out that year. (The total value of goods and services produced is called **gross domestic product**, which was $5,135 billion.)

Any additions to a firm's salable inventory is also investment. After all, a business cannot survive unless it has a stock of something to sell. In 1993 businesses invested $15 billion in their inventories of finished goods. These changes in **business inventories** are not always positive. (Inventories usually decrease during periods of weakness in the economy. For example, the change in business inventories in 1991, a recession year, was *minus* $1 billion; during

Table 16A

Investment Spending in the U.S. in 1993
(billions, 1987 dollars)

ITEM	GROSS INVESTMENT	AMOUNT CONSUMED	NET INVESTMENT
Business investment in buildings and equipment	$592	$472	$120
Change in business inventories	15	—	15
Residential construction	213	128	85
Total:	820	600	220

that year businesses did not replace all of the things they sold from inventory.)

Finally, government statisticians include **residential investment** in a nation's total investment figures. Residential investment consists of the construction of new places for people to live in (generally, houses and apartment buildings). It can account for as much as a third of total investment spending.

Why is housing construction counted as investment?

Housing construction is investment because houses and apartment buildings "produce" a service for residents. This service is the shelter people get from housing.

Like other types of investment, housing is part of capital stock because it provides shelter service for many years after it is constructed, just as computers and jackhammers continue to provide productive services long after they are made.

Is investment necessary just to maintain a nation's capital stock?

Capital stock is like an ice cube in a glass; it is always melting a little. *Capital stock is continually losing value* because of obsolescence, the ravages of time, or use. Today's fax machine or delivery truck will be worth less tomorrow even if it sits idle (like an ice cube sitting in an otherwise empty glass). In addition to losses due to time, capital stock may lose value as a result of the intensity of use (an ice cube placed in a glass of warm soda). Whenever a machine or structure is used, there is wear and tear. In the language of economics, the loss of value, from time and/or use, is called **depreciation**.

Depreciation of the nation's productive assets during 1993 is shown in the middle column of Table 16A. About three-quarters of all new investment made that year merely replaced depreciated assets.

Some investment is always needed to replace the loss of capital stock caused by depreciation. This means that the nation's capital stock always increases by *less* than the amount of investment that is going on.

To take account of the effects of depreciation, economists define **net investment** as total investment less depreciation. For the United States this net investment is shown in the last column of Table 16A. *Net investment is the actual change in a business's or nation's capital stock.* By contrast, the original sum of money spent on productive assets is called **gross investment**.

CECIL RUNS TO STAY IN PLACE: You have already met Cecil, who runs a taxi service. When he started his business, he invested $180,000 in new cars and office equipment. Three years later his original assets, because of age and use, had a market value of only $70,000; that meant his capital stock had shrunk by more than 60%. That year he invested $45,000 more in the business.

Over three years Cecil made *gross* investments of $225,000 ($180,000 when he started out plus $45,000 this past year) in capital stock. But over the same period this capital stock lost $110,000 in value because of depreciation. When you consider this loss, his capital stock totaled only $115,000, so this was his *net* investment.

Net investment is a better way of accounting for capital stock than is gross investment; it shows how much wealth the economy is actually gaining. Unfortunately, official quarterly investment data, such as those in Table 16A, report only *gross* investment spending.

Are depreciation allowances that investors take on their income tax returns good measures of losses of capital stock?

When a company owns capital stock, such as a fleet of taxis, two things happen. First, if the capital is used productively, it will produce income for the company, which adds to the owners' wealth. Second, part of the owners' wealth is lost to depreciation. It would be unfair to tax the company's entire income while ignoring the losses in wealth it experienced to get that income. Because of this, governments tax *net* increases in wealth. This is accomplished by allowing firms to deduct depreciation from taxable income before figuring the taxes they owe governments. The amount firms may deduct from income is called the **depreciation allowance**.

The depreciation allowance is determined by tax laws, which are related to political considerations and are only in part related to the actual (physical) deterioration of capital stock that takes place.

As an example of a political consideration, let's look at the U.S. federal tax-reform legislation of 1981. (Anytime legislators think of new ways to pull taxes out of people's pockets, they give it the sanctimonious label of **tax reform**, which is a bit like a dentist coming up with a new way of extracting teeth and calling it "dental reform.") The 1981 law provided for accelerated depreciation, which increases depreciation allowances in the early years of an investment project, thereby reducing the amount of income from the investment on which income taxes must be paid. This was done because the United States was in a recession. Government policy makers wanted to make investments more profitable so as to encourage businesses to spend more money, thereby accelerating economic recovery.

In the 1986 tax reform legislation these generous depreciation allowances were taken back because the economy was growing at a healthy rate. *Tax-related depreciation allowances have little or nothing to do with actual loss of wealth.* We could not say that the physical deterioration of a machine or factory was less rapid after 1986 than it was immediately after 1981. That is why economists cannot use depreciation allowances to determine net investment.

How much real wealth is there is the United States?

Year after year, investment builds up the real wealth of the nation. This real wealth is the total value of all the tangible property people and businesses own: land, buildings, machines, cars, appliances, furnishings, jewelry, etc.

We can only estimate this wealth because, while the government requires us to report our exact incomes every year, it does not require us to take an annual inventory of the *current* value of everything we own. But government economists at the U.S. Department of Commerce's Office of Economic Analysis occasionally make bold estimates of the value of a nation's wealth. Estimates of the wealth of tangible (man-made) property in the United States are shown in Table 16B.[6] The value of all tangible property in 1991 was judged to be about $9 trillion, when measured in 1987 prices ("constant dollars"). That comes to an average of just over $40,000 per woman, man, and child in the nation. Over half of this wealth belonged to businesses.

Table 16B

Estimated Net Private Capital Stock in the U.S., 1990 and 1991
(billions, 1987 dollars)

ITEM	VALUE IN 1990	VALUE IN 1991	CHANGE, 1990–91
Nonresidential	$4,773	$4,824	$51
Residential	4,385	4,434	49
Total:	9,158	9,258	100

IN THE NEWS . . .

"Report Links Growth and Natural Resources"

New York Times, May 11, 1994, page D2

Gross Domestic Product does not tell us everything about production of goods and services in the nation. In 1994 the U.S. Commerce Department started to estimate the value of all natural resources in America such as trees, lakes, coal and oil deposits, and fish. These figures will be used to show the value of our nation's natural resources that are being used up to produce goods and services. The result will be the so-called "Green GDP."

The figures in Table 16B do *not* include purely financial assets such as cash, bank deposits, stocks, and bonds. If they did, we would be double-counting a lot of wealth. That is because most financial assets represent tangible property. For example, the stocks you own are backed up by corporate property that is already covered by these figures.

Nonresidential property is the tangible assets owned by business and government. This includes buildings, machines, trucks, inventories, and tools. The residential property includes houses, furniture, autos, and so on.

How can we estimate the economy's net investment every year?

Generally, the more a nation invests, the faster it can grow. *A useful measurement of net investment is the increase in the market value of the nation's capital stock.* Table 16B shows us that the value of residential and nonresidential capital stock rose by $100 billion from 1990 to 1991. Changes in market value are the result of gross investment spending, depreciation, and changes in the usefulness of capital stock. As an example of a change in usefulness, an existing machine may lose value because it makes a product that consumers no longer want or its design becomes obsolete. Since government statisticians must estimate market values of capital stock, Table 16B gives us only an approximation of net investment, although it is a good one. One other drawback of this approach to estimating net investment is that changes in market value take some time to compute, so the data is not fresh.

Now, let us look again at the estimated net investment of $220 billion in 1993 reported in Table 16A. This type of annual net investment figure, which is published very soon after a year is completed and is widely followed, does not explicitly consider net changes in market value. It is based only on gross investment spending and depreciation. That makes it only a rough approximation of the increase in the nation's capital stock. Nonetheless, it gives us a quick and useful picture of investment.

What motivates business firms to make investments?

You have already read about several examples of capital stock. Investment is simply the way that we increase this capital stock. Because capital stock is costly to acquire and to maintain, a business firm wants only as much capital stock as it expects to use profitably. The capital stock a firm wants depends on two things: (1) the amount of product or service the firm expects to sell, and (2) the cost of this capital stock. Let's look at these factors.

SHELBI AND ED GROW A BUSINESS: This thirty-something couple runs a successful three-screen movie theater in their own building. Each theater screen has 160 seats. Because a new shopping mall will open across the street from the theater next year, they expect ticket sales to grow. Therefore, they decided to enlarge their building and to install an additional screen with 180 seats.

CECIL SCALES BACK: In his fourth year in the taxi business, Cecil had nine cars in service. But then fuel prices rose by 10% and car repair costs went up. These increases in the cost of using his capital stock cut his profits by one-third. Since his investment in cabs was now less profitable, he decided to decrease his fleet by three cars to give him more time and money with which to start another business. His capital stock was reduced.

If Cecil were running the only taxi service in a small city, he would expect to need fewer cars in his fleet than if he were running the only taxi service in a large city. His cars are part of his capital stock, and his demand for capital stock depends on his **expected sales**. *When a business expects its sales to rise, its demand for capital stock will increase.* The reverse is also true.

The total expenses a business would incur for *using* its capital stock is also important. In the language of economics this is called the **user cost of capital**, and it consists of any interest the owner pays on loans made to buy the capital stock and the expenses of using and maintaining it. For Cecil, the cost of capital consisted primarily of the money he had to spend for running his vehicles (he had no mortgage on them). *If the user cost of capital declines, demand for capital stock increases,* and vice versa.

When the cost of capital went up, Cecil's demand for capital stock went down.

How important is confidence?

Despite all the fancy computer models business planners use to forecast revenues and profits, decisions about expected sales come down to an ongoing tug-of-war between optimism and pessimism. If more of the rope is pulled to the optimists' side, businesses will invest in inventories and capital stock. If the pessimists prevail, demand for capital goods will fall and inventories will be worked down.

In the 1930s the great British economist John Maynard Keynes recognized the importance of the general optimism or pessimism that prevails in an economy. Keynes called this prevailing attitude

animal spirits and used this novel term to explain that mass mood swings in business were important in shaping economic conditions. If most business managers developed positive outlooks, they were likely to invest more money. This investment would put many people to work, increase the production of goods and services, and stimulate economic growth. If animal spirits were negative, the opposite would happen.

Animal spirits lead to a type of self-fulfilling prophecy. If businesses are optimistic, they will invest, and this investment will make the economy grow.

Today economists have replaced the term *animal spirits* with the more sophisticated label **business confidence**. They recognize that *business confidence is an important determinant of our economic future* because confidence triggers investment decisions. (I have some animal spirits in my classroom; they are called undergraduates.)

How do businesses *disinvest*?

Total investment spending is not always a positive sum of money. The higher costs for operating his taxis led Cecil to **disinvestment**, which means he reduced his capital stock. A firm can disinvest simply by selling off some capital stock. But as long as someone else in the nation buys it, the nation's capital stock will not change. For the nation as a whole, *disinvestment takes place when firms fail to replace depreciated stock.*

Remember that capital stock is like ice cubes: it melts a little each year because of depreciation. If firms fail to invest in enough new capital stock to replace what is depreciated, disinvestment takes place.

Fortunately, disinvestment of capital stock is rare. Fixed capital stock (buildings, machinery, and equipment) has not declined since the 1930s.

Business inventories, which are part of total investment, decline whenever the economy is weak, and a decline in inventory is also disinvestment. During the past twenty-five years inventories went down in 1975, 1980, and 1991, which were recession years. However, inventories also went down in 1982 and 1983, even though the economy was recovering from a recession, because business inventories were too large. The inventory part of investment is easier to adjust than is the capital stock portion. As a result, national *disinvestment usually takes the form of cutting inventories.*

Do tax laws influence investment?

The amount of money businesses put into investment depends on how profitable they expect investment to be. Any increase in **marginal income tax rates** on businesses has a dampening effect on investment spending. The marginal income tax rate is the amount of additional income tax a business must pay for each $1 increase in profits. When the marginal tax rate increases, the profitability of investment declines, and investment spending will decline. That will affect both the present economic environment (less spending on investment now) and, more importantly, the future economic environment (less capital stock means less growth in later years).

When an investor or business buys an asset for a price and later sells it at a higher price, she earns a capital gain. The U.S. tax laws include a **capital gains tax rate** that indicates the percentage of a capital gain an investor must pay as an income tax. Until the mid-1980s the capital gains tax rate was half the regular income tax rate. This was designed to make investing more attractive (profitable) because it allowed investors to keep more of their capital gains profits. The capital gains tax is actually a "discounted" income tax because it permits investors to pay less tax on each dollar of capital gain than they would have had to pay on a dollar of ordinary income.

Currently the capital gains rate equals the income tax rate on ordinary income. That means the discount has been taken away so that investment is no longer as profitable, with respect to taxes, as it once was. When the U.S. Congress raised the capital gains tax rate up to the level of the ordinary income tax rate, it made investments less profitable. Investors responded by reducing the amount of money they were willing to spend on investments.

The other way tax laws affect investment is through changes in **depreciation allowances**. This allowance is a percentage of an investment that an investor can shield from taxation. The allowance represents the investor's loss of wealth each year due to wear and age of a property. In practice it means that the investor can shelter part of her/his income from taxation. What an investor gets to keep from an investment is what the accountants call **cash flow**. Cash flow equals the after-tax income *plus* the depreciation allowance. That is because the depreciation allowance is part of the investor's income, but it is the part on which she does not have to pay taxes.

When the government reduces depreciation allowances, usually by lowering the percentage of an investment that can be written off each year, it makes investment less profitable. That is because a smaller depreciation allowance makes more income taxable and that, in turn, reduces after-tax profits. When investment is less profitable, investors will usually decrease their spending on new property.

ZOLTAN COLLECTS SPACE: Zoltan recognized that people in urban and suburban communities often need more private storage space than their apartments or houses provide. He has purchased properties on which he has constructed garage-type buildings that are divided into locked compartments. People rent compartments for storing their possessions. Each building costs Zoltan an average of $40,000 to construct, plus the land, and provides annual rental income of $6,000 when all compartments are rented. For the past ten years, under the old law, he was allowed to deduct one-twentieth of his investment from his taxable profits every year as a depreciation allowance. He was also charged a 28% marginal tax rate. This gave him a cash flow of about $4,520 per unit (11+% return on his investment), which was profitable enough to motivate him to construct four new buildings per year for a total investment of $160,000. Zoltan's accountant prepared Table 16C for you to see how his cash flow was calculated. Under the tax law passed this year the depreciation allowance was reduced to one-fortieth of his investment and his marginal tax rate became 39%. This decreased his yearly cash flow by 17% (during the depreciation period). The new tax law made the storage units less profitable, producing a return of only 9%, so Zoltan cut his annual investment to one new unit, spending only $40,000 per year.

You can see from this example that tax laws have a big impact on Zoltan's bottom line. His return on investment depends on his

Table 16C

Zoltan's Net Profit and Cash Flow from Each Storage Unit

TAX INFORMATION	OLD TAX LAW	NEW TAX LAW
Depreciation period (years)	20	40
Marginal income tax rate (percent)	28	39

INCOME AND EXPENSES PER UNIT	OLD LAW	NEW LAW
Yearly rental income received	$6,000	$6000
Less: depreciation allowance (untaxed income) on $40,000 unit	–2,000	–1,000
Less: expenses for upkeep	–500	–500
Equals: taxable income	3,500	4,500
Less: income tax paid	–980	–1,755
Equals: after-tax income	2,520	2,745
Plus: depreciation allowance	+2,000	+1,000
Equals: cash flow	4,520	3,745

Note to reader: The calculations in Table 16C are simplified and are not based on actual current accounting rules and tax laws.

depreciation allowance. When the tax law changed, by reducing his depreciation allowance, he invested less money. An increase in the tax rate would also have reduced his incentive to invest.

The U.S. federal Tax Reform Act of 1986 decreased depreciation allowances on structures (buildings) used by businesses. This reduced the demand for structures and may have contributed to a depression of commercial real estate values in the late 1980s. (Shortly thereafter the maximum marginal income tax rate was increased.) Lower real estate prices certainly did not lessen the savings and loan crisis of the late 1980s since many S&L's had mortgages on business properties; in some cases S&L's had to foreclose and take over properties whose values became less than the mortgage loans made on them.

In general, *less investment takes place when income tax rates go up or when depreciation allowances go down.*

What about investment tax credits?

Occasionally, during recessions, government calls on an old and generally effective device to stimulate investment, the **investment tax credit**. Like manufacturers' rebates, investment tax credits are offered for only a limited period of time; they provide a temporary stimulus to the economy.

Here is how tax credits work. Investors in new plant and equipment are permitted to use a specific percentage of new investment spending toward their tax liability in the year when the investment is made. The tax credit reduces the cost of capital and, therefore, makes investment more attractive. The effect of the tax credit is often to accelerate investment spending.

> **WILLIAM UPGRADES:** William is a professor of statistics who works part-time as a consultant to local companies on quality control. He uses an old personal computer exclusively for his consulting, but he wishes to replace it with a new, more powerful model. When the government passed a 10% investment tax credit, to be in effect for one year, he felt it would be advantageous to replace his equipment during that year rather than to do so later. So when the 10% investment tax credit came into effect, he bought a new PC for $4,000. This permitted him to reduce his ordinary income tax bill by $400. His immediate investment helped the economy.

Tax credits are intended to get businesses to order new machinery and to build new plants. They have no effect on business investment in inventories.

Unlike depreciation allowances, which are permanent, tax credits are temporary catalysts for investment spending. If investment tax credits were permanent or enacted frequently, they would not be as effective. *A temporary investment tax credit will often stimulate investment.* Depending on the size of the tax credit, it could be more powerful, or less powerful, than an increase in the depreciation allowance.

Do interest rates affect investment decisions?

Businesses often borrow funds to finance investments in inventory, major equipment, and structures. Interest is the most important cost of borrowing. *When interest rates go up,* borrowing for investment is more costly, and less profitable, so the *demand for investment goes down.* Lower interest rates increase investment demand. They are one component of the cost of capital.

Aside from tax law changes, how can government stimulate investment?

We have seen how government affects investment decisions by changing tax laws. By lowering marginal income tax rates, increasing depreciation allowances, reducing the taxation of capital gains, or providing investment tax credits, government can encourage businesses to invest in capital stock, structures, and inventory.

But government can do more. Most large investments by business are made with borrowed money. That makes interest rates important because low interest rates encourage borrowing and investment. Consequently, government monetary policies that reduce interest rates may stimulate investment spending (☞ Art. 18: The Federal Reserve, page 235). Recall that a nation's investment consists of building new assets by both businesses and individuals.

What determines investment in residential construction?

Residential construction is the creation of *new* houses or buildings where people will live. This type of investment spending does not take place when someone decides to buy a house that already exists.

The decision to invest in new housing is made either by individuals who want a new place to live or by landlords who want to go into the business of renting property where others will live. The amount of money people invest in new housing depends largely on three main factors. The first is income and wealth. Income and wealth give people the ability to buy new properties. If someone has a sufficiently high enough income to cover mortgage payments, or if she already has a house that can be sold for cash, she is more likely to build a new property than someone who does not have these advantages.

The second factor is the return people can get on nonhousing assets. If the interest rates on CDs, for example, are attractive, people will be less willing to tie up their money in a house.

CAROLYN STAYS PUT: Carolyn is a forty-year-old chemical engineer who holds a well-paying middle-management position. She is single, has no dependents, and currently rents a town house. Carolyn considered using $70,000 of her savings for a down payment on her own home. But when her bank offered her a juicy 8.5% return on a five-year CD, she decided to buy the CD and postpone building a new house, at least for another five years. If interest rates are much lower when her CD expires, she will have two incentives to build a house: the bank will no longer offer her an attractive CD rate and the cost of a mortgage loan will be low.

In general, residential investment is low when interest rates are high. As Carolyn's decision shows us, that is because mortgages would be costly and financial investments (as alternatives to housing investments) would be attractive. How powerful interest rates are in influencing investment decisions depends on a buyer's eagerness for owning her own home. If Carolyn had not been satisfied with her town house and felt that there were good opportunities for home building right now (building costs were low and available lots were attractive), she might not have been turned off by high mortgage loan rates.

A third factor is rents. Carolyn and other renters will be more inclined to build houses if they consider the rents they must pay to be high. Building one's own house is an alternative to renting.

People invest in new housing when their incomes or wealth rise, interest rates come down, and/or rents are high.

How do investors make the "invest or buy" decision?

The market for used assets is important. Smart investors look at existing assets before creating new ones. Housing construction decisions depend on what economists call existing **housing stock**, the current amount of houses potential builders can buy. People go to the trouble of building their own houses if they are not attracted by what is currently available.

Businesses that want to expand face the same choices. A business can grow by building a new plant (making a real investment) or by **mergers and acquisitions** (financial investment), abbreviated as M&A's.

From time to time businesses go through what seems like an M&A frenzy. The "robber barons" of the late nineteenth century were masters at it as they collected similar firms (generally, competitors) under a single management. A conglomerate-merger boom took place in the 1960s when it was fashionable for a large corporation to collect dissimilar businesses to create synergies. Another M&A boom took place in the 1980s using junk bonds and leveraged buyouts. Real productive assets (tangible wealth) are not created by M&A's, so they do not represent real investment. Businesses expand through M&A's only when the prices of existing assets are less than the cost of new ones.

The corporation will acquire existing assets only so long as the share price is under $15 (so all the shares would cost less than $150 million). Real investment (building new exploration capacity) would take place only if the shares were $15 or more. That is how stock prices influence real investment.

THE CORPORATION GOES SHOPPING: A petroleum refiner needs to expand its sources of crude oil. It can obtain its desired capacity by investing in a new oil-exploration division, which will cost about $150 million for surveys, wells, and production. Alternatively, it can obtain similar capacity by buying up the stock of an existing oil-exploration company that has 10 million shares outstanding at $12 per share. The acquisition would cost $120 million.

When companies expand by buying existing firms or equipment, they do not create new productive assets and no real investment takes place.

What is left out of official investment figures?

Official investment figures are available for the three categories of fixed business investment, inventories, and residential construction. These are tangible assets; you can see and touch them. However, there are three other categories that are also important. They are

- human capital
- research and development
- exploration

Human capital is discussed in another article (☞ Art. 8: Human Capital, page 88).

Many types of businesses must make expenditures on **research and development** (R&D). Without R&D we would have no new products or improvements in technology. Expenditures on R&D affect our nation's production, productivity, and income, although it may be hard to show exactly what the payoff from a particular R&D investment might be (and some do not pay off at all). Because successful R&D expenditures improve productivity, they are really investments.

Finally, there is money spent on **exploration** for natural resources. Petroleum, minerals, and other assets of the earth are essential for supporting much of our economic activity. Expenditures for exploration are investments because they enable economic activity to take place. For example, the more petroleum we find, the more our economy can support the production of goods and services that use oil.

Expenditures on human capital, research and development, and exploration are not included in our nation's investment figures. However, they produce benefits that are similar to those from investments in capital stock.

5

Money and Credit

For most of human history money was a rarity. Although coins were minted in biblical times, most commerce was handled through barter until after the Middle Ages. Money is useful only when it is widely accepted in exchange for goods and services. People put their wealth into money only if they have confidence in its value. That happens when money is backed by a strong government and when people trust the government, and their fellow citizens, not to counterfeit or to corrupt money.

As powerful and stable nation-states developed in Europe, their money played an expanding role in commerce. The earliest form of money was metal coins, often made of gold or silver, whose intrinsic value was evident to the user. (Of course, people who accepted coins had to be convinced of what they were made of. Gold and silver coins could be shaved or diluted with nonprecious metals. One can imagine the cashier in some medieval Kmart calling her supervisor to authorize acceptance of some out-of-town coins; she had to test and weigh the metal to be sure of its value.) This was money's childhood.

However, money grew into adolescence as an instrument of business when coins, which were bulky and difficult to protect, were replaced by bills issued by recognized banks or governments, at least for large transactions. This paper money was a convenience, but it was acceptable only if it could be converted into precious metal by bringing it into the bank or government agency that printed it. The development of trustworthy folding money was an important step in the growth of market economies.

Money reached early adulthood when coins and banknotes were replaced by checks drawn on bank accounts. Unlike bills and coins, checks are not money; they are, after all, only pieces of paper that anyone can write. What people spend are bank deposits, the wealth that they give to the bank for safekeeping. When you give a store a check in exchange for merchandise, you are transferring some of your wealth from your bank account to the store. The check gives the store the right to claim your money, and they want to be sure it is there. That is why some stores give me such a hard time when I try to pay by check. (I have had to produce identification tracing my origin to Adam and have even had my picture taken, probably to be added to some rogues' gallery if the check was not good.) The store wants the money in the bank that my check represents. Checking accounts require more trust than coins or folding money.

Now, in its middle age, money takes on yet more sophisticated forms. People hold their wealth in the form of certificates of deposit (CDs), government bonds, and other financial instruments. As money becomes more sophisticated, it becomes easier to use as a tool of finance.

Money is no longer a pile of coins; it is far more complex. The first article in this chapter, Article 17, will tell you about the most important forms of money that we use today. This article will explain why money is so important and how it does so much work in a market economy. How much money there is matters a lot. Therefore, this article explains, in simple terms, the complex process of creating money for the economy to use. You will learn how money is really "made." It takes more than a printing press.

Who are the players in creating money? Article 18 introduces you to the big and vitally important (and sometime mysterious) Federal

Reserve System, affectionately known as the Fed. It has a huge influence on the economy of the United States and on the economies in the rest of the world. If you really want the inside story of money, you have to know how the Fed operates and what makes it tick. This article is a little technical in spots, but it conveys the dynamics of the most important player in our financial system.

Article 19 introduces you to the financial markets. This is where money does its work. You will learn about the big players in financial markets and what they trade. The article describes the most important financial assets that are used in the market economy; these assets are imaginative ways of owning and using wealth. The article gives you a brief description of stocks, bonds, mutual funds, insurance, and more complex financial creations and tells you what they do for our economy.

Prices are vital to a market economy, and that is no less true in the world of finance. All of the important financial assets discussed in Article 19 have prices. Article 20 tells you why these prices are important and what makes them move up and down. This article is important to readers who are investors responsible for handling their own or others' wealth.

Now, get ready for a quick tour of the world of finance.

ARTICLE 17:

MONEY AND BANKING

How Money Is Really Made

Can an economy work without money?

One of the biggest problems facing emerging market economies, such as those of Eastern Europe and the former Soviet republics, is the lack of a stable and widely accepted money supply. However, market economies can work without money by using **barter**, the simple exchange of goods and services among residents of one country. The exchange of goods among nations (international barter) is called **countertrade**. Today countertrade represents a small but significant amount of global economic activity. Jamaican bauxite (the principal ore of aluminum) has been exchanged for cars, trucks, and food from the United States. Peru and Russia have exchanged oil for food and equipment; Russia has even exchanged its vodka for American soft drinks.

But barter and countertrade require traders to incur **search costs**. These costs are the time, lost production, and energy needed to find a coincidence of wants. If Russia wants farm equipment, for example, it must search for a trading partner who has exactly what it needs *and* who, at the same time, wants Russian oil. These deals are not easy to find. (Some people search for coincidence of wants in singles' bars.)

Because barter and countertrade limit trading opportunities, nations that do not use money for most of their trading have to produce a wider variety of the things they need. They lose the advantages of specialization.

Their need for self-sufficiency requires Madhu and his wife to devote considerable time and energy to tasks at which they are less productive, thus taking time from their carving and pottery making. If their local economy were fully monetized, they could devote nearly full time to what they do best. They could sell their carvings and pottery for cash, which would be used to purchase most of what they need.

While a market economy can exist without money, the use of money in trading allows an economy to be more productive.

What does money do?

Money is anything that can be used as a medium of exchange, as a means of storing wealth for future spending, and as a way of measuring the value of things.

As a **medium of exchange** money is readily acceptable in return for goods and services. You can use it to buy most anything you need. But if many sellers do not trust their nation's money, buyers will have a hard time making trades, and the vitality of a market economy does depend on trading.

As a **store of wealth**, money facilitates saving, which is important for economic growth. Many people may wish to postpone immediate consumption so they can accumulate purchasing power for a large purchase later or for investment.

How can the value of different things be compared? In a barter economy a pair of shoes has many prices: eighty loaves of bread, eleven audiotapes, seventy-five lightbulbs, two dental exams, four books, and so on. It becomes difficult to compare the value of an audiotape and a book, or a loaf of bread and a lightbulb, with such a system because every single item has many prices. But money is a common yardstick for valuing any one of these because it is a common **unit of account** that can be used for anything.

What do we use for money?

Our economy has invented and uses *several* things as money. The best-known money is **currency**, both paper and coins. Most currency is used as a medium of exchange because people carry currency primarily to spend it within a short time. However, a small part of our nation's currency is used by some people to store their wealth for future use. This currency might be kept in deposit boxes,

> **MADHU'S PLANTATION:** Madhu lives with his family on a tropical plantation. Because of the instability of the nation's government, few people use the local currency; a persistently high inflation rate causes its value to decline rapidly. Madhu has great skill as a wood-carver, and his wife has extraordinary talent in making decorative pottery. Since the plantation is a hundred miles from the nearest commercial center (a small city), and portions of the roads linking it to the center are unpaved, the couple must spend a large amount of their time growing most of the food the family eats, making much of their clothing, servicing their machinery, and providing home instruction for the children. Twice each year, when travel is practical, Madhu takes millet (his main crop) and some carvings and pottery into the city. Although their carvings and pottery are in demand, the couple have to confine their trading to dealers who can supply the shoes, tools, and other items the plantation cannot furnish.

in piggy banks, under mattresses, etc. Finally, currency can also be used to measure the value of things. Currency is used as money because it does the three things money can do.

But many of the things we buy, especially those with large price tags, are purchased by using a checking account. A check is only a printed piece of paper that we fill out; it is not money. When people use checks, they are receiving products in exchange for **checkable deposits**. It is the deposit that is money (medium of exchange), not the check paper. If you have ever gone through the hassle of showing a store clerk various forms of identification to make your check acceptable, you know that the seller is really interested in verifying the existence of sufficient deposits to support your check. Deposits are what makes a check "good," and you are really spending your deposits when you write a check.

Computer and communication technology is slowly changing the way checkable deposits are used. Many banks are issuing **debit cards** to replace paper checks. These look like credit cards, but when they are used for a purchase, money is immediately transferred out of the buyer's checking account and into the checking account of the seller. Debit cards are simply means for making it easier to use checking accounts and for speeding up the flow of funds into and out of these accounts. Besides, they save a lot of trees by cutting down on the use of paper.

Today there are many types of checkable deposits. They include the familiar checking accounts held in commercial banks, savings banks, and savings and loans. Other checkable deposits are share draft accounts in credit unions and checking privileges given by money-market mutual funds. And don't forget traveler's checks; technically, they are not deposits, but they are used as money.

Credit cards are often used, in place of checks or currency, to make purchases. But unlike currency and checkable deposits, they are not money. When you use credit cards, you are borrowing money from a bank by using that *bank's* checkable deposits; the charge slip you sign when making your purchase is essentially used as a check. Later you are expected to repay the bank by transferring some of your checkable deposits to the bank. Therefore, charge cards (which require quick repayment) and credit cards (which allow you to borrow money from the bank in return for paying it interest) are only alternative ways of drawing on checkable deposits, as are debit cards. They do not add to the nation's money supply, but they make the money supply work harder by giving more people access to checkable deposits.

The amount of money a nation has available is important and is carefully watched by economists. The total of currency and checkable deposits is called **M-1**, our primary measure of the **money supply**. *In its narrowest definition, the money supply consists of checkable deposits and currency that serve as mediums of exchange.*

Other things also serve as money, but they primarily perform the store-of-wealth function of money; they are places for "parking" wealth. These include noncheckable money-market funds and small savings deposits (certificates of deposit, CDs, under $100,000). There are also some arcane savings devices such as Eurodollar deposits (bank accounts held outside the U.S. but recorded in dollars rather than in the currency of the nation where they are kept) and repurchase agreements ("repos," in banking jargon). Repos are made when you loan money to a bank and get to hold on to government bonds, owned by the bank, as your security until the loan is repaid. (Repos are not insured bank deposits, as some sad investors in repos have learned when their banks failed.)

These parking places for wealth are important because most of this money will eventually be spent. These parts of the money supply are not as closely linked to spending as are the components of M-1, but they are worth watching. When they are added to M-1, economists have a broader indicator of money supply called **M-2**.

Table 17A gives you a recent picture of these two indicators of the money supply of the United States.[1]

There are still broader measures of the money supply that are watched by economists who specialize in monetary affairs. But M-1 and M-2 are the most widely used.

Table 17A

Components of the U.S. Money Supply, July 1994

Type of Money		Amount ($ billions)
M-1, a narrow measure of money supply, is made up of money people have available to spend now as mediums of exchange.	Currency in circulation	$340
	Checkable deposits	799
	Traveler's checks	8
	Money supply (M-1)	1,147
Add to this other types of money, being held (and earning interest) as stores of wealth, for possible spending later . . .	Money market funds	359
	Savings deposits	1,208
	Small time deposits	771
	Eurodollar deposits and repos	97
To get a broad measure of the nation's money supply.	**Money supply (M-2)**	3,582

Why can economists not settle on one measure of the money supply?

Indecision is not the reason we have more than one measure of money supply. Each measure of our money supply has a special significance.

For short-term forecasting, economists watch the narrowest definition of money supply, M-1. It is the amount of money available for spending right now. That is why any increase in M-1 is likely to have a fairly immediate impact on spending, and therefore on the nation's production and income.

For longer-term forecasting, M-2 may be helpful. If M-2 changes, but there is no change in M-1, some time is likely to pass before the change is felt by the economy. That is because changes in time deposits and savings accounts, which show up in M-2 but are not in M-1, often represent funds that are being stored awhile (and earning interest) before they are used for spending.

NEVILLE GETS PAID: Neville is an internationally known concert violinist whose annual income is substantial but whose paychecks arrive at irregular intervals. These paychecks come from concerts, recordings, and occasional lectures. This month he got a check for $15,000 for two solo appearances with a symphony orchestra in South America. He put $5,000 of this in his checking account in the U.S. and will use it for living expenses and to pay some credit card debts. He put the rest in a two-year CD issued by a savings and loan association located near his home in Philadelphia. The proceeds from this CD will be used later to pay his daughter's tuition bill when she starts attending college.

When Neville made his two deposits, M-1 of the United States (currency plus checkable deposits) went up by $5,000 and M-2 (M-1 plus savings and time deposits) went up by $15,000. The change in M-2 that did not affect M-1 was $10,000. An economist could confidently predict that spending will soon increase by $5,000 as Neville writes checks. Furthermore, there will be another round of spending after two years when he cashes in his CD.

It is easy to predict Neville's spending when you know as much as we do about his personal plans and needs. For the economy as a whole, prediction is trickier. We may see an increase in the nation's M-1, and we know that a substantial amount of this may be spent in the next few weeks, but we cannot predict exactly how much will be spent and when.

Economists use both M-1 and M-2 to give themselves clues about future spending in the economy.

Do changes in the nation's money supply affect credit?

We have already seen how changes in the money supply affect spending. But money supply also affects **credit**. *Additions to the nation's money supply can be used to provide credit.* When someone decides not to use all of her income for spending, she can use money for savings (store of wealth). As savings, money is idle and contributes nothing to the economy. But when savings are used to make loans to others (create credit), this idle money is freed to enable someone else to spend it; this creation of credit is what banks, S&L's, credit unions, etc., do with the savings they get. This spending leads quickly to the creation of new goods and services. *When money is used to create credit, a nation's output and income generally increase*, at least in the short run.

> **NEVILLE HELPS MICHELLE GET WHEELS:** Michelle applied to the same S&L that Neville uses and received a $12,000 loan to help her finance a new car. Neville's CD money was used to help give Michelle the credit she needed. With the $12,000 in hand, Michelle purchased her car. Right after selling her the vehicle, her car dealer ordered a new car from the factory to replenish his inventory.

Neville earned $15,000 in return for his work as a musician. He did not put all this money back into the economy by spending it himself. But by making two-thirds of it available to Michelle, Neville helped the economy to grow this year.

Do money and credit affect prices?

At any one time an economy has a limited stock of resources. There is just so much labor, machinery, equipment, and raw materials that can be used to produce what people want. When the demand for goods and services pushes against the economy's productive capacity, shortages occur and prices rise (☛ Art. 10: Price Changes, page 118).

Let's go back to Michelle and her new car. Suppose the auto plant was producing at full capacity so that car dealers could not quickly get new merchandise to replace sold vehicles. Car prices are likely to rise because demand exceeds supply. Neville's savings were used to create credit, but this credit increased demand for cars, which, in turn, led to higher prices. A general increase in prices is called **inflation**. *Using the nation's money supply to create credit might generate inflation* (☛ Art. 11: Inflation, page 128) *if the economy is producing at or near its capacity*. An increase in the supply of money may result in some mix of inflation and production.

Are interest rates affected by the money supply?

The **interest rate** is the "price" of credit; it is what people pay for using other people's share of the nation's money supply. As the price of credit, the interest rate (☛ Art. 13: Interest Rates, page 153) is determined by the demand and supply of credit. If the money supply grows, it is quite likely that more credit can be supplied to borrowers and interest rates will go down. Often interest rates will decline when M-1 or M-2 grows at a high rate.

The economic significance of interest rates is that low rates encourage borrowing. People, businesses, and governments do not borrow money just to look at it; they borrow money to spend it. This spending stimulates the economy.

As money supply goes up, it is likely that the supply of credit will increase and *that the interest rate (the cost of credit) will go down. Both events will stimulate demand for goods and services.*

What do banking firms have to do with our nation's money supply?

There are two types of people, firms, and governments in an economy: savers and borrowers. Banking is a simple business. A banking firm "collects" deposits from customers who are savers and lends this money to customers who are borrowers. Banking firms are important players in our financial markets (☛ Art. 19: Financial

Markets, page 252). The banking firm is a middleman (no gender bias implied here) who pays a certain interest rate to savers for the use of their money. At the same time, it charges a (usually) higher interest rate to borrowers and pockets the difference for its troubles (see "Neville Helps Michelle Get Wheels"). In doing this, *the banking firm uses savers' deposits to create credit.*

Today several types of banking firms conduct this important transformation. They include commercial banks, savings and loans, savings banks, and credit unions.

How does the nation's money supply grow?

Remember, the basic money supply of the nation, M-1, has two principal parts: currency in circulation and checkable deposits in banking firms. The sum of checkable deposits is the biggest of these parts. M-1 "grows" when banking firms receive new checkable deposits.

Banking firms are not free to lend all of the deposits they receive. A minimum percentage of the money they get for new deposits must be put aside as **required bank reserves**. These reserves must be available so that the firm always has some funds to pay withdrawals if any of their depositors demand them. Since 1980, banking firms in the United States have been required to hold reserves of at least 10% of their checkable deposits.

PAUL'S DEPOSIT FEEDS THE MONEY SUPPLY: Paul just got a gift of $1,000 in U.S. money from his Aunt Jolie in Liberia. (Liberia is a small West African nation that uses American money in its local economy.) Paul put the money in a checking account in a bank in Kentucky. The bank put aside 10% of this money to meet its required reserves obligation and loaned out the remaining $900 to Mark, who borrowed it to buy a large-screen TV. A TV dealership deposited the $900 it received from Mark in its checking account in a savings and loan.

As soon as Aunt Jolie's currency entered the United States, the American money supply (M-1) went up by $1,000. Then Paul transformed it into a checkable deposit. This deposit reduced the currency part of the money supply and increased the deposits part, so the money supply did not change. This is shown in the first two rows of Table 17B.

But Paul's deposit did not sit idle for long. After putting 10% aside as bank reserves, Paul's bank put most of it into action as a loan, which soon became another checkable deposit. At this point the nation's money supply had grown by $1,900: Paul's $1,000 deposit plus the TV dealership's $900 deposit. *The money supply grows each time a new checkable deposit is created.* Aunt Jolie's money is doing double duty, as you can see on the next line of Table 17B. It supports two checkable deposit accounts, each of which is part of M-1, our basic money supply.

PAUL'S MONEY . . . THE NEXT GENERATION: The savings and loan that received $900 from the TV dealership put some of it aside as a reserve. The rest did not sit idle. It loaned $810 to Trudi, who used it to pay for some dental work. Trudi's dentist put $810 into his credit union share draft account. (Share draft accounts are checkable.)

With the dentist's deposit, the money that came from Aunt Julie caused the U.S. money supply to grow by another $810, giving us a total of $2,710 at this point. And the money growth still does not stop. The credit union loaned part of the dentist's deposit to a student for college expenses; this resulted in a deposit in the college's bank. Later this money was used to make a vacation loan to pay a travel agency, a consumer loan used to buy jewelry, a bank overdraft loan used to pay a bill owed to a 900-number telephone service, and other loans of decreasing size. This activity is summarized in Table 17B.

If the bank, savings and loan, or other banking firm loans 90% of every deposit it receives, Aunt Jolie's $1,000 gift could expand the nation's money supply by a whopping $10,000. All of this new money would come from checkable deposits.

Table 17B

Expansion of the Money Supply

ACTIVITY	MONEY SUPPLY
Aunt Jolie sends money to U.S.: this raises U.S. money supply by . . .	$1,000
Paul deposits $1,000 in bank: money supply is still up by . . .	1,000
TV dealership deposits $900: money supply is now up by . . .	1,900
Dentist deposits $810: money supply has now grown by . . .	2,710
College deposits $729: money supply is now up by . . .	3,439
Travel agency deposits $656: money supply is now up by . . .	4,095
Jewelry store deposits $590: this brings the increase up to . . .	4,685
Telephone service deposits $531 . . .	5,216
Subsequent deposits. . . .	—
Maximum new money supply:	10,000

What determines how much the money supply will grow when someone makes a new deposit?

The bottom line of Table 17B shows you the *maximum* impact Aunt Jolie's $1,000 gift can have on the money supply in the U.S. But it is doubtful the gift would have increased M-1 by anywhere near $10,000. Too many roadblocks are likely to get in the way.

The behavior of banking firms is important. If Paul's bank had loan applications from persons it regards as risky borrowers, if it believed the economy was weak, or if it believed that better investments would come along later, the bank might have loaned out only $400 of Paul's deposit, even though it could have loaned as much as $900. In this situation the bank would have created **excess bank reserves** of $500. That is, it would have decided to keep $600 idle rather than the $100 it was required to hold back. You can see that this action would have made every subsequent line in Table 17B smaller, and the money supply would have grown far less than $10,000. *The growth of the money supply is slowed if banking firms decide to hold excess reserves.*

The behavior of depositors also counts. Suppose Paul decided not to put all of his $1,000 gift into a financial institution in the U.S. He might have kept some of it in currency or deposited some of it overseas. In either situation his bank would have had less money to lend and the expansion of deposits (the major component of money supply) would have been smaller. *When members of the public reduce the amount of their money placed in deposit accounts, potential growth of the money supply is reduced.* That is how you and I play a role in money creation. The less of our money we put into banking firms, the less ability these banking firms will have to expand the money supply.

Anyone who received any part of Paul's money could have slowed money growth. The TV dealership, the dentist, the telephone service, etc., could have decided to hold some of this money outside of banking firms. Money growth would also have slowed if any of the banking firms in the process increased their excess reserves.

Based on actual behavior of the public and of lenders in the United States over the past several years, we might expect Aunt Jolie's $1,000 gift to have expanded the money supply by between $2,500 and $3,000.

Is the money supply stable?

With so many people and firms able to influence the size of our nation's money supply, what is preventing money from getting out of control? This is an important matter because our money supply has such a powerful influence on our economy.

Happily, there are restraints to the creation of new money. First, any growth of the money supply must be based on additions or withdrawals of currency from the nation. The money growth traced in Table 17B started from an infusion of currency from outside the economy: Aunt Jolie's $1,000. Since *all American paper currency must first be created by a Federal Reserve Bank*, the "seeds" of money growth are in carefully controlled, limited supply. (Coins, which are a small part of currency, are minted by the U.S. Treasury). Even Aunt Jolie's money, although it arrived from Liberia, had to originate from a Federal Reserve Bank in the United States. By and large, the folks at Federal Reserve Banks are very responsible people.

Second, *no individual banking firm can create its own money*. When Paul put $1,000 of currency in his bank, the bank could loan no more than $900 to its customers. The bank could not simply give a loan customer a check for, say, $1,700, because it did not have enough currency to cover it. But the banking system can create money by passing deposits from one banking firm to another. The discipline in the banking system is that a banking firm must hold currency before it can make a loan; no bank can create a deposit unless the deposit can be made in cash, or by check that can be turned into cash. As a practical matter, most deposits are made by check. But a bank will accept a check only if it can be turned into currency. Also as a practical matter, banking firms make loans by check. But any borrower should be able to turn that check into currency by taking it to a teller's window. There is a special place in hell (and in jail) for a banker who cannot cash his or her own check.

Third, every time a currency deposit is made, a portion of that deposit is withdrawn from the public and put aside as bank reserves. This means that currency cannot wander from deposit to deposit indefinitely because with each deposit some of the currency is chipped away (put out of circulation as reserves). Eventually nothing is left with which to make new deposits. *There is a limit to the amount of deposits the banking system can create from new currency.* You can see this erosion as you move down Table 17B.

Does all growth of the nation's money supply start from currency?

Although money supply, as measured by M-1, consists of both currency and checkable deposits, these two parts play different roles. Currency is **high-powered money** because it can be used to create new deposits when it is taken out of circulation and placed in a checkable account in a banking firm that then uses it to make loans. These new loans are then spent and eventually become additional deposits when that money finds its way into other checking accounts.

Checking account deposits can lead to new deposits only because banking firms keep currency moving. Paul intended to let his $1,000 sit for a while, but his bank did not let that happen. As long as Paul was not using it, the bank loaned some of it to someone who would. But the bank could not lend out more than the currency it had. Paul's $1,000 in currency continued to create new deposits only while his currency lasted.

It would be awkward if all new deposits and bank loans had to be made with currency (although it would be great for the armored car business). Here is how the system gets around the need to do all of its business with paper money and coins.

All commercial banks must have an account with one of the nation's twelve Federal Reserve Banks. These special banks are "bankers' banks" and are part of the Federal Reserve System (☛ Art. 18: The Federal Reserve, page 235). Commercial banks' accounts at Federal Reserve Banks exist as a place for commercial banks to hold their required and excess bank reserves. They are like checking accounts (that pay no interest) except that banks must maintain a minimum balance in these accounts equal to their required reserves (generally 10% of their checkable deposits).

These accounts can be used by banks as checking accounts to shift funds from one commercial bank to another, or between commercial banks and the Federal Reserve Banks, in place of hauling around cash. The balances commercial banks have in these special accounts are merely computerized bookkeeping entries made by the Fed Banks. Commercial banks can use these balances as though they were currency to back up their own checks.

These balances that commercial banks have in Federal Reserve Banks can be used like currency because the Fed stands ready to back them up with currency; the Fed has the printing press and can turn any of the computerized entries into currency as needed.

A Federal Reserve Bank can create high-powered money by printing, and spending, its own currency or simply by making a computerized deposit to a commercial bank's reserve account. *Banks can only lend out currency, or Fed deposits that can be turned into currency.* Banks cannot create their own money. If a bank lends out money in the form of a bank check, rather than in the form of currency, that check must be backed either by currency in the bank's possession or by a deposit that bank has with a Federal Reserve Bank. A $1,000 Fed Bank reserve account deposit does the same job as Aunt Jolie's U.S. currency from Liberia. Only a Federal Reserve Bank has the legal authority to create high-powered money (currency) by printing new currency or by making a computerized deposit. (A jail cell awaits any adventurous printshop operator or computer hacker who tries to do the same thing.)

The growth of the nation's money supply is limited by the amount of currency in existence and by the Federal Reserve Bank deposits that the Fed has created. They are the only "seeds" that can be used to create money; their limited supply keeps money scarce enough to be valuable.

ARTICLE 18:

THE
FEDERAL
RESERVE

The Leviathan of Finance

Reading Suggestion: Please read or skim the preceding article before you read this one.

What are the jobs of a central bank?

Money is a critical resource in a market economy. That is because the supply of money has a heavy influence on economic conditions. Interest rates, inflation, and economic growth all depend on the money supply. The money supply is too important to be left in the hands of private interests. That is why most nations create a **central bank** to take responsibility for it.

The first job of a central bank is to conduct **monetary policy**. Monetary policy consists of deliberate actions of a central bank that are intended to influence the condition of an economy. For example, during a recession a central bank may wish to reduce interest rates to stimulate economic growth and recovery. The major tool of monetary policy is regulation of the amount of money (the money supply) in the economy.

The second job is to stand ready to help the nation's banks to operate smoothly. If a bank gets into trouble by running short of money, the central bank should stand ready to provide emergency relief (loans), not to protect the bank's owners, but to protect depositors and to preserve the soundness of the banking system.

To support this second job, the central bank often has responsibility for regulating and supervising privately owned banks that hold depositors' money. That means the central bank makes rules about what private banks can, and cannot, do with that money. Furthermore, the central bank is the watchdog that sees these rules are followed.

Beyond these important duties the central bank is typically the government's bank. A nation's government is a big business, and the central bank is where it does its banking.

A nation's central bank also plays important roles in international money markets. It generally handles financial transactions between its government and other governments and is often engaged in maintaining the status of its nation's money in world markets.

Because *a central bank regulates a nation's money supply and helps to maintain a sound banking system*, it has a powerful impact on the economy. Despite its importance, a central bank usually works in the background; it rarely grabs headlines. Like the oil in a car engine, you may not think about it unless it fails to do its job well.

Does the United States have a central bank?

*In the United States the role of central banker is played by the **Federal Reserve System**,* which the business community refers to as **the Fed**. Actually, the central bank of the United States is an organization of twelve banks headed by a Board of Governors. The twelve **Federal Reserve Banks** are located in Boston, New York, Philadelphia, Cleveland, Richmond, Atlanta, St. Louis, Chicago, Minneapolis, Kansas City (Mo.), Dallas, and San Francisco.

The Board of Governors is headquartered in a grand marble building in Washington. The Board has two important jobs. The Board coordinates the activities of the Federal Reserve Banks and participates in designing and implementing monetary policy.

At the base of the system are a few thousand privately owned commercial **member banks**. These banks own stock in their regional Federal Reserve Bank, although this is largely a symbolic investment. At one time a commercial bank that was a system member had special privileges and responsibilities. Since 1980 most of these privileges and obligations have been extended to all commercial banks, so membership in the Fed is no longer an important issue.

Why was the Fed needed to regulate the money supply?

The Fed was created by an act of the U.S. Congress in 1913. Before that, any nationally chartered bank (that is, commercial banks that had a federal license to operate) had limited rights to print money and to add to the nation's money supply. In other words, individual banks collectively determined our nation's money supply.

This led to some serious economic problems. During boom times, when a bank had the chance to make a lot of profitable loans to its customers, banks created money willingly. This generous lending may have been good for the bank, but it was often bad for the economy. Here is the reason. When many banks increased their lending, borrowers often were given the money to increase their spending faster than the nation could increase the amount of goods and services people could buy with their bank-supplied money. The result was that there were spot shortages throughout the economy, prices rose sharply, and this sudden inflation devalued the money people had.

JEREMY'S COUNTRY BANK: Jeremy owned and operated the only bank in a small agricultural community in the late nineteenth century. Legally, his bank could print and lend money only up to the amount of gold and silver it had on deposit. However, sometimes Jeremy got carried away and, in response to his customers' demands for loans, printed up more money than he should have. (After all, in his remote location, bank examiners rarely came around.) Once he did this when grain prices were high because local farmers borrowed heavily to plant larger crops. It was common for prices of all things to rise sharply during these times as the farmers freely spent the money they had borrowed. Jeremy was a popular guy in those heady days. But soon inflation became a real problem.

On the other hand, during tough times banks often refused to create more money and even reduced the money supply by refusing to renew loans. Their stinginess resulted in **credit crunches**, shortages of credit due to bankers' unwillingness to lend, and the crunches made the economy worse because businesses often could not get loans when they needed them most. While the banks were operating in their own best interests (they did not want to print money and lend it to businesses that might not be able to repay them), they were unintentionally hurting the economy.

JEREMY TAKES A TUMBLE: Eventually the farmers in Jeremy's part of the country expanded their grain fields too much. The resulting oversupply of grain sent farm prices crashing and many farmers failed. Then the bank could not get back all the money it had loaned to its customers. The bank's losses meant its depositors could not get all their money out of the bank when they needed it. (Insured bank deposits did not exist in those days. If a bank lost lots of money, its innocent depositors were left holding the bag.) The area's economy took a dive. To make things worse, the bank had no money to lend to those farmers who needed new loans to tide them over to better times. Worse still, there was no money from the bank to finance the planting of the next crop. Hard times followed and Jeremy was thrown out of the country club.

Most of the discussions in this book explain the benefits of free markets where private businesses are allowed to make important decisions about production. But it is too risky to leave money supply to the discretion of a large group of independent businesses (the banks and their customers). *If left solely to the decisions of profit-seeking banks, the nation's money supply could rise and fall in a way that would damage the economy.*

What do the twelve Federal Reserve Banks do for the economy?

To see how the Fed does its critical work of regulating the money supply and supervising the banking system, we must understand what the Federal Reserve Banks do. Each Fed Bank serves commercial banks in its district. For example, the Federal Reserve Bank of Boston serves District 1, which includes the New England states. Hawaii and Alaska are part of District 12 and use the Fed Bank of San Francisco.

The Fed requires all banking firms that hold deposits to keep bank reserves. This is uninvested money that the bank must keep available to meet any depositor's demand for withdrawals. By holding these reserves, banks are less likely to run out of funds. Reserves give banks **liquidity**; that means they have the ability to come up with cash as it is needed.

Every commercial bank must have a reserve account with its regional Federal Reserve Bank (which explains why they are called Federal Reserve Banks). This account can be used to hold reserves, although banks can also hold reserves on their own premises in the form of what is called **vault cash** (literally, the cash in the bank's vault).

Besides holding banks' reserves, the regional Feds can loan funds to banks. These advances are called **discount loans**. When a bank goes to its regional Fed Bank for a loan, it receives an electronic transfer of funds to that bank's reserve account. The commercial bank could then withdraw or transfer these funds at its discretion. Of course, banks have to pay the Fed Banks interest for these loans; the interest rate charged is called the **discount rate**.

The critical functions of the regional Federal Reserve Banks are to hold bank reserves and to make discount loans. These functions give the banking system the liquidity it needs.

They also perform a number of "housekeeping" services for banks such as providing shipments of paper money and coins, and arranging transfers of funds between banks here and abroad. Commercial banks' reserve accounts at the Fed Banks are also quite handy for clearing checks written by bank depositors. (Take a look at the back of a canceled check you wrote that was cashed by a firm or person in another part of the United States. The stampings may show what Fed Banks were involved in passing your funds on.) In addition, regional Fed Banks print the money you use. (Look at the stamp on the left side of a bill to see which Fed Bank printed the cash you have.)

Besides all this, regional Fed Banks supervise the operations of commercial banks in their districts. They periodically or sporadically send out teams of examiners to look over banks' books. The fear of a "surprise audit" is often enough to keep a banker on the straight and narrow path. Fed Banks have the authority to immediately close or impose other penalties on banks that do not conform to regulations.

How do Federal Reserve Banks increase or decrease the nation's money supply?

If the Fed wants to increase economic activity, it can always print currency and spread it around. A packet of newly printed $50 bills could be dropped out of an airplane, but this method of adding money to the economy would be controversial (people who are upwind would cry foul) and inefficient (some bills may be lost). The method the Fed actually uses was discovered by accident.

During its early years the Fed's major job was to take care of commercial bank reserves. Being a creation of the U.S. Congress, its patriotic instincts led it to invest these idle bank reserves in U.S. Treasury securities (mostly short-term Treasury bills). This had two benefits: it helped the government to finance its debt and earned interest on bank reserves. Some bright Fed official then realized that when the Fed bought government securities, it was pumping money into the economy. Since then, *the Fed purchases government securities whenever it wants to add to the nation's money supply.* Further, it gave the Fed an important new job. The Fed was no longer just a keeper of bank reserves and a lender of last resort for banks in trouble; the Fed became a maker of monetary policy as it deliberately regulated the size of the nation's money supply to influence conditions of the economy.

This process also works in reverse. Whenever the Fed sells government securities, it draws money out of the economy, which shrinks the money supply. That is because the Fed takes the money out of the economy that people pay it for these securities. So *the Fed sells government securities whenever it wants to reduce the nation's money supply.*

The activity of buying and selling government bonds, notes, and bills (types of government debt) is called **open market operations**. Policy decisions about buying and selling U.S. government securities are made by the **Federal Open Market Committee (FOMC)**.

Are there advantages to open market operations?

Open market operations are conducted almost daily by the Fed. This method of adding to, or subtracting from, the money supply is immediate and flexible. *The Fed can fine-tune the money supply by selecting the size of the adjustment it wants to make to the money supply (the amount of buying or selling it does) and its timing down to the day.* There is little wonder that the Fed uses open market operations as its primary instrument for conducting monetary policy.

What types of monetary policy does the Fed use?

The FOMC, as the Fed's policy-making body, will, from time to time, set **monetary policy goals** for itself. These goals are specific changes the Fed wants to make in the economic environment. For example, the FOMC may decide that the nation's inflation rate is too high. Therefore, it sets a goal of reducing the inflation rate from, say, 4% to a moderate 3–3.5% range. Its prescription for reaching this goal would be to reduce the rate of growth of the money supply. In the arcane lingo of "Fed-speak," this is called **monetary tightening**, which means selectively selling U.S. government securities so as to decrease bank reserves and money supply.

BRYAN HELPS THE FED: The FOMC is concerned about high inflation and decides to sell U.S. Treasury bills, which it had earlier purchased with reserves that were deposited by commercial banks. Investors like Bryan, who runs a company's pension fund, are not attracted by the bills' current yield of 6.5%. So the Fed gradually drops its asking price for the securities until the bills yield 7.2%; at this rate Bryan thinks it is a good deal and he buys the bills from the Fed.

U.S. Treasury bills have a maturity of up to one year and are sold in denominations of $10,000. To yield 6.5%, a one-year T-bill would have a price of $9,390. (Bryan would have bought it at that price and sold it back to the government for $10,000 when it matured, to give himself a profit of 6.5%.) But to yield 7.2%, and to get Bryan's money, the Fed has to lower the price to $9,330.

Bryan pays for the securities with a check for $38 million drawn on the Hill Bank, where Bryan's pension fund keeps its cash. The Fed collects on the check by taking $38 million from Hill Bank's Federal Reserve account.

Once the Fed drains these bank reserves from the economy, they are no longer available for private use. It is as though the Fed burned the money in a furnace. Bryan unwittingly helped the Fed to reach its monetary goal in two ways. First, he willingly gave it $38 million to buy the securities, not realizing that the Fed would take this out of the money supply. (In fact, if Bryan dealt through a broker, he probably never knew who sold him the investment.)

Second, Bryan helped the nation's interest rates to rise. The yield (interest rate) of a bond or treasury bill is inversely related to its price. When the price went down, to induce Bryan to buy the investment, the interest rate rose.

When interest rates rise, fewer people borrow money (and spend it), and this helps to dampen inflationary pressure. So the Fed used Bryan and other investors to deliver two punches against inflation: a lower money supply and a higher interest rate.

Suppose the Fed adopted a monetary policy goal of stimulating faster economic growth. In the Fed's lingo this goal would be called **monetary easing** and would require it to go out into the financial markets and buy government securities from investors; that is, it would conduct an open market operation. Its buying power would force security prices up, which would have the effect of lowering interest rates and also adding funds to the nation's money supply.

The Fed uses open market operations to reach its monetary policy goals.

How do people help to determine the money supply?

The nation's money supply (according to the narrow M-1 definition) consists of currency in circulation (cash in the hands of the public) plus checkable deposits. This is what people have available for spending.

How much of their wealth people keep in cash or checkable

deposits is a matter of choice. Often when people's trust in financial institutions is shaken, or for other reasons, they will decide to keep more wealth outside of the basic money supply.

A NEW SAVINGS PLAN: Christine and Beryl generally deposited their combined monthly take-home income of $3,100 in their bank. Their account had an average balance of $1,500. Recently they started planning for retirement and decided to put $300 in U.S. savings bonds each month. This reduced their average checking account balance to $1,200. Their decision also reduced the M-1 measure of the nation's money supply.

Christine and her brother Beryl showed you how individuals can affect the size of the money supply by shifting their wealth from one form to another. (Savings bonds are included in the broadest measure of money supply, called L, but L is far removed from spendable money.)

Whenever individuals make decisions about cash holdings, they influence the composition of the money supply (currency vs. deposits), even if they do not change it. The Fed cannot tell people how much cash to carry around, even though it has the power to print it.

A MATTER OF TRUST: Irwin likes the feel of cash; holding his money gives him a sense of its value and the security of controlling his property. Besides, his grandfather, who was a wealthy man, lost most of his money in an uninsured bank that failed in the Orient. This memory made Irwin shy away from heavy reliance on bank accounts. (He kept only a small checking account for use in his plumbing business.) Irwin often had $6,000 or more on his person and was known to hide cash. (He designed some clever hiding places in plumbing fixtures that no one ever disturbed.) When his customers paid him by check, he would cash it and keep most of the money outside banks. The result was that he reduced the nation's checkable deposits and increased currency in circulation.

Irwin's personal decisions influenced the composition of the money supply by reducing checkable deposits and increasing currency in circulation. *Members of the public make personal decisions that influence the size and composition of the money supply.*

How do banks influence the nation's money supply?

Banking firms also make decisions that affect the money supply. A banker may hold or lend any money deposited in a checkable account. If money is deposited in a checkable deposit and the banker who takes care of the money lends most of it to someone else, a round of spending will take place that could lead to another deposit. If the banker holds on to it, no new checkable deposits will take place. By holding on to the money, bankers are increasing bank reserves. Any increase in bank reserves (which are idle funds) reduces the potential money supply. *Bankers make decisions, in their own interest, that can enlarge or reduce the nation's money supply.*

Can the Fed put money into the economy even when private bankers are reluctant to make loans?

If you look in your wallet, you will notice that U.S. paper money you have, regardless of denomination, consists of **Federal Reserve notes**. (Coins are supplied by the U.S. Treasury Department, which does not run the Fed. But a lot more money is in bills than in coins.) Only the Fed has the legal right to print paper money in the United States. As we saw above, the Fed can use newly printed money, or more commonly computer transfers of money to banks, to purchase government securities. These open market operations inject funds into the economy through banks.

The Fed, as an independent government agency, can influence bankers to expand or to contract the money supply in accordance with the needs of the economy. It can often move them to do what they would not otherwise be inclined to do. If the economy is growing too rapidly, so that inflation becomes a real threat, the Fed can restrict the growth of the money supply. This slows the growth of bank deposits. When banks have less money to lend, credit creation and spending slows down. The bad news is that when banks become "mean" by refusing credit to some of their customers, many people will be disappointed at not being able to make the purchases they want. The good news is that less credit buying reduces upward pressure on prices in the economy.

On the other hand, during tough times the Fed can expand the money supply, thereby feeding more money into banks. Banks may be reluctant to make loans, but if deposits pile up with new Fed money, banks are likely to expand the amount of credit they give. After all, bankers have to pay interest on these deposits; deposits that just sit idle in the bank do not earn revenues that the bank can use to pay this interest. Of course, once banks decide they need to lend more ("move the money out"), they have to find people who want to borrow. Often this can be done by increased advertising and/or lower loan interest rates; sometimes banks have to run "loan sales."

SKIP'S BANK HELPS OUT: Skip is Jeremy's great-grandson and runs the same bank Jeremy owned over a hundred years ago. Since the regional and national economy are weak and his bank is afraid of losing money to insolvent borrowers, it has turned away many applicants for loans. This has hurt businesses in the bank's community. But the Fed has just begun expanding the money supply, and as a result, Skip's bank has received $50 million in new deposits on which it must pay interest. Under pressure from its directors and shareholders to raise the bank's revenues to cover these interest obligations, Skip gingerly expands lending. The bank does not have a shortage of loan applications. But its need for profits makes the bank willing to take more risks in lending. Some loans are given to people who would have been turned away at other times. These loans help local businesses to recover and to prosper. That is just what the Fed wanted!

Does the Fed really *control* the money supply of the United States?

We see that the public and private bankers have important roles to play in determining the money supply. What this means is that *the Fed can* influence *the money supply, but it cannot* control *the money supply.*

The actions of individuals and bankers can sometimes weaken the monetary policy that the Fed is trying to implement. Here is an example. Suppose the Fed's policy is to tighten bank reserves so as to reduce the nation's inflation rate. To carry out its policy, the Fed would most likely sell treasury securities in its open market operations. This would take money out of the economy. The banks would have less to lend, there would be less borrowing, and people would have less to spend. That would help to reduce inflation.

Here is the fly in the ointment. Now, let us assume that at the same time, members of the public decide to increase their checkable deposits by taking more cash out of wallets and cookie jars and putting it into banks, and that bankers decide to expand their loans. When banks lend more, the money supply goes up. This lending would tend to accelerate growth of the money supply just as the Fed is trying to reduce growth.

If the bankers went along with the Fed and reduced their lending, then they would be strengthening the Fed's actions, not weakening them.

Decisions of members of the public, and of bankers, can increase, or weaken, the Fed's effect on the money supply.

How does the Fed keep the banking system healthy?

Since banks have to pay interest to most of their depositors, pay salaries, and meet other expenses of the banking business, they need income. This income comes primarily from investing their depositors' funds. That means they have to tie up a large amount of money in loans, mortgages, bonds, and other investments. Suppose some of the depositors want their money back?

While banks have to invest depositors' money, sometimes they do a bad job of it. Banks do not trumpet their losses, but the fact is that some people do not pay back their loans. What happens when the bank loses some of its depositors' money?

In either of these cases a bank may be short of cash if some depositors ask for quick withdrawals. In the days before the Fed, this often was quite a problem. Banks had to sell off some assets quickly, at fire sale prices, to raise cash for these demanding depositors; this often meant the banks suffered losses and their selling drove down prices.

SUZETTE TURNS TO THE FED: The Hill Bank held $300 million of deposits of residents in its service area, where it was the dominant bank. It invested $270 million of this in credit card and personal loans, mortgages, and bonds, holding back a cash reserve of $30 million. This was usually more than adequate to provide for cash withdrawals by customers. But an earthquake in the area caused a massive run on the bank; depositors suddenly demanded withdrawals of $90 million to travel out of the area or to repair damages. Suzette, the bank's president and CEO, arranged for the bank to borrow $70 million from the Fed to meet depositors' needs for cash and to allow only $10 million in operating funds to remain in the bank. The Fed delivered the funds immediately.

Banking firms rarely hold much cash. On most days the amount of withdrawals demanded by their customers is more or less offset by the amount of deposits coming in. Suzette's situation was unusual. But banking firms can turn to the Fed at times such as this.

The Fed serves as an emergency provider of funds to banks so they can maintain their **liquidity**; this is the ability of the bank to provide cash for customers. Without this liquidity depositors' trust in the banking system would be shaken and banks' inability to pay depositors their money would create serious disruptions to commerce.

Does the Fed's lending authority really help the economy?

The Fed's lending authority may seem insignificant since, in practice, the amount of lending done by the Fed is small. But when these loans are made, they can be critical. The Fed is a kind of financial 911 number for banks in trouble. Suzette's bank would have suffered a huge setback if it had been unable to meet its customers needs for withdrawals. Its inability to honor its own customers' checks would have shaken confidence in it and in the banking system.

Sometimes the Fed's role as lender has dramatic nationwide implications. On October 19, 1987 ("Black Monday"), the U.S. stock market suffered its worst one-day decline in history, with a wipeout of about 25% of the value of stocks.[2] An immediate problem was that a large amount of stock was used as security to back up loans made to some businesses, individuals, and stockbrokers (for people who buy stocks on margin). As the value of this collateral declined, economists feared that lenders would be forced to sell much of it to prevent further losses, starting an avalanche of stock and bond selling that would lead to a huge financial collapse. What is more, a large number of people and companies have pension funds invested in stocks. Seeing the value of these funds drop so rapidly might scare many of them to dump their holdings on the market, which would add to a downward spiral of prices. Finally, a declining stock market would make it difficult for businesses to sell new stock to finance investments in new production facilities. This sharp decline in stock values could create serious damage to the economy.

Early in the day after the crash the Fed pledged to provide emergency discount loans to bank lenders if they would not dump stock collateral on the market. They agreed, and *the Fed's timely use of its bank lending ability helped to avert a serious economic disaster following the stock market crash of 1987.*

How might the Fed use the discount rate to implement monetary policy?

The twelve Fed Banks stand ready to make emergency loans to commercial banks to maintain liquidity in the banking system. The discount rate, Fed-speak term for the interest rate charged to commercial banks for these loans, can be moved up or down to influence bank borrowing. In addition, the discount rate can be used as a signal to let the financial community know what the Fed wants to happen in the economy.

Suppose the Fed decides to pursue a policy of monetary ease, Fed language for expanding the money supply to make the economy grow faster. To support this policy the Fed might reduce the discount rate. This would have two effects on the banking system. First, some banks might take advantage of this lower discount rate by borrowing money from the Fed. When the Fed makes discount loans, it gives banks the means to make new loans, thereby increasing the money supply and helping the economy to grow.

In reality the discount rate has little direct impact on the nation's money supply because very little is borrowed from the Fed. Discount loans by all banks in the nation generally total less than $1 billion. That is less than a drop in the bucket compared with a money supply of more than $1,000 billion. So any additional borrowing that might come from a lower discount rate would have a negligible effect on the economy.

Actually, banks rarely borrow money from the Fed. They prefer borrowing money from each other in what is called the **federal funds market**. Banks charge each other interest at the **federal funds rate**. The term *federal* is used only because loans among banks are made by transferring funds through Fed Banks. The Fed does not control this market. However, the federal funds market is an alternative to borrowing from the Fed and one that is much preferred by bankers. When a bank goes to the Fed for a loan, it may feel like Oliver Twist asking for more soup.

Second, the lower discount rate acts as a signal that the Fed is encouraging financial institutions to make more loans and that the Fed may be willing to support them in doing so. This purely psychological impact is called the **announcement effect**. Sometimes it works and sometimes it does not. If the announcement effect is successful, it will make lenders loosen their purse strings. When banks decide to lend more money to their customers, the money they put into the economy could have a noticeable impact on money supply and on the economy. Thus, *the main impact of a change in the discount rate is purely psychological. A drop in the discount rate may encourage financial institutions to lend more money; conversely, a rise in the rate may discourage credit creation.*

Monetary policy is never focused on the discount rate. If the Fed pursues a policy of monetary ease, it will rely more on open market operations, that is, buying government securities as a way of injecting funds into the banking system. Discount rate changes are only supplementary supports to policy.

Are there other tools available to the Fed?

The Fed controls the **reserve ratios**, which are the percentages of deposits banks must keep on reserve (inactive cash or deposits with Fed Banks). When the reserve ratios are raised, banks must increase their reserves and will have less money to lend. *Higher reserve ratios generally reduce bank lending activity, and lower ratios encourage lending.* Higher reserves would slow the growth of the economy.

The last major change in reserve ratios was made in 1980, although minor adjustments have been made since. *Because reserve ratios are so powerful,* and it is so costly for banks to adjust to new ratios, *they are rarely changed.*

Is the Fed free of political influences?

Political leaders would get great personal benefit by controlling the Fed. Imagine a president of the United States, running for reelection, who could promise to use the Fed to lower interest rates and to expand credit if he/she were continuing in office. Imagine a Congress or president who could order the Fed to print new money to finance a government budget deficit.

In both scenarios, compliance by the Fed would be inflationary because the nation's money supply would be used to create a flood of easy credit. Politicians never seem to want higher interest rates and tight money, even if that would be good for the nation in the long run. Giving politicians control of the Fed would be like holding AA meetings in a winery.

Back in 1913, *the wise designers of the Federal Reserve System tried to make it independent of the political establishment.* The seven members of the Board of Governors of the Fed, who coordinate the activities of the twelve Fed Banks, serve for staggered fourteen-year terms. They are appointed by the president of the United States and confirmed by Congress. If the design worked as planned, each president would make only two appointments during a four-year presidential term, which is not enough to give the chief executive "control" over the powerful Board. Furthermore, not more than one governor can come from a single Federal Reserve Bank's district, so the Board represents geographical diversity.

The Fed also is financially independent of politicians. When commercial banks deposit cash reserves in the Federal Reserve Banks, the Banks invest this money in U.S. government debt (Treasury bonds, notes, and bills). The U.S. Treasury must pay the Fed interest on this debt, and the Fed pays its expenses by using this interest income. That is why the Fed never has to go to Congress for money to keep its doors open. (Actually, the Fed gets more interest from the government than it needs, so at the end of every year it is required to turn over any unspent income to the U.S. Treasury as a "donation." This arrangement does not move the Fed Banks to be penurious, as you can see from their impressive buildings, office decor, professional staffs, and volumes of free publications.)

How much political influence can be exerted over the Fed?

Sam Goldwyn, famous for his turns of phrase, would probably say that if the designers of the Fed were alive today, they would be rolling over in their graves.

Most members of the Board of Governors have come up through the ranks of the Fed's bureaucracy or were academic economists; either way, they were generally folks of modest means. The position of governor gives immense influence, a wide range of impressive contacts, and invaluable experience studying and regulating the nation's financial system. A relatively modest salary, just above $100,000 per year, seems incongruous with the authority of a seat on the Board of Governors, especially when Fed governors give direction and advice to (and mingle with) private-sector executives whose incomes are several times as large. Little wonder that most of the governors succumb to offers of lucrative positions in the private sector, and they often do so before the expiration of their fourteen-year terms. Governors have left the board after consideration of their credit card balances, their mortgage payments, and their spouses' wardrobes.

As a result of resignations and expired terms, some U.S. presidents have gotten to appoint a majority of board members, and they are likely to have selected individuals whose viewpoints would support their own political agenda. Presidents Nixon and Reagan got to shape the Board in this way, and they will not be the last presidents to do so.

The Fed was created by the U.S. Congress. Fed governors are keenly aware that their powers can be changed by Congress. Congressmen have been quick to point this out to Fed boards whose actions are inconsistent with the direction of the political leadership. Occasionally the ax falls; in 1978 Congress passed a law requiring the Board to make periodic reports on its policies. But so far Congress has relied more on threats than on actual changes. Mindful of Congress's power, however, the chairman of the Board of Governors makes frequent appearances on Capitol Hill, to maintain a good working relationship, and keeps good contacts with the executive branch as well. (The U.S. Congress, like every parent, knows there is nothing wrong with having their grown kids call home every couple of weeks!) *Although the central bank of the United States is relatively free of political control, Fed governors generally are wise enough not to walk against a strong political wind.*

Nations whose political leaders exert direct control over their central banks have often had to contend with serious bouts of inflation brought about by continuously expansive monetary policies (especially around election time). Central banks in Argentina and Peru, among others, are not blameless when their nations experience inflation in the triple digits. But the U.S. economy has benefited from the relative independence of the Fed. In fact, we have probably gained from the efforts made (at times) to coordinate the economic policies of the Fed with those of the executive and congressional branches.

ARTICLE 19:

FINANCIAL MARKETS

Something for Everyone

What are financial markets and what do they do for the economy?

People, businesses, and governments in the economy can be divided into two groups. The first are savers. They are the ones who spend less than they earn, or the lucky ones who receive gifts or inheritances of money that they want to hold on to. These savers want their money to work for them to increase their wealth. They do this by becoming investors. Most investors are **lenders**, including banks and bondholders. Others buy pieces of a business, such as stockholders.

The second group consists of the **borrowers** and entrepreneurs. Some of the borrowers are consumers who want or need to spend more money than their incomes or savings currently provide. Others are businesses who need to finance inventories or expansions. The entrepreneurs are people who organize resources to create salable products and services; they want money to enable them to get the resources they need and often sell stock or partnerships in their businesses to do so. Finally, there are governments and government agencies who have budget deficits.

A financial market is where investors come together with users of funds. It can be a place, like a bank or a stock exchange, or it can be a way of communication that does not require a specific location, such as deal making over telephone networks.

Financial markets contribute to our economy by taking "idle" (unused) funds from savers and channeling these funds to people who use them. These users of funds generate economic activity either by consuming or by producing goods and services.

What do investors acquire in financial markets?

Investors go to financial markets to buy **financial assets**. These financial assets are pieces of paper (or just computer entries) that give them the right to make certain claims on persons or businesses. There are two types of financial assets: debt and equity.

An investor who buys **debt** becomes a **creditor** or lender. When an investor makes a loan, she gets a loan contract or **bond** as evidence of the borrower's obligation to repay the money lent, with interest added. The bond spells out the terms of the loan and the remedies the lender has in case the borrower does not keep his promises. The investor acquires the right to repayment of a loan plus interest. If the investor has the right to claim some specific property of the borrower in the event the borrower fails to repay, the bond is called a **mortgage**. (If you ever read a mortgage, you would know it is truly an awe-inspiring instrument worthy of Mephistopheles!)

For over 200 years bondholders got to hold on to elaborately printed certificates, which were evidence of their loan. Increasingly, bondholders are now getting nothing more than little slips of paper (if even that) that tell them the borrower simply made an entry in his computer to record the obligation. Computer entries make buying and selling bonds cheaper and more efficient . . . and they save lots of trees. (On the other hand, computer entries lack aesthetic appeal; in the old days colorful certificates often contained pictures of factories, mills, or other symbols of the borrower's business.)

Investors can also buy **equity**. This is part ownership in a business. The most convenient way of getting part ownership is to buy **stock** in a corporation. Then the investor becomes a **shareholder** because he owns a share of the business. Another way of buying equity is to purchase a **partnership**. Equity owners (stockholders or partners) have a claim on a share of the earnings and property of the business.

Entrepreneurs who organize corporations and sell stocks or bonds, and entrepreneurs who sell partnerships in (noncorporate) businesses, are creating and selling financial assets.

Financial markets bring together borrowers, who create financial assets, and investors, who exchange their money for these assets.

What do the borrowers bring to financial markets?

Of course, borrowers get the use of someone else's money. In return, they create and give to investors bonds, stocks, or loan contracts. The paper, or computer entries, borrowers sell to investors are **financial liabilities**. Every single transaction in a financial market creates a matching financial asset and liability.

TRISHA BUYS A BOND: The Upper Valley School District wants to build a new senior high school building on part of the district's huge sports field. To raise most of the $23 million construction cost, it makes the necessary legal and regulatory arrangements, prints bonds, and offers the bonds to investors. Trisha, an investor, takes $150,000 from her safe-deposit box and buys some of the bonds from the district. With this purchase she acquires a new financial asset, the bonds, and the school district acquires a new financial liability, its obligation to Trisha.

Borrowers get money in financial markets by creating and selling financial assets and taking on liabilities. But we should not lose sight of the fact that, while borrowers bring financial assets to market, they bring real activity to our economy. Trisha's funds were idle (nonproductive) until she let the school district use them to create jobs and incomes through its construction project.

What are the most important types of financial assets?

Most financial assets represent **debt**, which results from borrowing. Debt is a borrower's obligation to a lender. A financial asset that stands for debt is called a **debt instrument**. **Bonds** and **mortgages** are types of long-term debt instruments. They are IOUs that must be paid back after a period of years. The life of a debt instrument is called its **maturity**. A bond reaches maturity when the borrower, a corporation or government, has to pay back the money it borrowed and the debt instrument expires.

For part of the nineteenth century England issued special bonds, called consols, that had no stated maturity. Don't look for them now, though, since they have all been redeemed. In that same century some American corporations issued hundred-year bonds. Today's lenders (investors) are less patient, so bonds generally have a maturity of from ten to thirty years, as do most home mortgages. (Although their parents may not realize it, teenagers generally reach maturity before most bonds! Unfortunately, when they do reach maturity, their parents are still stuck with a mortgage.)

A relatively recent development in financial markets is the selling of mortgages and credit card debt as securities. This is called **securitized debt**. These new securities have been created by innovative financial intermediaries by bundling individual home mortgages, auto loans, or credit card debt. That way a savings and loan association, for example, can sell twenty $50,000 mortgages to a big pension fund as a single security. The fund spreads its credit risk among twenty borrowers, but it has only one investment to watch over.

Not all home mortgages and credit card obligations have been sold off as new securities, but the use of securitized debt is growing. If you owe money on your house, you may not even know that your mortgage has been sold by the bank you deal with; you will continue making your monthly payments to the same bank, but the bank simply passes your payments on to some invisible stranger who owns your mortgage. (Pity the poor borrower. It is getting so he no longer knows who owns him!)

People take out many kinds of loans in addition to mortgages, for cars, college tuition, credit lines, vacations, and so on. All bank loans are represented by loan contracts. These contracts, which represent borrowers' debts, are the bank's financial assets.

Large corporations frequently skip over banks when they want to borrow money. For long-term loans they sell bonds. For short-term borrowing they issue their own IOUs, called **commercial paper**, which they sell directly to big investors. Commercial paper has a maturity up to nine months and is often sold in units of $25,000 or more. Money-market mutual funds, insurance companies, and pension funds often invest in commercial paper.

Stocks are also financial assets sold in financial markets, but they are quite different from debt instruments because stocks represent ownership shares; they are not liabilities of the corporations that sell them. Stocks represent **equity**, not debt. Equity is the value of a stockholder's share of a business. The corporation that creates stock is a legal person. This legal person has the obligation to pass its profits on to humans who own it. When the corporation dissolves, it is obligated to distribute its remaining property among these shareholders.

Bonds, mortgages, loan contracts, commercial paper, and stocks are important financial assets.

How do financial assets differ from real assets?

It may seem somewhat affected, but in the language of economics *real* means only one thing: something that comprises tangible wealth and that satisfies a material need. A house or chair is real, so is a bushel of wheat or a hunk of gold. A **real asset** is a useful material resource. In business, real assets include machines and commodities that can be used to make goods or services.

As we saw earlier, stocks, bonds, etc., are financial assets; they are not real assets because you cannot eat them or otherwise use them directly to satisfy a human need. However, most financial assets are backed by some real assets. For example, a share of stock in Campbell Soup Company represents a small part of the processing plants, equipment, distribution facilities, offices, and other real assets of that firm. The attraction of financial assets is that they are expected to bring their owners income.

Financial assets are important in a market economy because the money that is paid for them is commonly employed to acquire real assets.

CANDACE AND DREW OPEN THEIR DOORS: Realizing a long-held dream, this fifty-something couple started a resort hotel in a semirural area that has a variety of popular ski slopes. To build their hotel and to acquire all the necessary furnishings and equipment, as well as to pay for a substantial marketing campaign, they needed $2.7 million. They pieced together the funds by putting up $300,000 from their pension funds (built up while they worked for a large corporation), took out a mortgage on the hotel property for $400,000, and got a bank loan of $200,000. In addition, they incorporated their business and sold stock to venture capitalists for $1.8 million.

Candace and Drew created some financial assets: a mortgage, a loan contract, and stock. With the money they got from these financial assets they acquired real assets: the hotel building, furnishings, etc.

What is direct finance?

In any financial market, money changes hands either directly or indirectly. *Money is obtained by **direct finance** when the investor and the borrower deal with each other.* Dealings in direct finance can be very personal.

A lot of money changes hands this way. Here are some examples of direct finance:

- You lend $75 to a coworker, who will pay you back at the end of the month.
- Your sister gives you a $12,000 loan to buy a new car.
- An investor buys a savings bond from the U.S. Treasury Department.
- A savings and loan association decides to become a corporation and sells its stock to investors at its offices.

- A furniture store raises some cash by selling a partnership to a local businessperson.

What are the advantages and disadvantages of direct finance?

The appeal of direct finance is that you, as the investor, get to decide who gets the use of your money. The other attraction is that it is usually cheaper to make investments directly. After all, you do not have to pay a middleman, who would otherwise get a cut somewhere.

BRUNO'S NEIGHBOR KNOCKS ON HIS DOOR: Bruno's friend and neighbor Max asked him for a loan of $10,000 to finance a car he needs for his sales work. Max could get a loan from his credit union for four years at 9% interest. Bruno has the money and he has the opportunity of investing the $10,000 in the same credit union, which is paying 5% interest. In place of this credit union deposit, Bruno could lend the money to Max at 8% interest. Max would be happy to get the loan at a lower interest rate than he would have paid to the credit union. Bruno would be happy to get more interest than he could earn from a CD, and he likes the idea of knowing where his money would go. He is thinking it over.

Now, Bruno has nothing against banks, credit unions, savings and loans, or other places where he could deposit his money. But if the credit union pays him 5% for the use of his $10,000 and then lends it to Max for 9%, the credit union gets a cut of 4% (9% minus 5%) for itself. Max would like to see some of that cut go into his own pocket instead.

But there are two important problems in direct finance. The first problem concerns an investor's need to get information about **credit risk**, which is the risk that the investor will not get all of the money he expects or is promised. A high credit risk means the investor may not get all of his money back. This is important because if credit risk is high, the investor might decide not to make the loan. Investors need information about credit risk to guide their financing decisions.

There are some things Bruno might want to know about Max to get a good picture of the credit risk he would be taking on by lending Max the money. What is his income and is it reliable? How much money does he owe already? Does he have a good record of paying financial obligations? Can Bruno claim any of Max's property if he fails to pay back the loan? Even if they are good friends, this information may be hard (or at least awkward) for Bruno to get.

The second problem with direct finance is the lack of **portfolio diversity**. (*Portfolio* is a classy word used by economists to mean all of the things people own. One's portfolio usually consists of both tangible property and financial assets.) Portfolio diversity simply means spreading the credit risk. If Bruno uses all his savings for Max's loan, Bruno has no diversity of financial assets; all his eggs are in one basket. If Max turns out to be a deadbeat, Bruno will be hit hard. If Bruno could lend his money to several people, he would diversify his portfolio; if any one borrower failed to repay his loan, Bruno would not lose his entire savings.

While direct finance often gives investors higher returns on their investments than they could get going through a third party, it gives them the burden of collecting information and it usually provides less portfolio diversity than they could otherwise get.

What is indirect finance?

Indirect finance takes place when another party brings investor and borrower (or equity provider) together. In technical jargon this party is called a **financial intermediary**. The financial intermediary collects money from investors and then parcels this money out to companies or individuals who apply for it. Often, in indirect finance, the investor never knows what borrower gets her money, and vice versa; it is very impersonal.

You are probably familiar with some of the most important financial intermediaries. Each one is a unique combination of sources of money and uses of money.

- **Commercial banks** get most of their funds from short-term and intermediate-term deposits (checking accounts, CDs). These deposits are primarily used to finance credit card balances, business inventories, and installment loans. Banks also buy very safe bonds and generally make few mortgage loans that they cannot sell quickly (☞ Art. 17: Money and Banking, page 221).

- **Savings and loan associations** have about the same sources of funds as do commercial banks, but most of their lending is for long-term mortgages. They compete with banks to do many other types of lending (auto, business inventories, etc.).
- **Credit unions** have deposits similar to banks, but generally specialize in personal loans, with some funds used for mortgages.
- **Insurance companies** raise money from policyholders who pay premiums. Most of the money is put into long-term investments such as mortgages, stocks, bonds, and real estate. Policyholders get some of these funds back from insurance companies in the form of policy benefits, such as the money the insurance company pays when a life-insurance policyholder dies.
- **Pension funds** get money from pension plan participants and make long-term investments similar to insurance companies'.
- **Mutual funds** collect money from shareholders and invest them in a variety of financial assets, especially stocks and bonds. **Money market mutual funds** are a special type of mutual fund that invests only in short-term assets that have little or no credit risk.
- **Finance companies** sell stocks, bonds, and other financial assets to raise money. They use this money mainly to make short-term and intermediate-term installment loans to businesses and individuals. This group of lenders includes automobile finance companies (often owned by carmakers), companies that provide money to retail stores to finance their customers' purchases, and "storefront" loan companies that provide small and large loans directly to individuals.
- **Investment banks** often buy newly issued stocks or bonds from corporations, as well as bonds issued by governments. The investment banks then sell these securities to investors. They are not commercial banks so they use their own funds rather than those of depositors.

Other financial intermediaries are less prominent members of the finance industry. But *all financial intermediaries exist to channel money from investors (savers) to borrowers and equity providers.* They are vital middlemen in our economy because they finance so much of our economic activity. Without them we would have fewer houses built, less consumer spending, smaller business inventories, and fewer new business enterprises.

What are the pros and cons of indirect finance?

By including the middleman, *investors often get a slightly lower return on their money by using indirect finance.* Remember that Bruno could only get 5% interest from the credit union, but he could get 8% by lending directly to Max (assuming Max paid off).

Middlemen always get a share. That is why banks, savings and loans, and credit unions always pay their depositors less than they charge borrowers. Mutual funds, pension managers, and insurance firms all take a small part of their earnings to cover their expenses and profits before passing their incomes on to the people whose money they use. Investment banks, like retail stores, add a markup to the bonds and stocks they resell to investors.

You pay for what you get. Suppose Bruno politely turns Max down and puts his $10,000 into the credit union. Max then has to turn to a financial intermediary such as the credit union. This gives the credit union the job of worrying about Max's credit risk. It will have to ask the tough questions (about income, past borrowing record, etc.) that must be answered before it can make good lending decisions. That is their business, and most credit unions, and other lending organizations, are good at it.

The credit union puts Bruno's $10,000 in a pool of money that is used to make loans to many people. So each depositor, such as Bruno, spreads his or her credit risk; everyone's eggs are in many baskets. Bruno and the other depositors benefit from portfolio diversity. So *the advantages of indirect finance are freedom from information gathering and lesser credit risk because of portfolio diversity.* Actually, investors enjoy zero credit risk when engaging in some types of indirect finance. If they place $100,000 or less in deposits in banks, savings and loans, credit unions, and savings banks (a hybrid between S&L's and banks) that have deposit insurance, they cannot lose their money. The deposit insurer, usually a government agency, takes all the investor's risk.

There is more. By putting his money into a credit union Bruno also reduces his **interest-rate risk**. This is the risk of loss if interest rates rise. When interest rates rise, the value of bonds or of other loans goes down; people who own bonds or other interest-paying assets will see their assets lose value. In addition, if they have their funds locked up in only one asset, they will not be able to get the benefits of higher rates. For example, if Bruno commits his money to Max for four years at 8% interest, he will not get more than 8% during that period if rates rise. By placing his money in a credit union or bank, Bruno will not have a risk of loss and may enjoy higher income over time if interest rates increase. Thus, *an additional advantage of indirect finance is that it may reduce interest-rate risk.*

Sometimes borrowers also benefit from indirect finance. Max may have preferred to make a friendly deal with Bruno and to pay a lower interest rate for his car loan. But by using indirect finance, he does not have to search so hard for a lender, and he develops an institutional credit record and a banking relationship that might do him some good in the future; credit unions, banks, and other lenders share information through credit-reporting agencies.

Are financial assets traded among investors?

Primary financial markets are ones where *new* financial assets are sold. For example, a corporation that issues stock and then sells it to new stockholders is raising funds in a primary market. All financial assets have to start out in a primary market. There are also some **secondary financial markets** in which "old" financial assets can be resold. Any time a financial asset is bought or sold after its initial sale, the buyers and sellers are using the secondary market.

Secondary markets are important because they make it easy to buy or to sell financial assets before they mature. That way an investor who buys a twenty-year bond, for example, can sell it anytime before it matures. Secondary markets are for people who don't want to wait until maturity.

When a secondary market exists for a financial asset, we say the asset enjoys **liquidity**. Investors prefer to put their money into financial assets that have liquidity because it gives them freedom to buy or to sell a financial asset at will at a reasonably predictable price; it also gives them continuous information about what their financial assets are worth. Because of these advantages, investors are willing to accept a lower rate of interest from liquid assets than from assets that have no secondary markets.

Not all financial assets have well-established and reliable secondary markets. Issuers of new securitized financial assets often promise to provide secondary markets for some debt instruments (mortgages, credit card debt, etc.) that previously did not have any.

Financial markets consist of primary and secondary markets for financial assets. Secondary markets give investors the important advantages of liquidity and of continuous information about the value of the financial assets traded there. Stock exchanges and the NASDAQ over-the-counter securities market are examples of important secondary markets. Prices realized in many secondary markets are reported in most daily newspapers.

How much debt is there in the financial markets?

Our nation's financial markets channel huge sums from investors (savers) to borrowers. *Total debt in the U.S. is at least $12 trillion* (that is $12 million million). Table 19A shows different types of debt in the United States in 1992.[3] This is a minimum figure, since official

Table 19A

Debt in the United States, 1992

TYPE OF DEBT	AMOUNT ($ BILLIONS)	PERCENT
U.S. government	$3,080	26%
Tax-exempt bonds	1,197	10
Corporate bonds	1,154	10
Home mortgages	2,923	25
Other mortgages	1,078	9
Consumer credit	809	7
Commercial paper	107	1
Other loans	1,393	12
Total:	11,741	100

figures do not report some private lending among relatives or friends, that comes to over $50,000 per person. For several years *the largest borrower in the United States has been the federal government*, claiming more than a quarter of the funds lent. Another 10% went to nonfederal governments and their agencies, who have the privilege of borrowing by issuing bonds whose interest is exempt from federal income taxes.

Closely behind the federal government in the money they borrow are homeowners who borrow to finance their castles (however humble or grand) through home mortgages. Other mortgages are used to finance farms, multifamily housing, and business properties.

Most of the consumer credit listed in Table 19A represents credit card borrowing, but a variety of other types of bank and finance company loans are aggregated in the last row of the table.

Businesses are large borrowers. They account for all of the corporate bonds, the nonhome mortgages, commercial paper, and a large share of the "other loans"; the last category includes bank loans to finance inventories and accounts receivables of businesses.

How do equity owners make out during hard times?

The total value of financial assets that represent equity is harder to determine, but it is somewhat smaller than the amount of debt. For example, the total value of stocks on the New York Stock Exchange, the nation's largest stock market, is only about $2.5 trillion.

Equity owners take bigger risks than do debt owners, but they have larger potential rewards. When things go badly for a business, the debt owners generally get first grabs (after the government) at whatever property the business has. The equity owners get whatever might be left.

Of course, when a business makes profits, the rewards to debt holders are capped at whatever they were promised: the repayment of the loan plus (and only) interest. The equity owners get everything else, with no limit.

During good times equity owners get higher rewards than do debt owners, but in hard times debt owners lose less.

ARTICLE 20:

PRICES IN FINANCIAL MARKETS

The Ups and Downs of Bonds, Stocks, and Other Investments

Reading Suggestion: Please read or skim the preceding article before you read this one.

Why is interest charged for loans?

Lenders have money to invest only because they deferred their own spending to provide funds for the use of others. *Interest payments are justified to compensate lenders for postponing consumption.*

A FRIENDLY LOAN: By the start of the skiing season Walter had saved $500 for a new set of skis. But before he could purchase them, his friend Gerard asked for a $500 loan to pay for an emergency furnace repair in his home. Gerard promised to repay the loan in a year, but by that time Walter would have missed the skiing season and would have to wait until next year to get a good selection of skis. Nonetheless, Walter was willing to use his savings to give Gerard the loan if he could buy a better pair next year in return for having to go through the current season with his present old and battered equipment. Gerard offered to repay Walter his $500 plus $20 interest (4%), for a total of $520, so he could buy better skis next year.

The interest payment of $20 would have given Walter a reward for waiting: the ability to buy better-quality skis than he could have purchased today. The interest rate Walter wants so that he can improve his purchasing power next year is called the **real rate of return**. The "real rate" is a recognition of the **time value of money**, which is the presumption that $1 today is worth more than $1 you would get next year. To give up $1 today Walter needs more than $1 next year and is considering asking for an interest rate of 4%. But he hasn't made a final decision.

Where does inflation come in?

Since the early part of the twentieth century inflation has become almost a constant condition in modern market economies. If the price of the skis Walter wanted went up next year by $25, Walter would not have gained anything for postponing his purchase. Suppose Walter anticipated 4% inflation. What deal would he have made with Gerard? He would ask Gerard to tack the cost of inflation onto his interest payment.

In modern lending practices investors ask for a rate of interest equal to the **expected inflation rate** plus the rate of increase in purchasing power they require. In the language of economics the increase in purchasing power lenders want from a deal is called the **real interest rate**. By adding this real rate to the expected inflation rate, lenders arrive at the **nominal interest rate**, which is the percentage rate you see on paper. *Investors include the anticipated inflation rate in their interest charges.* Lenders ask for a nominal interest rate that equals the real interest rate they want plus what they expect inflation will take away from their purchasing power.

Of course, the expected inflation rate is only a guess. Investors always take some inflation risk. Considering this, Walter is now thinking of asking for a nominal interest rate of 8% (4% for inflation plus 4% for a better pair of skis). If the skis go up in price by less than 4%, Walter would get a little surprise gift: more of an increase in purchasing power (a higher real rate of interest) than he had counted on receiving. If the price of the skis escalates by more than 4%, Walter would absorb a loss of purchasing power (a penalty for guessing incorrectly).

In the late 1970s inflation in the U.S. shot above the double-digit level. Investors were not prepared and had previously agreed to accept interest rates that turned out to be too low. In fact, in terms of purchasing power, many investors got *negative* interest. (In economic jargon we say they suffered a decline in their real wealth.) Maybe that is why interest rates in the early 1980s, when inflation was low, were so high. Lenders, once burned, were trying to catch up on their buying power. (Whether or not they were merely trying to recoup losses from the seventies, these higher interest rates did slow economic growth in the early eighties.)

But don't pity the investor/lender too much. Economists have discovered that in times of high and varying inflation investors often demand a sizable inflation risk premium.

Should investors get something to compensate them for risk?

By making the loan Walter would be sticking his neck out, at least a little. Suppose Gerard does not repay all or part of the loan. That is what we call **credit risk**. Unless an investor buys U.S. government bonds or makes a government-insured deposit in a banking firm, credit risk is always there. Walter deserves some payment for risk taking, just as an insurance company wants a payment before agreeing to cover your automobile.

We will not go into the complexity of calculating a fair payment to get Walter to take on the risk. (Insurance companies employ highly trained actuaries to do this type of work.) However, let us assume Walter decided he needed $20 (4%) as a fair fee for credit risk and built this into his interest fee. With this in mind, he decided to ask Gerard for 12%. *Compensation for risk taking is part of the interest rate lenders demand.*

How are interest rates determined in financial markets?

An interest rate is really made up of three separate rates: the real rate of return, the expected inflation rate, and a premium for credit risk. Walter's interest rate of 12% was made up of a 4% real rate to boost his purchasing power, a 4% rate to cover expected inflation, plus 4% as an "insurance premium" to cover credit risk. (That 12% rate would still beat most credit cards.)

This means that interest rates can change in financial markets if any of three things happen:

- Economic conditions improve or deteriorate so as to change credit risk faced by investors.
- Investors anticipate a higher or lower inflation rate than what had been expected previously, or inflation rates become more (or less) volatile.
- Investors' appetite for savings change so that they demand a higher or lower real rate of return as their reward for postponing their own consumption (☞ Art. 13: Interest Rates, page 153).

What is meant by discounting, and what does it have to do with prices of bonds and stocks?

Investors buy bonds and stocks because they expect to receive income from them in the future. For example, the issuers of bonds usually promise to pay their bondholders $1,000 per bond when the bonds mature, plus interest payments (usually paid twice a year) until that time. The maturity value of a bond is called its **face value**. The total interest payments made each year are usually expressed as a percent of this face value and are called the bond's **coupon rate**. For example, a bond with a coupon rate of 8% promises to pay interest of $80 (8% of $1,000 face value) per year, in semiannual installments of $40.

Corporations that sell stocks are expected to pay **dividends** to stockholders as well as a lump-sum payment (a share of what the corporate assets are worth) when the corporation is dissolved. These dividends, usually paid quarterly, are intended to partially compensate the investor for risking his money, expected inflation, and postponing spending. The rest of this compensation, any increase in the price of the stock, is a **capital gain**.

The current prices of these financial assets are always lower than the future payments that are expected. Otherwise there would be no incentive to buy them. Investors get rewarded for buying financial assets by getting them at a discount. This discount is the interest the investor gets on his money.

SIBYL'S DEAL: Sibyl manages a trust fund for one of her bank's customers. A corporation offers to sell the trust a promissory note for $1 million, payable in one year. Since Sibyl also has an opportunity to invest the trust's money in an uninsured bank certificate of deposit for one year at 6% interest, she feels that the corporate borrower should pay her customer at least this much interest; she offers to buy the corporation's note for just under $943,400.

Sibyl's reasoning is sound. If $943,400 were invested at 6%, it would produce $1 million in one year. The sum of $943,400 (actually, $943,396.23) is called the **present value** of the $1 million promissory note. The present value is also known as the **discounted value** because the present price of the financial asset includes a discount from its future (maturity) value.

Because of the time value of money, *financial assets always have prices equal to their present value*, if the financial market is efficient (see below).

What did Sibyl do to find the present value of the note?

In the example above, the present value of a single payment of $1 million, to be made in one year, is equal to the amount of money you would have to put in a bank account today at 6% to get $1 million in a year. You can find it using a pocket calculator. The formula is $1,000,000/(1.06) = $943,396.23. If you put $943,396 in a bank account at 6% interest today, then in one year you would have $1 million.

How are bond prices established in financial markets?

The major contribution well-functioning financial markets make to a market economy is that they channel money from those who save it to those who have good uses for it. But there is more. Financial markets also provide **price discovery**. This elegant term means the ability to find out what an asset is actually worth. Discovery happens whenever an asset is bought in a financial market because the buyer and the seller must settle on a price.

To see how bond prices are established, think of a bond as a financial asset that promises to give its owner certain income on specific future dates. An investor has to decide on the present value of this asset because that is what it is worth. This present value depends on the **yield** investors demand.

Unlike the promissory note that was considered by Sibyl, most bonds have a maturity of more than one year and pay interest during that time. For these bonds the formula for present value is more complex than the one Sibyl used, but it is built into many sophisticated pocket calculators and computer programs. Some actual bond prices (present values) are given in Table 20A, along with the annual payment the owner of the bond would receive and the annual yield that would be received if the bond was held until maturity.[4]

These bonds promise to give their owners annual payments plus $1,000 at maturity. (The $1,000 maturity value is a well-established custom for corporate and federal government bonds, although there are exceptions.) The bonds expire after that last payment, and after paying the owners the principal of $1,000, they become worthless (but make neat wallpaper). On October 18, 1994 (a typical market), a U.S. Treasury bond was traded that promised to pay its owners $60 per year ($30 every six months) for the next five years plus a lump sum of $1,000 on the maturity date in October 1999. The total income would be $1,300 spread over this period. How much were investors willing to pay for such a package that day? The answer is the market price, or present value, of $947.50.

Investors in financial markets customarily express the total return

Table 20A

Some Bond Prices and Yields on October 18, 1994
(All Bonds Worth $1,000 at Maturity)

Issuer of Bond	Yearly Payment	Maturity Date	Price	Yield
U.S. Treasury	$60.00	October 1999	$947.50	7.27%
Pacific Gas & Electric	72.50	March 2026	832.83	8.83
Lockheed Corp.	67.50	March 2003	912.47	8.21
Ford Credit Co.	62.50	February 1998	961.40	7.57

they get from an asset as **yield to maturity**, or just "yield." The Treasury bond shown in the table gives the investor a capital gain of $52.50 when it matures (that is the maturity value of $1,000 less the $947.50 paid for the bond) in addition to $60 per year. If you spread this gain over the five-year remaining life of the bond and add the $30, semi-annual income, and reinvested interest payments, the investor would get a yearly yield (or average annual return) on her investment of 7.27%. The yield is an important number and should always be shown along with price when information is given about a financial asset. If the price of the Treasury bond were lower, the yield would have been larger, and vice versa. Investors actually set the price of a bond according to yield they want.

On that same day trading took place in bonds issued by Lockheed, an aircraft manufacturer, by Ford Credit, which finances customers' purchases of Ford cars, and by Pacific Gas & Electric, a utility. Their yields were higher because they were riskier than the government bond; in addition, two of these bonds required their owners to wait longer for the final lump-sum payout.

Basically, the price or present value of a bond depends on the interest rate investors demand. If bonds all have the same yearly payout, then *bonds that pay higher interest rates would have lower prices, and bonds that pay lower rates would have higher prices.*

If all bonds made the same annual payments to bondholders, then those bonds with longer maturities would have lower prices because long-term bond investors demand higher interest rates. The reason is simple: the longer an investor has to own a bond before its final payout, the higher the risk the investor takes. Another reason the longer maturity bond would have a lower price is because that is the way you would induce the investor to tie up her money for a longer period of time; the lower price compensates for the lower liquidity of the long-term bond.

If any two bonds had the same maturity and degree of risk, the bond with the higher yearly payment would have a higher price.

Are bonds ever sold for less than their present value?

Sellers of bonds are usually as smart as the buyers. They can calculate present value, too. So if the present value is the top price buyers would pay, sellers will ask for it. Beside that, in an active bond market there are always speculators ready to buy any bond that happens to slip below its present value. The speculators' demand for such bonds would quickly push its price back up to the present value. If the price were to drift above the present value, sellers of bonds would quickly push the price back down. That is why *prices in an efficient bond market are kept equal to their present values.*

What makes bond prices rise or fall?

Bond prices equal their present value, and present value depends on yield. So bond prices change when yields change. Suppose conditions in the bond market change such that yields from the particular type of bond that Sibyl was offered fell from 6% to 5%. In that event the price of her one-year bond would rise to $952,381 ($1 million divided by 1.05). If the price of the bond *had* remained at $943,396, it would not have stayed there long; like sharks smelling blood in water, sharp investors would rush into the market and try to snap the bond up because it would be paying 6% when other bonds like it were paying only 5%. These investors would demand the bond in such force its price would soon be pushed up to the new present value. *Bond prices rise when yields fall and decline when yields increase.*

Under what circumstances will yields change?

Yields on bonds depend on supply of bonds and on demand for bonds (☞ Art. 9: Prices and the Economy, page 102). Demand and supply depend on many factors, but in the bond market the most important are the outlook for inflation and business confidence.

If investors think that the nation's inflation rate will rise, their demand for bonds will fall, pushing bond prices down (☞ Art. 11: Inflation, page 128). We have already seen that lower bond prices push yields up. To get the higher yields the investor will demand when inflation rises, bond prices must fall.

On the other hand, borrowers (corporations and governments) would increase the supply of bonds now if they expect yields will increase in the future. The reason? They will want to borrow money at today's yields rather than risk having to pay higher yields later.

Either falling demand *or* rising supply will depress bond prices.

The result of both events is unambiguous: bond prices will fall and yields will rise.

Confidence plays an important role. By confidence I mean the faith that investors have that borrowers will be good credit risks. If investors believe that business conditions will deteriorate, so that borrowers are less likely to be able to pay their debts, their demand for bonds will fall. This means that borrowers will have to lower the prices of bonds (raise their yields) to induce investors to part with their money and take on added credit risk. Just like a store with overstocked inventories, prices will have to be cut to move the goods.

Inflation and confidence both reflect economic conditions. Therefore, *bond prices change when people change their expectations of what will happen to the economy.*

How do the markets determine what stocks are worth?

Stocks give their owners shares of corporate profits. The price of a stock depends on the stream of profits the corporation is expected to make over the remaining life of a corporation (which is usually indefinite) and the payout stockholders will get if the corporation dissolves. In addition, just as in the bond market, the price also depends on what yields investors can get elsewhere for investments of comparable risk. This yield is used to calculate present value. *The price of a share of stock is the present value of the income investors expect to get from it.*

If new information influences investors to expect higher income from a stock, the present value of the stock will rise; its price will go up. Because stocks exist for much longer periods than do bonds, and because expected income from a stock fluctuates much more than does the income from a bond, stock prices tend to be more variable than bond prices. That is one reason stocks are generally riskier investments.

Do expectations really move markets?

One of the most important developments over the past twenty-five years in the way economists view the workings of our economy is their new concern with the way *expectations* affect economic events, especially financial markets. This new view is expressed in the theory of **rational expectations**. Although this theory is intricate, its meaning is that

- People gather all the information they can about the economy and about financial markets.
- They analyze this information, calling upon their experience and education.
- They use this analysis to form forecasts about prices or economic conditions and act on these forecasts by buying or selling assets in financial markets.

Economists have recognized the importance of expectations for a long time. After all, people buy products, go to specific restaurants, buy stocks or bonds, even select marriage partners, on the basis of what they expect from them. Sometimes expectations are not realized (which is why there are divorces), but *expectations motivate behavior*. The more experience and information people have, the better (more accurate) their expectations will be.

Economists' interest in rational expectations is heightened by the information explosion; technology is making so much news available to so many people so quickly. Radio, television, computer networks, and satellite transmissions deliver data to millions of market participants around the world almost as quickly as events occur. Because of the importance of expectations in moving markets, many economists are studying the way people formulate expectations from the masses of information they receive.

HECTOR QUESTIONS AUTHORITY: The president of the United States, facing a reelection campaign, issues campaign statements expressing his determination to reduce the federal deficit so as to cut down on government borrowing. He states that less borrowing would generate lower interest rates. In turn, lower interest rates would stimulate the economy and increase prosperity. But Hector suspects that the president, and the U.S. Congress, will actually *increase* deficits, by raising government spending and cutting taxes, as a way of "buying" votes in critical election districts. Higher deficits mean higher yields and lower bond prices, so Hector decides to sell bonds.

Hector suspects the president's statements are merely designed to make people believe yields would drop. In fact, the president is probably counting on a trusting public to stimulate demand for bonds, which, by itself, would drive bond prices up and interest rates down, even if the government did nothing to change spending.

Of course, what might be rational to some might not be rational to others. Some investors might have believed the president and, based on their education and experience, rushed out to buy bonds. (Hector would have considered their credulity as evidence of Abraham Lincoln's conviction that you can fool some of the people some of the time!)

Will Rogers observed that the difference of opinion makes horse races. This is true in financial markets, too. Trades occur only when opinions differ: someone buys and someone else sells. In this information age most everyone has access to the same information. What motivates some to buy, and others to sell, is the difference in the way they form their expectations based on this information.

What happens to bond prices and yields depends on the weight of traders' expectations on one side or the other. If the big money goes with Hector, bond prices will fall. *Bond prices change as a result of rational expectations.*

Can rational expectations explain anomalous behavior in financial markets?

To a casual observer price changes in the stock and bond markets are sometimes hard to figure out. When a corporation announces good news and the price of its shares rise, we tend to think the market is being rational. But what about cases where good news makes prices decline? The theory of rational expectations gives us a consistent explanation of the behavior of stock prices.

> **DAVE SELLS OUT:** Dave has invested most of his family's wealth in shares of Potter Crystal Corp. Last week the stock had a price of $125 per share. This week the company announced that earnings for the year were up 15%. This announcement was made with some fanfare and pride by the company because it was their best earnings increase in ten years. But Dave, and many other investors who were interested in the stock, expected earnings to grow 20% because the particular markets Potter serves are expanding rapidly. Disappointed in the company's performance, Dave and others sold their stock, and this selling caused the share price to drop quickly to $110 per share.

Since most investors had anticipated a 20% growth in earnings, these expected earnings determined their calculation of the present value of $125 per share. When earnings went up by only 15%, these investors had to recalculate their assessment of the present value of the stock. The new value investors placed on the stock was $110 per share, so the share price quickly dropped to this level. Apparently the company was not able to get as much out of its growing markets as investors had expected it would.

This illustration highlights the fact that, in a free market for corporate shares, *stock prices are based on rational expectations, not on historical events.* Crystal's earnings rose (historical event), but when this information was analyzed by investors in the market, their rational expectations led them to sell the stock and that selling caused its price to fall.

If I understand rational expectations, can I make a small fortune in the market?

It has always been possible to get a small fortune out of the stock market . . . if you start with a large one! Sad to say, the theory of rational expectations puts a wet blanket on dreams of easy riches from the stock and bond markets. Perhaps Thomas Carlyle was right when he said economics was the "dismal science."

Within seconds after Potter Crystal reported its earnings, the news was spread across computer screens, announced on television, and fed to telephone lines and fax machines. Other computers calculated the new present value, and using the same rapid communications technology, traders sped their orders to the stock exchange. The few who could react quickly enough made a little money. But those who paused a few moments, waited for an analysis in the morning newspaper, a call from their broker, or the next issue of a stock market newsletter lost out.

Traders will make above-average returns on Wall Street if they have relevant information before *it is shared with others.* If Dave had known about Potter Crystal's earnings before anyone else, he could have sold shares at $125 and then waited to see the stock price tumble as others got the news. He would have forecast a price of $110 while everyone else was still forecasting $125 as the stock's value. But his better forecast would not have been based on superior skills; it would have been based on better data. Ivan Boesky would have been proud of him.

Dave's advantage would have been his ability to get and trade on **inside information**. It is not illegal to have inside information; after all, someone is always among the first to know, whether it is the corporation's accountant, CEO, or mail room clerk. But in the United States it is illegal to make trades based on inside information. By making such trading illegal, markets are made more efficient.

Are the major financial markets efficient?

Economists argue persuasively that our economy benefits from **efficient markets**. Efficient markets are level playing fields where all market participants have equal access to information and equal opportunities to trade. In an efficient market no trader has an advantage over others: no insider trading, no front-running (where brokers execute trades for some customers ahead of executing orders entered by less favored customers), and no giant traders whose buying or selling forces prices in a particular direction. Efficient markets embody perfect competition.

Government regulation and supervision of major financial markets in the United States, and in other leading market economies, enhance the efficiency of these markets. Our financial markets are still not as efficient as they could be. There is still occasional insider trading, front-running, and dominance by major market players.

Does our economy gain anything from efficient financial markets?

The advantages of efficient markets are their openness and fairness. Efficient markets gain the confidence of investors. Because they are fair, investors are more likely to channel their money through them. Entrepreneurs are also more likely to use financial markets to find the money they need for productive projects. Therefore, *the growth and level of our nation's economic activity are greater with efficient markets than they would be without them.*

Gambling casinos exist to create risks for the sake of risk taking. By contrast, financial markets exist to collect money and to channel it to constructive uses. They finance real economic activity: the creation of goods and services. The more efficient these markets are, the better they can perform that task.

Can investors make money in efficient stock and bond markets?

The overall performance of the stock market is measured by market price averages, such as the widely reported Standard & Poor's Corporation Index of 500 Common Stocks. See Table 20B for some recent values of this important indicator.[5]

The last column of this table shows you the average annual return, from both capital gains and dividends, that you could have received if you had invested in all the stocks in the **S&P 500**. For example, you would have made a capital gain of about 3.7% from holding stocks from 1989 to 1990 plus a dividend yield of 3.6%, for a total return of 7.3%. This was not bad considering that the U.S. economy slid into a recession in late 1990. (However, there was a brief, dramatic plunge in prices at the very start of the recession.)

The 1980s were very good for stocks. During some years the investor could have earned double-digit returns. The only down years shown in Table 20B were from 1981–82 and from 1987–88. The latter period included the most dramatic one-day plunge in stock market history, in October 1987. But the market quickly recovered and continued to produce gains, even through the recession of 1990–91. (A sum of $10,000 invested at the average price

Table 20B

Standard & Poor's 500 Stock Index, 1980–92

YEAR	INDEX VALUE	CAPITAL GAIN	DIVIDEND YIELD	TOTAL RETURN
1993	451	8.4%	2.8%	11.2%
1992	416	10.6	3.0	13.6
1991	376	12.2	3.2	15.4
1990	335	3.7	3.6	7.3
1989	323	21.4	3.5	24.9
1988	266	−7.3	3.6	−3.7
1987	287	21.6	3.1	24.7
1986	236	26.2	3.5	29.7
1985	187	16.9	4.3	21.2
1984	160	0.0	4.6	4.6
1983	160	33.3	4.4	37.7
1982	120	−6.3	5.8	−0.5
1981	128	7.6	5.2	12.8
1980	119	—	5.3	—

level of 1980, with all dividends reinvested, would have grown to more than $59,600 by 1993.)

These results show you that, since stock prices rise more than they fall over long periods, *investors can make money in an efficient market, over the long run, merely by joining the crowd and following the average.* Of course, the average performance changes. The 1970s was a nearly flat decade for investors. But over just about any period of ten or more years since the 1930s, the "average" investor would have done well. (Think of the long run as ten years or more.)

Can investors "beat the market" if the market is efficient?

In economics, beating the market means getting a return on your money that exceeds the average return, as illustrated in the above question.

As evidence of the efficiency of markets, economists point to the long-term performance of mutual funds that invest in stocks selected by professional investment managers. During any one year most of these **managed mutual funds** do not have rates of return that beat the returns of the S&P 500. Of course, every year some funds do beat the average, and when they do, they advertise their performance heavily. But the efficient-markets theory says that performance superior to the stock average is a fluke; although some stock market mutual funds get lucky and beat the average, a large group of funds has returns poorer than the average.

It is hard to find a professionally managed mutual fund that beats the average year after year. Why? Because the stock market is efficient, these managers do not have any advantage in stock selection over the long run. That means that *in efficient markets investors can make money over the long run, but their average returns will be close to those of the overall market.*

The efficiency theory purists argue that *over the long run the best way to make money in the stock market is to simply "buy the averages."* Economists have been getting their message across during the past twenty or so years because a number of mutual funds have been started that try to do just that. These **index funds** do not pick stocks based on the judgment of managers. Instead, they pick a broad portfolio of stocks that, based on computer models, are highly correlated with one or another stock market average. (The S&P 500 is the most widely used average for this purpose.) These funds are also cheaper to run because they do not have to pay big bucks to hotshot fund managers.

For investors who prefer a more dramatic approach, efficiency theorists suggest tossing darts at a list of all stocks in the market and investing in the stocks hit by the darts. Some studies have shown that professional managers often fail to beat the stocks randomly selected by the darts. The dart approach is not advisable unless you can invest in a rather large number of stocks. Index funds should do the same job.

How do economists explain the success of a small number of leading fund managers and investors who beat the market?

Efficiency theory economists have been annoyed in recent years by reports that some professional investors and fund managers beat the stock market averages consistently for several years. To add insult to injury, many of these pros have become rich while the academic economists' learned essays on the impossibility of beating the markets contribute nothing to their own bank balances. The economists' explanation has been to dismiss these folks as being just lucky.

One efficiency theory economist and professor illustrates the success of a few wealthy stock pickers by giving fifty of his students a coin and having them toss it. Everyone who tosses a "tail" drops out and the remaining persons toss again. Once more the "tails" drop out. This is done until only one or two people remain. This shows that with efficient, fair markets, as with fair coins, there will be a few big winners by chance alone.

Now, some dissident economists have a different way of explaining the consistent successes of a few stock pickers. These economists argue that *there are pockets in the financial markets that are* not *efficient, and these pockets provide profit-making opportunities for those who seek them out.* Successful traders are the ones who find these pockets and profit from them until markets become more efficient (competitive).

HUNTER THE ROCKET SCIENTIST: Hunter was an engineering professor at an eastern university when he decided to apply his skills in mathematics, physics, and statistics to studying price changes in the bond market. He designed a complex computer-driven model (a set of equations) to show that a certain combination of an increase in the prices of utility company stocks, and a drop in the price of gold tended to precede increases in the prices of government bonds. Working with a Wall Street investment banking firm, he formed a team to apply his model to forecasting bond prices and trading. The model was successful for the firm and its clients for nearly three years, after which time Hunter retired, having earned bonuses of $83 million.

Efficient markets are ones in which people have equal access to information and to trading. However, people do not have equal access to brains. Hunter had figured out a way to use public information that had not been discovered by others. Soon the word about Hunter's approach got out, and others with equal skills developed their own methods. Some started forecasting prices of utility stocks and gold to get a jump on Hunter, and when their methods were perfected, his approach lost its value because they beat him to the profits.

It has become fashionable for Wall Street firms to hire promising young academics with skills that enable them to develop new ways of forecasting prices in financial markets. Since many of them have a background in applied physics, they have been called rocket scientists. Like Hunter, some of them will make big profits while they have a monopoly on a method of forming rational expectations. During this time they will be exploiting a kind of "insider information" that makes the markets inefficient. Eventually free competition will restore efficiency. Rocket scientists often have short, but profitable, careers.

6

Government and the Economy

oviet-style economies are examples of what economists call **command economies** because most decisions about what is produced, and who gets it, are made by central government agencies. The governments of command economies run the most important factories, farms, and service organizations. These agencies *command* most of their nation's productive resources because they own them (except for labor). By contrast, market economies are sometimes called **capitalistic economies** because most productive resources are in private hands and decisions on their use are based on market forces. Decisions about what to produce, and who should get it, are made in response to economic incentives such as prices and profits. Profit-seeking private businesses reply to what the markets *demand*.

The United States and other leading industrialized nations are not purely capitalistic economies. That is because many important functions are performed by government, as you will learn in this chapter.

While these nations are far closer to capitalism than to command economies, their economies are actually mixed.

The breakup of Soviet-style economies in Europe and Asia, and attempts to rely more fully on the market when making economic decisions, have led some people to expect that government is somehow inconsistent with the market economy. They believe that "big government" is more of a hindrance than a help to economic growth. This is far from the truth. Government has an important place in a market economy; it helps to make capitalism work.

A significant part of economic literacy is familiarity with what government does (or should do) and an understanding of how it facilitates the market economy. This chapter explains the role of government. It starts with a job description of government. In this first article of the chapter, Article 21, you will learn where markets fail to meet some basic needs and how government steps in to fill the breach. Most of this book explains what markets do well and how they do it. This article covers the important exceptions: economic needs that the market cannot provide efficiently.

Of course, government has to be supported. Over the years our political leaders have devised a variety of taxes to pay for the programs they have created. Article 22 looks at the major types of taxes used by governments and introduces the important subject of tax incidence, which is the analysis of where the burden of a tax really lies. One of the most intriguing findings of economics is that the person who pays a tax to the government is not necessarily the one who carries the load. Read this article to find out into which pocket government dips its hand.

Taxes do more than pay for government. Different *types* of taxes have different effects on the economy. In Article 23 we learn how taxes influence the condition of the economy. Some taxes influence people's spending and savings. Other taxes influence the motivation of businesses to grow. Still others are believed to affect the amount of work people do. A dollar raised from one type of tax may have quite a different impact on the economy than would a dollar raised in another way.

The chapter concludes with Article 24 on economic policy. While government is primarily a unique provider of services, economists recognize that the *combination* of government spending and taxation may have significant effects on the health of the economy. Government budgets have even been regarded as a curative agent for some economic problems.

Economists and politicians have become quite concerned with the effect that the growing government debt in the United States has on the economy. Article 24 concludes with a discussion of the "evils" of debt. Is it a real ogre or a paper tiger?

ARTICLE 21:

THE BUSINESS
OF GOVERNMENT

A Job Description

Does a market economy need government?

Most of what you purchase are **private goods** and services. What makes them "private" is that you enjoy all the benefits they provide. A restaurant meal, a toothbrush, a haircut, are private goods. (In common usage in the language of economics, private "goods" means goods and services, although the word *services* is often omitted.) Anyone who does not pay for a private good will not receive a benefit from it. Since you get all the benefits of a restaurant meal, for example, you are generally willing to pay the full cost of it.

But our economy must also provide many useful things that economists call **public goods**. Public goods are special because you benefit from them only if they are shared with others. That is, if they are there for your benefit, you cannot prevent others from getting the same benefit. National defense is the classic example of a pure public good. You cannot enjoy the peace and security provided by national defense without having the same benefits given to your neighbors. Other (less pure) examples of public goods are highways, education, and even clean air.

Because the benefits of public goods must be shared, you should not have to pay the whole cost of them; fair is fair. Governments provide a solution. Society gives governments the power to tax, and this taxing authority is the means for getting others to share the expenses of public goods. That is why *governments are our main suppliers of public goods.*

In most cases public goods are provided by both the private market and by the government. National defense is a pure public good in that there is no private market for it. But education can be obtained from either public or private schools.

Why must public goods be shared?

Public goods generate **externalities**. Externalities are the benefits people get from a public good even if they do not use it themselves. An important example is schooling. Think of what your education does for your neighbors, your economy, and your society. Educated workers often have skills that enable them to support themselves rather than being a burden to society. Educated workers may also make important discoveries and improvements that benefit us all; think of the products and services we enjoy that are made possible by the education others received. Educated citizens help to make intelligent choices of policies and of politicians to run government (most of the time, anyway). Even though it may seem as though the nation were run by C students, we are all better off by living in a society where we, our neighbors, and leaders are educated.

Because of these shared benefits, schools even enrich the lives of those who do not attend them. That is why families that do not include students help to pay for public schools through taxes. The externalities justify our system of financing public education.

Our nation's transportation infrastructure is also a public good. Let us see what it does for a business.

A WINDOW OF OPPORTUNITY: Alberto operates a warehouse that distributes specialty windows to home builders. His company delivers most of its products to construction sites in three small metropolitan areas located twenty miles north, fifty miles south, and seventy miles east of the warehouse. Just-in-time delivery of windows is important to the business because builders want to avoid the expense and risk of storing windows before installation; they also need to "close up" a new house as soon as possible to protect its interior. Because delays in construction are costly, they need to avoid late deliveries. Alberto's facility is one mile from the intersection of two limited-access highways that enable him to deliver windows in 30% less time, and at less cost, than he could using other roads.

The highway is a public good because it creates externalities. Builders in the metropolitan areas get the benefits of quicker delivery, and lower prices for windows, than they would have otherwise. Home buyers also benefit from lower building costs. To make things fair, the government employs its taxing authority to require both users (Alberto's company) and nonusers of the highway to cover the costs of the road through taxes. The nonusers include Alberto's customers, home buyers, and the many other persons and firms who benefit from the homes that are constructed.

Governments provide public goods because they can collect money from most everyone who benefits from them. In a private market many beneficiaries of public goods could avoid paying for them.

How does the provision of public goods reduce the number of free riders in society?

People who benefit from public goods without paying anything for them are called **free riders**. (This refers to more than highways!) The private market often cannot exclude free riders. For example, our society has accepted the view that the existence of an educated population benefits even those who do not acquire education themselves. If all schools were private, those who paid tuition would, in effect, be paying for the benefits received gratis by nonstudents. Society would consider such an outcome unfair. Governments that provide public goods can reduce the number of free riders by requiring everyone to pay school taxes.

Can private markets supply us with public goods?

There are private market alternatives for many public goods that are commonly provided by governments. In the field of education public and private schools exist side by side. Other examples are less common. Businesses and wealthy individuals may employ their own security forces in place of relying on public police. Some families or groups of homeowners have their own private parks, roads, and lakes that they can enjoy while excluding those who do not pay for them.

Our society places high values on access to education, transportation, protection, and recreational facilities. *Private market alternatives for public goods are not practical or affordable for most people. Yet society feels that they are too important to let anyone be deprived of them.*

Can governments do anything about externalities that are bad?

Education, highways, and protection create benefits for users and nonusers; that is why we call them *public goods*. But many private market activities create externalities that are costly for people who are not directly involved. Some economists refer to these as **public bads**, which is not just a play on words. Suppose my neighbor hires a hard rock band (which she gets from the private market) to play loud music at a backyard party to which I am not invited. The music benefits her guests who come to hear it, but if I do not like it and want to go to bed before the party ends, my suffering from noise pollution is an externality that is a public bad.

Private market activities frequently generate more serious public bads. A factory that dumps pollutants into a river is creating a public bad. People outside the plant may have to bear the costs of water pollution; they might include fishermen, recreational water users, or nearby residents. Those who get the plant's products or receive income from the plant may feel that their benefits make the bads justifiable, but the others will get no compensating advantages for their suffering.

Markets fail to work well when they create public bads that harm inno-

cent people. Public bads give the polluter, its customers, and its employees all the benefits while other people pay for them. As long as people who get no benefits suffer, the polluter underpays for what he/she uses. That is when the market does not work. My neighbor pollutes the air with noise and does not have to pay for the disturbance it costs others. A manufacturing plant may pollute the water without having to pay for lost fish catches, foul odors, and other costs that society must bear.

If people or businesses that create externalities underpay for the resources they use, they are likely to use more resources and create more pollution than they would otherwise.

Private market arrangements could be made, without government intervention, to cover the costs of public bads. My noisy neighbor might offer to take me to dinner to compensate me for my sleepless night. The owner of the plant might make payment to fishermen whose catches were diminished by water pollution. But these arrangements are not easy to make. One reason is that it may not be clear exactly who is harmed and what the extent of their damages are.

Here is where government can often help. In response to water pollution, it might levy a tax or fine on the plant to cover society's losses from the pollution. If this tax is set correctly, it will make the polluter pay for the full value of any damages he causes. Alternatively, it might make him reduce pollution. *Government helps the economy's markets to work fairly if it makes a polluter pay the total cost of what the person or business takes away from society.*

THE NONORGANIC FARM: Ruth and Lyle run a truck farm on the borders of two housing developments. The homeowners in these developments all get water from deep wells. The pesticides Ruth and Lyle use seep into the ground and contaminate the well water pumped by the homes. When these damages were discovered, the government ordered Ruth and Lyle to share the cost of constructing a water treatment plant and to lay water lines to the developments. They cut down on the use of pollutants, treated their water, and continued farming. But faced with these new costs, the truck farm became less profitable.

Originally the two farmers were getting a free ride at others' expense. Once the government forced them to pay the full cost of their farming operation, which included the damage caused to others, they paid their fair share for the resources they were using.

How about my noisy neighbor? Government could help with laws about public disturbances, enforced by the local constabulary. Here prevention, rather than compensation, would be the remedy.

Governments can help to prevent, or to compensate society for, damages created by public bads.

Should the government stop all public bads from being created?

If you are like most people, you do not junk a car because it has a bad muffler; you fix it. The economy would be a lot poorer if we shut down all activity that created any public bads. What good government can do is to make polluters reduce the public bads they create or to pay for the damages. That is why automobile inspection laws require car drivers to replace faulty mufflers that create air and noise pollution. These laws motivate drivers to correct problems they might not otherwise be motivated to correct. If the privilege of driving were valuable enough, drivers would pay to fix or to replace their cars and continue driving. (A few profligate drivers might be content to just go on paying fines, although if the fines were high enough, a new muffler would be cheaper.) However, for some drivers the added cost of fixing their cars would not be worthwhile; they would stop driving. In either case, pollution would be reduced.

Suppose Ruth and Lyle spent $1,200 to grow a ton of lettuce, which they could sell for $1,600 and earn a profit of $400. When the government required them to pay the cost of water treatment, they figured their production costs rose to $1,450 per ton. Although their profits were sharply reduced, from $400 to $150 per ton, they continued growing lettuce. If the government had simply forbidden farming on the land, jobs on the farm would have been lost, incomes would have dropped, and the supply of food would have been reduced. Of course, if the lettuce had not been valuable enough to provide the revenue needed to cover the cost of water treatment, Ruth and Lyle would have shut down their operation. In an efficient market economy, that would have been fair and beneficial to society, although it would have caused some personal hardship for Ruth and Lyle.

If an economic activity creates public bads and innocent parties have to pay for these externalities, producers are poaching from society. Economists use the term **market failure** to describe such a taking of social resources, whether intentional or not. *Governments should intervene in private markets to make producers pay the full costs of the resources they use, but it would be wasteful to cut off their use just because there are externalities.*

How else should government intervene in private markets?

There are other ways that governments help markets to work. Economists have argued for decades that fair **competition** brings consumers the best products and prices. Fair competition means that markets must be open; anyone who has a better product or service, or who can provide goods more cheaply, should be free to serve customers in the market.

Governments have **antitrust laws** to promote competition. These laws generally make it illegal for existing firms in a market to restrain new competitors from entering a market.

TANYA CANS THE COMPETITION: For twenty years Jimmie ran the only trash collection firm serving all of the residents in a group of communities. His company charged each household $340 per year for weekly pickups, with a two-can limit. Tanya and two college friends felt the firm was offering poor service at an inflated price, so they bought a used garbage truck and solicited customers for $290 per year, with a four-can limit. Jimmie lobbied local dump sites to get them to refuse to accept trash from the upstarts, in effect preventing the three friends from doing business. Tanya and her partners filed an antitrust suit against Jimmie's firm and the dump sites. They won and were soon collecting new customers, and their trash.

Tanya used antitrust laws to enable her new company to get into a market, resulting in lower prices and improved service for customers. Antitrust laws do not forbid monopoly; if no one wanted to compete with Jimmie, we could hardly accuse him of being an unfair competitor. Antitrust laws are designed only to allow competition;

they make it illegal for existing business firms to bar others from trying to compete with them. *Governments can promote competition in markets by making markets accessible.*

While antitrust laws promote new competition, other laws try to support the market economy by creating barriers to unfair competition. Copyright and patent laws are examples. If a company patents one of its products, another firm cannot offer the identical product, nor can two publishers sell the same book. The reason for these laws is to promote innovation. By protecting a patent owner, for example, government helps an inventor to get the rewards of her/his work. Patent protection in the U.S. is provided for only seventeen years. Nonetheless, without patent protection inventors would not have as much incentive to make new discoveries and to create better products. In the long run, less innovation means less competition. In effect, patent laws help inventors to get the full and fair price of their works. *Governments make laws to promote competition by preventing others from claiming part of the rewards (the inventor's or author's "price") for inventions and writings.*

Governments also provide court systems and agencies, such as the U.S. Department of Justice, to support the laws that help to make the market economy work.

Can governments lessen poverty?

The idea of **income redistribution** is at least as old as the story of Robin Hood. Income redistribution is the job of taking some money from those who have it and giving it to those who have little or nothing. In a pure market economy, income redistribution is handled by charitable organizations. Religious and civic groups collect money from donors and distribute money, food, or services to those in need.

But society has come to feel that private market solutions to the problems of needy individuals are not enough. The slack must be taken up by government.

Government activity in income redistribution is not new. Readers of Charles Dickens's novels are familiar with his moving descriptions of British government poorhouses in the nineteenth century. Germany, under Bismarck, started a government-run retirement plan in the 1890s. But it has only been since the Great Depression of the 1930s that national governments have become seriously involved in redistributing income.

The U.S. federal government is the nation's major provider of **social insurance** programs. Social insurance programs are intended to provide financial safety nets for those who would be unable to meet their needs through the private market (earnings, savings, and nongovernment aid). However, most social insurance benefits are not just given to those in need. Social security is the largest federal social insurance plan. Medicare is the huge health insurance component of social security. Both programs are available to participants regardless of income. (By contrast, medicaid is a program available only to persons with low incomes.) To pay for social security and medicare, payroll taxes are taken from employers and employees and are distributed to those who qualify for benefits. Another federal social insurance program gives food stamps to low-income persons.

Social insurance is not the only way governments redistribute income. The federal government provides or subsidizes public housing and veterans' benefits. Unlike social insurance, these are services, rather than cash payments. But the intent is the same. They supplement a person's ability to meet her or his needs.

At the state level wage earners and/or employers are required to contribute to state unemployment compensation funds, whose moneys are used to give income to unemployed persons. State and local governments also provide public assistance (welfare) and spend more money on health care than does the federal government.[1]

The rationale for most of these programs is to enable people to consume more services or goods than their incomes would permit, or to allow them to enjoy them without depleting all of their own assets. *People would be much poorer and would have to forgo many necessities if they lacked the social insurance and other benefits governments provide.*

Government redistribution of income is one important approach to reducing the incidence of poverty. While private charities still play important roles in income redistribution, the role of governments has grown substantially and is now larger. Because of their taxing authority, *governments are the major providers of income redistribution.* Robin Hood is now part of the system.

What does government produce?

Governments are a big part of most market economies. But governments make only a small part of the goods and services they dispense. *Governments serve as purchasers of many things that are made by businesses.*

Governments produce few of the things they distribute to the public; governments are major shoppers in markets supplied by business firms. For example, school districts generally do not construct their own school buildings; they contract for building projects with private business firms. States may contract with private firms to lay down highways. Military and police forces do not make their own weapons, with a few exceptions. *Governments acquire most of what they need by buying from businesses in the market.*

In addition to making purchases, governments make **transfer payments**. A transfer payment is money paid to an individual for which nothing is demanded in return. Most income redistribution programs involve transfer payments. For example, Aid to Dependent Children (welfare) programs make cash payments to low-income households; the recipients are not required to perform any government services for these payments when they are received. When making transfer payments, governments act as agents, collecting money from taxpayers and passing it on to beneficiaries. Some recipients of transfer payments will have made contributions to government programs at other times. Examples of such programs are social security, medicare, and unemployment compensation, which are supported by payroll taxes (☞ Art. 22: Taxes and Tax Burdens, page 298, for a discussion of payroll taxes). However, benefits from these programs are still considered to be transfer payments because these benefits are based on need at the time they are received, not on the amount of past contributions recipients may have made. (The social security program provides benefits that are partially determined by past contributions.) *Large shares of government budgets are used to make transfer payments.* Governments serve more as money handlers than as producers.

Look at Table 21A to compare government expenditures with purchases.[2] Although the federal government spent $1.5 trillion dollars, only about 30% of that sum represented its direct contribution

Table 21A

Government Purchases vs. Government Expenditures in 1993 ($ billions)

ITEM	FEDERAL	STATE & LOCAL
Expenditures	$1,507	$865
Purchases	444	705
Purchases as a percent of expenditures	29%	82%

to the nation's output of goods and services created during that year; most of these goods and services were created by private business firms for the government. The federal government is a big customer of our nation's businesses. The rest of the money spent by the federal government was distributed directly to the private sector of the economy in the form of transfer payments, grants-in-aid, interest on debt, and subsidies.

State and local governments create or distribute relatively more goods and services. They also employ many of the crews that build and maintain roads, they own and run the schools, which provide education, and they employ their own police forces; these governments rely less on purchases of final goods and services from private businesses. The difference between the federal and nonfederal governments, with respect to both direct production and distribution of goods and services, is primarily due to the different jobs they do.

Our nation's most comprehensive measure of the value of production is the gross domestic product (GDP). It totaled $6,343 billion in 1993, of which $1,149 billion ($444 from federal government plus $705 from state and local government) came from governments. *Governments directly purchased only about 18% of the value of all goods and services created in the United States.* Most of the money going to governments is merely passed through to others.

How much money do governments spend?

Now that we know most of the jobs governments are expected to do, let us look at the numbers. Table 21B summarizes the expenditures of the United States federal government for one typical year.[3] Notice how the federal budget is distributed among purchases, transfer payments, grants, interest payments, and subsidies. *The largest share of the federal government budget is used to make transfer payments.* About 30% of the budget is used to finance purchases.

Interest payments on the national debt claim about an eighth of the total expenditures, and this figure grows every year as the federal government adds to its debt. The federal government deficit in 1993 was $241 billion.

Payments to state and local governments under a variety of intergovernment programs claim another eighth. Finally, a small percentage of the budget goes to make subsidy payments. Examples of subsidies are agricultural price-support programs.

The distributions of state and local government budgets are quite different. Look at Table 21C, which adds together expenditures of all nonfederal governments.[4]

Purchases of goods and services by state and local governments (including payrolls) are relatively larger than those of the federal government. The

Table 21B

Federal Government Expenditures in 1993 ($ billions)

ITEM	AMOUNT	PERCENT
Purchases	$444	29%
Transfer payments	658	44
Grants to state and local governments	186	12
Net interest payments	184	12
Subsidies	36	2
Total:	1,508	99*

*Total is not equal to 100 due to rounding of values.

Table 21C

All U.S. State and Local Government
Expenditures in 1993 ($ billions)

ITEM	AMOUNT	PERCENT
Purchases	$705	82%
Transfer payments	250	29
Net interest paid	–53	–6
Dividends received	–10	–1
Subsidies less surpluses	–27	–3
Total:	865	101*

*Total is not equal to 100 due to rounding of values.

second-largest expenditure category is for transfer payments (e.g., welfare, unemployment compensation).

While many nonfederal governments borrowed money to build highways, schools, etc., the interest on their debt is not a major budget item. Nonfederal governments paid out $65 billion in interest. But they also received a larger sum in interest payments (from the federal government and others) of $118 billion. Putting these interest payments and receipts together, their net interest *added* $53 billion to their income.

State and local governments, in aggregate, generated a budget surplus of about $26 billion in 1993.

Is there anything else in the job description of government?

The 1930s can be considered the dawning of big government in the United States. Many of our largest social insurance and other "entitlement" programs were started. But there was another sea change in defining governments' missions in the economy. During the Great Depression some radical economists began to realize that government, because of the size of its involvement in the nation's markets, could become a therapeutic agent for the nation's economic health. Government could use its spending and taxation to regulate economic development. The deliberate use of taxes and spending for the purpose of fostering employment, incomes, and growth (or to control inflation) is called **fiscal policy**.

Since those dark years of depression the federal government has added fiscal policy to its job description. This new task is responsible for some of the huge growth of the federal government since that time. State and local governments have generally been excused from practicing fiscal policy, largely because their borrowing capabilities are more limited and the impact of their spending is localized.

Fiscal policy is a special and controversial topic, so it is left for a separate article (☛ Art. 24: Fiscal Policy and Government Debt, page 325).

ARTICLE 22:

TAXES AND
TAX BURDENS

Who Really Pays the Bills?

Are taxes fair?

In the private market, prices are "fair" because you pay only for what you get. The price we pay for something corresponds to its value . . . or at least to the value we *expect* to get from a good or service. (Unfortunately, the reverse is not always true. Sometimes we get stung. That is why we use the Latin term *caveat emptor*, meaning "let the buyer beware," when talking about markets. The ancient Romans probably originated the term when they did business with used-chariot dealers.)

Taxes are the contributions we make to support government. Government provides many public goods that cannot be fairly or efficiently distributed in private markets, such as defense, schooling, highways, and law enforcement (☛ Art. 21: The Business of Government, page

285). The price system does not work for supporting all of these government services because many people might not choose to pay for some of them. Furthermore, many people who need government services cannot afford to pay. That is why all taxes cannot be like prices. But that does not mean that taxes are unfair. There are many kinds of taxes. *Most taxes are designed to follow one of two principles of fairness: the benefits principle or the ability-to-pay principle.*

What is the benefits principle of taxation?

Some taxes are designed to conform to the **benefits principle of taxation**. These taxes are very much like prices you pay in the private market because you pay them only if you get some benefit in return. The federal gasoline tax in the United States is based on the benefits principle. The money from this tax is used exclusively to pay for the construction and maintenance of highways. You pay this tax only when you buy gasoline; the government assumes that if you buy gasoline, you use government highways. The gasoline tax is a means for getting highway users to pay for these roads, and it is a lot more convenient than having tollbooths all over our highways. The rationale is that the more you use public highways, the more you should pay for them. Fair is fair.

User fees are taxes that are based on the benefits principle. Like the gasoline tax, these are fees you pay only when you use some government service. Turnpike charges and bridge tolls are user fees that drivers pay for the use of some government-run facilities. Airport boarding fees are charges intended to help governments pay for airport facilities. Some municipal governments sell water and sewage services; in most cases users of these services pay government in accordance with their volume of use. Despite its name, a user fee is a tax because it is a payment to government.

Taxes based on the benefits principle are fair because these taxes are paid only by those who benefit from certain government services.

What is the ability-to-pay principle of taxation?

The lion's share of government revenue comes from taxes that are based on the **ability-to-pay principle of taxation**. What you pay in such taxes has little to do with your use of government services; it depends only on what you are assumed to be able to pay. The higher your income or wealth is, the more tax you pay (not considering any tax loopholes you might be able to slip through). *The fairness of an ability-to-pay tax is that people are made to contribute to government in accordance with their means.*

The best example of an ability-to-pay tax is the **income tax**, which is the major source of revenue of the U.S. federal government and of many state governments. Supporters of the income tax claim that the more money you receive each year, the more you are able to pay to support government.

Payroll taxes are paid by employers and employees on the basis of wages or salaries. The most important payroll tax is your contribution to the social security fund, which is used to provide benefits to retirees, survivors, and other beneficiaries. Contributions to unemployment compensation funds and medicare are also made through payroll taxes. Payroll taxes follow the ability-to-pay principle because what you pay depends on what you earn.

Sales taxes are important sources of revenue for most state governments, and for some local governments as well. Sales tax payments are not linked to the benefits you receive from government services; they are based on income, although not directly. The rationale for the sales tax is that the more income you have, the more money you are likely to spend, and the amount of sales tax you pay depends on what you spend. Special taxes that some cities and counties charge for theater tickets, hotel rooms, and restaurant meals are essentially sales taxes, although they may not be called that. (There will be more to say about sales taxes below.)

Other ability-to-pay taxes are based on **wealth**. (Economists use the term *wealth* to describe the total value of anyone's possessions, regardless of how humble or grand they may be.) **Estate and gift taxes** are based on the wealth a beneficiary receives. **Property taxes** are charged to owners of real estate, investments, and other forms of wealth. Property taxes have been the traditional source of revenues for local governments in the U.S.

One of the curiosities of local taxes in the United States is that real estate property taxes are expressed in **mils**. A property tax mil is one-tenth of one percent of the **assessed value** of a property (land and buildings). For example, if the property tax millage charged on all real estate property in a town is fifty mils, and a particular residential property is assessed at $80,000, then the owner must pay a yearly property tax of $4,000 (which is 50 × 1/10% × $80,000) on that property. The assessed value of a property may be larger or smaller than the market value an owner could get when selling it.

ERIC AND HANNA ARE CHILD-FREE, BUT NOT TAX-FREE: Eric and Hanna, who are in their sixties, never had children to benefit from the local public schools. Twenty years ago, when they had an annual income of $20,000, they bought a house for $60,000. Due to inflation, this house is now assessed at $150,000, and they pay 2.5% of this assessed value ($3,750) every year to the school district. That is because their house is part of their wealth and is regarded as showing their ability to pay. Inflation and work experience also increased their employment income to $50,000. However, they just retired and their income is now only $35,000 per year; with this income the property tax hits them hard. At the same time, their younger neighbors across the street pay the same amount of school tax, even though they have four children in the schools.

Some politicians and economists argue about the fairness of the property tax, claiming that it is a poor indicator of ability to pay. Eric and Hanna bought their house many years earlier for a fraction of the $150,000 it is worth now, and they are retired on a modest income that would not permit them to buy the same house today. But the property tax is blind to their circumstances.

A lot of people have been forced to pay a high portion of their current income for property taxes as a result of the dramatic escalation of property values that we experienced from the 1950s to early 1980s. In addition, a growing percentage of our aging population is living longer on retirement incomes than when the property tax system was put in place. There is little wonder that many policy makers regard the property tax today as less fair than the income tax because the property tax base (property values) may no longer accurately measure one's ability to pay taxes.

While most income or wealth taxes are collected from persons, *corporations pay taxes that correspond to their income (profits).* Some states also charge taxes based on net worth or on some other measure of the property owned by a firm. Both types of taxes are based on an assessment of a corporation's ability to pay for government.

How do economists measure the fairness of ability-to-pay taxes?

Not all ability-to-pay taxes are equally fair. Economists measure the degree of fairness by the **progressivity** of a tax. A **progressive tax** is one that takes a higher *percentage* of the earnings of high-income persons, or corporations, than it does from others. The graduated income tax used by the U.S. federal government is a progressive tax.

> **ANDY AND CLYDE PAY THEIR TAXES:** Andy and Clyde are professional wrestlers who travel around the nation to participate in wrestling matches. They are employees of a firm that promotes matches. Their earnings depend on their win/loss records and on their ability to attract spectators. Andy earned $115,000 last year, after expenses, on which he paid a federal income tax of $28,200; this was about 25% of his income. Clyde, who is less well known and whose theatrical techniques are not well developed, earned $45,000 and paid $7,800 in federal income tax; this came to only 17% of his income.

The federal income tax is a progressive tax because it took a larger share of Andy's income than of Clyde's earnings. The federal income tax rate rises as income rises.

But not all income-based taxes are progressive. Andy and Clyde also pay a social security (SS) payroll tax. The SS tax paid by an employee is 6.2% of income up to a ceiling amount that rises every year. (The employer pays an equal amount.) During the year when Andy and Clyde earned the amounts listed above, the maximum income on which SS taxes were collected was $55,500. So Andy paid a SS tax of over $3,400 (6.2% of his first $55,500 of income, with the rest not taxed), which was about 3% of his total income that year.

At the same time, Clyde paid the full SS tax of 6.2% on all of his earnings since his income was below the maximum subject to the SS tax that year. The SS tax is an example of a **regressive tax** because the *share* of one's income used to pay the tax declines as income rises. The burden of a regressive tax actually falls as one's ability to pay rises.

It is not always obvious that a tax is regressive. Sales taxes are actually regressive, even though they claim the same percentage of one's spending, regardless of income. The reason that sales taxes are regressive is that high-income persons generally spend a smaller share of their income than do low-income persons. In other words, high-income earners save a greater percentage of the income they receive, and the income they save is not touched by the sales tax.

ANNETTE AND GLENDA PAY SALES TAXES: Annette and Glenda live in a state that charges a 5% sales tax on all purchases. As the associate director of marketing research for a large consumer products distributor, Annette earned $120,000 last year. She put away a significant percentage of this income in a pension plan, tax-sheltered annuities, and in purchases of government savings bonds. In addition to rent and some other things that are not covered by the tax, Annette spent $70,000 of her income on items that were subject to the sales tax, resulting in payments of $3,500 to the state. That came to a mere 2.9% of her income. During the same year her secretary, Glenda, earned $28,000. Glenda could not save much from that income and spent $22,000 on taxable purchases. The sales taxes she paid came to $1,100, or 3.9% of her income. The sales tax claimed a larger share of Glenda's smaller income. That is why the sales tax is a regressive tax.

If the sales tax exempts major basic purchases such as rent, food, clothing, and health care, it will be less regressive than a sales tax that covers all of the goods and services people buy.

The property tax is often a regressive tax. How regressive it is often depends on your age. When Eric and Hanna, whom you met above, retired, their income fell about 30%. Despite their loss of income, their property tax did not decline. As a result, during their retirement it claims a larger share of their income than it did before. That makes it regressive.

The regressive effect of the property tax is not only felt by retirees. People in their twenties and thirties often buy houses that are worth three or more times their current income, counting on their future rising incomes to lessen the burden of mortgage payments. People in their forties and fifties often have incomes that are closer to the value of their homes. Yet the property tax rate ignores these differences in income. The result is that the property tax usually takes a larger chunk of the lower income of younger homeowners than of the higher incomes of middle-aged homeowners.

If an income or wealth tax always results in taking the same share of one's annual income, we say it is neither progressive nor regressive. It is a **flat tax**. Some states and cities have simple income taxes that are flat taxes, meaning that these taxes claim the same percentage of high incomes as of low incomes, and they do not have loopholes that favor high-income earners. *The fairness of an ability-to-pay tax can be judged by whether it is progressive, flat, or regressive. Regressive taxes are often regarded as less fair than other types of taxes.*

Taxes that follow the benefits principle can also be judged on the basis of their progressivity, but it is often hard to do so. For example, a user fee such as a bridge toll may be regressive if the same toll is paid with equal frequency (say, five times per week) by car-driving commuters who have different incomes. But it may not be regressive if lower-income commuters generally take the bus across the bridge, or carpool, so that each individual pays only a small share of the toll.

Is a progressive tax the fairest type of tax?

Some people feel that progressive taxes are the fairest type of ability-to-pay tax because of what economists call the **diminishing marginal utility of income**. This ornate term means that each dollar of income you get means less to you as your income rises. In other words, the more income you have, the less of a burden a dollar of tax is to you.

The notion of diminishing marginal utility of income means that if you added an extra 10% to the income of a $100,000-per-year executive, you would improve her well-being and lifestyle no more than you would if you gave, say, only an extra 5% to her $20,000-per-year au pair. That is because the au pair has fewer dollars to start with so that an extra 5% would mean more to her than an extra 10% would mean to her employer. If that is true, it might be fair to tax the executive at twice the rate you tax the au pair. Perhaps the two women would be making equal sacrifices for government if the executive were taxed $10,000 (10% of her income) and the au pair were taxed only $1,000 (5% of her income).

We have no proof that the value of money diminishes as you receive more of it (although I would be happy to sign up for an experiment). But it is a persistent notion that economists and policy makers have held for years. *Many people feel that progressive taxes are fairer than regressive or flat taxes because they believe in the diminishing marginal utility of income.*

How can income or wealth taxes be used to help a market economy to grow smoothly?

Taxes exist to pay for government. But the economy gets a side benefit from ability-to-pay taxes. They are not just a fair way of supporting government, they help a market economy to grow smoothly. This is not their purpose, but it is a kind of bonus. (This may be like saying that while making love is an important expression of emotional bonding, it is also good exercise!)

Ability-to-pay taxes make a nation's economic growth smoother because they act as **automatic stabilizers**; *income and wealth taxes slow down rapid growth and cushion economic declines.*

When the economy is growing, incomes and property values rise, with the result that larger amounts of income are taken away from taxpayers by income and wealth taxes. This means that consumer spending might not increase as much as it otherwise would. That is good for the economy because rapid increases in spending often result in inflation (☛ Art. 11: Inflation, page 128). By taking more dollars out of people's pockets when incomes rise, the government softly pushes against inflation.

But when the economy declines, income and wealth taxes take fewer dollars away from taxpayers, leaving more dollars to spend when they are most needed. Because tax burdens fall when incomes decline, periods of economic downturn are softened because people can spend some of the dollars they would otherwise have to pay in taxes. That spending may help put the economy on the path to recovery.

There are other types of automatic stabilizers. When people become jobless, their lost incomes may be partly replaced by government benefits such as unemployment compensation, welfare payments, and food stamps. Some economists even propose that the federal government provide a **negative income tax** plan. Under such a plan, tax filers whose incomes fall below the poverty level should be able to file for cash payments from the government, not just tax refunds or credits (☛ Art. 23: Taxes and Tax Reform, page 311).

Where do the taxes come from?

Now let us see how important different types of taxes are. Table 22A shows receipts of the U.S. federal government in a typical year.[5] The largest single revenue source is income taxes. *Most of the revenue collected by the federal government comes from taxes that are tied to income.*

Wealth taxes play a minor role in federal government finance. Customs duties and estate and gift taxes are wealth taxes because they are assessed on the value of property.

While half of federal revenues come from income taxes, income taxes contribute only a fifth (personal plus corporate income taxes) of the revenues of state and local governments. See Table 22B for the details.[6] Sales taxes, which are related to income, account for another 24%. One-fifth of nonfederal government revenues come

Table 22A

Receipts of the U.S. Federal Government, 1993

SOURCE	AMOUNT ($ BILLIONS)	PERCENT
Personal income taxes	$520	41%
Corporate income taxes	143	11
Indirect taxes (customs, excises, gift, etc.)	85	7
Social insurance programs, including social security	518	41
Total:	1,266	100

Table 22B

Receipts of State and Local Governments, 1993		
Source	Amount ($ billions)	Percent
Personal taxes and nontax revenues	$166	19%
Corporate income	30	3
Sales taxes	212	24
Property taxes	184	21
Social insurance	68	8
Federal grants-in-aid	186	21
Other taxes	44	5
Total:	890	101*

*Total is not equal to 100 due to rounding of values.

from property taxes. *Nonfederal governments rely on a mix of income-related taxes and wealth taxes.*

Who really carries the burden of a sales tax?

One of the most important contributions economics makes to the study of taxes is to identify the **incidence of a tax**. Tax incidence is the analysis of who actually carries the burden of a tax. Often the one who gets the tax bill is not the one who winds up paying all of it.

Let us look at a state sales tax of 5%. If I bought a pen that had a store price of $20, I would get a bill for $21: $20 for the pen and $1 for the state tax. Although I am charged for the full 5% tax, do I really pay all of it myself? Generally, I would not. In practice, the store shares the tax with me by charging a lower price for the pen than it would otherwise. Of course, it does not announce this fact, but it happens. In other words, the store absorbs part of the tax by accepting a lower price for itself. This is called **tax sharing**. It means that part of the burden of the tax falls on the buyer (whom the state actually charges) and part of the burden is carried by the seller. The amount of tax sharing that takes place between buyers and sellers depends on how the customers are likely to react to higher prices.

How large a share of the tax is put on the buyer depends on the **price elasticity of demand**. This is the sensitivity of buyers to prices. If buyers are sensitive to the price of a product, then economists say the demand is elastic; buyers will cut back purchases significantly if the price rises. If buyers are not fussy about price, demand is inelastic; they will not cut back much on their buying if prices go up (☞ Art. 9: Prices and the Economy, page 102). The more elastic the buyers of a product are, the larger the share of a sales tax that will be picked up by the seller. Smart sellers will have a sense of their customers' elasticity of demand, and they will use this sense to decide how to share a tax with customers.

> **REYNOLDO SIZES UP HIS CUSTOMERS:** Reynoldo owns an appliance dealership in a city near the borders of three states. His state charges a 5% sales tax. Dealers in the two nearby states, which do not impose sales taxes on home appliances, charge $1,250 for a certain popular set of clothes washer and dryer. All dealers in the tristate area have the same net factory cost for the appliances. Reynoldo's dealership charges $1,220 for the pair, for an after-tax price to his customers of $1,281, which is less than 2.5% above his competitors' prices. He accepts a lower markup for his dealership after passing on the sales tax (5% of the $1,220 price) to the state.

If Reynoldo added the full 5% tax to the appliances, he would be asking customers more than $1,310 for the pair. This would hurt his sales for two reasons. First, he would be going into the next $100 range, which would make his higher price more noticeable. Second, he knows that his customers are sensitive to price (they have an elastic demand) and that they see the ads run by the other merchants in the tristate area. They would readily cross the state borders to save as much as $60, but they might be willing to pay up to $31 more than his out-of-state competitors' prices so they can enjoy the convenience of dealing with a local merchant for sales and service. He feels that his lower profit is better than losing sales.

In Reynoldo's case the incidence (or burden) of the 5% sales tax is half on buyers and half on the seller. That is, Reynoldo's buyers really pay only half the sales tax. In general, *the more sensitive buyers are to price, the less of the tax they will bear themselves.* To look at it from the other side, the more sensitive buyers are to price, the greater will be the incidence of the tax borne by sellers.

If Reynoldo had no competition from tax-free state dealers, he might have made his customers pay the full amount of the sales tax. They would probably have paid it because they had no less costly substitute to turn to.

Who carries the burden of an excise tax?

An **excise tax** is a tax the government charges the seller. The federal gasoline tax, mentioned above, is an example of an excise tax because the government charges it to the seller for each gallon of gasoline sold. Excise taxes are not as widely used as are sales taxes.

The seller who has to pay an excise tax will have to decide how much of this tax burden can be shifted to the customer. If the customer is sensitive to price and will cut back sharply on purchases if the price goes up, the seller will bear most or all of the excise tax. Otherwise the seller will pass it on to the buyer.

> **GASOLINE BUYERS PAY THE DEALERS' TAB:** A new 4% gasoline excise tax was charged to all gasoline dealers in a given region. To keep their profit level the dealers simply raised gasoline prices from the former average of 95¢ per gallon for 87 octane ("regular") gasoline up to 99¢. Of course, at the higher price some sales were lost. But, since the dealers were located in a prosperous region, their customers did not react significantly to the price rise. The volume of gasoline pumped stayed at about the same level as before the excise tax was imposed.

The dealers got their customers to carry the burden of the new tax that the government actually imposed on sellers. (In fact, the dealers collected more than 4% in additional revenue per gallon, since a 4¢ rise above 95¢ is a 4.2% boost in price. But the dealers felt the extra amount was fair compensation for their additional paperwork for paying the new tax.)

Sharing of an excise tax is no different from sharing of a sales tax. *If buyers are not sensitive to price, they will bear the larger burden of either a sales tax or an excise tax. In a free market it makes no difference whom the government actually holds responsible for paying the tax.*

Is the incidence of a tax based only on the price sensitivity of buyers?

So far our discussion of tax incidence has focused on the demand side of the market, i.e., the responses of buyers. But the supply side is also important. Sellers also have price sensitivity that influences their decisions about how much to sell. If sellers are hit with an excise tax that reduces their profits, they may cut back on production. If the cutback causes a shortage, customers may become willing to pay more for the product to get back the old amount.

HELMUT SHORTENS HIS WEEK: Helmut runs a busy one-chair barbershop. His fee for a standard cut is $10. When his state imposed a 6% sales tax on services, his profit fell by 60¢ per haircut. Since he now made less profit, he decided to cut back his shop hours from fifty hours per week to forty-five hours so he could enjoy some additional leisure time. But his many loyal customers complained. So Helmut raised his price to $11 and, with the incentive of higher profits, went back to a fifty-hour week. He lost no customers because of the higher price.

Initially the new sales tax made Helmut reduce the supply of his services. But his customers had little sensitivity to price changes, so he raised his prices and increased the supply of haircuts. *A tax on sellers of goods or services may cause them to reduce the quantities that they supply if they are sensitive to the prices they receive.* In such cases sellers may try to shift the burden of the tax onto buyers as a condition for going back to their old levels of supply.

Are excise and sales taxes the only kinds of taxes that can be shared between buyers and sellers?

In a market economy any type of tax can be shared between buyers and sellers. It makes no difference whom the government requires to pay the tax, buyer or seller. If a bus company has to pay higher tolls (user fees) to drive a bus through a tunnel or across a bridge, it may be able to raise its fares to pass some or all of this new tax burden on to its passengers; the bus company is charged the toll, but the passengers will bear part or all of the burden. If a corporation has to pay higher taxes on its income (profits), it may try to raise the prices of its products or services to restore its former level of after-tax profits. No matter what it is called or how it is charged, a tax is a cost that will be paid by either buyer or seller, depending on the price sensitivity of the buyers and sellers.

ARTICLE 23:

TAXES AND TAX REFORM

Footprints on the Economy

How do taxes affect the economy as a whole?

Taxes can strongly influence both the level and the type of activity in a market economy. The actual impact that a tax has depends on its type and its size. *Taxes affect employment of workers, the willingness of people to work, business investment, and savings.* Let us look at these things separately.

How do taxes affect hiring?

Hiring employees is a cost of doing business. Businesses try to make profits, and these profits depend, in part, on what it costs to have people working for them. How many people businesses hire is affected by taxes. If new or higher taxes make workers more expensive to hire (less profitable), employers will try to reduce their payrolls by replacing some of them with other resources (computers, robots, etc.) or by redesigning jobs to make work more efficient.

The two types of taxes that affect hiring are payroll and income taxes. **Payroll taxes** are amounts of money taken out of your paycheck. How much you pay in payroll tax depends on how much income you receive. The higher your wages or salary, the more payroll tax you pay. Your required contributions to the social security trust fund (FICA) are payroll taxes; they are paid equally by employer and employee. Payroll taxes also include employees' payments for medicare and unemployment compensation funds.

In the current work environment many employers are trying to make their workforces more flexible by switching from payroll workers to temporary workers. "Temps" are technically not on the payroll of the firm that uses them because they are hired under contract, either directly or through an agency. But that does not hide or diminish the effects of payroll taxes. Someone has to pay them. If regular workers are on the payroll, then both the firm and the employee pay the payroll taxes. If they are temps working for an agency, the agency and the employee pay. If they are self-employed private contractors, the workers pay. Regardless of who hands the tax money over to the government, higher payroll taxes are passed on, at least in part, to the businesses that employ workers.

Payroll taxes have a direct impact on the cost of employing workers. For example, if the social security tax that must be paid by an employer rises, workers become more expensive. To an employer, higher payroll taxes are like increases in the wage rate (but unlike higher wages, employees do not get the benefit). How do employers typically react to higher payroll taxes? They may try to cut back on new hiring or reduce their current payroll by dismissing some employees.

Businesses pay other types of taxes such as income taxes on profits, excise taxes on some of the resources they use, property taxes on their stores, offices, and plants, and so on. The impact of these non-payroll taxes on employment is less direct and more difficult to identify. However, more taxes of any kind mean lower profits and less incentive to hire workers. *Higher taxes may lead to a reduction in the number of people working in the economy.*

Do taxes affect the amount of work people are willing to do?

You, like most workers, probably have some control over the amount of work you do. You can always choose between working and not working. However, too much leisure cuts down on your standard of living, unless you married well or were born to rich and generous parents. Even those who are employed can often decide how much they will work. The salesman can make one extra sales call, the office or factory worker may work overtime, the manager may bring work home over the weekend.

When personal income taxes rise, work becomes less profitable because what we get to keep (after taxes) from our extra efforts goes down. Economic theory tells us that *workers may respond to lower take-home pay by working less or not at all.* The spouse who wanted to earn some money for the family may decide to stay home. Some workers may drop a second job. The college professor may decide not to write that book.

However, economists have little evidence that higher taxes cause people to work less. In fact, some suggest that higher taxes may make people want to work more so that they can keep up their standard of living. *But most of the evidence we have suggests that higher tax rates have no more than a small negative effect on the amount of work people do.*

Do taxes affect business investment decisions?

Economists use the term **investment** only when they talk about businesses' acquiring the productive assets, or **capital stock**, that are needed to make goods and services (☞ Art. 16: Investment, page 197). The economy is strengthened whenever businesses make investments in capital stock because that enables the economy to produce more goods and services. This is how an economy grows. In fact, about half of the growth the United States has experienced over the past fifty years came directly from the accumulation of productive assets. The rest was due to investment in **human capital**, by which we mean the skills and capabilities of human beings. Human capital makes the difference between a bookkeeper and an accountant, and between a baseball rookie and a superstar. Both kinds of investment (in equipment and in human skills) are essential to make an economy grow.

How much businesses invest in capital stock depends on how profitable it is to do so. After all, businesses need to earn profits; profit is the food they live on. Taxes help to determine the profitability of investment. Lower taxes let businesses earn and *keep* more profit so *lower business taxes usually result in more investment.*

The income tax has a direct effect on investment. If the corporate income tax rate goes down, businesses become more profitable and are willing to make more investments.

Some tax laws can be specifically designed to stimulate investment, such as when they provide for an **investment tax credit**. An investment tax credit is a percentage of the cost of an investment that the government lets a firm use to reduce its taxes. It is a powerful tool. The U.S. Congress occasionally gives the nation temporary tax credits to stimulate a weak economy. Tax credits have to be temporary (they may be provided only for two or three years), otherwise they would not be such an effective quick pickup for the economy. A permanent tax credit would be like a constant diet of uppers; eventually the lift wears off. Here is how Ed made the tax credit work for him and for the economy.

Remember that the whole economy has millions of individual businesses like Ed's. So what they do collectively influences the economy. *An investment tax credit is an effective way to stimulate investment throughout the economy.*

Investment tax credits are great for boosting investment. That, in turn, creates jobs in the businesses that make capital stock. These are the companies that make computers, software, machinery, etc. What is more, the new equipment companies buy will make them more productive and profitable; that might motivate them to hire more employees and expand their businesses. Investment snowballs as it travels through the economy. The tax credit is an old and effective tool for energizing the economy.

AUTOMATING THE NEWSROOM: Ed runs a weekly newspaper that now serves three suburban towns. Its circulation of fifteen thousand has been static for many years. Ed wants the newspaper to grow by attracting readers from two additional nearby towns, which he estimates will boost circulation to a more profitable level of 25,000. His strategy is to expand the newspaper's coverage of local sports activities (a strong feature of local weekly community papers). Since he cannot afford to increase his staff of three, he is thinking about purchasing a computer software program that can produce background information and formats for sports stories. He would also have to buy a new high-power desktop computer to run the sophisticated software. With the new software and computer a writer would only have to enter some specific information into the program, such as the type of sport, scores, and the names of local teams and players, and the software would help to calculate statistics and compose the stories. With the software one of Ed's writers could double her/his output of newspaper copy, and what is more important, proofreading and correction costs would be sharply reduced. This is the only way Ed could expand his news coverage to include the two new towns he wants to target. But at a cost of $3,500 for the software and $4,000 for the computer, he thinks the total $7,500 investment might be too costly for his paper. That is why Ed has postponed this investment so far.

Ed's investment would not replace workers, but it would make his writers more productive. Now suppose new legislation provided for a two-year 15% tax credit. That means that, anytime during the next two years, 15% of whatever Ed invested in new capital stock could be used to reduce his income tax liability by the same amount. The tax credit

> would enable Ed to deduct $1,125 (15% of $7,500) of the software and computer costs from his income tax. In effect, this would make the investment $1,125 cheaper.
>
>   Ed decided to make the two investments because he could, in effect, do so at a hefty discount. At this lower cost, the investment would be profitable. In effect, the government offered to put up $1,125 toward the cost. Ed could not turn down this opportunity.

As great as it is, the investment tax credit is one-sided; it targets only investment in capital stock as a source of economic growth. Unfortunately, governments do not yet provide equally powerful tax incentives to influence investment in human capital, which has historically contributed just as much to growth as does capital stock.

For example, Ed will not get a tax credit for the money he will have to pay to a trainer who will teach his writers how to use the new computer and software. (Ed's costs would be tax deductions for his business, of course, but this would mean much less than a tax credit.) Perhaps when government policy makers recognize how much investments in human capital actually contribute to economic growth, we will have tax laws designed to stimulate investment in human beings just as we encourage investment in machinery. (In 1994 President Clinton proposed a tax credit for college tuition that would encourage investment in human capital.)

Governments promote investment in human capital in many ways, such as by providing public schools and financial assistance for college students. But governments do not use the tax system to provide temporary booster shots for a weak economy by encouraging investment in human capital.

Do taxes affect savings?

How does an economy pay for its investments? Most money for investment comes from **savings**. Savings is the difference between the income you receive and the amount of that income you spend. When people and businesses save part of their income, this money becomes available for investment. The saver can use her or his money to buy capital stock, or the saver can put it in a bank or buy stocks or bonds so that others can use the money to make investments.

The more money that is saved in an economy, the more funds there are for investment. A good prescription for growth is for an economy to encourage savings. Savings come from income that is not spent. The way to encourage saving is to make it more attractive than spending. Taxes can help.

The American tax structure does a lot to make savings *less* attractive. That is because an American earner must pay taxes on both the income he spends and on the income he saves. Then, when these after-tax savings are invested, any earnings these investments produce are also taxed, which amounts to a double hit on savings.

But the news is not all bad. Lawmakers in the U.S. have occasionally used taxes to encourage savings. The Tax Reform Act of 1981, which was the keystone of President Ronald Reagan's economic game plan, fostered increased savings by providing a novel tax incentive, the **individual retirement arrangement** (the initials *IRA* are often used to refer to an individual retirement *account* in a financial institution). This is a restricted account that can be built up by making contributions from one's current income. The hook is that the saver does not have to pay income taxes on the portion of his income contributed to the IRA, within certain limits. The approach is similar to that of the tax credit; what you save reduces your income tax bill. (But the IRA contribution merely reduces your taxable income, it does not give a credit.) The IRA worked well in the early eighties and encouraged large amounts of new savings, which then became available for investment in the economy.

Unfortunately, the later Tax Reform Act of 1986 put a ceiling on the level of income a saver could have to qualify for tax-free contributions to IRAs. (Of course, people at any income level can still make *taxable* contributions to an IRA, and the income earned in the IRA remains untaxed until benefits are withdrawn.) Part of the motivation for making fewer people eligible for tax-free contributions to IRAs was the discovery that IRAs were used more heavily by higher-income folks than by those of more modest means.

What was really surprising was that this response to IRAs was a surprise to lawmakers! After all, low-income people pay lower tax rates, so for them the tax appeal of the IRA was less. In addition, economists have known for decades that higher-income people can afford to save a greater chunk of their incomes without sacrificing their immediate material well-being. (That is why the rich worry about the price of gold bullion while the poor worry about the price of gold fillings.)

An economy that can encourage savings among its citizens will have more investment than one that encourages consumption. *Tax incentives can be used to encourage savings as well as investment. Economies that can increase their savings and investment can usually increase their rate of growth.*

How do income taxes influence interest rates?

In the United States people who own nonfederal government bonds do not have to pay federal income tax on the yearly income they receive from them. These **tax-exempt bonds** are issued by states, cities, school districts, sewage and water authorities, and other government agencies. In the language of finance, any nonfederal government bond is called a **municipal bond** (or simply a "municipal"). As an added benefit, investors who live in the state that issues a municipal bond they own may also be exempted from state income taxes on the bond's interest payments.

The tax exemption of interest payments on municipal bonds makes them attractive to many investors. That means that nonfederal governments can sell their bonds more easily, and at lower interest rates, than can issuers of other bonds, such as corporations. Let us see how this appealed to Nickie.

CATCHING THE BEAT WITH BONDS: Nickie is a member of a heavy-metal rock group. Her income this year will be in the upper six figures, so she will pay a marginal income tax rate (for state and federal income taxes combined) of 45%. She has about $500,000 invested in high-grade bonds of blue-chip corporations. This corporate bond portfolio gives her a yield of 8.2%. After paying 45% in income taxes she gets a net return of only 4.5% on her savings, which she reinvests. Stu, her financial manager, urges her to switch her money into tax-exempt bonds issued by governments in her home state. Recently school district bonds there were paying 6.2%, which is free of income taxes, so Stu expects Nickie to get 1.7% more than her current return on corporate bonds. That would give her an additional investment income of $8,450 next year. Nickie likes Stu's idea and plans to send this unexpected additional income to her mother, who needs the money to pay off the trailer in which she lives.

State and local governments realize that they can pay less interest on their bonds and still give investors a larger after-tax return than the investors would get from taxed bonds. Consequently, *municipal bonds pay lower interest rates than investors can get on other bonds of comparable risk because interest payments of municipal bonds are tax-exempt.* After all, why should they pay investors more than necessary to borrow their money? Governments want to save taxpayers' money.

How do taxes influence government spending?

The above tax advantage (some people call it a tax "loophole") has facilitated and encouraged government projects such as the building of roads, schools, airports, and water-treatment plants. *By exempting interest payments of municipal bonds from federal income taxation (and some state taxation), the U.S. government has given local governments a powerful incentive to make important investments in infrastructure.*

THE BOARD GOES TO MARKET: A suburban public school district has a growing population of young people. As a result, its school buildings have been overcrowded for several years. The district's school board has been reluctant to start construction of a new school building because borrowing costs on the bonds it would issue would be so high that the district would have to raise property taxes, which would have substantial local opposition. However, recently federal income tax rates rose. As a result, investors around the nation increased their demand for tax-exempt municipal bonds (which are tax loopholes), and this new demand pushed the rate of interest on these bonds down to a level that the school board felt it could afford. Shortly after the federal tax hike, the school district issued bonds and broke ground for a large new building. The construction of the building created a lot of work for local builders, craftsmen, and suppliers.

Because the interest payments made by municipalities are exempt from some income taxes, any increase in federal income tax rates makes them even more attractive to investors. That is why *an increase in income tax rates generally leads to lower borrowing costs for nonfederal governments.* With this incentive, state and local *govern-*

ments may borrow more and engage in new activities that help the economy to produce new goods and services.

Do taxes affect some industries more than others?

The building construction and housing industries are sensitive to tax changes. One reason is that the interest borrowers pay on mortgages is currently deductible from income before paying federal (and some state) income taxes. This is true of mortgage interest paid by businesses and by homeowners. If this tax deduction were taken away, as is occasionally suggested by some lawmakers, there would be less borrowing for construction and home buying. With less demand for houses, the prices of existing homes would fall; in time, these lower house prices would discourage new home building, too, because new houses would be less profitable to put up.

Many other taxes favor or disfavor specific industries. A federal excise tax is currently charged on gasoline; when this tax goes up, gasoline producers and dealers are hurt.

Import tariffs (taxes collected whenever certain goods are brought into the country) are charged on some goods, such as automobiles and steel. *Import tariffs partially protect certain home industries from foreign competition,* whereas other industries are left to fend for themselves. Tariffs make imports more costly so they hurt those who want to buy them. Of course, one man's poison may be another's feast; for example, higher import tariffs on autos help to stimulate the business of domestic automakers while they hurt both importers and buyers of foreign cars. *Changes in the type or level of taxation imposed by government has an uneven impact on the economy.* Some industries will be helped and others will be hurt.

Some states do not extend their sales taxes to specific types of items, such as food, clothing, or medicines. This favors those who make or produce the exempted goods and helps people who spend a large share of their incomes on these products.

What changes are likely to take place in the tax structure of the United States?

The **tax structure** of government is the term we use to describe the system of taxes used to raise revenues. In the United States the tax structures of the federal, state, and local governments are different. The federal government relies heavily on income taxes paid by individuals and corporations. Most state governments use sales taxes to raise the revenues they need. However, state income taxes are becoming increasingly important as state governments have expanded their activities and as the federal government in the 1980s reduced its support of state budgets.

By contrast, local governments (towns, counties, school districts, sewage and water authorities, etc.) have traditionally relied on property and other wealth taxes to raise money. But this, too, is changing. Because the property tax is regarded as being too regressive (see discussion above), *state and local governments will probably increase their use of income taxes.*

But the federal government is also seeking to change its tax structure. A popular European revenue raiser, the **value added tax (VAT),** is being eyed by policy makers in the U.S. *The U.S. federal government wants a new source of income and it will probably be the value added tax.*

How does the VAT system work?

The VAT is a percentage tax charged on the increase in the value of any item as it is manufactured and distributed. If you buy potted flowers for $5 each and then sell them on a street corner before Easter for $9 each, you have added a value of $4 to your product. As the seller, you pay a VAT only on the $4 of **value added** to the product.

Under the conventional American sales tax system, the sales tax is paid only by the *buyers* of a final good or service, and the amount of tax collected depends on the total value of that item. The VAT, by contrast, is paid by all *sellers*, regardless of whether they are selling raw materials, semifinished goods, or final products. The VAT is paid only on the value each person adds to the product. *The VAT assesses all types of economic activity when they result in a market transaction.* Under the VAT system, each seller pays a sales tax that depends only on the contribution that seller made to the product.

HEINZ MAKES A PIN: Heinz was a wholesale custom jeweler in Germany, which had a 14% VAT. One of his customers, a retail merchant, ordered fifty commemorative gold pins. Heinz deals in his nation's currency, deutsche marks (DM). Let us trace the steps in filling this order.

1. To make each pin Heinz purchased seven grams of eighteen-karat gold (about one-fourth ounce) for DM 165 (which was worth $100 at that time). By the time he bought the gold all of the firms that had previously handled it, paid total value added taxes of *23 marks* (14% of DM 165) for the metal to be used in each pin.
2. Heinz also purchased other materials for DM 55 per pin, bringing his materials cost up to DM 220 each (DM 165 plus DM 55). All of the firms that had previously handled these materials, at their various stages of manufacture, paid value added taxes that totaled about *8 marks* per pin (14% of DM 55).
3. After molding each pin, adding a fastener, and inscribing it, Heinz sold the pins to the merchant for DM 500 each. This meant that Heinz's work had a value added of DM 280 (DM 500 minus DM 220). Therefore, he paid a VAT of *39 marks* (14% of DM 280) per pin to the government on the sale of each pin.
4. Finally, the merchant whom Heinz supplied individually packaged and sold the pins for DM 800 each. Ignoring the cost of packaging materials (which was minor), the merchant added a value of DM 300 to each pin. For this he paid a VAT of *42 marks* (14% of DM 300).

To help you to follow the government's share of each transaction, the VAT payments are italicized. In all, the transactions provided the government with revenue of 112 marks per pin.

The VAT is essentially a sales tax. But to avoid double taxation, *each seller pays tax only on what he or she did to increase the value of a product.*

But do not be fooled by the small amount of tax (42 marks) paid by the final buyer. She really may not be getting out of paying the burden of the VAT. That is because all of the VAT payers try to pass some of the tax they paid on to their customers in the form of higher prices. The 800 marks the final customer paid for each pin included a lot, if not all, of the VATs paid along the way. Without the VAT payments, the pin would have been cheaper than 800 marks; in fact it might have been 112 marks cheaper.

What is the attraction of the VAT system?

The VAT requires that each contributor to the value of a product pay something to the government. This piecemeal approach to taxation means the government does not lose revenue if one party destroys or diminishes the value of the final product. Let us see how that benefits government.

CARL IS STUCK WITH THE PINS: Carl is the merchant who paid Heinz DM 500 apiece for fifty commemorative pins. The pins honored a popular soccer team that had many fans, many of whom had substantial incomes. Carl ordered the pins well before the soccer season began. Much to his surprise, the team lost most of the games it played during the season. This made the team's fans less enthusiastic in their displays of loyalty. Carl sold only ten pins at DM 800 each, earning 420 marks in VAT payments (300 × 14% × 10) for the government. (Had he sold all fifty pins, he would have turned over VAT payments of 2,100 marks.) His suppliers felt that Carl did not work hard enough to market the product.

Under a simple American-type sales tax system the government would have collected tax only on the ten pins Carl sold to final users. (In most states, sales taxes are not charged on the sale of materials that are used to make final products.) The revenues from a sales tax, which is imposed only on the final buyer, make the government's tax collections depend exclusively on the last value given to the product, despite all the work done beforehand.

However, by collecting some tax payments at every step of the manufacture and distribution of the pins, the government got VAT revenue from all of the pins before the final sales were made. This is fair because the value of the work done by Heinz (and for which a VAT was collected) was not diminished by any errors of judgment Carl might have made in selling the final product.

Now let us look at the effect of the VAT on savings. Some economists might argue that *the VAT encourages savings* more than does a simple income tax. That is because the VAT is voluntary in the sense that it is paid only if one chooses to buy something. One can *avoid* paying the tax simply by saving income, rather than by spending it. (This is also true of all types of sales taxes.)

As a national sales tax, the VAT conforms to the ability-to-pay principle of taxation. After its long and successful use in Europe and elsewhere, look for it to make its appearance in the U.S.

IN THE NEWS . . .

"The Many Vexations of a Vat"

U.S. NEWS & WORLD REPORT, April 26, 1993, Vol. 1. 114, No. 16, page 60

The Clinton administration proposed a value added tax to raise the huge amount of money it would need for its proposed health care program. The VAT, used in many other nations, is flexible. For example, a lower VAT could be charged on food than on luxuries. But the VAT is a regressive tax because it would fall heaviest on persons who must spend a large share of their incomes, such as the poor and elderly.

ARTICLE 24:

FISCAL POLICY AND GOVERNMENT DEBT

Spending and Taxing
Our Way to Economic Health

Reading Suggestion: After reading this article you might wish to read or skim the material on monetary policy in Article 18: The Federal Reserve.

Is the government supposed to help the economy?

A 1940s melodrama, *Mighty Joe Young,* told the story of a huge African gorilla who was brought to America to star in a nightclub act. In the course of his travels Joe's handlers came upon a burning orphanage where, to everyone's surprise, this hulking animal became a superhero by gently rescuing children from the blaze.

Governments were established to provide certain services that the market economy could not effectively furnish. These were mundane activities such as maintaining national defense, a justice system, schools, parks, roads, and so on (☛ Art. 21: The Business of Government, page 285). The ups and downs of a market economy were considered to be the business of the **private sector**, that part of the economy consisting of households and businesses. The **public sector** (government) was expected to stay in the background when it came to economics.

It was not until the Great Depression of the 1930s that attitudes on this matter slowly changed. A prominent British economist, Lord John Maynard Keynes (rhymes with Hanes), boldly suggested that government use its awesome buying power to spend money until the economy turned around. He urged Western governments to undertake massive building projects to put people to work and, most important, to put money into their pockets. The method of this economic nostrum was that the people who got this money would spend it to meet their needs, and this spending would create more jobs, and more income, for others.

It was a radical idea at the time. Imagine trusting the economy's recovery to politicians! At one point during the 1930s Keynes traveled to the United States to personally sell his ideas to President Franklin D. Roosevelt. As the Great Depression worsened, some of the Keynesian prescription was cautiously adopted and woven into Roosevelt's economic policies.

But the massive military spending brought about by World War II did more to lift Western nations out of the depression than did the relatively moderate government programs initiated earlier by Keynes's followers. Nonetheless, the outcome was just as Keynes had forecast: spending in the public sector led to prosperity in the private sector. By the mid-1940s Keynesian economics became de rigueur.

One of the major contributions of the Keynesian reformation was the conviction that government could be an agent for improving the economy. We found that it had a heart and a will to help, just like the mighty Joe Young.

How does government change economic conditions?

The Keynesian remedy for economic distress has two parts: government spending and taxes. Compare them to two parts of a car. Government spending is the accelerator that can speed up the economy by pumping money into the economic system. Taxes are the brakes that pull money out of the economy to slow it down.

Suppose we are in an economy whose income is declining, a condition we call **recession** (☛ Art. 4: Business Cycles, page 35). One of the painful effects of recession is unemployment: idle people, machinery, and other resources. Higher government spending (pushing down on the accelerator) can be a remedy for recession. *Government spending is one way of putting unemployed resources back to work and raising income.* Another remedy is to cut taxes (loosening the brakes). If taxes are reduced, people and businesses can keep and spend more of their income. *Lower taxes lead to higher spending in the* *private sector, and this also raises income.* If desperate moves are called for, government can do both, increasing government spending and cutting taxes at the same time.

Why do we need brakes? When the economy grows too fast, it may run short of resources. What happens to a rapidly growing economy is that it can run short of manpower (inclusive of both genders), machinery, or raw materials. It takes time to increase all of these ingredients of economic growth. Meanwhile, spot shortages develop that push prices upward.

When a wide range of prices move up, the economy experiences **inflation**. When inflation is high, it has enough harmful effects on people to call for a government remedy. Inflation often occurs when people, businesses, and government spend too much; it occurs when they try to buy more goods and services than the economy can produce (☞ Art. 11: Inflation, page 128). *The principal Keynesian remedy for inflation is to raise taxes.* When taxes go up, people and businesses get to keep less of what they earn. If they have less, they spend less.

An alternative remedy for inflation is to cut government spending. But this remedy may be milder because it would have direct impact on fewer people than would be affected by a broad tax increase. A government budget cut would primarily hurt people who sell goods and services to government. A tax increase would hit just about everyone.

Economists have coined the term **fiscal policy** to refer to the government's use of taxes and spending for the purpose of changing conditions in the economy. A fiscal policy to attack a recession might call for increased government spending and/or reduced taxes so people have more money to spend. *More spending is the elixir for a weak economy.* A fiscal policy to reduce inflation might call for just the opposite: lower government spending and/or higher taxes. *Less spending is the elixir for inflation.*

IN THE NEWS . . .

"How a Capital Gains Tax Cut Can Help the Economy"

U.S. NEWS & WORLD REPORT, December 9, 1991, Vol. 111,

No. 24, page 65

Both Democrats and Republicans were pushing tax cut proposals as catalysts for recovery from the 1990–91 recession in the U.S. Democrats wanted a temporary middle-class tax cut that would stimulate consumer spending. But Republicans argued that consumers would only use tax savings to cut households' debts rather than to spend. Republican Sen. Phil Gramm and Rep. Newt Gingrich lead an effort to reduce the capital gains tax and to expand IRA's, expecting these tax cuts to promote investment.

How does deficit spending affect the economy?

The government runs on a budget that includes spending and revenues, mainly from taxes. When government spending in any year exceeds its revenue, we say that the government is engaged in **deficit spending**. As you can imagine, *deficit spending stimulates the economy because it means government is putting more money into it than it is taking out.*

A fiscal policy that calls for deficit spending will speed up the economy. But the impact of deficit spending does not depend on whether or not it is deliberate. Deficit spending accelerates economic growth even if it is merely the result of the failure of political leaders to control government spending. As we will see later in this article, the U.S. economy has been consistently energized by unintended deficit spending for the past couple of decades.

Government debt is the cumulative result of deficit spending, just as your credit card balance is the result of your charged purchases.

Government debt is important not just as a memorial to past spending. The legacy of deficit spending is debt and interest payments must be made for that debt out of every subsequent government budget.

Is deficit spending always necessary to jump-start a weak economy?

A fiscal policy designed to stimulate the economy is called an **expansionary fiscal policy**. (By contrast, a fiscal policy that is designed to reduce inflation by reducing or eliminating deficit spending is called a **contractionary fiscal policy**). *A fiscal policy that increases spending and/or reduces taxes at the same time, to put more money into the economy, could result in deficit spending.* If it does, the government would have to borrow money to cover the deficit.

But an expansionary fiscal policy does not have to result in borrowing. The government could avoid borrowing by raising taxes enough to pay for its spending. That means there would be no deficit spending. It is not obvious at first, but this type of balanced budget fiscal policy could actually do the trick. *A larger government budget could jump-start a lagging economy even without deficit spending.*

Suppose the government increased its total spending by $100 billion and at the same time raised taxes by the same amount. This policy would certainly not create more debt, but it would help the economy. To see why, let us see how the tax increase would hit Sally.

SALLY'S MONEY COMES OUT OF RETIREMENT: Sally earned $70,000 last year as district manager of information systems for a credit-rating agency. With an average tax rate of 20%, after her deductions and exemptions, she took home $56,000, from which she plans to save $10,000 and invest it in foreign-government bonds. Because her company had a bad year, Sally will still earn only $70,000 this year (no raise). But the legislature surprised her by raising tax rates. Because of this Sally will pay a rate of 24% and take home just over $53,200. Since she is not able to reduce her contribution to her household's expenses ($46,000), she will manage to save only $7,200. That means the government will take and spend $2,800 that Sally would have put aside.

At the old lower tax rate Sally would have saved $10,000 of her money and, in effect, retired it (not put it back into the economy). The tax increase changed all that by putting $2,800 of that money to work in her nation's economy because she will be able to save only $7,200.

An expansionary fiscal policy can actually stimulate the economy, without deficit spending, simply by taxing and spending money that individuals would not have spent. In other words, the government can design an effective fiscal policy that "pays for itself."

Who makes decisions about the nation's fiscal policy?

Decisions on government spending and on taxation, the two tools of fiscal policy, are embodied in the annual budget of the federal government. The budget is the responsibility of the executive branch of government. The budget is put together by the president's staff (specifically, the Office of Management and Budget, or OMB, in the White House). This budget is submitted to the U.S. Congress, which, after negotiations and changes, writes the budget into law. *Congress passes the legislation that authorizes spending and taxation.*

We saw that government gradually recognized, beginning in the 1930s, its obligation to keep the economy sound by fostering growth and tempering inflation. This recognition was formalized after World War II when the U.S. Congress passed the Employment Act of 1946. The legislation called on the executive branch to use government to help the nation's economy. In accordance with this act, *the president of the U.S. has a **Council of Economic Advisors (CEA)**, which analyzes the economy and makes recommendations on economic policy.* The CEA is headed by a chairperson and consists of a small group of professional economists. The CEA is generally not an "all-star" team of economists, but its members are accomplished and recognized in the field. Most of them are economics professors.

Each president forms his own CEA and generally selects economists with whose views he is comfortable. CEA members who develop divergent views, as did CEA chairman Martin Feldstein under President Ronald Reagan, are generally banished back to the classroom, where, of course, there is less income and prestige. Some presidents have selected economists from the business community;

Presidents Ford and (after Feldstein's resignation) Reagan favored nonacademic leaders of the CEA.

The CEA is the group that is expected to deliver fiscal policy initiatives. By contrast, the president's Office of Management and Budget (the OMB) is a more political entity. Over the years the relative influence of the CEA and the OMB on fiscal policy has varied.

How much deficit spending has there been in the United States in recent years?

Table 24A gives you some snapshots of deficit spending in the U.S.[7] (Because the purpose of the table is to compare federal deficits with federal budgets each year, the dollar amounts have not been

Table 24A

U.S. Federal Spending and Deficits, Selected Years (years with two or more quarters of recession are shaded)

Year	Federal Spending ($ billions)	Federal Deficit ($ billions)	Deficit as % of Spending
1970	$ 196	$ -3	2%
1971	210	-23	11
1973	246	-15	6
1974	269	-6	2
1975	332	-53	16
1979	504	-40	8
1980	591	-74	13
1981	678	-79	12
1982	746	-128	17
1983	808	-208	26
1990	1,253	-221	18
1991	1,324	-270	20
1992	1,381	-290	21
1993	1,408	-255	18

adjusted for inflation; they are nominal values.) The last year in which the federal government had a surplus was 1969. That means that *following the 1960s, continuous deficit spending has been a permanent pep pill.* We have become hooked on the stuff!

The table highlights recession years and includes the years that followed them. Deficits tended to expand just *after* the onset of recessions (these are the years that are shaded in the table). Here is why. First, a recession is not recognized by policy makers until after it is well under way; that is, it takes time for even the brightest folks in Washington to see a need to help the economy. Second, once the need is recognized, it takes time for political wranglers and their advisers (in the White House and on Capitol Hill) to design a stimulative fiscal policy and to push it through Congress. Third, it takes time after passage of budget and appropriations bills for the government to disperse its money throughout the economy (place orders and pay bills). Often these lags are so long that the economy almost nurses itself back to health before help arrives.

Although the budget deficit was large during the recession of 1974–75, a string of serious budget deficits began in the 1980s. The deficit got as high as 26% of the government budget (which meant the government spent 26% more than it took in).

There were back-to-back recessions in 1980 and in late 1981 to 1982. The government's response was to initiate large tax cuts, Ronald Reagan's "supply-side" plan for prosperity. The logic behind **supply-side economics** was that tax reductions, especially for high-income persons, would give people more after-tax dollars with which to boost savings. Lower tax rates would also make investment more profitable. (Of course, tax cuts would also give everyone more money to spend, but the long-run objective of supply-side economic policy was to stimulate savings and investment.) This investment would create jobs and new incomes, and the resulting increase in the supply of goods and services would usher in prosperity.

The expected outcome of this prosperity was that government income-tax collections would rise enough to shrink the budget deficit. In other words, the supply-side gurus (mostly a small group of young economists and dilettantes) claimed that cutting taxes would actually increase government tax revenues in the future.

The supply-siders' predictions of balanced government budgets were never realized. Their tax cuts did not create enough new income and tax collections to erase the annual budget deficit. Deficit spending escalated and stayed rather high. The economy prospered in the 1980s, but not for the reasons the supply-siders gave us. The huge deficits helped the economy to grow because they were really just the old Keynesian elixir; deficit spending was stimulating economic growth. Supply-side economics did not fulfill its promise of closing the government budget gap; it seemed just to give us old wine in new bottles. Meanwhile, *budget deficits as a percentage of the federal government budget remain in the 15–20% range.*

If an expansionary fiscal policy does not have to include deficit spending, why does the government continuously run deficits?

We saw earlier that even a perfectly balanced government budget stimulates the economy because it spends some money that the private sector would not have spent. A really "neutral" government budget (one that neither helps nor harms the economy) would be one that shows a small surplus.

Even a balanced government budget is hard to achieve because *it is politically easier for legislators, presidents, and governors to raise spending than it is to raise taxes,* especially in election years.

Politics aside, the government could avoid debt in the *long run* if, after running deficits when the economy was weak, it put together government budgets that would result in a surplus when the economy was strong. By carefully planning for budget surpluses when the economy is strong, the nation could offset deficit spending when the economy is weak.

A budget surplus is actually a type of contractionary fiscal policy because a surplus would sap some energy out of even a strong economy. Government policy makers are always reluctant to put any brakes on economic growth, except to combat serious inflation. Policy makers have the same attitude toward brakes as do teenage drivers.

Another reason why an expansionary fiscal policy generally calls for deficit spending is that deficit spending is a lot more powerful than is a balanced budget.

What effect might deficit spending have on interest rates and on the availability of credit?

Anytime the government increases its spending or reduces taxes (or both), the economy gets a boost. Either way, the economy grows in the short run.

But fiscal policy always has a side effect. The culprit is the interest rate. The interest rate is the price of borrowed money. When it wants to borrow, the government has to compete with the private sector to get the money people have to lend. As a result of this competition for funds, *deficit spending often pushes the interest rate up.* That makes borrowing more expensive for everyone.

> **DENNY AND ELISSA PUT OFF THEIR DREAM HOME:** Denny and Elissa have a combined income of $35,000. They are planning on building a three-bedroom house for their growing family. They want to construct a house on a lot they inherited from Elissa's parents. Their bank will give them a mortgage as long as the monthly payments do not go over $700 per month, which is what the bank feels they can reasonably handle on their income. Three months ago the fixed interest rate for mortgages was 9%. This would have allowed them to borrow $85,000, which is what they will need for their dream house. But while they were locating a builder, the government increased its borrowing to support a massive deficit. Interest rates shot up, so that when Denny and Elissa went back to their bank for the loan, the mortgage rate was 11%. At that rate a $700 monthly payment will support a mortgage of only about $75,000. The young couple postponed building their dream house until their income rises or they can come up with a larger down payment.

When interest rates rise, many borrowers are reluctant or unable to borrow. That cuts down spending and incomes in the private sector.

Higher interest rates lock a lot of people and businesses out of the credit market. When people cut back on borrowing, spending goes down and the economy suffers from it.

A lot of money is borrowed in the United States. Table 24B gives you a sense of how much is involved.[8] The table shows the amounts of money that were owed by various types of borrowers during the first three months (first quarter) of 1993 and of 1994.

(These were formal credit market debts and do not include informal lending, such as the $100 you might have loaned to your son to finance his prom date and that he promised to repay out of his summer job earnings.)

The largest debts were accumulated by households such as yours. Most of the household debt (about 70%) consists of home mortgages; the rest is for such things as auto loans and credit card balances.

The U.S. government is the next biggest borrower, followed by corporations and then by state and local governments. Most of the $248 billion the U.S. government added to its debt between 1993 and 1994 went to cover the official budget deficits during this period. This borrowing is not sensitive to interest rates; the U.S. Congress never seems to cut back on anything just because the cost of financing is too high.

But other borrowers do pay attention to interest rates. The $1 trillion+ of nonfederal government (mostly tax-exempt) securities are IOUs issued by state and local governments. These governments often accelerate or delay projects on the basis of borrowing costs. Corporations that borrow money are also influenced by the interest rate because borrowing costs cut into their profits.

Mortgage borrowing is sensitive to interest rates because these rates determine how large borrowers' monthly payments are. Lenders are very concerned about that, as Denny and Elissa found out.

Aside from mortgages, household debt covers loans for automobiles, vacations, and a variety of other purposes. Many of these loans are discretionary, which means they can be put off if interest rates are too high. Auto dealers and bankers, for example, know how consumers react to interest rates, and that is why lending rates are often displayed so prominently in dealer showrooms and in bank lobbies (especially if they are low).

A lot of money is borrowed by financial service organizations. The federal government has agencies that borrow money to finance mortgages. Finance companies borrow money to help people buy automobiles, furniture, appliances, and other things. Banks and savings institutions are also big borrowers.

Some debt in Table 24B appears twice. For example, a finance company, such as General Motors Acceptance Corporation (GMAC), may raise money by borrowing it in the financial markets and then

Table 24B

Credit Market Debt in the U.S., 1993 and 1994

BORROWER	1993 Q1* ($ BILLIONS)	1994 Q1 ($ BILLIONS)	CHANGE ($ BILLIONS)
NONFINANCIAL BORROWERS			
U.S. government	$3,140	$3,388	+248
State and local government	1,007	1,073	+66
Corporate business	2,419	2,482	+63
Farms	133	137	+4
Other businesses	1,145	1,135	−10
Households	3,981	4,265	+284
FINANCIAL INSTITUTIONS			
Government related	1,756	1,952	+196
Financial firms	1,218	1,332	+114
All borrowing:	14,799	15,764	+965

*Q1 = first quarter of the year.

relend it to a car buyer (household) for the purchase of an automobile.

Borrowing in 1993 was a little below average (especially among unincorporated small businesses) because this was a year of slow economic growth following the recession that ended in 1991. Total net borrowing was equal to about 15% of the gross domestic product that year, which is the value of all goods and services produced.

Federal government borrowing to finance the deficit puts upward pressure on interest rates, and this, in turn, discourages some private-sector borrowing and spending. The loss of some private-sector (borrowing and) spending cancels out some of the stimulation deficit spending gives to the economy. If consumers, corporations, and nonfederal governments are very sensitive to interest rates, this backlash can be strong.

Higher interest rates are not the only reason for the backlash. When the federal government borrows huge sums of money, it is taking a big chunk of the cash lenders have to give. This leaves less money for others to borrow. Now, the federal government is the nation's safest borrower; in fact, it is the world's soundest debtor. No one fears that the U.S. government will renege or default on its debt. That means it moves to the head of the line formed by borrowers; others get what money is left after the federal government is done borrowing. This situation is called the **crowding-out** effect.

Economists are not sure how big the crowding-out effect is, although *the crowding-out effect is certainly not large enough to reclaim most of the benefits the economy gets from deficit spending.* A more important effect of crowding out is that it takes money away from business investment and uses it for government spending; more about this later.

How efficient is deficit spending as a remedy for economic weakness?

If there is a crowding-out effect from government borrowing, its size depends on how sensitive borrowers are to interest rates and how much credit lenders have to give. If credit is tight, deficit spending could drive interest rates up significantly. If borrowers are sensitive to interest rates, they will cut back borrowing and spending on credit. That could make the crowding-out backlash zap a lot of the benefit out of deficit spending. *Deficit spending will not be an effective remedy for economic weakness if interest rates rise sharply and if borrowers are sensitive to these rates.* If borrowers are not sensitive to rates and if there is plenty of money available for lending, deficit spending can be very helpful for the economy.

How does deficit spending influence investment?

Deficit spending certainly adds spending to the economy. But does government borrowing help us as much as borrowing in the private sector? This issue goes to the heart of economists' debate over the real burden of deficit spending and debt.

Businesses generally borrow money for investment. They use it to get new machinery, equipment, buildings, and other assets that help the economy to produce more, and to grow, in future years. In fact, sophisticated investors would not lend any money to businesses without knowing that it will be used to increase production and income.

Most of the money lent to individuals is used to buy long-term assets such as houses and automobiles. Much less money is lent for pure consumption, such as for vacations.

Just like an individual or business, the government can spend its borrowed money on consumption or investment. If the government borrows and spends money on investment, it will buy assets that will produce goods and services in the future, and the economy could get long-term benefits. But consumption is a temporary economic stimulant.

When the U.S. government borrows money, it does so to help finance its entire budget. Unlike the corporate investor, the buyer of a U.S. Treasury bond does not know exactly how her or his money will be used. It may help to pay for a new office building, health care, bullets, foreign aid, employee pensions, or statues.

Businesses produce annual income statements and balance sheets that make distinctions between money spent on operations and money spent to acquire assets. But in the United States governments do not have separate budgets for operating expenses (consumption) and for capital expenditures (investment); all the money is lumped together. But we can get a general idea of how governments use borrowed money by looking at their budgets. For example, in 1993 the federal government spent about $1,500 billion. Only about 30% of this amount went to nondefense purchases, as shown in Table 24C.[9] Furthermore, only a small fraction of the purchases went for durable goods (tangible assets that last three years or more) and for structures.

Most federal money was spent on transfer payments (money just passing through government hands as it goes to individuals, businesses, or other governments to be spent by them). Most of the federal money spent on purchases went to government employees as salary and benefits. (If you want a breakdown of government spending, look at Tables 21B and 21C in Article 21.) As you can see, the federal government does little investing.

The story is much the same for nonfederal governments, which are also represented in Table 24C. Employee compensation, operating expenses, and transfer payments got most of the money.

An important implication of this is that *the crowding-out effect of government borrowing reduces the nation's investment.* That is because

Table 24C

Purchases by Governments in 1993

Type of Purchase	Federal ($ billions)	Percent	Nonfederal ($ billions)	Percent
National defense	$303	68%		
Nondefense	141	32		
Total purchases:	444	100		
Durable goods	78	18%	$37	5%
Nondurable goods	17	4	63	9
Services (primarily employee compensation)	333	75	506	72
Structures	16	4	100	14
Total purchases:	444	101*	706	100
Total expenditures:	1,507		865	

*Total is not equal to 100 due to rounding of values.

businesses borrow money primarily to make investments. Governments (especially the federal government) primarily borrow money for consumption. Borrowing for consumption does not contribute much to the nation's economic growth. But borrowing for investment might increase future long-term growth. Governments borrow money to buy corn and eat it; businesses buy seed corn and plant it.

What has deficit spending done to the national debt?

By the early 1960s the federal government had accumulated a debt of just under $300 billion, most of which resulted from World War II in the 1940s and the Korean War in the early fifties. This debt more than tripled, to $1 trillion (one thousand billion), in the next twenty-two years, although only a small part of this new debt was due to the Vietnam War. Then the deficit spending of the 1980s caused the debt to take off; in only ten more years the debt tripled again, passing $3 trillion in 1992. *The net federal government debt is going to pass $4 trillion in the late 1990s, which will come to about $16,000 per adult and child.*

Actually, these figures do not tell the full story because they only represent the official "net debt." In truth, the government's "gross debt" passed $4 trillion in the middle of 1992. But about one-quarter of this debt is held, as investments, by government agencies and trusts. The largest owner of debt is the Social Security Administration; your retirement money has been loaned to Uncle Sam. This part of the debt is what the government owes to itself. Some economists consider the net debt (total debt minus the debt that the government owns) to be more important. A great way to keep your creditors quiet is to owe the money to yourself!

To whom does the federal government owe its debt?

As we just learned, the U.S. government owes a large chunk of money to itself. But what about "outsiders"? When the federal government engages in deficit spending, it finances it by selling securities such as bonds. Currently just under one-fifth of these securities are owned by foreign investors, but this foreign share is slowly and steadily growing. Another 10% of the debt is owned by Federal Reserve Banks.

The rest of the debt is owned by American individuals, pension funds, investment companies (e.g., mutual funds), and businesses. We might say that Americans owe a lot of their government's debt to themselves, in addition to what the government owes to itself. That does not mean, however, that it is unimportant. *The federal debt takes money from the private sector and diverts it to the public sector (government).* The public sector uses the money differently from the way it would be used if it were in private hands.

We should be concerned if the share of U.S. federal debt owned by foreigners continues to grow. There is no justification for being xenophobic just yet, but to the extent the U.S. government is reliant on foreign investors to get money, it is subject to economic conditions and political pressures in other nations.

Has the federal debt become more burdensome?

While the federal debt in the United States is very large in absolute numbers, many economists prefer to compare it to the nation's income. The burden of the debt lessens if the nation's output grows faster than its obligations.

Table 24D

Total Federal Debt of the U.S. and Gross Domestic Product, Selected Years

YEAR	DEBT ($ BILLIONS)	GDP ($ BILLIONS)	DEBT/GDP
1950	$257	$266	97%
1960	291	505	58
1970	381	985	39
1980	909	2,644	34
1990	3,206	5,482	58
1995*	4,960	7,022	71

*Estimated debt and GDP.

In the early 1950s the United States government was carrying a huge debt, relative to its gross domestic product, as a result of the costs of fighting World War II and the Korean War. The federal debt grew much more slowly than did the nation's income during the 1960s and 1970s, despite the Vietnam War and the recession of 1973–75. The low point was reached in the early 1980s when the federal debt was about one-third of GDP. The massive deficits that resulted from the tax cuts and defense spending of the Reagan administration, and subsequent government budget deficits, rapidly increased the debt load, which is shown in Table 24D.[10]

For many years some economists argued that the growing debt was not an increasing problem because, while it grew, the nation's economy was growing faster. This is no longer true. By comparing the debt to the nation's output of goods and services, it is evident that *the burden of the national debt has increased since 1980.*

Has the U.S. government done anything to reduce the federal debt?

If political rhetoric about deficit spending were legal tender, we could have paid off the national debt long ago. The only way to reduce the debt is to develop federal budgets that have *surpluses.* If you take another look at Tables 24A and 24D, you will see that the U.S. government is a long way from doing that.

The most we can expect to do over the next several years is to reduce the deficit (that is, add less to the debt). To this end the nation's most ambitious and realistic government budget policy makers are just trying to reduce the *rate of growth* of the debt by shrinking the annual deficits.

The Gramm-Rudman-Hollings Act of 1985 (GRH) was an ambitious attempt to legislate the government into balancing its budget, and it even set forth a deadline of 1991 for doing this. For a while everyone felt secure that they had snared the deficit monster. But the law had no teeth. It might have worked had the members of Congress required that they incarcerate themselves (or at least cut their own salaries) for failing to meet their targets. So in what was a quiet gesture of defeat, the U.S. Congress passed the Deficit Reduction Act of 1990, which put GRH out of its misery and declared the good intentions of our lawmakers to reduce deficit spending when they can get around to it.

There was a vocal group of frustrated lawmakers and other citizens who called for a **balanced budget amendment** to the U.S. Constitution in 1995. It would have made it illegal for Congress to pass a federal budget that had a deficit. This is equivalent to forcing someone to cut up her/his credit cards (a kind of economic plastic surgery). The benefits would be clear. First, budget makers would have to exercise fiscal responsibility just as consumers do. Second, the national debt would stop growing. Many taxpayers probably think that paying annual interest on the debt that was built up from past deficit spending is like buying oats for a dead horse. The third benefit is that taxpayers could look forward to seeing this interest obligation freeze or even shrink. But the attempt to pass such an amendment went down to a narrow defeat.

But some of the opponents of a balanced budget amendment have a good point, too. They argue that this would take away fiscal policy as a tool to combat recessions. It would reduce government's ability to help in times of economic distress and put us back in the same mind-set that prevailed before the 1930s (see the first question in this article).

Is fiscal policy still a good way of improving the condition of our economy?

An economist would point out that the U.S. economy has been fed by growing deficit spending for the past few decades. It would be hard to quit this stimulant cold turkey. Deficits would have to be cut gradually until they disappear.

The continuous diet of deficit spending the United States has had for so long has taken the punch out of fiscal policy. Deficit spending has been so large and so consistent that there is not much more fiscal policy can do to foster economic growth, although it may still be useful for curbing inflation.

Fiscal policy had its heyday from the 1940s to the mid-1970s. That is when overconfident Keynesian economists felt they had mastered the chemistry of fiscal policy so well that serious economic distresses were not to be feared; they had the economy under control. The sharp recession of 1973–75 was a blow to their egos. They are a humbler group now. But they have sharpened their tools (their theories about how the economy works), and these neo-Keynesians are enjoying some fame today, even though they do not have the same attention of political leaders that they once had.

Fiscal policy was powerful from its initiation in the 1930s through the 1950s because it added a new stimulant to the economy. However, fiscal policy has now become a less potent weapon against economic hardships simply because we have overdosed on it.

However, the weakening of fiscal policy does not leave the economy defenseless. *Monetary policy has evolved as an alternative approach to waging war against inflation and recession.* The ascendancy of monetary policy is due to weakening of fiscal policy and the expertise that has developed in monetary policy's use. While recent innovations in financial institutions and markets, such as the development of financial derivatives and the growing variety of savings vehicles available to people, may have made monetary policy a little more difficult to implement, it remains a useful tool. (☛ Art. 18: The Federal Reserve, page 235).

7

International Trade
and Finance

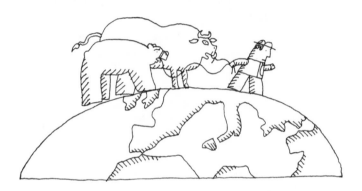

As an undergraduate in the 1960s, I was one of only two students who signed up for my college's course in international trade and finance. The subject was an afterthought in economics, something tucked away in the remote corners of textbooks. This attitude was shared by businesses in America and in other large countries. An assignment in the firm's foreign branch was more of a career dead-end than the path to the executive suite that it often is today.

Since then many of the world's economies have matured into strong competitors who have outgrown the confines of their home markets. International trade and finance are important issues in the political arena and (which may be even more telling) have gotten airtime on the evening television news shows. Most informed persons today are aware of the trade deficits of many leading industrial nations, of the General Agreement on Tariffs and Trade (GATT), of the European Community (formerly known as the Common

Market and the European Economic Community), of the value of the dollar, of the acquisition of domestic businesses by foreign companies, and of protectionism.

But awareness is not understanding. The two articles in this chapter explain what is behind the now-familiar words and introduce some new terms and concepts that are basic to understanding the nature and complexities of international economic relationships.

Article 25: Trading in the Global Village starts with an explanation of how the global village evolved. It then explains what nations have to gain from trading with each other, and what they would lose if that trading were impeded. You will see why even the least powerful nations have something they can contribute to foreign trade.

Since imports (the buying of foreign goods and services) and exports (selling abroad) play leading roles in most economies today, the article explains what determines the amount of importing and exporting that nations do.

The growth of global trading is the result of the success of competitors in one country in penetrating the markets in another. But one competitor's success in the rough-and-tumble global marketplace almost always threatens someone else's prosperity. That is why there are loud calls for protection against competition that some claim is unfair or that jeopardizes a nation's economic security. Protectionists call for the erection of barriers against such foreign competition. Article 25 evaluates some of their arguments.

However, more work has been done in the last couple of decades in breaking down barriers to trade than in building them. This second article concludes with a discussion of efforts to level the playing field.

Article 26: International Finance is about money. Almost all international trade involves more than one type of money, and that adds a variable that is absent in domestic trade. If an American manufacturer buys machinery from France, dollars must be converted into francs. If a capitalist in South Korea purchases a factory in Turkey, the transaction must involve both the Korean won and the Turkish lira, which are the moneys of those nations.

A nation's money has its price, and changes in the price of money are a major influence on both trade and investment. The core of this article is an explanation of changes in the prices of the various moneys used in the global village and of the impact these changes have. You will learn why a nation wants a *weak* money to promote trade but why a *weakening* money may jeopardize the flow of investment funds.

From this foundation the article turns to the efforts nations can make to change the value of their moneys so that they can bring about specific changes in their economic environments. This discussion is extended to include the critical matter of coordinating economic policies among nations because of increasing economic interdependence.

The article concludes with a discussion of America's huge and persistent annual trading deficits, which have caused it to become the world's largest debtor nation. You will learn why it is important and the efforts that have been made to lessen this deficit.

ARTICLE 25:

TRADING IN THE GLOBAL VILLAGE

Can Everyone Win?

Why has international trade become so important to nations like the United States?

International trade takes place whenever any goods or services move across national borders. International trade generally plays a big role in the economies of small nations. Small countries such as the Netherlands get as much as half of their income from selling goods and services to foreign customers.

For many years international trade was not a major part of economic activity in the U.S. The first reason international trade played only a minor role was that the nation was so large and so rich that it provided its own market for most of what was made here. Second, other nations' economies were so small or poor by comparison that they were not good customers. Third, these other nations did not seem to produce much that Americans wanted to buy.

Remember the movie *Gigi*? It is the story of a young girl who got little serious attention from adults until they discovered that, under their noses, she had grown into a bright and charming woman.

In a way, many countries with which we now trade were like Gigi. *In the two or three decades after World War II, nations such as Japan and (West) Germany "grew up" quickly and demanded attention from the major economic powers because they began to offer to the world competitive goods.* They became significant players in global markets. An early symbol of this new competitive posture was worldwide acceptance of the Volkswagen Beetle automobile in the 1950s. Later Japan entered the global marketplace with high-quality steel and electronics (after briefly experimenting with cheaper, lower-quality products). Soon after, they were joined by other serious newcomers in the world marketplace such as Taiwan, South Korea, Singapore, and Mexico.

But that was only half the story, for in addition to becoming significant producers and competitors, *their new prosperity made these nations attractive markets in which to sell American products.* The world had matured into a global village of sophisticated and powerful sellers and buyers.

Table 25A gives you a quick look at foreign trade in the United States over the past half century.[1] **Exports** are the goods and services that are sold abroad by our nation's businesses, individuals, and

Table 25A

Foreign Trade of the U.S., Selected Years ($ billions)

Year	GDP	Exports	Imports	Exports as a Percent of GDP
1929	$103	$6	$6	6%
1953	370	15	16	4
1973	1,350	92	91	7
1993	6,343	659	724	10

governments. **Imports** are the goods and services we buy from other nations. Gross domestic product (GDP) is the total value of the things we make in the nation. Exports are part of GDP. *The U.S. exports more than 10% of what it makes.* That may not seem like much, but as you will see below, exports are more meaningful than they appear to be.

Americans currently import slightly more than they export. Imports are not part of GDP because they are not part of what is made in the U.S.

How did the new contenders in the international marketplace become so important so soon?

War-weakened economies, emerging from World War II, became powerful for three reasons. First, their ability to produce peacetime products had been so reduced that they had to build their economies practically from the ground up. This vacuum, along with the help of rich nations like the U.S., enabled them to construct new plants with the most modern and efficient production methods. They were not saddled with the aging and dated factories that dotted the American landscape. Second, these upstart economies had good teachers; they could copy the best of what the leading nations had to offer. Third, their governments were actively involved in fostering commercial growth through aggressive **industrial policies**. These policies consisted of government investment, tax incentives, and pro-competitive laws and regulations designed to benefit specific industries for whom their nations saw special opportunities for growth.

Today the global village has many giants. These include the economic powerhouses of Western Europe and the Pacific Rim. The list of major international traders will soon also include nations such as Mexico, several countries in South America, Russia, and in time the developing countries of Eastern Europe. *Since World War II international trade has become more meaningful because nations developed their ability to compete in producing goods and services and also in their ability to buy what their trading partners had to offer.* As the world economy grew, differences in wealth lessened, and barriers to trade gradually lowered, so that now many nations are competing on a more level playing field.

How important are exports?

Today many American industries are highly dependent on the customers they have in other nations. From Table 25A we see that the money they earn from exports contributes over 10% to the nation's gross domestic product (a measure of all the goods and services made during a year), but this figure understates the importance of exports. Exports are vital to specific industries. For example, foreign sales account for more than a third of all machinery produced in the U.S. and about 15% of transportation equipment. Many companies count foreign buyers among their biggest customers. We should also recognize that exports make both direct and indirect contributions to the economy.

MAXWELL STARTS A SNOWBALL: Maxwell founded a successful American business making and distributing snowmobiles. Because his product is designed as a working vehicle, there is little domestic demand for it (Americans use snowmobiles primarily for leisure). Nearly all of his output is exported. His firm employs most of the workers in its community and has a payroll of $8 million per year. Because his workers spend about 60% of their income locally, Maxwell's payroll is responsible for about $20 million of annual income in the community. Local businesses such as grocery stores, hair salons, the cable TV operator, restaurants, card shops, gasoline stations, and others might not survive, or would be smaller, without the business they get from Maxwell's employees.

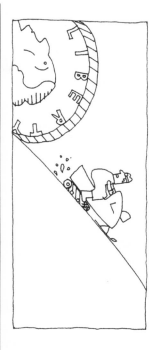

The $20 million that Maxwell's firm brings to the community, from its payroll of $8 million, is not economic legerdemain. It results from what economists call the **export multiplier**. Here is how it works. When Maxwell pays employees $8 million, they spend

60% of this amount in local businesses, and that comes to about $5 million. The next thing to happen is that the people who get this $5 million spend 60% of it locally, which rings up sales in the community of about another $3 million. So far we can see that Maxwell's company brings the local economy 8 + 5 + 3 = $16 million. But the dollars keep rolling as 60% of this last $3 million finds its way into the town's cash registers, and so on for round after round. The total gets to $20 million before the additional spending disappears. This whole process is like a snowball rolling down a hill, picking up new snow as it goes. But unlike a real snowball, the export snowball picks up a little *less* snow every time it rolls over, until nothing is left to pick up and it reaches its full size.

The export multiplier shows us that *the money that exports bring into an economy creates far more income than can be seen by the exports themselves.* Like seedlings, export dollars "grow" as they pass through the economy.

Can a nation do anything to increase its income from exports?

As you see, exports can mean a great deal to a nation's economy because they bring new income into the economy and that new money creates income as it travels through the economy.

A nation can do some obvious things to promote its exports. *The country can try to design and sell innovative products,* such as American television programs, and to produce a basic good at low cost, such as American wheat and corn. One way to do both of these things is to invest in research and development (R&D). This is just as consequential as investment in new factories and machinery.

Buying something from another nation is more complex than buying things in your neighborhood; you have to buy another nation's money first. Most sovereign nations have their own money, and that money comes at a price. The cost of foreign money is called the **foreign exchange rate** (or simply the exchange rate).

A STRONG YEN TO SEE NEW YORK CITY: Takashi is a Japanese tourist visiting the Big Apple (a promotional name for New York City, in which it is hard to find an apple orchard). His hotel room, in midtown Manhattan, costs $150 per night. But the hotel does not take Japanese money; it wants dollars. Japan's money is the yen (for which the symbol is ¥). Before he could pay for his hotel accommodations, Takashi knew he would have to buy dollars, which can be done at most banks. When he planned his trip, the exchange rate was ¥110 per dollar. That would have made his room cost ¥16,500 per night. At that rate he made the decision to stay for four nights. When he got to the United States, he was delighted to find that the exchange rate had changed to $1 = ¥100, which put the nightly hotel bill at only ¥15,000. The cheaper dollar also meant his food, souvenirs, and other items (he bought a camera in an electronics store near Times Square) cost less than he had planned. Because of these lower prices Takashi decided to stay an extra day and to spend more money.

When a Japanese tourist has to pay ¥110 per $1, the dollar is costly and so are the things he needs the dollars to buy. When the exchange rate drops to ¥100 per $1, the dollar is "cheaper" and so are American goods and services. Another way to look at it is that the Japanese yen became stronger so that Takashi required fewer yen to buy each dollar. A nation's exchange rate is important. For example, *when the exchange rate of the dollar goes down, the United States will export more goods and services because they become cheaper for foreigners to buy.* Tours are exports because they bring money into the country. Notice that the exchange rate does not affect prices in dollars, only what foreign customers must pay.

Products and exchange rates are meaningful, but they are still not the major factor in exports. *Exports are primarily determined by the income levels in other countries.* For example, when Japan's economy is strong and its citizens enjoy high incomes, they can afford to buy more American goods. That means that a nation has an interest in seeing its trading partners become prosperous. The recession the Japanese economy experienced in the early 1990s harmed American exports and made American political leaders vocally encourage the Japanese government to do more to help its own economy. The best way to promote exports is to have prosperous foreign customers.

Does a nation also have to import goods and services?

Political leaders boast about their nations' exports because they bring money in from other nations. The ability to sell abroad is a sign of success. But these same leaders worry about the other side of international trade, imports. Imports are what we buy from other nations. Some people seem to believe that when we buy things abroad, it is a sign of weakness; it means some other nation can make something that is better or cheaper than what we can make for ourselves.

However, it is wrong to think that exports are good and imports are bad. That is because *international trade is a two-way street; we cannot sell anything to other nations unless we also buy from them.* The reason is that most every nation uses its own money. When you want to buy something from another country, you must generally first buy that country's money so you can pay for your purchases. We saw above that when you sell something to another country (or to its citizens like Takashi), you want to receive *your* nation's money because that is what you can spend at home.

> **VAJAY MEETS THE SHIPS:** Vajay makes a good living selling beautiful locally made scarves on an island in the Bay of Bengal. His shop is near the dock used by tourists from cruise ships that visit the island. The tourists' visits are too brief to make it worthwhile to buy the Indian rupee, which is the island's money. To accommodate his customers Vajay accepts payment in British pounds (among other major currencies). But he cannot spend these British pounds on the island, since local merchants only want rupees. Therefore, Vajay uses most of his pounds to buy radios from Britain, often purchasing them from members of the ships' crews who bring them to him from England. He then sells the radios to local merchants, who pay him in rupees, for resale. By importing radios and exporting scarves Vajay is a true international trader.

Because most nations have their own money, *the money a nation receives from selling abroad must be used to buy things from abroad.* A nation cannot continue to export goods or services without also buying from other nations. *Unless we had imports, we would have few or no exports.* That is why imports are important. In the international marketplace trade must flow both ways.

Despite this, nations that sell abroad do not buy things from other nations just to use up their foreign money. There is another reason to trade. Most countries rely on imports as a way of freeing their own time and energy so that they can focus on doing what they do best. This is the issue we turn to in the next question.

Does every nation have something worth trading in the world market?

The reason for trading among nations is no different from the reason that individuals trade among themselves. The only reason I buy my shoes is that someone can make them better and cheaper than I can make them myself. That is why I do not bake my own bread, sew my own clothing, or build my own car. That is also why I go to others to deliver my mail, dry-clean my clothes, and fix my broken VCR. Fortunately, I can do some things better, such as teach and write about economics. That is why the mail carrier, dry cleaner, baker, and others come (or send their kids) to me to learn. International trade takes place only if it makes nations better off than they would be without it. It is easy to see that *trade should take place between two nations if each one is good at something the other nation cannot do as well.* For example, suppose oil could be sold more cheaply by Kuwait than it could by Taiwan, simply because oil is easier to find and to extract in Kuwait. On the other hand, Taiwan can supply textiles and television sets much more cheaply than they could be made in Kuwait. Rather than trying to find at home all of the oil it needs, Taiwan devotes its resources to making television sets and textiles. Rather than using its workers, factories, and raw materials for making textiles and television sets, Kuwait uses them to produce (and perhaps refine) oil. Then Taiwan can trade textiles or television sets for Kuwaiti oil and vice versa. Both nations are better off because they are striving to use their resources in the most profitable way.

But some people and nations may not be superior at producing *any* product or service. Would anyone want to trade with them?

> **SHARON'S HOT KEYS:** Sharon is a real estate attorney for a midsize law firm. With the help of high school courses and steady practice, she became an expert typist. Later she developed proficiency in the use of personal computers for word processing. Today she can use a word processor with more speed and accuracy than can her legal secretary, Linda. While Linda can put together standardized contracts, she has difficulty with more complex legal documents and has less ability in contract writing than does Sharon. Despite Sharon's superior skills as a lawyer and as a typist, she has delegated nearly all typing tasks to Linda and relieved her of responsibility for drafting all but the most routine documents.

In her office Sharon is a wizard at both typing and law while Linda is less expert at both skills. However, Sharon is much more adept at contract writing than is Linda, but only a little better at typing. The women have agreed, therefore, to let Sharon do all the contract writing and to let Linda take care of typing tasks. Each person specializes in the job in which she has a **comparative advantage**. Sharon specializes in law because her comparative advantage is greater there than in typing. To allow her to devote herself to this task she lets Linda specialize in typing. (Furthermore, this arrangement will give Linda more experience and opportunity to improve her typing skills.)

So far we have ignored the fact that Sharon probably receives a higher salary than Linda gets and that typing contributes less value to the firm than does contract writing. But when you consider these things, the comparative advantage argument is even stronger. Sharon's employer, the law firm partnership, will get more for their money by paying her to specialize in the task for which she has the greater advantage.

People and nations could improve their economic well-being if they would each specialize in producing the goods and services for which they have a comparative advantage and then trade among themselves to satisfy their diverse needs.

What do the imports and exports of a major trading nation such as the United States look like?

Let us first look at goods. As we can see from Table 25B, the U.S. exports more foods, especially wheat and corn, than it imports.[2] It may import such products as Swiss chocolates and Polish hams, but it is one of the world's major providers of basic food staples. The U.S. has a comparative advantage in agricultural goods. (Table 25B does not include military items, which were included in the totals in Table 25A.)

It also has a comparative advantage in capital goods, which is the term economists use to cover machinery and equipment that can be put to work making other things. The U.S. is a preeminent supplier of agricultural machinery, oil-drilling and construction equipment, and aircraft.

When it goes shopping around the world, the U.S. buys a lot of industrial supplies such as fuel, metals, and nonmedicinal chemicals. Although it is the birthplace of computers, it actually buys more computers and parts than it sells abroad. In the consumer-goods category, the U.S. imports billions of dollars worth of household appliances and clothing. In 1993 it imported over $100 billion worth of vehicles and parts, primarily passenger cars.

Table 25B

U.S. Exports and Imports of Merchandise, 1993 ($ billions)

Category	Exports	Imports
Food and beverages	$41	$28
Nonfood consumer goods	55	134
Automotive and related items	52	102
Industrial supplies	112	152
Capital goods	182	152
Other	15	20
Total:	457	588

Table 25C

U.S. Exports and Imports of Services, 1993 ($ billions)

CATEGORY	EXPORTS	IMPORTS
Travel	$58	$41
Passenger fares	17	11
Port services, freight, and other transportation	23	25
Royalties and fees	20	5
Other services	55	32
Total:	173	114

In all, *the United States imported far more merchandise than it exported.* This resulted in a deficit in foreign trade in goods. But there is more to the story of foreign trade. *The U.S. is a winner when it comes to exporting services.* This is seen from Table 25C.[3]

The U.S. is a successful exporter of travel, including tourism. When foreigners come with their camcorders and cameras to see New York City, the Grand Canyon, Washington, D.C., and other attractions, Americans are exporting services in exchange for their money. America is clearly a world resource for ideas, and these ideas are sold for royalties and fees: payments received by the nation's writers, inventors, and entrepreneurs. Businesses that earn fees for the U.S. include McDonald's, Hollywood film studios, and pharmaceutical companies.

The "other services" category includes substantial export income received by American insurance firms, credit card companies, and by colleges and universities. The U.S. is a leader in education and collected over $7 billion in tuition and fees from foreign students in 1993; that was nearly ten times what Americans spent that year for schooling abroad.

How does a nation put a curb on spending abroad?

When a person spends more money than he receives as income, some remedies are to cut up his credit cards, to turn off the home-shopping television channel, or to make it hard for him to get out to the stores. When people think that a nation's residents import too many goods or services, they might also call for serious action.

The least imaginative way to clip imports is to put up **trade barriers**. The most popular barrier is a **tariff**. A tariff is simply a tax a government collects on things that are brought into a country. For example, the United States government collects a tariff on every ton of steel and every foreign-made car that is brought into the country.

What is the rationale behind tariffs? *Tariffs make imports more costly to buy, and this is supposed to make them less attractive.* If buyers are sensitive to prices, the tariff will work; if not, imports will continue and the government simply increases its revenues. (However, governments generally do not use tariffs just to fill their treasuries.)

A more severe method of cutting imports is for the federal government to enact **import quotas** on specific items. For example, the U.S. limits the number of automobiles that can be imported from Japan each year. The tariff gives the import buyer a choice; she can pay it (buy the import) or not. The quota puts an absolute ban on imports of a product beyond a certain amount, regardless of how eager people are to buy it.

A more subtle import barrier is the specification of **product standards** that are costly for a foreign seller to satisfy. Suppose a nation treats the fruit it grows with a certain insecticide that is widely accepted in its own country. Another nation that wants to discourage imports of this product might ban any fruit treated with that same insecticide. The importing nation hopes that it will be too troublesome for the seller to meet this condition for selling its fruit, so that imports would be sharply reduced or eliminated.

Some nations employ draconian measures to keep out imports. These include **currency controls**. *Currency* is a special term economists use to represent easily spendable forms of money, such as paper money and coins. There might be a limit on the amount of local currency that a nation is permitted to turn into another currency during a given time, or citizens might be required to go through bureaucratic inconvenience to buy foreign currency.

Trade barriers are erected by governments to discourage imports.

What reasons are there for reducing imports of specific goods or services?

On the surface it seems as though import restrictions are intended just to keep more money at home, like clipping the wings of a shopper who spends too much money. But import quotas usually have a narrower reason. *Import barriers are intended to benefit specific industries in a nation* rather than to reduce the nation's total bill for imports. Any government effort to restrict the competition that imports give to one of its home industries is called **protectionism**.

> **THERESA KEEPS THE WORK AT HOME:** Theresa is the president of a union representing several thousand workers in the watch industry of a leading Western industrial nation. Inexpensive quartz watches, made in eastern Pacific Rim nations, have been gaining shares in the domestic watch market. As watch imports increased, local watch firms lost business, and when they downsized, they dismissed members of Theresa's union. Through extensive lobbying, in cooperation with senior executives of her nation's watch manufacturers, Theresa's union has succeeded in getting the government to impose a 25% **ad valorem tariff** on imported quartz watches. With this tariff, imported watches are more costly than locally made watches of comparable quality. The result is that imports are sharply reduced and two thousand members of Theresa's union are called back to work. Theresa is given a new luxury car by her grateful union members.

A 25% ad valorem tariff is a tax equal to 25% of whatever price exporters charge for their products. If a foreign seller charges an importer $160 per watch, the tariff would bring the importer's cost up to $200 (25% over $160), assuming the seller passes the full tariff on to the importer. The purpose of the tariff is to make the import so costly that domestic substitutes (watches made at home) become more attractive to buyers. That would be good for the nation's employment. Of course, the effect of a successful tariff is to lose business and jobs for the exporting nation. In practice, *if your country imposes a tariff, it shifts jobs from a foreign nation to your nation.*

Can import barriers be used to nurture a developing industry?

One of the oldest rationales for protective trade barriers is the **infant industry** argument. This states that a small industry in a nation can compete successfully against imports if it is temporarily protected from competition until it can mature.

JOSEPH NEEDS SCALE: Joseph manufactures jitneys, a specialty vehicle for transporting small groups of people. He markets his product to tour operators and school districts. Some companies have also bought his product to help their employees commute to their jobs. There are significant scale economies in the industry: plants that turn out a thousand or more vehicles per year have a much lower average cost of producing a vehicle than Joseph could attain with his annual sales volume of only two hundred jitneys. Because of his higher cost, and selling price, his price was being undercut by a few large foreign jitney makers whose costs are much lower. However, once his nation's government placed a low import quota on foreign jitneys, which sharply reduced his competitors' sales, Joseph's sales rose to twelve hundred per year. At this level of production he could produce vehicles at a lower price than foreign competitors could offer, even without the quota. Later, when the quota was lifted, he competed successfully.

If there are strong scale economies in an industry, a protective tariff or quota may help the domestic producers to grow so that they can compete with imports after the protection is removed. Under the infant industry argument, protection is meant to be temporary. Of course, a protective tariff or quota is not intended to shield a local industry that remains inefficient.

National security is another reason protectionism is sometimes evoked. Unlike the infant industry argument, it has little to do with economics. Advocates of protection would argue that a particular industry, such as aircraft manufacturing, should be nurtured because the home nation may need a domestic source if it is ever at war and cannot rely on foreign suppliers. Trade barriers are put up to let the home industry prosper while being shielded from foreign competition.

Can economists justify protectionism?

Free competition generally gives buyers the lowest prices and best selection for their money. That is why competition is good for an economy, and many former members of the Soviet bloc are learning this lesson well in the 1990s. That is also why most economists have little to say in support of protectionism, which makes for less competition.

Although temporary protection of an infant industry is justified if it really has a chance to become competitive (if it can achieve economies of scale), we should note that *protectionism always means that domestic customers pay higher prices* for imports than would otherwise be the case, and higher prices for the domestic products that are sheltered from foreign competition. Arguments for protection of so-called infant industries is often specious because a protected industry really has little incentive to become efficient for the same reason an overly protected child may have difficulty maturing. Protectionism may only delay efforts to make an industry or a workforce more efficient.

The national security motive may have some merit, but it may call for perpetual protection of a bloated or inefficient industry. Exactly which industries are essential to a nation's security is also difficult to judge.

Is the world moving toward free trade or toward protectionism?

Our world is moving in opposite directions at the same time. During the past decade several nations have come together in **free trade associations**. These are groups of two or more countries who formally agree to eliminate trade barriers among them. The most famous is the **European Economic Community**, popularly known now as the **EC** or **European Community** (in trade circles the term **Common Market** is still occasionally used). In 1992 all border restrictions to trade among the current twelve (and growing) EC members, such as tariffs and quotas, were removed. The EC is currently trying to make progress toward eliminating differences in money, which would make international trade easier. The EC expects to have a common currency within the next few years.

The EC members enjoy free trade (that is, free from government restrictions) among themselves because they recognize the advantages of open competition. In the Western Hemisphere, Canada, the United States, and Mexico have formed the North American Free Trade Association (NAFTA), which will eventually become a North American "Common Market."

Free trade visionaries see the eventual formation of a free trade zone that encompasses all of North and South America. Some progress is also being made toward a free trade association of Asian Pacific Rim nations.

Not all of the interest in lowering trade barriers is resulting in the formation of free trade associations. For over forty years most of the nations of the world have been formally discussing chipping away trade barriers through the loosely structured General Agreement on Tariffs and Trade (GATT), which promotes multinational efforts to reduce trade barriers. Furthermore, on a one-to-one basis, nations are striving for **most favored nation** (MFN) designation from their trading partners. When a nation grants MFN status to another nation, it is pledging not to charge any tariffs against the other nation's goods that are larger than the lowest tariffs it charges anyone.

Growing interest in free trade associations, in GATT negotiations, and in MFN status are clear indications of an interest in reaping the benefits of fair and competitive trade among nations. Insightful leaders are striving to avoid the constraints imposed by protectionism.

When grade school children see some of their peers forming clubs that exclude them, they often turn around and form their own clubs. There is no doubt that some of this new fraternization among trading nations is retaliatory. For example, some of the advocates of NAFTA feared that the EC would isolate the nations of North America. NAFTA would give these nations a chance to enjoy the same type of benefits the EC nations were giving themselves. NAFTA is a "club" formed by three nations in North America who were afraid of being excluded by the Common Market club.

The downside of free trade associations is that they are likely to set up trade barriers against outsiders. So *while international trade will increase among members of free trade associations, trade might be reduced among members of different associations.* In a world racing toward development of regional common markets, GATT is significant because it goes beyond the interests of regional multinational blocs of trading partners. It is an effort to gather everyone under one umbrella.

How did the United States get such large trade deficits?

In the mid-1980s the United States became a debtor nation. That meant the world's largest economy owed more to others than they owed to the U.S. This happened because *for many years Americans had imported more goods and services than they exported.* It simply means Americans spent more overseas than they earned there and lived beyond their means.

When a nation spends more abroad than it takes in, it goes into debt, just as you and I would if we charge $300 of purchases on our credit card every month but make monthly payments (to the credit card issuer) of only $200.

The reason for the deficit is that foreign sellers offered Americans a lot of goods and services that were more attractive than what they could buy at home. In addition, the U.S. could not offer these foreign sellers enough attractive American products to offset its purchases.

What is the source of the current trade deficit?

There are three types of foreign transactions: merchandise, services, and transfers. Merchandise trade consists of the buying and selling of tangible goods, and this is the popular conception of imports and exports. In fact, until early in 1994 the U.S. government gave us monthly figures on just this part of the international trade picture. In 1993, Americans exported $457 billion worth of merchandise and imported $588 billion. The result was a merchandise trade deficit of some $131 billion, which is listed in Table 25D.[4]

Table 25D	
Balances on Foreign Transactions of the U.S. in 1993	

ITEM	BALANCE ($ BILLIONS)
Merchandise trade	$ –131
Services	+59
Unilateral transfers	–32
Investments	+4
Current account:	–100

We hear somewhat less of the fact that *the U.S. is a winner when it comes to services.* The nation sold nearly $173 billion of services. This included airplane fares, travel services, insurance, royalties earned, entertainment, and a variety of other activities. The nation bought services worth $114 billion and generated a surplus on its services account of $59 billion. The U.S. government formerly reported imports and exports of services only four times per year, and this infrequency might account for the relatively scant attention that was given to this most successful U.S. activity in world markets.

Now the U.S. government reports the total of merchandise and service exports every month.

Americans make investments abroad (stocks, bonds, partnerships, and property), and those that are successful earn income that comes back to the nation. In 1993, Americans received investment income from abroad of $114 billion. Foreigners also invest in the U.S., and in return for this they are paid profits and other income every year. Foreigners received $110 billion in payments for their U.S. investments. Putting these together, Table 25D shows that the U.S. had a net gain on investments of about $4 billion.

Unilateral transfers, the third item in Table 25D, were payments made abroad for which nothing was received. They include foreign aid and other grants of the government, money sent by U.S. residents to relatives or friends in other countries, and other items.

Table 25D shows the final result. America is a generous nation; its (net) unilateral transfers of $32 billion made a big contribution to its deficit on current account. However, the U.S. had a net deficit of $100 billion on its foreign transactions. *Most of the U.S. deficit is due to a lack of competitiveness in merchandise.*

How does the trade deficit affect foreign investment in the U.S.?

When the U.S. continually imports more than it exports, something must happen. The initial result of a trade deficit is that foreigners accumulate a lot of dollars. When that happens, they can do only two things with these dollars: buy American goods and services (demand exports from the U.S.) or buy American property (make investments). Foreigners who want neither American exports nor American property can change their dollars into another currency only if they find someone outside the U.S. who *does* want something from America. Otherwise, passing dollars around the world would be like the children's game of "hot potato."

The deficit itself occurred because foreigners apparently did not want a lot of the goods and services the U.S. had to sell. They had all the American exports they wanted. They had no alternative but to buy American property, and they did, in grand style. Investors from Great Britain, Germany, Japan, and other nations with a surplus of dollars went on buying sprees. They bought cattle ranches and farms, publishing companies, manufacturing and service firms, stocks, government bonds, and even a piece of Rockefeller Center in New York City. One way to say this is that foreigners seem to prefer buying stock in General Motors rather than a Chevrolet. Currently about 20% of the U.S. federal debt is owned by foreign investors, and this proportion is growing. The United States needs foreign investment to cover its excess spending.

Alarmists in the American media warn about what seems to be a foreign economic invasion. But this is no sinister plot to take over the nation. The citizens of other countries were merely using the dollars that American buyers of their goods and services gave them.

Its accumulated foreign trade and government deficits made the U.S. a debtor nation because foreign investors were willing to finance them. *A foreign trade deficit eventually results in foreign investment in the nation that created the deficit.*

What has been done about the trade deficit?

About ten years ago Washington came up with a solution: devalue the U.S. dollar. (Remember that a weak or "cheap" dollar makes it easier for the U.S. to sell exports.) The Federal Reserve, with the cooperation of other central banks, aggressively sold dollars (most of which were newly created for the occasion) to force exchange rates down. The results were dramatic. From a high of ¥260 per dollar in 1985, the yen exchange rate went to just over ¥100 in 1993. During the same period the German mark went from $1 = DM 3.20 to $1 = DM 1.60 (it even flirted with DM 1.40 for a while). *The dollar weakened substantially against all major currencies between 1985 and 1993.*

Exports increased and imports declined, for a while. The tourists came in droves because the cheap dollar made America a travel bargain.

The medicine helped, although it did not bring a complete cure. A dollar that is too weak can backfire on the economy. After all, some things must be imported, and cheap dollars make them more costly. (Even though oil, America's largest import, is priced in dollars, oil imports still send money out of the economy.) *The only permanent solution to closing America's foreign trade deficit is to make U.S. goods and services more attractive.*

ARTICLE 26:

INTERNATIONAL FINANCE

What Is That Strange Money Worth?

Why does the world have so many different kinds of money?

International trade takes place whenever someone buys or sells goods and services across national borders. But it is harder to do than buying or selling in the same country. That is because more than one type of money has to be used. If a food-processing firm in Mexico wants to buy one hundred tons of soybean meal from a dealer in the United States, it must first use its Mexican pesos to buy the U.S. dollars it needs to purchase the meal. That is part of the cost of doing business abroad.

Most sovereign nations have their own money. It is often the first thing a new nation will create, even before it designs uniforms for its army. As an army is a symbol of political independence, a nation's money is a mark of economic independence. A nation individualizes its money by printing currency (the most spendable form of money) with a unique selection of colors, designs, and sizes, just as it individualizes its flag. (In that sense the bland design of the U.S. dollar, and the uniformity of color and size for different denominations, make it one of the world's most unimaginative and impractical currencies. It is easier to miscount.)

But having one's own money is more than a symbol of sovereignty. How much there is of it matters. The ability to control the **money supply** gives a government a powerful influence on the nation's economy (☛ Art. 17: Money and Banking, page 221). We might call it the power of the printing press. The money supply is the quantity of a nation's money in circulation in that nation.

If a nation wants to galvanize its home economy, it could increase its money supply. That gives its banks more money to lend, and this lending gives its citizens more cash to spend. But that power may be abused, for despite the allure of easy credit and fast growth, too much money can create inflation.

The art of controlling the money supply is the ability to walk on that fine line between economic stimulation and inflation. But there is more to controlling the supply of money. Changes in a nation's money supply have international consequences.

What is the foreign exchange rate?

The money of another country is called **foreign exchange**. The French franc is foreign exchange in the United States, and elsewhere, and the U.S. dollar is foreign exchange in any nation that does not use the U.S. dollar for its money. Therefore, the price of a foreign nation's money in terms of your own nation's money is called the **foreign exchange rate**, or simply the exchange rate. In the United States, when people speak of the exchange rate, they generally mean the amount of foreign money you can get per U.S. dollar. For example, if the exchange rate for the Mexican peso was

Table 26A		
Exchange Rates on a Thursday in November 1994		
NATION	CURRENCY PER $1 (U.S.)	
Canada	1.36	dollars
France	5.21	francs
Germany	1.52	marks
Japan	98.00	yen
Mexico	3.43	pesos
United Kingdom	0.62	pounds

3.31 in May, it means that at that time one dollar could buy 3.31 pesos (3.31 units of the Mexican currency). *Exchange rates determine what you must pay for the foreign money you need to buy things abroad. The exchange rate also influences what foreigners have to pay for your nation's goods and services.*

Exchange rates are listed daily in many major newspapers. For a sample of exchange rates see Table 26A.⁵ On that day one U.S. dollar bought 1.36 Canadian dollars (which are more colorful than the U.S. dollar), 5.21 French francs, 1.52 German marks, 98 Japanese yen, 3.43 Mexican pesos, or two-thirds of a British pound.

If you find yourself with a group of international traders or bankers, you have to be careful about language because many nations use the same name for their money. The dollar is the official money of the United States, Canada, Australia, Hong Kong, Taiwan, New Zealand, and Singapore. But they are different dollars. For example, on one Friday in November 1994 one U.S. dollar equaled 1.35 Australian dollars, 26.05 Taiwanese dollars, and 1.36 Canadian dollars. The peso is another common designation. It is used in Argentina, Colombia, Mexico, the Philippines, and Uruguay, although each of these pesos is unique to its nation. Also, do not confuse the liras of Italy and Turkey and Malta, the francs of France and Switzerland, the dinars of Bahrain and Jordan and Kuwait, the rupees of India and Pakistan, and the pounds of Britain and Lebanon. So when you are traveling and a suspicious character asks you, "Wanna buy some francs?" don't fall for a bait-and-switch game!

Why are exchange rates important?

The exchange rate is the price of foreign currency. Like other prices, it can go up or down. If the exchange rate for the Mexican peso, which was 3.31 in May, went to 3.43 in November, we would say that the peso has *weakened.* That means Mexicans must come up with more of their pesos to buy a U.S. dollar. If $1 cost Mexicans 3.31 pesos last May, that meant that one peso was worth 30¢; the calculation is $1 divided by the exchange rate of 3.31, 1/3.31 = 0.30. When the exchange rate rose to 3.43 pesos per dollar in November, a peso was worth only about 29¢, so each peso had lost about a penny, which was about 3% of its value.

Now let us look at this from the American side. The dollar bought more pesos in November than it did the previous May, because $1 got 3.43 pesos rather than 3.31. That is why we say the dollar *strengthened.* When one nation's money weakens, another nation's money is strengthened. That is the way they talk in the foreign exchange business.

Exchange rates are significant in commerce because they represent the purchasing power of money in international trade. When the peso weakened, it meant that Mexicans could buy less from the U.S. with their money. But it also meant that, because the dollar strengthened, Americans could buy more from Mexico with dollars. In other words, a stronger dollar meant that Mexican imports from the U.S. are likely to decline while U.S. imports from Mexico might rise. In general, *a higher exchange rate for a foreign nation's money means that nation's money has lost some of its value and its residents can buy less of your country's exports with it.*

Why are exchange rates written with so many numbers?

The exchange rates in Table 26A have been rounded off to make them more readable. But in the real world of international business, exchange rates are usually written with four or five decimal places, such as $1 = 5.2100 F (F is the symbol for the French franc). Those extra numbers on the right side make a big difference in large transactions. If you bought 3 million French francs on the first Thursday in November 1994, when the exchange rate was $1 = 5.2100 F, it would have cost you $575,816. (That is, 3,000,000 F divided by 5.2100). On the preceding day, Wednesday, the exchange rate was $1 = 5.1925 F. On that day the 3 million francs could have been purchased for $577,756. The value of 3 million French francs changed enough in one day that had you purchased them on Thursday, rather than Wednesday, you would have saved enough dollars to buy yourself a round-trip flight to Paris, with something left over for souvenirs. For bankers and foreign exchange dealers who do these trades all day long, small changes in the exchange rate can add up to big profits or to big losses.

Tourists can feel the effect of foreign exchange changes, too. For example, during my last trip to Germany, I got DM 1.64 per U.S. dollar on the day I arrived. (DM means deutsche marks, the German currency. Although the symbol DM is still used, they are now simply called marks. The old designation of DM was necessary to designate West German currency when East Germany and West Germany were separate nations, each with its own brand of marks.) Near the end of my visit, three weeks later, each dollar was worth DM 1.68. When changing $200 into deutsche marks at the higher rate, the extra money I got, worth about $4.75, was enough to buy lunch in a *Schnellimbiß*, a fast-food shop commonly found in Germany.

What does a stronger dollar mean for exports?

We just saw that when the peso weakens, and the dollar strengthens, it may be hard on folks in Mexico because it means that Mexican buyers must come up with more pesos to buy anything in the United States. It is worth repeating that a strong money is not necessarily good for a nation's foreign trade, contrary to the conventional expectation that something that is strong is preferable to something that is weak. *A stronger dollar makes American goods and services more expensive for foreign customers to buy.* The impact is not necessarily immediate, but in general, when the dollar strengthens, exports are likely to decline after a while as soon as foreign buyers find substitutes for American goods.

JOSE WORKS FOR HIS MEAL: José is an international buyer for a foods processor in Mexico. It is his job to get the raw materials his firm needs to make its products, and to do so at the least cost. At the current price of $200 per ton in the U.S., one hundred tons of soybean meal will cost the firm $20,000. José must use Mexican pesos to buy these dollars before he can buy American soybean meal. Last November he needed 3.25 pesos per dollar, so $20,000 cost him 65,000 pesos. At this same time he could have purchased Mexican soybean meal for 68,000 pesos, so he decided to buy the U.S. meal to meet his firm's need and to save it money.

However, the dollar strengthened the following October (became more costly) so that $1 cost 3.60 pesos. His firm would have had to pay 72,000 pesos for the same number of dollars needed to buy the U.S. soybean meal. With that turn of events José decided to buy the Mexican meal for only 68,000 pesos. The U.S. lost a customer.

A stronger dollar is generally bad for American exports, but good for foreign businesses. We saw this as José turned away from American exports to meet his needs. There was a bright side, of course. A stronger dollar meant a Mexican firm got José's business. When the exchange rate (pesos per dollar) goes up, American products get more expensive for Mexicans. A strong dollar is good for domestic businesses in other nations.

What does a strong dollar do to imports of foreign goods and services?

Now let us look at the import side. Imports are what we buy from other nations. Imports include the money Americans spend on foreign goods whether they make the purchase at home (buying a Polish ham in a supermarket in Kansas) or away from home (an American buying a Polish ham in a store in Poland). A strong dollar means $1 buys more foreign money, and that means it can buy more things abroad. *A strong dollar makes imports cheaper.*

Using a pocket calculator, it is easy to find the effect that exchange rates have on the cost of foreign items. You just *divide* the foreign price by the exchange rate.

Suppose you are interested in flying from Bremen, Germany, to Vienna, Austria, and back, and you learn that the round-trip airfare on a German airline is DM 850. Last year $1 would have bought 1.66 German marks. Therefore, the U.S. traveler in Europe would pay DM 850 ÷ 1.66, or $512 for the airfare. Suppose the following year the dollar strengthened so that $1 equaled DM 1.85. Then that same Bremen-to-Vienna plane fare (get out the calculator) would be DM 850 ÷ 1.85 = $459. For the American traveler this amounted to a price cut of 10%, even though the German price did not change. Some American customers might be influenced by this and would increase their air travel abroad. These ticket purchases would be counted as American imports from Germany. *A strong dollar usually means that Americans will buy more imports.*

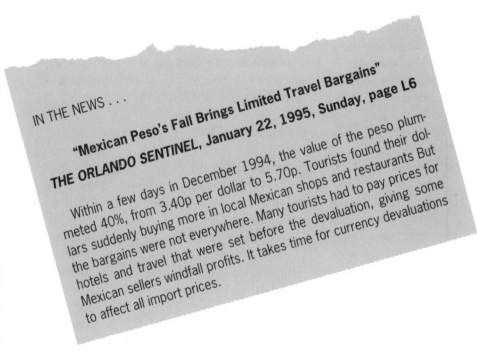

IN THE NEWS . . .

"Mexican Peso's Fall Brings Limited Travel Bargains"

THE ORLANDO SENTINEL, January 22, 1995, Sunday, page L6

Within a few days in December 1994, the value of the peso plummeted 40%, from 3.40p per dollar to 5.70p. Tourists found their dollars suddenly buying more in local Mexican shops and restaurants But the bargains were not everywhere. Many tourists had to pay prices for hotels and travel that were set before the devaluation, giving some Mexican sellers windfall profits. It takes time for currency devaluations to affect all import prices.

What makes exchange rates move down?

A nation's money is like a commodity; its price (the exchange rate) depends on supply and demand (☛ Art. 10: Price Changes, page 118). If the demand for the Mexican peso goes down, the exchange rate will go up. No, that statement is not a misprint. The fewer pesos that are demanded by international traders, the fewer American dollars (or other money) you have to pay for them. That means a dollar buys more pesos.

José was on the short end of a weakened Mexican peso. In November the exchange rate was 3.25 pesos per dollar. That meant that each peso was worth 31¢. By October the demand for pesos had gone down, so each peso was worth only 28¢. That made the exchange rate go up to 3.60 pesos per $1, and José's pesos could buy less. (Remember that when one money becomes weaker, such as the peso, another becomes stronger, such as the dollar.)

The demand for a nation's money depends, in part, on the demand foreigners have for the goods and services the nation has to sell. If Americans want fewer goods and services from Mexico, the exchange rate for pesos goes up, which means that the cost of pesos goes down.

How does a lower exchange rate help exporters?

Free markets have all the balance and harmony, as well as the intricacies, of a Mozart concerto. Just as there is beauty in the orderliness of artfully composed music, there is a beauty in the orderliness of free markets, including the market for foreign money. This orderliness actually helps a nation to maintain its prosperity. Here is one reason why: when the demand for American products goes down, its money loses value. That makes the U.S. dollar cheap in the rest of the world, and that automatically lowers the price of American exports. If the cost of America's exports goes down enough, foreigners will increase the amount of things they want from the U.S. *When the demand for a nation's exports decreases, its money becomes cheaper. This weakened (lower-priced) money can restore some or all of the demand for what the nation has to sell.*

EVA'S ROLLER-COASTER RIDE: Eva exports orange juice concentrate from Florida. Her main competitors in the world market are orange growers in Brazil. Wholesale orange juice concentrate prices in the U.S. have been stable at about $1 per pound. She sells 500,000 pounds per year to a major customer in Japan. With an exchange rate of $1 for ¥110, that 500,000 pounds costs her customer ¥55 million. But when Brazilian orange juice prices fell because of a bumper crop there, her Japanese customer canceled its order. This loss of business hurt. Shortly thereafter, a drop in Japanese demand for a wide range of American exports caused the dollar to weaken. The exchange rate became $1 for ¥95. Although the wholesale price of orange juice concentrate stayed at $1 per pound, that drop in the exchange rate meant that 500,000 pounds would now cost her former Japanese customer only ¥47.5 million, or 14% less than previously. That was enough to beat the Brazilian competition. Eva won back her original order and saved her business, so her son could stay at an expensive boarding school in Georgia.

Eva was lucky. The drop in demand for her product coincided with a drop in the demands for enough other American exports that the exchange rate was pushed down. The beauty of the foreign exchange market is that changes in the exchange rate, which result from changes in demand for a nation's products, help the nation as a whole. The weaker dollar boosted American exports across the board, and Eva was able to go along for the ride. Had Eva's lost business been the only casualty hitting U.S. exports, the exchange rate would not have changed enough to help her bounce back.

How else does a stronger money affect the economy?

When the exchange rate moves up, a nation's currency is strengthened. A stronger money is both good and bad. Let us take the bad news first.

If the demand for U.S. exports goes up, so does the cost of the dollars foreigners have to buy to get these exports. *A higher exchange rate makes a nation's exports more expensive.* After that happens, the quantity of exports demanded by the world may actually go down, with the resulting loss of jobs in export industries. If the dollar strengthened so that $1 equaled ¥120, then Eva, and her employees, could be put out of work, even though they did nothing to bring this about. They would suffer from changes in the economic environment. If the dollar becomes very strong, the entire U.S. economy could suffer significantly.

LEON COMPUTES MORE PROFIT: Leon assembles and markets laptop computers in the United States. His chassis for these PCs are imported from South Korea and cost 120,000 won each. Last year the exchange rate was $1 per 800 won, so each chassis cost him (120,000 ÷ 800 =) $150. But a stronger U.S. dollar pushed the rate to one dollar per 1,100 won. This reduced his cost to $109 per chassis. With the slim profit margin he had in this competitive business, this lower supply cost increased his bottom line significantly. With this extra income he could send his daughter to an expensive private boarding school in Georgia where she met Eva's son. (They are doing nicely.)

Now the good news. *A stronger dollar makes imports, and foreign investments, less costly.* That helps Americans who have to buy abroad.

Another economic benefit is that *a strong dollar tends to contain inflation.* Because the strong dollar makes imports more competitive with American goods, American producers will keep prices down. Then there is the impact on American export industries. With less business from abroad, firms like Eva's will fight harder for customers in the United States. This also puts a damper on raising prices.

Despite these benefits, the loss of income that comes from a stronger money makes the net outcome generally bad for the economy. This is particularly true if a nation is battling with a **foreign trade deficit**, which is aggravated when exports decline and imports rise. A deficit occurs when a nation exports less goods and services than it imports.

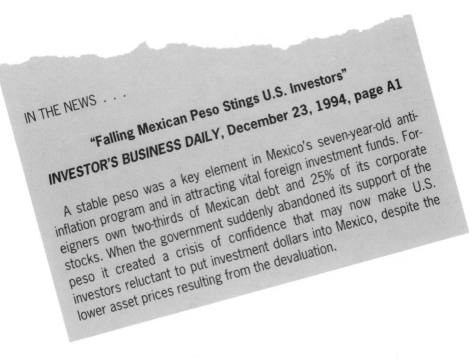

IN THE NEWS · · ·

"Falling Mexican Peso Stings U.S. Investors"

INVESTOR'S BUSINESS DAILY, December 23, 1994, page A1

A stable peso was a key element in Mexico's seven-year-old anti-inflation program and in attracting vital foreign investment funds. Foreigners own two-thirds of Mexican debt and 25% of its corporate stocks. When the government suddenly abandoned its support of the peso it created a crisis of confidence that may now make U.S. investors reluctant to put investment dollars into Mexico, despite the lower asset prices resulting from the devaluation.

What keeps all the world's exchange rates in line?

The international marketplace is awash in exchange rates. Every nation's money has an exchange rate for every other nation's money. Are they related in some way? Economists have shown that they are. They all hang together by what is called **purchasing power parity**. This mouthful simply means that *all exchange rates are aligned so that any particular item has the same price in any money*, allowing for transportation costs. That means exchange rates give you equal purchasing power in all nations.

ANNABELLE SEIZES THE MOMENT: Annabelle is a gold trader in New York. When she arrived at her office at 7 A.M. one morning, she noticed that gold had suddenly slipped to $380, but that the exchange rate had stayed at $1 = DM 1.66, which it was the night before. Furthermore, her associate in Frankfurt told her that gold in Germany was still at yesterday's price of DM 664. She got on her telephones and bought 10,000 ounces of gold in the U.S. for $3,800,000. At the same time she had her German associate sell an equal amount of gold in Germany; that got her DM 6,640,000. With another telephone call Annabelle converted the DM 6,640,000 into dollars, and this sale of marks brought her (6,640,000 ÷ 1.66 =) $4,000,000. In a matter of a few minutes Annabelle had made a profit of $200,000 and had not even had her morning coffee. She sensed it was going to be a great day.

Suppose an ounce of gold costs $400. If the exchange rate for the German mark is $1 = DM 1.66, then gold should cost DM 664 per ounce in Germany because that is what $400 is worth in marks. (The calculation is 400 × DM 1.66 = DM 664.) If the price of gold were to drop to $380 in the U.S., but remain at DM 664 in Germany, the exchange rate would be out of alignment. Fortunately, the working of the private market would bring it back quickly.

Annabelle's story is a bit dramatic, but it describes what the armies of professional traders in our financial markets do for a living. She noticed that prices, in relation to the exchange rate, were out of line. You may be sure that she was not alone in this discovery. As these traders did their work, they forced changes to occur in the foreign exchange market. All of the selling of German marks made the mark weaker. This pushed the exchange rate upward, above $1 = DM 1.66. How far up would it go? It would rise until gold costs the same in both countries.

If gold stayed at DM 664 per ounce in Germany, the new exchange rate would be $1 = DM 1.75. That new exchange rate is just what it takes to make gold cost the same in dollars as in marks; DM 664, the price in Germany, divided by $380, the price in the U.S., gives 1.75. What this means is that *exchange rates change when prices in one nation change more than prices in another nation.* Inflation also plays a role, which I will discuss below, but this basic principle of exchange rates will remain true.

In what way does competition keep orderliness in the foreign exchange market?

Time for a reality check. Chances are slim that Annabelle could have done quite as well as this, because she would have had lots of competition. Actually, as soon as gold slipped below $400 (assuming the exchange rate did not immediately go up), people like Annabelle would have jumped into action. Financial markets are now global, so that at any hour of the day or night these slippages and opportunities for profit would be noticed by someone in New York, Hong Kong, London, Bombay, or elsewhere. Although each location has its own business hours, international trading never closes because at any moment of the day some traders, somewhere, are open for business. These markets are the "7-Elevens" of finance.

What is more likely is that Annabelle and her peers would have made tinier profit margins in large volume. She would have started her gold buying in New York at, say, $399, with simultaneous sales in Germany at DM 664. (However, all that gold selling in Germany would almost certainly have pushed the German price below DM 664 quickly.) Her profit on 10,000 ounces of gold would have been closer to a few thousand dollars or even less. *Intense competition in the international foreign exchange and commodities markets usually keeps exchange rates from moving dramatically up or down over short periods, so markets remain stable.* This competition would have shaved Annabelle's profits. But if she is good, Annabelle could still make a nice living.

Let us not forget the exchange rate, which started at DM 1.66 per dollar. Suppose all the selling of gold in Germany and the buying of gold in the U.S. settled the American price at $390 and the German price at DM 655. Then the exchange rate would have settled down at DM 1.68 because at that rate gold would have the same value in both countries and no more trading profits could be made by moving the metal across the ocean.

How does inflation influence exchange rates?

Annabelle's experience trading gold showed us that exchange rates can change if a price in one nation does not change as much as the price in another nation. The same is true for the full range of prices in a country.

Inflation is a general increase in the level of prices in a nation (☛ Art. 11: Inflation, page 128). It is an erosion of the purchasing power of a nation's money. Suppose that the inflation rate is 2% per year in the United States and in Germany, and the exchange rate is $1 = DM 1.66. Then, for one reason or another (we will discuss this later) the inflation rate in Germany rises to 4%. That means that prices in Germany are now rising faster than those in the U.S. The result is that prices will be unbalanced; German goods and services will quickly become more costly than American goods and services. International competition is sharp enough that the higher prices of German products will result in a lesser quantity of them being demanded. Buyers will turn to the products of other nations, such as the U.S., whose prices rose less.

That brings us back to Eva's experience selling orange juice. She found out that when the demand for a nation's goods and services drops, so does the exchange rate. Now, with respect to the U.S. and Germany, the lower demand for German products will mean less demand for marks and a weaker mark. The increased demand for American products will mean more demand for dollars and a stronger dollar. The result will be a new, higher exchange rate reflecting the 2% difference in inflation rates. *The value of a nation's money will decrease if its inflation rate increases beyond that of other nations. The value of a nation's money will go up if it experiences a relatively low inflation rate.*

What makes foreign investment attractive?

Investors put their money where they can get the best return (profit), consistent with risk. Suppose a risk-free U.S. government bond paid a return of 5% per year, and a risk-free German bond paid a return of 7%. Other considerations aside, *investors will select a foreign investment if it is more profitable than a domestic one.* This difference in returns will draw investment money out of the U.S. and into Germany.

But to make an investment in another country an investor must first buy the money that country uses. This is important because it means the investor who goes abroad really winds up investing in both foreign property (stocks, bonds, real estate, etc.) *and* in the country's money.

We have already learned that the value of a currency changes. Therefore, changes in the value of the money will add to, or subtract from, the return he/she gets from sending money abroad. Suppose the American investor buys German marks and uses them to buy the German bond. If the German mark goes up in value by 5%, the investor would get a total return of 12% per year, 7% from the bond and 5% from the money. The profit from the mark would be realized when the American investor sells the German bond and converts the proceeds back into dollars. If the mark goes down by 5%, the investor would end up with a modest 2% return.

How do investors make decisions about foreign investments?

When deciding on investments outside one's own country, a special consideration must be made of the **expected exchange rate**. The expected exchange rate is what you believe the foreign currency will be worth when you go to sell a foreign property. This makes foreign investing a little more complex (and exciting). As you learned from the previous answer, *when you make an investment in another country, your return is made up of two parts: the local profits (received in the foreign country) from your investment property, and the change in the value of that nation's money that you get when you convert back to your nation's money.*

> **WAYNE AND KEN SIZE UP MEXICAN STOCKS:** Wayne and Ken are
> sophisticated investors who have to decide how to invest $50,000 that
> they will need back in two years to build a house. They are attracted to a
> Mexican utility stock that they expect will go up 15% over the next two
> years. They compare this to an American utility stock they expect to gain
> 12% in the same period. But there is the matter of the Mexican peso. To
> make the Mexican investment they would have to buy pesos first. In two
> years, when they sell the Mexican stock, they would have to sell for dol-
> lars the pesos that they get for the stock. There are two possible out-
> comes. If the peso depreciates, the Mexican investment would not be as
> attractive because they would gain 15% on the stocks but lose on the
> peso. However, if the peso appreciates, their investment return would be
> increased. Wayne and Ken have to make a decision about pesos.

The two get out their calculator and do some work. The exchange
rate is $1 = 3.31 pesos now; each peso they would have to buy costs
30¢. Suppose the dollar were to *depreciate* so that the exchange rate
moves to $1 = 3.00 pesos; the pesos they would get back would be
worth just over 33¢ each, which would be 10% more than they paid
for them. This means their total return for the two years would be
over 25%: a 15% gain in the stock plus the 10% more they would
get for their Mexican pesos. A good deal. The Mexican investment
would then be superior to buying the U.S. stocks, which would have
increased their savings by only 12% over the two years.

On the other hand, suppose the dollar were to *appreciate* relative to
the peso such that the exchange rate in two years would be $1 = 3.60
pesos; each peso bought for 30¢ now would be worth just under 28¢
when turned back into dollars. That means the men would "give
back" 8% of their investment when they sold out and would end up
with a net return of only about 7% for the two years (15% gain minus
8% loss). The U.S. investment would have been the superior choice.

It is hard to tell them what to do. But one thing is clear. The foreign investment is less certain because of what is called **exchange
rate risk**. This is the chance that investors in foreign property will
lose money because of changes in the exchange rate. *All foreign
investment involves exchange rate risk. Exchange rate risk gives the
investor abroad a chance for extra profits, but it could also result in losses
that would not have been incurred by investing at home.*

How do business owners handle financial risk?

Exchange rate changes create only one type of financial risk faced by businesses. Before saying more about exchange rate risk, let us look at a more familiar kind of financial risk. Financial risk is a part of many business activities. It never goes away. But people often try to share some of this risk with others who are willing to take it, for a price. A good example is **insurance**.

> **MARTIN'S TRUCKS HIT THE ROAD:** Martin owns two refrigerated tank trucks that distribute milk in a metropolitan area. He carries casualty insurance for which he pays $4,000 per truck per year, with a $500 deductible for each damage claim. Last year Truck No. 1 hit a highway guardrail, causing damage to the truck and the rail that cost Martin $20,000. The insurance company paid Martin $19,500, which he used toward these repair costs.

Martin faces a financial risk every time his trucks hit the streets and highways. By paying $4,000 per truck each year he gets an insurance company to share this financial risk. When the accident occurred, Martin's insurer paid out $19,500. Martin picked up the rest of the cost, which included the deductible, the time and effort getting the repairs done, and the loss of business while the truck was out of service. It is important to notice that the insurance company's obligation was purely financial; it did not repair his truck nor did it deliver his milk, it only paid out some money.

Martin's Truck No. 2 ran during the same year without incident. Nonetheless, Martin also paid $4,000 for insurance on that vehicle. Had he only known with certainty that that truck would not have any accidents, he might have saved himself $4,000 by not paying for this coverage, but he was not prescient.

Businesses buy insurance coverage to share their financial risks.

What are financial derivatives of foreign currency?

Foreign exchange risk is always present when people deal in investments outside of their home country. That is because exchange rates constantly change. But mutual funds, and other sophisticated investors, that deal in global investments often try to protect themselves from exchange rate risk, at least partially, by shifting that risk to others who are willing to take it. One way to do this is to buy or sell **financial derivatives** that are linked to foreign exchange rates.

Financial derivatives are contracts whose values are determined by some financial asset, such as a nation's currency. The oldest and most widely used financial derivative is a **financial futures contract.** (Although the term *financial derivatives* came into vogue only recently, financial futures contracts have been around for more than two decades. Futures contracts on agricultural commodities have been traded in the U.S. for over 150 years.) Futures contracts are created when a seller of an asset, such as the British pound, agrees to sell that asset to a buyer on a specific future date, but at a price set now.

Futures contracts on foreign currency are traded on organized exchanges that operate much like stock exchanges. The most important financial futures market in the United States is the Chicago Mercantile Exchange, where trading volume often amounts to tens of billions of dollars' worth of currencies each day. Thousands of market participants come together there through their brokers. These brokers meet on the floor of the "Merc" to make futures contracts for Canadian dollars, deutsche marks, Japanese yen, British pounds, Swiss francs, and Australian dollars. Standardized futures contracts can be written for delivery of a foreign currency in March, June, September, or December following the date they were made. That means traders can contract to buy or to sell foreign currency as far as a year in advance.

Table 26B shows you some exchange rates for both the spot and futures markets on a typical trading day in November 1994.[6] The currency **spot market** is the term given to trading in actual currencies for immediate delivery, whether traders make deals on an exchange, over telephone lines, or by other means. The currency **futures market** refers to trading in contracts for future delivery of a currency. On that day a trader could buy ¥100 for immediate delivery in the spot market for $1.023 of U.S. currency. But the futures market provided contracts for delivery of Japanese currency the following December, March, June, and September. You could have contracted for delivery of yen at a price of $1.027 per ¥100 for delivery in December, a price of $1.036 per ¥100 for March delivery, and so on.

Let's look at the total costs. Each standardized futures contract for

Table 26B

Futures Prices (in U.S. Dollars) for Foreign Currency on a Trading Day in November 1994

DELIVERY MONTH	JAPAN PER ¥100	GERMANY PER DM 1	SWITZERLAND PER SwF 1
Current	$1.023	$0.658	$0.788
December 1994	1.027	0.659	0.790
March 1995	1.036	0.661	0.793
June 1995	1.046	0.662	0.798
September 1995	1.056	0.664	(not traded)

Japanese yen calls for delivery of ¥12.5 million. A package of this much currency could be obtained for $127,875 immediately in the spot market. At the same time the futures market offered contracts for delivery of this package for $128,375 in December, or for $132,000 if you wished to wait until September.

While the delivery months and contract amounts (such as SwF 125,000 or DM 125,000 or ¥12.5 million) are standardized, the prices (exchange rates) change continually. On that day in November traders in the futures market for Japanese currency expected the value of the yen to drift upward continuously over the next several months. That is why the prices of yen they wanted for delivery in later months were higher than were the prices for earlier delivery. Similarly, prices for German marks and Swiss francs were sequentially higher for later delivery. (On that day no one traded the September contract for Swiss francs.)

The prices that are quoted for these futures contracts are traders' forecasts, carefully crafted guesses of what they expect the foreign exchange rates to be when the contracts call for delivery. These forecasts sometimes turn out to be way off the target. For example, early in 1994 futures traders created futures contracts for December 1994 delivery of Japanese yen for prices as low as 95¢ per ¥100. When December arrived, those on the selling end of these contracts had to deliver yen that were, at that time, worth more than the 95¢ per ¥100 they had to accept, whereas futures market buyers of yen turned out to get a bargain.

How do investors try to reduce their foreign exchange rate risk?

Here is how a financial derivative can be used by an investor to reduce foreign exchange risk.

> **MARY HEDGES:** Mary manages a global stock mutual fund. She is interested in profiting from what she expects to be robust growth of the British economy. To do so she buys $30 million of British currency and uses it to purchase shares in British firms. She is willing to speculate on the growth of the value of these shares. But she does not want to risk losing money if the value of the pound falls, so she hedges against changes in the value of the pound by selling 290 British pound futures contracts for $1.65 per pound for delivery in six months. These contracts are worth £18,125,000 (290 contracts at £62,500 each). That comes to a tad over $29,900,000 (£18,125,000 at $1.65 each).

Using the futures market, Mary's broker found buyers who were willing to commit themselves to paying Mary $1.65 per pound for the £18,125,000 that she will deliver in six months, regardless of what the pound may be worth then. If Mary's fears are realized, that the value of the pound declines, these contracts will grow in value and pay her money she can use to offset foreign exchange losses.

Now let us suppose six months pass. Mary's British stocks have risen 10%, confirming her expectations. But the pound fell to £1 = $1.50. When she sells these stocks for pounds and then converts these pounds back into dollars, she will have a net gain of only 1%: a 10% gain on the stocks and a 9% loss on the British currency. Her mutual fund investors would be disappointed, and she would be unlikely to get a performance bonus. Fortunately, she protected her investment by making contracts in the futures market in which she was a seller. These contracts gave her a profit of 9% that she applies to offset the foreign exchange losses. Her fund realized the full gain of 10% on its British investment.

Mary and Martin, the milk-truck operator, both experienced losses. Martin got money from his insurance policy that covered some of the losses he suffered from the truck accident. Mary got money from the futures market that she used to reimburse her fund for the losses it incurred when the pound lost some of its value. *Financial futures contracts are used to reduce exchange rate risk, just as insurance policies are used to reduce a person's potential losses in business or personal life.*

Do foreign currency futures eliminate foreign exchange risk?

Mary used the futures market as a kind of insurance against losses resulting from any decline in the value of the pound. Her results illustrated what economists call the "perfect hedge"; that is when gains in the futures market almost exactly offset losses in the foreign exchange spot market. (There was a slight difference only because the standardized futures contracts covered fewer British pounds than she actually invested.) But such perfect hedges are rare. *In most cases gains in the futures market are larger or smaller than are spot market losses, and vice versa, because price changes in futures markets do not exactly parallel price changes in spot markets.*

Hedging in the futures markets works only because futures prices and spot prices tend to move in the same direction over time, but they are determined by different factors. Remember that the prices of futures contracts are only traders' guesses about the future value of a currency; futures prices depend on expectations. However, foreign exchange rates in the spot market are determined by the actual supply of, and demand for, a nation's currency. Let us go back six months and retell Mary's story.

MARY HEDGES (THE REMAKE): Mary converted $30 million into pounds when £1 = $1.65. She then got about £18,200,000 (actually, £18,181,818), which she used to buy British stocks. Suppose futures market traders at the time expected the pound to fall in value; accordingly, they set the price of a pound in the futures contracts Mary wanted to £1 = $1.63, which was lower than the spot market price at the time. To offset possible losses in the value of the pound, she sold 290 futures contracts worth £18,125,000 (290 contracts for the standardized amount of £62,500 each).

At the end of six months her stocks had gained 10% in value while the spot market price of the pound had fallen to £1 = $1.50. But futures traders, who then felt the pound was about to rise again, were offering to buy futures at £1 = $1.52. After selling her British stocks for £20 million, Mary bought back her futures contracts for a profit of 11¢ per pound, which came to just under $2 million ($1,993,750) on the £18,125,000 her contracts represented.

However, the actual spot market price of the pound fell by 15¢. Because of the decline in the British currency, the 20 million pounds she got from the British stock market were worth only $30 million, about what she paid for them. Currency losses offset all of her stock market gains. However, adding her profit in the futures market, Mary's transactions in the stock and the currency markets netted her fund about $2,000,000, for a gain of just under 7% in 6 months. Her fund's stockholders were happy with that.

Like Martin, Mary learned that her insurance did not cover all of her losses.

Before leaving our discussion of foreign currency futures markets, let us consider what would have happened if the pound's value had gone up. Suppose that at the end of six months the spot price of the pound moved up to $1.75. Mary's fund would have made two profits, 10% from the increase in British stock market prices and 6% from the increase in the value of the British currency. Her fund's $30 million investment would have grown to $35 million.

But the fund could not send all of this money home. As the pound gained value on the spot market, the futures prices went up as well. Mary would have to buy back her futures contract after six months at, let us say, £1 = $1.76. That means she would have to buy back at

$1.76 contracts she sold at $1.63, losing 13¢ per pound. This would amount to just over $2,350,000. Taking this into account, her mutual fund would get back approximately $32,650,000 on its $30 million investment, for a profit of just under 9%. (The loss in the futures market was moderated by the fact Mary sold futures contracts on fewer British pounds than she actually invested in stocks.)

As steep as it would have been, Mary's loss in the futures market must be considered as the fee she would have paid for the protection the futures market offered against a decline in the pound's value. It is analogous to the $4,000 Martin paid for his insurance on Truck No. 2, which had no accident.

Are there other financial derivatives global investors use?

The financial community has been quite innovative in its creation of financial derivatives. After futures contracts, the second most widely used financial derivative is **options**. There are two types, put options and call options. Put options on currencies are contracts that give their owners the right to sell a foreign currency at a preset price at the end of a specified period of time (technically, these are so-called European-style options). Call options give their owners the right to buy a specified quantity of a currency at a set price.

In place of dealing in the futures market, Mary could have purchased put options to sell her British pounds at, for example, $1.60 each at the end of a six-month period. Futures contracts put her under the *obligation* to sell currency when the contracts expired. Put options would have given her the *right* to sell her pounds, but the choice would have been hers. The options she needed to cover her £18,200,000 investment might have cost her an up-front fee of several hundred thousand dollars. The fee would not have been refunded if she failed to use the option as a place to sell her pounds, but the put options would have saved her a bundle of money if the value of the pound plummeted while her fund owned British stocks. That is because the put options would have guaranteed her a minimum price for the currency. Another advantage of options is that their cost is fixed, regardless of what happens to the underlying currency.

At present the market for options is far smaller, and less flexible, than that for currency futures.

Another type of financial derivative is options on futures contracts. This financial derivative is complex because it includes the characteristics of both options and futures. While overshadowed by the huge market for currency futures themselves, there is an active market for options on currency futures on the Chicago Mercantile Exchange.

In addition to financial futures contracts, financial derivatives include options on currencies, options on futures contracts, and other types of contracts.

How are exchange rates influenced by investments?

Foreign investments result in movements of money across borders, just as do imports and exports.

> **CARLOS PLAYS THE MARKET:** Carlos is a real estate developer in Argentina who has some savings to invest. A few years ago, to diversify his investments, he sent Argentine pesos to the U.S. to buy dollars with which he purchased $500,000 worth of stock in an American corporation in the retail business. Every year the corporation pays him a dividend of $27,000. Sometimes he sends this dividend back to the U.S. to invest in more American stock. Other times he converts the dollars into Argentine pesos to spend at home.

When foreign investors like Carlos want to buy stock, real estate, businesses, or any other property in the United States, they increase the demand for U.S. dollars. If there is a great demand for American investments, the resulting *demand for dollars by investors might push up the exchange rate and make the dollar stronger.* That means that purchases of American money for investment purposes can have an effect on the U.S. economy. That is because a stronger dollar lessens American exports and increases imports. Later we will see that it might have another economic impact as well.

DARLENE BUYS A PIECE OF THE ORIENT: Darlene is a successful business owner in California who wants to profit from what she expects to be rapid economic growth in the Pacific Rim. She purchased a junior partnership in a Taiwanese engineering company for $140,000, after first purchasing the equivalent amount of the Taiwanese dollar. Each year she expects to receive a partnership income of about $10,000 from her Taiwanese investment, which she will repatriate (bring back to her home country) and invest in her California business.

When Darlene made her investment, she had to sell U.S. dollars on the foreign exchange market to get Taiwanese money with which she made her investment. *Selling U.S. dollars to make foreign investments will make the U.S. dollar weaker (dollar exchange rates will fall).*

Putting together all you learned so far in this article, you see that a nation's exchange rate is affected by both trade and investment. For example, U.S. dollars are demanded by foreigners who want to buy American exports (goods, services, and spending by foreign tourists) or American property (stocks, bonds, real estate, and businesses). On the other side of the foreign exchange market U.S. dollars are supplied (sold) by Americans who want to import goods and services from abroad or who want to buy investment property outside the United States.

What can governments do to influence exchange rates?

The supply of a nation's money is determined by the amount of it created by that nation's central bank. We have seen that the world's demand for money depends on the amount of it that people want to purchase goods, services, or investments in that nation. The foreign exchange market brings together buyers and sellers of a nation's money to establish its free market price (exchange rate). The market exchange rate is the value foreign exchange traders put on the money.

When exchange rates are allowed to move up or down in accordance with the demand for, and supply of, a nation's money, they are **floating exchange rates**. A free (unconstrained) foreign exchange market allows a nation's money to find its market value where the supply of a nation's money equals the world's demand for it.

But a nation can be hurt by exchange rates that move in a direction that is bad for its economy. Whenever a nation's money becomes too strong, its exports fall and its imports rise. This means that jobs and incomes will be lost in businesses that export, and the whole economy will take a hit. On the other hand, when foreigners *expect* a nation's money to become weak, investment funds will flow out of the nation. The loss of this investment money could also hurt the economy.

Because of the damage exchange rates can do to an economy, many governments intervene in the foreign exchange market to prevent the exchange rate from going too far in what they consider to be the wrong direction. This intervention results in what is called **managed float**, in which the government lets the market determine its money's exchange rate, but within limits. That is, the government puts a fence around its exchange rate.

A government can use its central bank to influence exchange rates (☞ Art. 18: The Federal Reserve, page 235). A central bank has the authority to create its nation's money, just as the U.S. dollar is provided by the Federal Reserve Banks. (The Federal Reserve acts as the central bank of the U.S.) A central bank also often owns large quantities of the money of other nations with which it deals. *If the central bank wants to promote its nation's exports, it can make its money weaker by selling newly created money in the foreign exchange market.* When the central bank of a nation weakens its money, we say the money has experienced a **devaluation** (or been devalued). The same action will also discourage imports, making it advantageous for its citizens to buy things at home rather than abroad.

Heavy demand for goods and services pushes prices upward. *If demand for its country's goods and services is so great that there is danger of high inflation, a central bank can buy its nation's money, revaluing it so as to lessen the demand for exports.* That is, it reduces the supply of its money available to the rest of the world. When the central bank of a nation strengthens its money, we say the money has experienced a **revaluation** (or been revalued). This is hard medicine for fighting inflation because it hurts people in the home country who make exported products, but it often works.

Does a managed float ever conflict with other economic goals?

A government, through its central bank, will often influence its money's exchange rate to help it improve exports, attract foreign investment, or to reduce inflation. But sometimes the pursuit of these goals harms the economy in other ways. The reason is that governments can influence the exchange rate only by raising or lowering the nation's money supply (☛ Art. 17: Money and Banking, page 221).

Suppose the central bank feels that exports are too low, or imports are too high, and concludes that its nation's exchange rate is too high. The way to correct this situation is to devalue its money by driving down the exchange rate. The way to do that is to print up new money and to sell it to the world. The weaker money will make exports cheaper and imports more costly; foreigners will buy more exports, and the nation's own citizens will buy more domestically made products in place of imports (which will have become more expensive). It all sounds so neat there must be a catch.

There is. When the central bank lowers the exchange rate by creating more money to help exports, there is a real danger of creating inflation at home. (Remember that inflation can occur if there is too much money going after more goods and services than the nation can produce.) This inflation erodes its citizens' purchasing power, and that, in turn, reduces the quantity of things they can buy and enjoy. *When a central bank weakens its nation's money to promote exports, it may, at the same time, give up its ability to hold down inflation.* The best way to prevent inflation is to restrain growth of the money supply. The export goals and inflation goals may be in conflict.

Another dimension of the problem of managing exchange rates is the effect on interest rates. The interest rate is the price of borrowed money (☛ Art. 13: Interest Rates, page 153). Like other prices, it is determined by supply and demand. *When a central bank increases its nation's money supply to devalue it, domestic interest rates are likely to fall.* That may discourage foreign investment that the economy needs. It may also make it easier for the nation's citizens to borrow money, spend it, and cause inflation.

Managing a nation's exchange rate is not easy and may involve some painful side effects. Yet *most central bankers seem to believe the condition of their nation's economy is too vital (or fragile) to be left at the mercy of uncontrolled fluctuations of exchange rates.*

What is being done to coordinate economic policies?

Most of the world's economies are tied to each other in some way. Exports and imports and investments bind nations together. For example, your nation's economic environment may depend very much on its exports to other nations. As another example, your nation's exchange rates may be tied to other nations' interest rates; if other nations have higher interest rates, the demand of investors for their currencies will weaken yours. However, when one nation is in need and asks another for help, the welfare of both nations may depend on the response. The same is true among individuals.

Market economies go through business cycles, which are sequences of expansions and recessions. However, these cycles are not simultaneous (☞ Art. 4: Business Cycles, page 35). One nation can be struggling to pull itself out of a recession at the same time that a second nation is fighting off inflation. Similarly, one nation may have an urgent need to cut its imports while another nation may need to expand its exports. *That is why an economic policy that would be good for one nation may conflict with the immediate needs of another.*

Sometimes the exchange rate can get in the way. For example, in the early 1990s the U.S. was quite concerned about its trade imbalance with Japan. Americans were buying far more from Japan than Japanese were buying in the U.S. The U.S. pressured Japan to revalue its money so that the exchange rate, which was around $1 = ¥110, could go down. Some economists believed an exchange rate of less than ¥100 per dollar (which was reached in late 1994) would be a big help to American business because a stronger yen, and a weaker dollar, would spur exports to Japan and cut back on U.S. imports.

However, at this same time Japan was battling a recession at home. Japan felt it needed strong export demand, which a weak yen would provide, to help lift its income. Consequently, it resisted efforts to revalue its yen.

At about this same time the U.S. tried to persuade Germany to increase the growth of its money supply to get it to grow faster. The motive? If Germany and other European nations grew faster, they could buy more goods and services from the U.S. and help it to grow, as well as to cut its trade deficit. But Germany had just increased its money supply to facilitate the integration of West and East Germany. Germany was afraid that any further efforts to increase the pace of its economic growth would risk raising its inflation rate. Germany felt it had a stronger obligation to the economic health of its own economy than to the United States. (Germany is perhaps more wary of inflation than are most other nations. It had a serious bout with high inflation in the 1920s, which wrecked its economy and strengthened the nascent Nazi party.)

Nonetheless, cooperation is common, especially for making minor adjustments in exchange rates. In early 1994 the U.S. dollar was sold heavily by speculators who believed the United States was doing too little to reduce its trade deficit with Japan and to reduce its large government deficit, which was requiring the nation to borrow heavily in world financial markets. Dollar exchange rates dropped sharply. While a weaker dollar may have promoted exports, a rapidly falling dollar would scare potential foreign investors (who would lose money on American investments such as government bonds). The U.S. and other nations favored a more stable foreign exchange market. Fifteen central banks quickly came to the aid of the Federal Reserve in buying dollars to prop up the currency. In addition, Germany's central bank lowered interest rates in its country, which made investments in the United States look more attractive. The dollar regained much of its lost ground.

National leaders today recognize that the globalization of trade and finance has made economies more interdependent than they were in the past. One result of this recognition has been the creation of the **Group of Seven**, or **G-7** as it is known in the press. G-7 is an informal discussion group of economics ministers (including the U.S. secretary of the treasury) from the major industrialized nations (and market economies) of Britain, Canada, France, Germany, Italy, Japan, and the United States. (Although Russia would like to become a full member, in 1994 it was permitted to attend the G-7 meeting as a guest.) They meet from time to time to discuss their respective economic goals and to consider policy coordination. The G-7 is a voluntary association with no power to enforce coordination or to supersede each member's sovereignty. The communiqués it usually issues after each of its meetings are often vague. But this effort to come together is a step in the right direction.

Is the world moving toward a common currency?

Recall that a nation's money is a mark of its sovereignty. A nation is loath to surrender the control of its money supply to an external agency. To do so would be to surrender its ability to use its money supply to affect interest rates, availability of credit, and exchange rates.

However, *the notion of folding the moneys of two or more nations into one common currency* persists because it *is a logical result of economic interdependence.* Currently one proposal that is quite alive is the effort to adopt a common currency for all members of the European Community (the Common Market) by 1999 (☞ Art. 25: Trading in the Global Village, page 346). At this writing this proposal is working its way through the legislatures of Common Market members and is likely to be in place on schedule. The common currency would eliminate the need for currency conversions, and exchange rates, among Common Market nations. This will certainly promote trade and investment among member nations because it would eliminate exchange rate risk. However, the final agreement for a common money will probably contain some clauses that give individual nations some limited control over their domestic economic environments.

Commencement

Students who complete a degree program in a college or university are heralded in a graduation ceremony called commencement. Commencement does not celebrate the end of a course of study. It celebrates the beginning of a new stage of personal development in which the degree holder is equipped with a deeper understanding of his or her environment and with new ways of thinking about events and challenges. Had this book been presented to you in a multimedia format, this closing section might be accompanied by a fully orchestrated rendition of Elgar's Pomp and Circumstance March because this is *your* commencement.

If you have read this entire book, you have completed a short course about the economic environment in which you live, work, and invest. Rather than a parchment wrapped in ribbon, your diploma is your new familiarity with the terms and concepts of our modern market economy.

The many vignettes that were used in this book were intended to show that the economy is made of individuals like you and me and that their collective decisions and activities in the marketplace shape economic conditions. This way of learning economics brings the subject closer to what is familiar, and that makes it easier to understand.

The charge to graduates is an important part of any commencement ceremony. My charge is that you keep your new skills honed. Stay current by reading reports on economic conditions written by well-informed reporters. You can find them in such business publications as *The Wall Street Journal, Investor's Business Daily, The Financial Times, The Economist, Business Week, Fortune,* and *Forbes.* Informed writing on the economy can also be found in many of the better general-interest publications such as *The New York Times, The Christian Science Monitor,* and many other large metropolitan newspapers. You can also get useful information about the economy in magazines such as *Newsweek, Time,* and *U.S. News & World Report.*

There are some excellent and relatively inexpensive sources of information for the serious student of the economy who wishes to dig deeper. Throughout this book material for tables and discussions was taken from one of the best of them, *The Survey of Current Business,* a monthly publication of the United States Department of Commerce. Each issue contains brief summaries of the state of the economy as well as special studies on specific economic activities. The heart of the *SCB* is a large collection of continually updated data tables and graphs that cover the economy in great detail. Used along with the explanations in this book, the *SCB* gives you the most comprehensive information about the U.S. economy available at low cost.

Another excellent source of information about economic conditions is the *Annual Report of the President,* published early each year by the U.S. government. The "Annual Report" itself is a brief document, signed by the president of the United States, containing some useful commentary on the state of the general economy and a bit of political rhetoric highlighting the accomplishments of the president's administration. However, while the president's statements get top billing in this book, the "Annual Report" is bound with a much meatier document called "The Annual Report of the Council of Economic Advisors." The CEA report is a "must read" for many economists (☛ Art. 24: Fiscal Policy and Government Debt, page

325, for a discussion of the CEA). The CEA report consists of a number of brief analyses of current economic conditions including economic growth, the job market, inflation, international trade, finance, and articles on special topics of current interest (the 1994 report discussed health care reform). The analyses are carefully and well written, although they tend to be favorable to the president's political agenda. The last section of the report of the CEA consists of updated tables of historical data on the American economy; some of these data were used for tables and discussions in this book.

Each of the twelve Federal Reserve Banks offers a monthly or quarterly publication. They include articles on special topics such as foreign exchange rates, inflation, specific financial markets, government economic policies, and other subjects. The articles are scholarly, but well written and useful. In addition most Fed Banks publish reader-friendly reviews and analyses of current conditions. Among the best is "Economic Trends" by the Research Department of the Federal Reserve Bank of Cleveland (about twenty pages per month). Each of these reviews focuses on the economy of the Federal Reserve district served by the bank that publishes it, but most also contain information about the national and international economies. Federal Reserve Banks are located in Boston, New York, Philadelphia, Richmond, Atlanta, Cleveland, Chicago, St. Louis, Kansas City (Mo.), Minneapolis, Dallas, and San Francisco. Most of these publications are free and can be found in many public and college and university libraries.

You can use this book to provide background information for reading any of these publications. That is why this is a book for your desk, not for your bookshelf. Look through one of its articles anytime you want to review a subject that relates to a current topic in economics that is important to you. With this book you have developed the one skill that is essential to learning about markets, money, business, and policy: your economic literacy.

Notes

PREFACE

1. Dennis Kelly, "Knowledge of Economy Lacking," *USA Today*, September 14, 1992, D1.

CHAPTER 1: AERIAL VIEWS OF THE ECONOMY

1. U.S. Department of Commerce, "National Income and Product Accounts," Table 1, *Survey of Current Business* (SCB) 74, no. 7 (July 1994).

2. U.S. Central Intelligence Agency, *The World Factbook 1993* (Washington, D.C.). The U.S. GDP figure from this source, shown here, is an early estimate that differs slightly from the revised 1992 GDP figure shown elsewhere in this book.

3. *SCB* 74, no. 7 (July 1994): 56.

4. David C. Colander, *Economics* (Homewood, Ill.: Richard D. Irwin, Inc., 1993), 177.

5. Ibid., Chapter 37, "Growth and Economics of Developing Countries."

6. *SCB* 74, no. 7 (July 94): Table 1 in this and earlier issues.

7. Calculated from data in U.S. Department of Commerce, Bureau of Economic Analysis, *Business Statistics 1963–91* (1992), Appendix II (*Bus. Stat.*); and from U.S. Department of Commerce, *Survey of Current Business*, 74, no. 7 (July 1994): 54.

8. *SCB* 74, no. 3 (March 1994): C-2; *SCB* 74, no. 7 (July 1994): C-2.

9. *SCB* 73, no. 4 (April 1993): C-2; Table C.

10. CIA, *Factbook 1993*. The U.S. growth rate given in this source, and shown here, is an early estimate that differs slightly from the revised U.S. growth rate shown elsewhere in this book.

11. *SCB* 73, no. 11 (November 1993): C-48.

12. *SCB*, various issues (1990–94).

CHAPTER 2: JOBS AND WAGES OF PEOPLE AT WORK

1. *SCB* 74, no. 7 (July 1994): Table 6.

2. U.S. Bureau of the Census, *Statistical Abstract of the United States, 1990* (Washington, D.C.): Table 645.

3. *SCB* 74, no. 3 (March 1994): S-11, S-12.

4. Ronald G. Ehrenberg and Robert S. Smith, *Modern Labor Economics: Theory and Policy*, 5th ed. (New York: HarperCollins, 1994), 27, 585.

5. *SCB* 74, no. 3 (March 1994): S-10; *SCB* 70, no. 5 (May 1990): S-10.

6. J. R. Clark and others, *Macroeconomics for Managers* (Boston: Allyn & Bacon, 1990), 298–301.

7. *SCB* 74, no. 3 (March 1994): S-9.

8. *SCB* 74, no. 7 (July 1994): C-13.

CHAPTER 3: PRICES

1. *SCB* 74, no. 7 (July 1994): C-3, and earlier editions; *Business Stats.*, 24.

2. Colander, *Economics*, 150–51.

3. *Economic Report of the President* and *The Annual Report of the Council of Economic Advisors* (Washington, D.C., 1994), 335–37 (ERP).

4. These rates were calculated from figures in *SCB* 74, no. 7 (July 1994): C-3; *SCB* 73, no. 11 (November 1993): C-3; also in *ERP* and *Report of the CEA*, 338, 341.

5. Federal Reserve Bank of Cleveland, *Economic Trends* (September 1994): 6.

6. "USA Snapshots: Core Inflation Rate Low," *USA Today*, July 14, 1994, B1.

7. *SCB* 74, no. 7 (July 1994): C-3.

8. Ibid., 54; Federal Reserve Bank of St. Louis, *National Economic Trends* (July 1994): 14.

9. Jeffrey D. Sachs and Felipe Larrain, *Macroeconomics in the Global Economy* (Englewood Cliffs, N.J.: Prentice-Hall, 1993), 327–29.

10. "Yield Comparisons," *The Wall Street Journal (WSJ)*, October 6, 1994, C19.

11. "Treasury Bonds, Notes & Bills," *WSJ*, January 27, 1990, and October 6, 1994.

CHAPTER 4: HOUSEHOLDS AND BUSINESSES

1. *Bus. Stats.*, 1; *SCB* 74, no. 7 (July 1994): 62.

2. *Bus. Stats.*, 2; *SCB* 74, no. 7 (July 1994): 62, 63.

3. Clark, *Macroeconomics*, Chapter 9, "Consumption," especially pp. 212–20.

4. Ibid., 223–24.

5. *SCB* 74, no. 7 (July 1994): 81.

6. *SCB* 72, no. 8 (August 1992): 39.

CHAPTER 5: MONEY AND CREDIT

1. Federal Reserve Bank of St. Louis, *Monetary Trends* (July 1994): 2–8.

2. Frederic S. Mishkin, *The Economics of Money, Banking, and Financial Markets*, 3rd ed. (New York: 1992), 433.

3. Board of Governors of the Federal Reserve System, *Federal Reserve Bulletin* (December 1993): vol 79, A43.

4. "Treasury Bonds, Notes & Bills" and "Bond Market Data Bank," *WSJ*, October 19, 1994, C17, C21.

5. *ERP*, 377.

CHAPTER 6: GOVERNMENT AND THE ECONOMY

1. Colander, *Economics*, 677–81.

2. *SCB* 74, no. 9 (September 1994): 6, 11.

3. Ibid., 11.

4. Ibid.

5. Ibid.

6. Ibid.

7. *ERP*, 359.

8. Board of Governors of the Federal Reserve System, *Federal Reserve Bulletin* 80, no. 10 (October 1994): A43.

9. *SCB* 74, no. 9 (September 1994): 11, 12.

10. *ERP*, 359.

CHAPTER 7: INTERNATIONAL TRADE AND FINANCE

1. *SCB* 74, no. 9 (September 1994): 38.

2. Ibid., 82–83.

3. Ibid., 84.

4. Ibid., 79.

5. "Key Currency Cross Rates," *WSJ*, November 4, 1994, C15.

6. "Futures Prices" and "Currency Trading: Exchange Rates," *WSJ*, November 4, 1994, C14, C15.

Bibliography

Board of Governors of the Federal Reserve System. *Federal Reserve Bulletin* (December 1993), volume 79, number 12.

———. *Federal Reserve Bulletin* (October 1994), volume 80, number 10.

"Bond Market Data Bank," *The Wall Street Journal*, October 19, 1994, p. C21.

J. R. Clark, et al. *Macroeconomics for Managers*. Boston, Mass.: Allyn and Bacon, 1990, pp. 298–301.

David C. Colander. *Economics*. Homewood, Ill.: Richard D. Irwin, Inc., 1993.

"Currency Trading: Exchange Rates," *The Wall Street Journal*, November 4, 1994, p. C15.

Economic Report of the President and *The Annual Report of the Council of Economic Advisors*, Washington, D.C., 1994.

Ronald G. Ehrenberg and Robert S. Smith. *Modern Labor Economics: Theory and Policy*, 5th ed. New York: HarperCollins, 1994.

Federal Reserve Bank of Cleveland. *Economic Trends*, September 1994.

Federal Reserve Bank of St. Louis. *Monetary Trends*, July 1994.

———. *National Economic Trends*, July 1994.

"Futures Prices," *The Wall Street Journal*, November 4, 1994, p. C14.

Dennis Kelly, "Knowledge of Economy Lacking," *USA Today*, September 14, 1992, p. D1.

"Key Currency Cross Rates," *The Wall Street Journal*, November 4, 1994, p. C15.

Frederic S. Mishkin. *The Economics of Money, Banking, and Financial Markets*, 3d ed. New York: HarperCollins, 1992.

Jeffrey D. Sachs and Felipe Larrain. *Macroeconomics in the Global Economy*. Englewood Cliffs, N.J.: Prentice-Hall, 1993.

"Treasury Bonds, Notes & Bills," *The Wall Street Journal*, January 27, 1990; October 6, 1994; and October 19, 1994.

United States Bureau of the Census. *Statistical Abstract of the United States*. Washington, D.C., 1990.

United States Central Intelligence Agency. *The World Factbook 1993*. Washington, D.C.

United States Department of Commerce, Bureau of Economic Analysis. *Business Statistics 1963–91*. Washington, D.C., 1992.

————. *Survey of Current Business* (monthly publication), various issues, 1990–1994.

"USA SNAPSHOTS: Core Inflation Rate Low," *USA Today*, July 14, 1994, p. B1.

"Yield Comparisons," *The Wall Street Journal*, October 6, 1994, p. C19.

Index

Note to reader: All of the terms in **bold-faced type** throughout the book appear in the index. This feature will make it easy to use this index to locate quickly the information you want.